# Activity Theory and Social Practice

# Activity Theory and Social Practice: Cultural-Historical Approaches

*Edited by Seth Chaiklin,*
*Mariane Hedegaard and Uffe Juul Jensen*

AARHUS UNIVERSITY PRESS

Published with financial support from the
Danish Research Council for the Humanities

AARHUS UNIVERSITY PRESS
University of Aarhus
DK-8000 Aarhus C
Fax (+ 45) 8619 8433

73 Lime Walk
Headington, Oxford OX3 7AD
Fax (+ 44) 1865 750 079

Box 511
Oakville, Conn. 06779
Fax (+ 1) 860 945 9468+

# Foreword

This book is the first in a series from the Fourth Congress of the International Society for Activity Theory and Cultural Research, held in Aarhus, Denmark in June 1998.

Around 600 delegates from 37 different countries attended the congress. The number of presentations at the congress was around 400; their diversity was fascinating. These presentations represented several disciplines including anthropology, pedagogy, philosophy, and psychology.

The contributions in this book are revised versions of keynote lectures and invited panel presentations. Two of the keynote speakers, Vasily Davydov and Marx Wartofsky, unfortunately both died in the year before the congress. This is a great loss to the cultural-historical traditions in the human and social sciences.

Davydov was an active and central person in establishing contact between Eastern and Western researchers working within the tradition of Vygotsky and Leontiev, and an active and engaged member of the Standing Committee of the International Society for Cultural Research and Activity Theory. His untimely death in the spring 1998 came as a shock for all of us working within the tradition of activity theory. We were all sad that we had to miss him at the Fourth ISCRAT Congress. But fortunately he had prepared his keynote lecture for the congress and the participants had the luck to hear this lecture read by Joachim Lompscher, his friend and colleague through many years.

Marx Wartofsky was invited as a keynote speaker because his cultural-historical work in philosophy has been an important source of inspiration for many researchers in understanding the relation between social practice, activity, and a person's development. The organizing committee was happy when he accepted to participate in the Congress. His untimely death in spring 1997 was a big loss for philosophy and for cultural-historical research and activity theory. We hope that his work will continue to be an inspirational resource in activity theory and cultural-historical research.

I want to thank the University of Aarhus and especially the Head of the Administrative Department Per Møller Madsen and Vice-Chancellor Henning Lehmann for their advice about and support for this Congress, which was part of the University of Aarhus's 70th anniversary celebration. I also thank the Department of Psychology at the University of Aarhus for secretarial support in preparing this book for publication

Seth Chaiklin made a tireless and tremendous effort in editing the papers and preparing them for publication, and I am sure that all the authors in the book will support me in thanking him.

*Mariane Hedegaard*                                          Aarhus, February 1999
President, Fourth ISCRAT Congress

# Contents

## Gendered Social Practice

## Cultural-Historical Approaches to Development and Personality

## Institutions and Organizations as Mediators Between Subject and Society

# List of Figures

# Contributors

*Amelia Álvarez*, Faculty of Social Sciences, University of Salamanca, Spain

*Jerome Bruner*, School of Law, New York University, U.S.A.

*Seth Chaiklin*, Department of Psychology, University of Aarhus, Denmark

†*Vasily V. Davydov*, Russian Academy of Education, Moscow

*Pablo del Río*, Faculty of Social Sciences, University of Salamanca, Spain

*Ritva Engeström*, Center for Activity Theory and Developmental Work Research, University of Helsinki, Finland

*Yrjo Engeström*, Academy of Finland and Department of Communication, University of California, San Diego, U.S.A.

*Bernd Fichtner*, University of Siegen, Germany

*Fernando L. González Rey*, Faculty of Psychology, University of Havana, Cuba, and Institute of Psychology, University of Brasilia, Brazil

*Mariane Hedegaard*, Department of Psychology, University of Aarhus, Denmark

*Uffe Juul Jensen*, Department of Philosophy, University of Aarhus, Denmark

*Vera John-Steiner*, Linguistics and Education, University of New Mexico, Albuquerque, U.S.A.

*Vladislav A. Lektorsky*, Institute of Philosophy, Russian Academy of Sciences, Moscow

*Martha C. Nussbaum*, The University of Chicago Law School, U.S.A.

*Vitaly V. Rubtsov*, Psychological Institute, Russian Academy of Education, Moscow

*Anna P. Stetsenko*, Department of Psychology, University of Berne, Switzerland

*Ethel Tobach*, American Museum of Natural History, New York, U.S.A.

*Peeter Tulviste*, Department of Psychology, Tartu University, Estonia

*Terence Turner*, Department of Anthropology, Cornell University, Ithaca, N.Y., U.S.A.

*Ghita Vygotskaya*, Moscow, Russia

*Tarja Vähäaho*, Center for Activity Theory and Developmental Work Research, University of Helsinki, Finland

# 1 Activity Theory and Social Practice: An Introduction

*Mariane Hedegaard, Seth Chaiklin,*
*and Uffe Juul Jensen*

Activity theory and the cultural-historical approach to psychology have their roots in the theory and research of Lev S. Vygotsky and Alexei N. Leontiev. Contributors in many countries around the world have developed this approach further, with active research going on in anthropology, communication, computer science, pedagogy, philosophy, and psychology.

The chapters presented in this book were developed from the keynote lectures and some presentations from invited panel sessions at the Fourth Congress of the International Society for Cultural Research and Activity Theory. At the Congress's opening ceremony Ghita Vygotskaya (this volume) told about her father, Lev Semonovich Vygotsky's life and engagement in science. She described how he united life with his family, colleagues and students to create a social practice in which their shared activities became part of his development of a cultural-historical approach to human science (see also Vygotskaya & Lifanova, 1996).

In this introduction, we would like to give a perspective for interpreting the chapters presented in this book. The first part of the chapter gives a historical account of some problems that captured the attention and interest of contemporary researchers in Northern Europe in the 1970s and early 1980s. These interests led to a series of European conferences that were forerunners to the Congress from which the chapters in this book originated. We then consider the Congress's main organizing theme "Activity Theory and Cultural-Historical Approaches to Social Practice," commenting briefly on how activity was presented at the Congress, and then elaborating on the meaning of social practice in relation to activity theory, and interpreting some of the present chapters in relation to this issue. Finally, we review some issues raised in these chapters that we consider important for further development within the activity theory and cultural-historical tradition.

* We thank Harris Chaiklin for comments on a previous draft.

## Thematic and Historical Origins of the ISCRAT Congress

The initial cell of the ISCRAT congress was a series of informal Scandinavian research seminars which started in 1980. These seminars were organized occasionally to discuss different questions in the cultural-historical tradition. Here we would like to review briefly some of the main ideas that either motivated these seminars, or captured interest and attention at that time. In particular these themes included the relation between man and animals, the nature of institutional practice in human development, forms of knowledge, and pedagogical methods for developing theoretical forms of knowledge.

### *Conceptualizing Human Nature*

The key problem that organized Vygotsky's research was the establishment of a cultural-historical science about humans. An important problem for Vygotsky was to explain the differences between man and animal (Vygotsky, 1929). His explanation focused on the human ability to construct tools, which are used in social interaction, and to act on and transform conditions for living. Humans hand over their tools and procedures for using them (knowledge) to the next generation, thus children's development can be seen as a social and cultural-historical process (see Stetsenko, this volume). This understanding and explanation of development was central in Vygotsky's thinking. It is expressed, for example, in two of his central concepts: the zone of proximal development and the genetic law of cultural development. Here is Vygotsky's (1931/1997b) classic formulation:

We can formulate the general genetic law of cultural development as follows: every function in the cultural development of a child appears on the stage twice, in two planes, first, the social, then the psychological, first between people as an intermental category then within the child as a intramental category. (p. 106)

Leontiev (1932) wrestled with the same problem of explaining the specific aspects that distinguish humans from animals. Through his attempt to solve this problem, Leontiev (1975/1978) formulated the concept of activity, characterizing human motives and consciousness as culturally and historically developed, and thereby qualitatively different from animal motives.

In his theoretical conceptualization, Leontiev focused on human production and communication, a focus he shared with Vygotsky. Leontiev conceptualized activity as a collective process, with actions as goal-oriented processes of individual subjects, and operations as psychic functions conditioned by the prevailing material conditions and available tools.

Leontiev's formulation of the concept of activity includes the concept of leading activity, which is the organizing principle for personality development. Work was taken as the prototype of activity, and other types of activity were developed though human history as derived from work. The relation between the collective and the individual, though central in both Vygotsky's and Leontiev's theories, was not clarified sufficiently. It is still a problem with which followers continue to wrestle.

## Conceptualizing Institutional Practice

Elkonin (1972) saw institutional practice as the main source of psychic development. Different institutions — home, daycare, school — were dominated by different activities; the dominating activity in an institution acquired the role as leading activities in different periods in a person's life. With Elkonin's theory the focus shifted from explaining general characteristics of psychological development to understanding the diversity of human development as it related to practice traditions in societal institutions. Furthermore Elkonin (1978/1988) explored the development of play activity and its transition into learning activity. This transition is based on the unity of development of motives and cognition. Together with Davydov, Elkonin formulated pedagogical principles of developmental teaching, which aimed to help students to appropriate learning activity.

## Epistemological and Psychological Aspects of Knowledge

Drawing on Ilyenkov's (1977) formulation of the ideal, Davydov (1995) distinguished between epistemological and psychological aspects of knowledge, which clarified the distinction expressed in Vygotsky's genetic law, between collective aspects of activity and individual subjective aspects.

For traditional psychology the ideal (if it was recognized at all) was situated in the consciousness of an individual. Vygotsky looked on the ideal in a quite different way. (p. 15)

The ideal cannot be discovered or understood at the level of consciousness of a single person; the ideal is an aspect of culture. Behind the ideal, behind the world of culture, and determining it, stands the objectively practical activity (first and foremost work activity) of a social subject in its historical development. (pp. 15-16)

From this point of view, in psychology one cannot talk about the determination of consciousness by activity and ignore the plane of the ideal or the cultural. In speaking about the ideal (or the cultural) as a determinant of individual consciousness, one has to recall the superindividuality of the ideal. (p. 16)

So the outline of the formation of individual consciousness that Vygotsky created could be represented in the following way: "first, collective activity, then culture, the ideal, sign or symbol, and finally individual consciousness." (p. 16)

Through the epistemological distinction between "the ideal" (knowledge) and individual consciousness, Davydov (1972/1990), in his dissertation, described and analyzed empirical and theoretical forms of knowledge. Empirical or categorical knowledge has dominated science and education for centuries and continues to dominate school teaching even today. Theoretical knowledge includes both conditions and procedures and abstract characteristics of conceptual relations in its knowledge system.

Davydov's dissertation was translated into German in 1977, making these ideas about different epistemological forms of knowledge and pedagogical principles for promoting theoretical thinking more accessible to researchers in Europe. In particular, his theory of theoretical knowledge and thinking and his theory about developmental teaching became an inspirational source for several Scandinavian researchers working within pedagogical psychology.

*Ascending from the Abstract to the Concrete*

These researchers organized several Scandinavian research seminars in the early 1980s. Fundamental for these seminars was the problem of transcending the understanding of activity as solely or primarily social interaction. This led to an understanding of activity as a societally and historically conditioned collective process. The discussion of these problems resulted in the First Activity Conference (with a focus on learning and teaching activity) held in 1982 in Espoo, Finland. This European conference was organized by Yrjö Engeström with invited participants including Vasily Davydov.

The following year Mariane Hedegaard and Vagn Rabøl-Hansen organized the Second Activity Conference in Aarhus, Denmark. The conference theme was "Teaching on a Scientific Basis — Ascending from the Abstract to the Concrete" (Hedegaard, Hakkarainen, & Engeström, 1984). Several problems were debated at this invited conference, which included participants from Scandinavia and Northern Europe. One of the central problems came from Davydov's distinction between the epistemological and psychological aspects of knowledge for teaching in school. How could theoretical epistemological (scientific) knowledge become psychologically useful knowledge for schoolchildren? The principle of instruction formulated by Joachim Lompscher (1984) of ascending from the abstract to the concrete was related to this discussion. The method of the formative teaching experiment (Markova, 1982) was debated as the methodological way to move forward in both research and implementation of research into practice (Hedegaard, 1990; Hedegaard & Chaiklin, 1995).

The Third Activity Conference followed in 1984 in Utrecht, The Netherlands with Eduard Bol as president. At this conference, educational researchers who worked with related theories were invited, so that a discussion between activity theory and other related theories could be accomplished (Bol, Haenen, & Wolters, 1985).

### Confronting the Societal Subject: The ISCRAT Congresses

Several of the participants at the Third Activity Conference thought that the time had come to expand the meetings from being an invited event with a focus on educational research to an open meeting for all topics in activity theory and sociocultural research. This resulted in the First International Congress on Activity Theory, organized by Georg Rückreim and Alfred Messman at the Berlin University of the

Arts in 1986. In addition to teaching and learning activity, the Congress themes included research on activity, communication, pedagogy, and psychology (Hildebrand-Nilshon & Rückreim, 1988).

The goal of the congress was to gather all researchers working within activity theory, therefore this first congress was organized in cooperation with the critical psychologists, Martin Hildebrand-Nilshon, Klaus Holzkamp, Valter Volpert and Arne Raeithel. As part of realizing this goal, a special panel session was organized composed of representatives from different lines within activity theory including the American sociocultural approach, critical psychology, different branches of activity theory in Russian psychology, as well as Scandinavian and European researchers. Vasily Davydov was invited but was not granted a visa to travel into Germany. At this congress, an International Standing Committee for Activity Theory was elected, hence the ISCRAT name.

The second international congress, now named ISCRAT, and held in Lahti, Finland in 1990 with Yrjö Engeström as president. Beginning with this congress, a specific topic was chosen as a focus for each meeting. The idea with these topics was to transcend different disciplines that would challenge activity theory and give direction for the development of new research activity. The theme for the second congress was "Individuality and Transformation" (Engeström, Miettinen, & Punamäki, 1998).

The theme of the third ISCRAT conference was "Activity Theory and Social Practice." This congress took place in Moscow in 1995 with Vasily Davydov as the president. Several sessions were devoted to different forms of social practice (communication; politics; economics; education; culture and art; social work; technology and telecommunication; and sport). The Fourth ISCRAT congress took place in Aarhus in 1998, with Mariane Hedegaard as president.

## Intellectual Concerns of the Fourth ISCRAT Congress

Having considered some of the intellectual issues that preceded and motivated the present Congress, we would now like to turn our attention to consider the issues and problems that were important in motivating the present Congress, and its special focus on the idea of social practice. In the following, we comment briefly on the meaning of social practice, sketch some of the relations between an activity concept and social practice, and indicate some implications for further investigation and clarification of these relations.

### Activity as Object and Methodology

Lektorsky (this volume) describes the historical change of the notion of activity as a methodological approach. Historically, activity has been viewed as individual attempts to gain knowledge through our actions on objects. Through Marx and Vygotsky, we can now start to conceptualize as activity as a collective process, dependent on interaction and communication. Among other things, this clarifies the need for developmental experiments.

In Davydov's keynote lecture (this volume), a concern for the methodological aspect was also put forward. His presentation focused on the structure of activity and the cell of this activity structure, elaborating Leontiev's conceptualization of the activity structure by adding desire, emotions, tasks, plans, and will. The cell of activity has a certain kind of integrity, which is always present in any activity (play, learning, work, sport, etc.) Transformation and communication are the components that create the integrity of the cell.

Davydov's distinction between activity structure and activity cell parallels Fichtner's (this volume) distinction between activity as object and activity as methodology.

Fichtner writes that the particular methodological potential of activity is constituted simultaneously on three levels: philosophical, individual science, and pedagogical-practical. These three levels can be found in Vygotsky's work: the philosophical level is described in "The Historical Meaning of the Crises in Psychology" (1927/1997a), the individual science level can be found in Vygotsky's genetic method, and the pedagogical-practical level is found in Vygotsky's work on didactics in school. As Fichtner notes, Vygotsky did not achieve any methodological discussion of how to act pedagogically. This was accomplished by Vygotsky's followers, such as Elkonin and Davydov's didactics of developmental teaching, Rubtsov's (this volume) didactics of cultural-historical teaching, and in general in the idea of the formative teaching experiment.

## The Concept of Social Practice in the Social Sciences

The idea of social practice has always been a part of the cultural-historical tradition, both in its marxian philosophical roots, and in the explanatory concepts that have organized the tradition. Social practice is not an appendage to activity theory; it lies at the heart of the theory's conceptual structure — but it is only in recent decades that it has started to receive the attention that it deserves.

The notion of social practice, as an analytic concept, is theoretically unsaturated. That is, no particular ontological or epistemological position is entailed by the general notion of social practice, defined as structured human traditions for interaction around specific tasks and goals. Therefore, the concept can be used with various conflicting philosophical and theoretical perspectives, and in practice, the term *social practice* is not unique to the cultural-historical tradition. Within philosophy, one can find it used by Wittgensteinians, phenomenologists, social constructivists and marxists. In the social sciences, science studies (e.g., Latour, 1987; Pickering, 1995) have argued that science has to be accounted for as a social practice. There is an anthropological tradition known as "social practice" theory, that shares some similar ideas (Lave & Wenger, 1991).

## The Importance of Social Practice in the Cultural-Historical Tradition

Research in the cultural-historical tradition, from the very beginning, has tried to understand the influence of social practices on human development (see Tulviste, this volume, for one example). The activity concept has been so important within the cultural-historical tradition because it provides a way to characterize those aspects of social practice that are believed to provide the conditions for psychological development. In other words, not only can one point to the importance of social practice, as other research traditions have done (e.g., Bronfenbrenner, dialectical psychology), but with the activity concept (and associated concepts such as action, motive, goal, leading activity, and motive hierarchy), it is possible to provide an elaborated set of concepts that can be used to give a differentiated theoretical analysis of social practice. Whether there is any surplus meaning for the concept of "social practice" that exceeds the notion of activity deserves further consideration.

The central use of the notion of activity is seen in many chapters in this volume. Stetsenko (this volume) reviews some of the main components of the process by which social practice contributes to human development, namely the acquisition of cultural tools, through social interaction in the zone of proximal development. She points to the importance of understanding the transformations that occur in activity in this process, viewing transformations of activity as the key synthetic concept for relating social interaction, cultural tools, and the zone of proximal development. The scope of Stetsenko's chapter does not permit consideration of the origins of these activities, but it is clear from the chapters by Tulviste (this volume) and Bruner (this volume) that activities must be understood as being formed through societal practices. Tulviste emphasizes the importance of recognizing the explanatory nature of activity, a topic that also figures centrally in Fichtner (this volume).

The integral relationship between activity and social practice is implied, for example, when Fichtner suggests that we must study concrete activities on an empirical level, or in the suggestion for the need to make a systematic inventory of human practices made independently by Tulviste (this volume) and Álvarez and del Río (this volume). We agree with the spirit of these observations, and would suggest in an even stronger way, that these descriptions need to address the institutionalized nature of practice more explicitly and directly in the development of the activity concept.

## Intervention in Social Practice

The institutionalized aspects of social practice become more salient when we consider another common meaning of social practice, namely that associated with the idea of intervention into ongoing social practices. As mentioned before, the concept of social practice is used in many different theoretical traditions; this would suggest that the concept of social practice is not compatible with a normative concept of social practice (i.e., where one is concerned with the content of the social practice, as well as acknowledging its central role in human functioning and development). The normative concept of social practice involves commitment to particular views about the goals and purposes of institutionalized human actions. Some ask justifiably whether a normative concept of social practice is mere camouflage for powerful groups which impose their values upon others? In other words, how does one consider the relation between theory about social practices and the content of the social practices themselves?

The chapters in this volume by Turner, Nussbaum, and Tobach confront this issue explicitly. Turner's chapter, "Activism, Activity and the New Cultural Politics," considers the implications of the global expansion of capital on the conditions for indigenous peoples in South America. One understands clearly from his chapter that one cannot intervene in social practice without theorizing about that practice, and in particular to understand that many local issues may reflect consequences of global capitalist market forces, which are often difficult to recognize explicitly in local conflicts. The embedded nature of the theorist's practice also comes forward in Nussbaum's chapter, "Public Philosophy and International Feminism," where she describes how her own philosophical analysis is challenged and strengthened by examining directly the specific practices about which she philosophizes. Moreover, she argues for the importance of recognizing that much theory is already in practice, such as the consequences of development economics for the living conditions of women in India. In other words, the traditional separation of theory and practice may never have existed. Similarly, Tobach in her chapter, "Evolution, Genetics and Psychology," describes the contradictions that arise between conducting psychological research in a market-dominated society and an interest in serving the welfare of all. In each case, these chapters illustrate the tension between expert perspectives and perspectives of the groups which the social practice aim to support, develop or emancipate. And in each case, it seems that a recognition of the embedded nature of the theorist and the need to theorize about one's practice are part of understanding the nature of the practices that one is investigating.

In the following, we want to indicate some reasons why we think these two senses of social practice — the interventive meaning and the focus on activity as a way to describe social practice that has more traditionally characterized research in the cultural-historical tradition — reflect a conceptual unity that is not always recognized sufficiently in the cultural-historical tradition.

Aristotle was the first of the classical Greek philosophers to argue "that philosophical reflection and teaching on ethical and political topics have a practical goal" (Nussbaum, 1994, p. 48). These activities should promote "the good life" or "human flourishing." To find the roots of the significance of social practice in the cultural-historical tradition, one turns to Marx's (1964) *Economic and Philosophical Manuscripts of 1844*, where one is struck by the reflections and analyses of the conditions needed for a worthwhile human life.

We mention Marx's work for several reasons. It is well-known that the first generation of cultural-historical theorists were directly inspired by Marx's theoretical concepts (e.g., Vygotsky 1927/1997a, pp. 330-331). Second, there are many important ideas in Marx's work that still need to be understood and integrated into activity theory (e.g., alienation, the historical construction of categories, the relation between the abstract and the concrete). Third, this specific relation between theory and practice was addressed in an interesting and productive way in Marx's work. The idea that research should be used to change social practices is expressed epigrammatically in Marx's (1845/1970) Eleventh Thesis on Feuerbach.[1] Knowing this thesis, one could draw the simple conclusion, by association, that if one is going to work with activity theory, then one must also be interested in social change.

Unfortunately, this associative argument serves mostly to confuse and obscure some important underlying arguments about the relations between social practice and activity theory. It is important to understand more clearly how the interventive component emerges as part of a general logic.

Jensen (this volume) explores this idea much more systematically, arguing that changes in practices must be understood as part of the theoretical work itself. A case can be made for the idea that Marx in his "Theses on Feuerbach" and his later theoretical and philosophical work developed a theoretical framework within which the analytic concept of social practice and the normative or interventive concept are united.

By using his analytic techniques, Marx was able to look ahead. These techniques included reflections on human history and about peoples' ability to develop new possibilities for action, to change conditions and transform themselves through this process. Marx did not espouse or presuppose particular norms or values in the theses. But the theory he sketched of the human condition, of our potentialities, and of our capabilities for change and development contain/imply reasons for his use of the normative concept in the eleventh thesis. To give a unified picture of Marx's thinking as expressed in the theses, the activity category

---

1.  "The philosophers have only *interpreted* the world, in various ways; the point is to *change* it"(Marx, 1845/1970, p. 123).

must, it can be argued, be given a central role. Jensen (this volume) starts in this direction.

Questions about the relation between research, intervention, and decent human conditions echo explicitly through the chapters by Nussbaum, Turner, and Tobach. Similar concerns are often seen in the background of the chapters about different forms of social practice. For example, Álvarez & del Río's analysis of cultural identity is part of the societal process of developing a cultural identity among the people in the Castilian region in Spain where they are working. Engeström, Engeström, and Vähäaho mention the ethical dimension as an essential part of understanding the changing configurations between professionals and patients in a medical setting. Hedegaard writes explicitly about the interest of using her analysis of immigrant parents' conceptions as part of a foundation for making interventions into the practices of Danish schools. Rubtsov's review of current developments in educational practices and policies in Russia can be understood as reflecting an interest in developing interventions in relation to social practices that are motivated by an analysis of those practices.

### Social Practice as the Key to Understanding Cultural, Ethnic and Gender Variations

Cultural, gender, ethnic and national differences are classic topics in the social sciences. Activity theory and cultural-historical research based on activity theory have not addressed these issues to any significant extent, even though they are topics which one might expect to be well-developed within this approach.

The concept of social practice, interpreted as activity located in different institutions, gives a possibility to focus on the dynamic between traditions for collective activity and the realization of collective activity in institutions through a subject's actions. This creates a way to transcend categories of culture, gender, and ethnicity as fixed or natural qualities, and to understand persons as participating in several different activities in different institutions. Being involved with activities in different societal institutions creates possibilities for persons to appropriate different capacities. Both Tulviste's and Hedegaard's chapters (this volume) argue that to transcend the dichotomized description of culture and capacity, one must consider a person's involvement in many different institutionalized activities throughout life.

Tulviste turns the question in Luria's classical research around and instead of asking how conceptual differences between persons belonging to different cultural traditions can be explained, he asks how the activities in which a person has been involved influences a person's mode of thinking.

Hedegaard discusses the relations and conflicts between different institutional practices, cultural positions and personal motives. She focuses on the different traditions for social practices in home and school, which become more visible when the traditions for social practice are exaggerated through a person's association to different cultural positions. She describes how conflicts in parents' expectations to social practice in school can create different conditions for children's school activity.

Both John-Steiner (this volume) and Nussbam (this volume) raise issues of gender. John-Steiner notes that there are many common points to be found between cultural-historical and feminist theory, particularly the idea of interdependence in developmental processes. She discusses several examples of differences in practice traditions depending on whether men and women are involved, reflecting on the need for cultural-historical theory to take these historical differences more clearly and explicitly in the future. Nussbaum, by considering traditions and practices in India, raises a series of questions for Western feminists to consider, and reflects on the importance of the social practices in formulating ideas about the quality of life. One can see that the attention to historically-contingent social practice raises new challenges and issues for the cultural-historical tradition.

## Directions for Further Development

### Relating Activity and Social Practice to Other Traditions

The task of relating the notions of activity and social practice found in the cultural-historical approach to other social scientific traditions (including philosophy) needs to be continued. For example, Lektorsky (this volume) has noted similarities between the cultural-historical concept of activity and the idea of self-organizing systems as described by Prigogine and Stengers. John-Steiner (this volume) notes the relevance of recent feminist scholarship, especially in relation to epistemological issues, and the value in considering its integration into the cultural-historical tradition. We can also mention the narrative approach to social practice as another possibility (e.g., Bruner, 1986), and Marx Wartofsky's cultural-historical philosophy, which contributes to the development of activity theory through his conceptualization of the relation between person and world as dialectic and nondeterministic.

Wartofsky (1983) describes the person's construction of the world and its objects as a construction that goes through social practice:

Since this cognitive history involves the making and use of artifacts, that is, of tools, and language, and social structures, and also involves the ramified historical forms of such activity, one may argue that the objects of cognition are not alien, external objects, but are already invested with human intentionality, with the sociality and historicity of their genesis, and with the specifically historical character of the human life-world in which these objects function or in which they arise. (p. 196)

Wartofsky also conceptualizes the development of the personal subject, his self and intentionality as a construction through social practice the same way as external objects and the world are created. He clearly brings the individual as an agent in social practice and his/her development, and thereby transcends a critique of the cultural-historical approach as culturally determined.

Wartofsky pointed out that cultural-historical theory is not only a theory about society, but it also plays a role in shaping the actions and self-conception of that society's members: "the theory in effect, changes the very artifact it studies" (p. 212). This point is central to Bruner's (this volume) discussion of the history of research on infants and the researchers' contribution to "creating" the idea of the information-seeking, competent, social, intentional-oriented infant. Bruner's "story" tells us, in line with Wartofsky's point, that cultural conceptions of a child conditions the research that is conducted on children, but at the same time research can change cultural conceptions, and thereby change children's developmental conditions.

*Elaborating the Activity Concept*

Several chapters in this volume have attempted to move beyond, what now is starting to become a commonplace assumption within the tradition, and started to explore dimensions of activity that have not received sufficient attention. Three dimensions that are discussed in this volume are communication, the collective, and emotions.

The relation between activity and communcation is an issue that still needs further analysis and clarification. González Rey criticizes the traditional activity approach for taking too narrow a view of the process of communication, viewing communication as an object-based activity. In contrast, Fichtner, citing Davydov, argues that communication is always occurring within activity. Both González Rey and Fichtner, as well as Lektorsky, note that communication must be understood much more broadly than conscious, verbal language, with González Rey mentioning the importance of the communication process in developing intentions and emotions, and Fichtner noting the communicative structures of preverbal children.

Davydov (this volume) also considers the importance of communication in relation to activity, emphasizing what he considers an overlooked point, namely that communication is always conducted in relation to a collectivity and in relation to our ideal conception of the capabilities of others in that collectivity. Lektorsky (this volume) makes a similar observation, and starts to consider the implications for how we should understand activity.

The importance of the integrating the concept of the collective more explicitly into activity theory was a major theme for Davydov, and in recent years he expressed repeatedly and vigorously the importance of addressing this issue. Davydov emphasizes the importance of considering the collective, in the form of a team, and the ways in which collective activity become individual activity. From this perspective, one can understand the work reported by Engeström et al. as either moving in the direction of Davydov's vision, or alternatively as a denial of the universality of collective activity being internalized. The Engeström et al. idea of knotworking suggests that individuals are constantly composing and recomposing collectives in work settings. Whether these local compositions can be understood as reflecting more general collectives remains to be explored.

To this point we have focused primarily on the relationship between activity and social practice. The issue of the relation between the individual and the collective often gets misunderstood or misinterpreted as providing a deterministic model of individual development. One meets, all-too-often, the misunderstanding that activity must be a deterministic theory, because it postulates that humans develop in relation to societal demands and processes. The individual disappears into the societal "stamping factory," which simply reproduces new individuals.

This understanding is simply wrong. It does not reflect the cultural-historical tradition, which from the start has focused on the interactions between persons, such as in Vygotsky's discussion of the zone of proximal development, and between persons and society. For example, the relation between objective meaning and personal sense discussed in Leontiev (1975/1978), and used by Hedegaard (this volume), provides a way to understand societal demands as a necessary framework within which people function. But this framework does not determine the specific form of development. Rather it creates a frame of possibilities.

A similar issue is raised concerning the role of emotions in activity theory. Fichtner (this volume) praises the productive final period of Vygotsky's work. John-Steiner (this volume) views the same work as inadequate in its understanding of emotions. Similarly, González Rey (this volume) argues that the classical cultural-historical approach has been too cognitively oriented, while Davydov (this volume) argues for the importance of introducing desires and emotions into the general theoretical model of activity.

Ultimately, we do not see any fundamental conflict here. It is clear that there has always been an interest in questions of emotions and needs and the subjective development of activity within the cultural-historical tradition. The problem has been to develop theoretical concepts that can be used to productively investigate these questions, while maintaining the basic insights about the historically-constructed nature of these phenomena

González Rey (this volume) takes up the problem of subjectivity in activity theory and debates Leontiev's and Elkonin's conception of personality development as determined by the leading activity in different developmental periods. He points out that the core of personality is a subjective phenomenon, which is always a synthesis of many different objective social facts and situations. Objective social influences become subjective through their emotional constitution by the subject. Therefore, development does not follow any standard rules that lead to regular transitions from one stage to another according to an age criterion.

### Conclusion

We take this volume to be a sign that the cultural-historical tradition is healthy and growing. While there are many points of general agreement in this book, there are also many points where sharp criticisms are made about the research that has been conducted within the tradition. This is a positive sign in our view, because it indicates the development of a tradition of practice that is self-sustaining, and less dependent on an "enemy-based" identity (see Álvarez & del Río, this volume).

Intervention into ongoing social practices is an important area for further reflection and action by activity theorists. If our suggestion about the unity of social practice in both its interventive and theoretical meanings is accepted, then activity theorists will have to confront an issue that has long been problematic in academic research institutions where much of the research is conducted. The traditional conception is that one cannot mix academic research and scholarship with intervention and advocacy of particular points of view. Activity theory may have important theoretical resources for developing arguments for why it is necessary to make interventions into social practice as a part of the method for the articulation and development of concepts and categories that are used to analyze and develop social practice.

### References

Bol, E., Haenen, J.P.P., & Wolters, M. (Eds.). (1985). *Education for cognitive development*. The Hague: SVO.

Bruner, J. (1986). *Actual minds, possible worlds*. Cambridge, Mass.: Harvard University Press.

Davydov (Dawydow), W. (1977). *Arten der Verallgemeinerung im Unterricht* (K. Krüger, Trans). Berlin: Volk und Wissen. (Original work published 1972)

Davydov, V.V. (1990). *Types of generalization in instruction* (J. Kilpatrick, Ed.; J. Teller, Trans.). Reston, Va.: National Council of Teachers of Mathematics. (Original work published 1972)

Davydov, V.V. (1995). The influence of L.S. Vygotsky on education theory, research, and practice (S. Kerr, Trans.). *Educational Researcher, 24*(3), 12-21.

Elkonin, D.B. (1972). Toward the problem of stages in the mental development of the child. *Soviet Psychology, 10,* 225-251.

Elkonin, D.B. (1988). *Legens psykologi* (J. Hansen, Trans.). Moscow: Sputnik. (Original work published 1978)

Engeström, Y., Miettinen, R., & Punamäki, R.-L. (Eds.). (1998). *Perspectives on activity theory.* Cambridge: Cambridge University Press.

Hedegaard, M. (1990). The zone of proximal development as basis for instruction. In L.C. Moll (Ed.), *Vygotsky and education: Instructional implications and applications of sociohistorical psychology* (pp. 349-371). Cambridge: Cambridge University Press.

Hedegaard, M., & Chaiklin, S. (1995). Building cultural identity of minority children through social studies education. In J. Hjärno (Ed.), *Multiculturalism in the Nordic societies* (pp. 231-242). Copenhagen: Nordic Council of Ministers.

Hedegaard, M., Hakkarainen, P., & Engeström, Y. (Eds.). (1984). *Learning and teaching on a scientific basis.* Aarhus, Denmark: University of Aarhus, Department of Psychology.

Hildebrand-Nilshon, M., & Rückriem, G. (Eds.). (1988). *Proceedings of the First International Congress on Activity Theory* (Vol. 1-4). Berlin: Druck und Verlag System Druck.

Ilyenkov, E.V. (1977). The concept of the ideal (R. Daglish, Trans.). In *Philosophy in the USSR: Problems of dialectical materialism* (pp. 71-99). Moscow: Progress.

Latour, B. (1987). *Science in action.* Cambridge, Mass.: Harvard University Press.

Lave, J. & Wenger, E. (1991). *Situated learning.* Cambridge: Cambridge University Press.

Leontiev, A.N. (1932) The development of voluntary attention in the child. *The Pedagogical Seminary and Journal of Genetic Psychology 40,* 52-83.

Leontiev, A.N. (1978). Activity, consciousness, personality (M.J. Hall, Trans.). Englewood Cliffs, N.J.: Prentice-Hall (Original work published 1975)

Lompscher, J. (1984). Problems and results of experimental research on the formation of theoretical thinking through instruction. In M. Hedegaard, P. Hakkarainen, & Y. Engeström (Eds.), (1984). *Learning and teaching on a scientific basis* (pp. 293-357). Aarhus, Denmark: University of Aarhus, Department of Psychology.

Markova, A.K. (1982). Das ausbildende Experiment in der psychologis-chen Erforschung der Lerntätigkeit. In V.V. Davydov, J. Lompscher, & A.K. Markova (Eds.), *Ausbildung der Lerntätigkeit bei Schülern* (pp. 74-83). Berlin: Volk und Wissen.

Marx, K. (1964). *Economic and philosophic manuscripts of 1844* (D.J. Struik, Ed.; M. Milligan, Trans.). New York: International Publishers.

Marx, K. (1970). Theses on Feuerbach. In C.J. Arthur (Ed.), *The German ideology* (pp. 121-123). New York: International Publishers. (Original work written 1845)

Nussbaum, M.C. (1994). *The therapy of desire.* Princeton, N.J.: Princeton University Press.

Pickering, A. (1995). *The mangle of practice.* Chicago: University of Chicago Press.

Vygotskaya, G., & Lifanova, T. (1996). *Lev Semonovich Vygotsky.* Moscow: Smysl.

Vygotsky (Vygotski), L.S. (1929) The problem of the cultural develop-ment of the child. *The Pedagogical Seminary and Journal of Genetic Psychology 36,* 415-434.

Vygotsky, L.S. (1997a). The historical meaning of the crisis in psychol-ogy: A methodological investigation. In R.W. Reiber & J. Wollock (Eds.), *The collected works of L.S. Vygotsky: Vol. 3. Problems of the theory and history of psychology* (pp. 233-343). New York: Plenum Press. (Original work written 1927)

Vygotsky, L.S. (1997b). *The collected works of L.S. Vygotsky: Vol. 4. The history of the development of higher mental functions* (R.W. Reiber, Ed.; M.J. Hall, Trans). New York: Plenum Press. (Original work written 1931)

Wartofsky, M. (1983). The child's construction of the world and the world's construction of the child: From historical epistemology to historical psychology. In F.S. Kessel & A.W. Siegel (Eds.), *The child and other cultural inventions* (pp. 188-215). New York: Praeger.

# 2 On Vygotsky's Research and Life

*Ghita Vygotskaya*

More than one hundred years ago, in the city of Orsha, Lev Semonovich Vygotsky was born.

He was destined to live a short life, only 37 years, but in this brief time he accomplished so much that even now his thoughts and ideas, his name and character, his life itself continue to attract the attention of the best scholars worldwide. Unfortunately, there is no one still alive who knew Lev Semonovich well and who could speak about him truthfully. I am the only witness to the last years of his life. We didn't simply live together, we shared the same room and therefore all of his life of that period unfolded right in front of me.

Of course, I could not understand (and did not understand) those discussions that Lev Semonovich had with his colleagues, students and friends at that time. But, probably, because I loved him very much, I always understood him. I knew what he liked and what he didn't like, what pleased him and what distressed him. I always sensed his mood and even, at times, his spirits and thoughts. I understood him and related to him not through my mind, but through my heart. Usually one best remembers the things that are loaded with strong emotions. All of my childhood, when Lev Semonovich was alive, has been very happy. It was so flooded with feelings that to this day I have preserved in my memory all that had happened in those distant years, even details that now might seem insignificant.

I remember an amusing episode. I am five years old. Lev Semonovich has guests, but I don't remember who exactly is there that night. They are talking and I am quietly preparing to go to bed. Suddenly Leontiev sneezes loudly, and everyone pretends not to notice. In my eagerness to be a good, polite young lady, I say to him loudly, "God bless you! Grow up to be big and smart." Leontiev laughs. Luria and Mama laugh too. I am surprised at their reaction. I glance at Lev Semonovich and realize that he is embarrassed. But why? Looking at him I understand that I have done something improper. But what? I only said what people always told me in similar situations and still I have done something improper. I know this from looking at Lev

Semonovich's face and from his reaction to my words. Mama interrupts my thoughts. She tells me to go to sleep, and I, reluctantly, obey. In the morning when I wake up, I see that Lev Semonovich is getting ready to leave. All the same I ask him what I did wrong the night before. He does not get angry with me and says smiling: "Well, you see, that's really not the way to talk to grownups. It's not appropriate. You can just wish them good health." "But why?" I ask, bewildered. Lev Semonovich is in a hurry and as he says goodbye, adding: "Figure it out for yourself. Think a while and you'll understand." And he leaves. I keep thinking about what happened the whole day long and it tortures me — Suddenly it becomes clear! I wait impatiently for Lev Semonovich to return to test the accuracy of my conclusion. Finally, he arrives and I come rushing up to him with the words, "Adults think that they are as smart as they can be?! And that they don't have to get smarter?!" Lev Semonovich laughs, hugs me and says, "Well, on the whole, you're right. You understood correctly."

I couldn't possibly explain at that time what kind of scholar Lev Semonovich was. I was unable to understand this when he was alive but I understand it now, just as you do, from his works. But there is something that only I know now. It is how he lived and worked and what kind of person he was. Anyone who thinks this is important will find, I hope, something interesting in my story.

Science was at the center of his life. He devoted his whole life to it. If I were to describe his relationship to science in one word, it would be obsession. Having begun his scientific studies when still at school, he never abandoned this path. He continued his studies in any settings and under any circumstances. Even when the doctors gave him only a short time to live, since his condition was considered hopeless (and he was aware of this!) he wrote, in the most trying circumstances "The Historical Meaning of the Crisis in Psychology." "I do not know anything that is distinguished by such remarkable clarity of thought, such beauty of logic, as this work," said Luria. "Lev Semonovich Vygotsky wrote this piece in a tragic situation, when he was struck with tuberculosis. The doctors gave him three or four months to live and put him in a sanatorium. Here he began to write enthusiastically so as to leave behind some fundamental work."

His interest in science took many forms. It could be work on theoretical or methodological questions, where he carefully thought through and wrote his papers regardless of what was going on around him (children were playing just a foot away from his desk). It could be discussions on scientific matters with colleagues and students about how to interpret findings gained in experimental research and how to plan future research. It could be delivering lectures, which always included both theoretical and empirical issues. And always, each hour of his life, he thought about science and was in its service. He served science with devotion and faith, without taking any days off. He worked even during holidays and summer vacations. His colleagues recall his "remarkable attitude to science. He devoted his whole life to it, forgetting about food and his own well-being. He was constantly working." His "intense involvement in his work ... verged on a total neglect of all other things, including his own health."

He worked on manuscripts at his desk. The desk was large, inherited by Lev Semonovich from his father; it stood near the windows. It was probably Lev Semonovich's sole private possession. When I entered school, he shared it with me so I could do my school tasks, and I, too, became it is rightful owner. From that moment on, we often sat next to each other, while I prepared my school tasks, or was reading and drawing, and he kept working. He would sit at the desk for hours, often deep into the night. In the evening, when I prepared to go to bed, he would still be writing. I would close my eyes...and fall asleep. Some time during the night I would wake up. It was silent in the room, the overhead light was off, my little sister was breathing heavily in her sleep, Mama was sleeping quietly...But at his desk, illuminated by the desk lamp, bent over, Lev Semonovich would be working. Sometimes I called him in a whisper and he, alarmed, immediately came up to me, touched my forehead, asked if I had a bad dream and whether I needed something and caressed my head tenderly. I would tell him "Go to bed, it's already the middle of the night." "Yes, yes," he would answer, "I'll go to bed soon. I'll just work a little while longer. You just go back to sleep, please." And again he sat down at the desk...

When he was working I was not allowed to call him or disturb him in any way. I tried not to violate this rule. But sometimes I urgently needed his advice or help. I remember very well how once I wanted to know right away whether God existed and, of course, I could not wait. Another time I wanted to convince him to give up such unappealing, from my point of view, work as he had and become instead a policeman on the boat. And I also was very impatient at times. It could be for any reason that I suddenly had to talk to him! At such times I "invented" a special tactic how I could get his attention without violating the rule. I simply approached him from the back, almost touching him and waited patiently until he noticed me. Most often he sensed my presence, turned around and, seeing that I was right next to him, put down his pen. Then he would put his arm around my shoulders and ask what happened. He never once became angry that I interrupted him.

There were unforgettable moments when Lev Semonovich invited me and my cousin (who grew up with us) to participate in his experiments. We always waited impatiently for this to happen. He seemed so cheerful and relaxed that we were both absolutely convinced that it was simply interesting for him to play with us. For some reason, I remember especially well how we participated in experiments similar to those that Köhler had previously conducted with primates. On the floor of the room a labyrinth was constructed whose walls took the shape of various objects, including low, narrow boxes with bibliography cards. In the center of the labyrinth was an orange. We really wanted to get this orange and we tried as hard as we could. If we were successful, Lev Semonovich was as happy as we were.

I remember, too, how I am sitting at the desk, next to Lev Semonovich or opposite to him, and in front of me are colorful experimental materials. Lev Semonovich calmly and at the same time cheerfully offers me various tasks to solve and takes notes on little pieces of paper of everything that I am doing and saying as I try to solve the tasks. This is how he conducted an experiment on the formation of scientific concepts using Sakharov's method. The subject of Lev Semonovich's scientific analysis was not only experiments conducted with our participation, but also many observations of our behavior, of our games and spontaneous reactions. His notebooks have plenty of such detailed observations.

If he needed to clarify or verify something, he created unique situations and posed specially formulated "tricky" questions. So, for example, probably wanting to find out how a child can defend his or her own answer, he once said to me: "Well, someone had a dog. Dog's name was Jack. When the man was getting ready to leave, he always said to the dog: 'Jack, are you coming or staying?' And Jack always either went or stayed!" I swallowed the bait: "But that's the only thing the dog could possibly do!" "But that's exactly what the dog always did!" Lev Semonovich argued. I understood the situation, but could not formulate the idea that "there is no third option." I got all worked up, trying to explain to my father that I did understand, but he only smiled. On the other hand, he was really amused by my younger sister's reaction to this story. She had listened to him calmly, then sighed and said thoughtfully, "Such a smart dog. It must have been trained."

It was a rare evening that his colleagues or students did not come to visit him. He would work with them all through the evening, but after they left, he would again sit down to write.

These talks with colleagues and students could last for hours. It was during these discussions, which seemed to me to be so boring, that I would go to bed and fall asleep. I remember the time when Lev Semonovich was writing *Thinking and Speech*. I am sick; my bed has been moved right up to the side of the bookshelf. I am lying in the same room where Lev Semonovich is working and I can observe him for hours. In my bed are toys and books to keep me busy and I play silently with them, so as not to disturb my father. A stenographer, who comes every morning, sits at the desk. Lev Semonovich is walking across the room with his hands behind his back, and dictates the text. He dictates without pauses, without faltering, at the same even pace. As he dictates, he pronounces the word *chelovek* (Russian for a human being) as *chek*, which seems terribly funny to me. When I get tired of playing, I begin to count how many times he pronounces this word. Around every hour or hour and a half, the stenographer stops to take a break and have a cup of tea. During such breaks, Lev Semonovich comes up to me and asks what he can do for me and whether I need something. At the same time I tell him the results of my calculations and we both laugh. He keeps working this way until evening. His work does not end when the stenographer leaves. He sits at his desk until deep into the night. In the morning everything begins all over again. What is the source of his strength?!

Lev Semonovich was such a riveting lecturer! Many people remembered this and told me about it. "His lectures were always a great event. For him, it was quite ordinary to read a lecture for three, four, even five hours in a row, using only a sheet of paper with notes," Elkonin recalled. "During his lectures, Vygotsky would toss around great blocks of information like in a fairy tale, incorporating scores of names and quotations, at the same time maintaining a high theoretical level," Shif added. "The way Lev Semonovich gave his lectures and taught how to think astonished me and has remained in my memory until this day," said Elkonin. And he continued:

Usually the entire department of pedagogy and psychology went to these lectures, although they were meant for students only of one particular grade level. Lev Semonovich's speech, without external affectation, with a minimum of gestures, but at the same time extremely emotionally expressive, rich in thought, precise and flowing, captivated the audience from the first to the last minute. It never occurred to anyone to talk to each other during his lectures, to take notes or whisper. But we not only listened to him during his lectures, we were thinking intensively. I heard a series of lectures and saw how each time they changed, enriched by new ideas.

Never, not in any circumstances, did he lose his interest in science. Here are a few excerpts from Vygotsky's letters. The first two letters were written during an acute attack of tuberculosis, when he was so sick that he had to stay in bed. He writes to one of his students:

For a whole week I have been in the hospital in a large room that accommodates six gravely ill people. Noise, shouting ... the beds are lined up with no space in-between, as in a barrack. I am in excruciating pain and morally dispirited.

Yet, a little later on in the same letter he writes:

I really want to know what you'll begin with first. It seems to me (between us), that now you have to experiment with the transformation of reactions... You have to experiment on the simplest forms, to demonstrate what constitutes a transformation in a given instance. An experimenter must be a detective, inventor, contriver, creator of traps, always flexible and bold. Be well. Your L.V.

In another letter:

Dear Aleksandr Romanovich, I have wanted to write to you for a long time, but all around me the situation was such that I felt ashamed and uneasy to take up my pen and unable to think calmly. I feel myself being outside of life, or rather, between life and death... And so my thoughts are not focused on questions of my future life and work.

Yet, just a little bit later, he expresses interest in Luria's life and plans, reflects on and evaluates the latter's work. He writes:

This is an important contribution to the foundation of your previous work. It is a justification of its methods... For me, the primary question is one of the method, which is a question of the truth, that is, of scientific discovery and invention. But theoretically, I see many dangers in the new experiments for your earlier conclusions: the boundary between emotional (affective) reactions and all others is erased, the source of emotion (affect) disappears and your theory of emotions is challenged. How I would like to exchange thoughts on this in a "private talk" at your seminar! Write if you can. What is new in foreign and Russian literature?

And in yet another letter: "I am suffering from tuberculosis and the anticipation of what seems to be an unavoidable operation in the fall (in one lung the caverns refuse to close!)." Later on he writes:

There is only one truly serious matter: each person working with the instrumental method in their discipline. I am investing all my future life and strength in this ... I shake your hand warmly and urge you to prepare (spiritually, of course) for our work together.

Lev Semonovich had great respect for his scientific predecessors (even if he didn't share their views) and taught this to his students. Morozova recalled having once received from him a book by Groos with an inscription that read "this is the best that has been said about play, and it must be mastered, because it is the naturalistic theory of play." Later on he wrote: "Don't forget that we are standing on his shoulders. We are higher, we see further, but we see because of what he did before us."

Elkonin could never forget how Lev Semonovich related to his students. Daniil Borisovich said that Lev Semonovich possessed

an extraordinary ability to give support, to find behind each thought something new, sound and progressive, and an ability to correct mistakes sometimes imperceptibly. For a long time we did not notice how he gave shape to our inadequately formulated, raw ideas ... and presented them back to us as our own creative thoughts. I have probably never met a single person who was so little interested in proclaiming his own authorship as Lev Semonovich. It was the extraordinary generosity and scope of ideas of the kind of person who gave everything to everyone. Ideas erupted from him like a volcano.

Lev Semonovich brought his students together into scientific groups. Morozova recalled that Lev Semonovich created an unusual moral climate around himself, where people were very closer to one another.

His students retained a feeling of love, loyalty and gratitude toward their teacher. They kept these feelings to the end of their lives. Now they are gone. Not one of his students is now living. It is their students and students of their students who are now working in science. They are continuing his ideas, developing and specifying them. This is how the school of Vygotsky lives on. My father was the dearest, closest person of my childhood. I admired him, he seemed so strong to me. I loved him very much. He always understood me, always was prepared to answer my endless questions, always helped me out and devoted his attention to me... I still admire him. And I still love him. If someone were to ask me to tell briefly what he was like, I would find no better answer than in the words from his beloved work: "He was truly a human being, a human being in every aspect, I will never again meet anyone like him..."

Death awaits every person. Unfortunately, this is inevitable. But some do find immortality.

# 3 A New Approach to the Interpretation of Activity Structure and Content

*Vasily V. Davydov*

The subject of my present report is a new approach to the interpretation of activity structure and content. It is up to you to judge to what extent the approach is new. But in my view there is a certain novelty in what I am going to tell you today.

Theories of activity have been in the process of development for a considerable time. It was the focus of philosophical and sociological studies in the 19th century, and psychological aspects of activity were expounded by the efforts of our prominent scholars, Sergei Leonidovich Rubinshtein and Alexei Nikolaevich Leontiev early in the 20th century. Their theories of activity are similar in some aspects and different in others but at present those theories of activity can be considered classical.

Still it took much time to master those theories after they had been formulated. But during the last decade, in my view, there have been several advances in activity theory. One of those was made by Vladimir Solomonovich Bibler, our well-known philosopher, logician, culturologist and somewhat a psychological theorist. He presented his views on activity in several lectures read at the Institute of Psychology in Moscow in 1982.

The second important advance in interpretation of activity in its global meaning was made in Andrei Vladimirovich Brushlinsky's works and especially in his book *The Activity Subject*. The book was published quite recently. Not only did he give the most essential and important characteristics of activity, based on many recent research results, but those who read the book closely can also come to a new interpretation of some important characteristics of activity.

* This chapter is the keynote lecture that Professor Davydov prepared for the Fourth Congress of the International Society for Cultural Research and Activity Theory. The editors thank Joachim Lompscher for his help in preparing the manuscript for publication.

In recent years, Yuri Vyatcheslavovich Gromyko has published several books and articles. They are not as well-known as the previously mentioned ones, but in my view, Yuri Vyatcheslavovich has quite a special way of defining activity, *thought-activity (mysledeyatelnost)*, in his terminology, on the plane of methodology. This concept of thought-activity was formulated by Gromyko's teacher, Georgi Petrovich Shchedrovitskii, who also had a very special theory of activity.

Then. In my view a very interesting theory of activity was presented by the Finnish psychologist Yrjö Engeström who did not refute Rubinshtein's or Leontiev's ideas but assimilated many of those and worked out his own interpretation of activity in his marvelous book published in 1987. His publications in our country are scarce unlike in the U.S.A. where a considerable number of his works have been published.

A specific type of activity is investigated by Elkonin's school, that of learning activity. Activity being of many types, aspects and forms, it is difficult to orient oneself in its structure and content and work out an abstract theory unless one type of activity is extensively and thoroughly studied.

Nevertheless there have been some advances made in the activity theory within the recent decade and I have tried to outline the most important ones as well as to present the authors' names.

My own report will consist of two parts.

First. I will try to describe and then — as far as I can — ground the proposed activity structure, because its general structure can be found both in Rubinshtein's theory and in Leontiev's theory. But many consequences may be derived from the proposed activity structure.

Second. The main part of my report will be concerned with a cell of activity content. There are many things here that are new for me. I am still unable to expound some of them, but the cell is what I will try to present to you.

But I have not succeeded yet in connecting the structure I am going to tell you about with the cell because to do this requires a new and original approach in understanding activity. I am searching for this new approach but until now I have not found any. Therefore, I will present the two new ideas — the structure of activity and the cell of activity content — separately (and you will realize they are separate).

Further I will rely on the activity structure presented by A.N. Leontiev. He considers activity as consisting of needs, tasks, actions and operations. I agree with this activity structure but I extend it as follows:

A.N. Leontiev did not consider a *desire*[1] as an element of the psychological structure of activity. In my view activity structure cannot be psychological, it is interdisciplinary, that is why only a certain aspect of it can be studied in psychology.

Unlike the above the desire is essential in the interdisciplinary structure of activity which can come into any human science. A desire is a core basis of a need. As far as biological, or human organic, needs are concerned — and the fact is medically established — there are mental diseases in which persons deny to eat food. There are cases of certain people who would have died if they were not given artificial nutrition because any food caused not only aversion but various kinds of excretions. There is no nutritional need but there is a bodily desire of organic substances! The problem is to find the way that desire is usually transformed into a corresponding organic need.

Nobody has seriously investigated transformation of certain desires into needs not even in the organic. But, while observing people, one can find that those who have, for example, no aesthetic needs show a desire for beauty — however pervertedly perceived — in certain ways and by certain behaviors. The topic deserves a special and long discussion but the observations provide us with the grounds for the following statement: a person has not only spiritual needs but also desires of humanitarian nature, not of organic, but of humanitarian nature. Take the desire of beauty as an example, the desire that was not transformed into a certain aesthetic need. By the way, that is the particular issue classical aesthetics is investigating while psychologists make no attempts to solve it. How is the spiritual desire of beauty transformed into an aesthetic need? Or into the need to enjoy music, poetry, prose or sculpture?

In my view nothing can be said about activity unless one understands spiritual or organic desire and how it is transformed into a need.

A.N. Leontiev also argued, and quite rightfully, that a need is the basis of activity but he repudiated the necessity of psychological and humanitarian investigation of a desire (or desires). I believe that the desire should be considered as an element of activity structure.

Needs and desires make the basis on which emotions function. The term *sphere of needs and emotions* emerged in psychology not without reason. From our observation of real life and certain research data we

---

1. The Russian word in the original manuscript was *nuzhda*. In German an appropriate translation might be *Bedarf*. (Eds.)

can understand that emotions and needs cannot be considered separately, the latter showing themselves in emotional manifestations.

The term *desire* hits the very essence of the matter: Emotions are inseparable from a need. While discussing a certain emotion we can always identify the need the emotion is based on. And when we are discussing a certain kind of need we have to define the emotions that stem from it to specify the above.

Now I will briefly outline the functions of emotions.

Emotions enable man to set vital tasks for himself and I mean human activity only. I admit activity in man only, animals cannot have any. Activity is, in my view, a phenomenon of social-public nature, of human nature.

Every person who regards himself as a supporter of the activity approach cannot but consider task as an important element of activity structure. The fact was acknowledged both by Rubinshtein and by Leontiev. Whatever differences there were in their views on other points, they interpreted the meaning of task in the same way: a task is a unity of a goal and the conditions to achieve the goal. I agree with this also. Setting oneself a task the person is setting a goal to be achieved in the specific conditions. There are some problems with this formulation, but I am not going to dwell on those. Anyway — if the conditions for goal achievement are changed while the goal is not, the task is change as well. So it is quite a problem to get insight into the nature of the task.

But the achievement of any human goal is invariably connected with transformation of certain fields of material or social reality. There can be no reality without transformation. It may be transformation of nature (another matter is whether the transformation is right or wrong), a forced change of nature or of social reality (also right or wrong).

A task is fulfilled through some special actions, this thesis can also be found in Leontiev's structure of activity. Some special motives correspond to acting, and the actions performed in the process are connected with using certain means (or tools if the material plane is meant).

So actions, motives and means can be included as constituent elements in the activity structure alongside with task. And this is the point of divergence from Leontiev's structure.

Leontiev states in his writings that actions are connected with needs and motives. It cannot be so. Actions as integral formations can be connected with nothing but needs based on desires, and the actions aimed at fulfilling certain tasks stem from motives. Motives in their turn are specific forms of needs in the case when a person has set himself a task and is undertaking certain actions to fulfill it. Thus motives are consistent with actions. Actions are based on motives, and acting is possible if certain material or sign and symbol means are available.

But the tasks can be on the plane of perception, or memory, or thinking, or imagination, and psychologists who adhere to the activity approach in their studies have been carrying out numerous investigations into peculiarities of tasks and ways of fulfilling them. What kind of tasks? The tasks in question are perceptual, mnemonic, thinking, and tasks connected with imagination or creativity. These are cognitive processes. Through such processes, or fulfilling of tasks, one finds a way to one's goal on the plane of perception, memory, thinking, and imagination. Additionally, there is a thing that helps one achieve one's goal through fulfilling certain tasks and this can be called *will*.

Will is always connected with the realization of a plan to achieve the goal. The plan is formal in the process of fulfilling perceptual, mnemonic, thinking, creative or other tasks.

This is the specified activity structure I tried to present to you. I am not going to present any drawings here, especially because it is very difficult to do it on only one plane, but I can enumerate the structural elements. They are: desires, needs, emotions, tasks, actions, action motives, means used for actions, planes (perceptual, mnemonic, thinking, creative) — all those refer to cognition and also will.

Piotr Iakovlevich Galperin's investigations of activity structure specified orientation, executive, and control elements of action. Yes, those elements are present in action. But I believe these three structural components can also be correlated with activity.

The executive part is an integral activity aimed at achieving a goal and satisfying a need.

The orientation part comprises the above planes.

P.I. Galperin exhibited his insight when he interpreted control as attention and, from this point of view, will as implementation of a plan to achieve a goal can also be called control. Will is control through attention. And it can now be understood why attention is not regarded as a cognitive process in many textbooks on psychology. Attention is a certain phenomenon on quite a different plane. It is a control mechanism functioning in the process of realizing the plan to achieve a goal and it relates to will.

From this point of view the problem of setting up a typology of activity types, patterns and forms emerges. It is the most difficult task and I am not going to dwell on it. There are different principles to be assumed as the basis for a typology of activity and two of those can be named.

First, the activity types which were developed in the course of human history. What are those types?

The fundamental kind of activity is work; next is artistic activity, then activity in the field of morals, of law, of religion and in my view sport has emerged as an activity within the past century. The reference is not made to specialized mass sport but to sport as a kind of human activity. I have enumerated the activity types that are present for the majority of civilized people.

The second basic principle is the activity types that emerge in the ontogenetic process. In my writings those activities are referred to as reproductive ones. They are: object manipulatory activity, play activity (though the latter is present in adults as well, it has emerged in human history and is characteristic to a vast majority of people. I just failed to mention it alongside with productive, religious and sporting activities as being specified on the same basic principle.) Another one is learning activity. All the above emerge in ontogeny.

There are more specific basic principles. I believe one of those is the principle by means of which there can be specified the scientific activity which is formed first within a small number of people and then within an ever-growing number of people. Because this activity has a social-mass character, the number of people who participate productively in this activity is important.

For me, according to the activity structure I have outlined, there does not exist activities with broad, commonly-used titles: no perceptual, no mnemonic and no thinking activities.

There are thinking actions — because they are aimed at fulfilling thinking tasks. There are motives to perform those actions, but the very thinking tasks stem from human needs and emotions. And that is why from the very beginning, since the middle and late 1950s I have been arguing with Georgi Petrovich Shchedrovitskii who introduced the concept of *mysledeyatelnost* (thought-activity) into the methodology used in those days.

The *thought* part of the compound word can be deleted, but *activity* with its general and integral characteristics will stay and can be used, even in the way Shchedrovitskii prescribed.

I use the term *thinking activity* quite rarely. I do use the term *thought* or *thinking action*, but not thinking activity.

Then the question arises — and what about science? Most probably there is a scientific activity or it is in the process of formation. In the 19th and especially in the 20th centuries a specific kind of activity emerged — the scientific activity as an integral activity. So one can specify the desire, need, corresponding emotions and all other characteristics of thinking activity. It is quite clear from this point of view that the most important thing in scientific activity is not reflections, nor thoughts, nor tasks, but the sphere of needs and emotions.

When I read a collection of articles that will be published, I encountered the fact that some authors — thank God — do not relate creativity or giftedness to intelligence or cognition. For intelligence and cogitation are a kind of a fifth wheel with respect to creativity or giftedness; you see I certainly exaggerated the situation. And that is why an artist is poor in cognition but brilliant in painting. A writer could be no philosopher, but a genius, like Leo Tolstoy, a true genius.

The point is that integral activity is based on desire, need and emotion in their many-sidedness. But as far as real human emotions are concerned practically nothing is known.

Incidentally, in this point of view emotions are more fundamental than thoughts, they are the basis for all the diverse tasks a man sets for himself, including thinking tasks. For the first time I found a statement (a brief one) of emotions being more powerful than thinking in an unpublished article by Vladimir Dmitrievich Shadrikov, the only scholar who noted the fact. I liked the statement because it agrees with the activity structure I propose.

Actually nobody has painted a picture — at any level of detail (but details are not yet the point) — of the integral activity including desires, needs, emotions, tasks, actions, motives, means, cognition planes and will (e.g., attention as control).

Such specifications are vital and the laboratory I head is working on a rather specific but not particular kind of activity, that is the learning one. We encounter many problems in our studies and the further we advance the more numerous they become.

The activity that is the most primordial and the most fundamental on the sociophilosophical plane — that is work activity — has not been described by anybody. It is believed that in our country it was the field that Marxist scholars studied. Yes, they did, but for some unknown reasons they were not allowed to study work activity as a whole, as an integral entity. Psychotechnics was also prohibited in those days and alongside with prohibitions on the psychology of labor, sociology of labor and interdisciplinary studies of labor.

This is my hypothesis about activity structure. It is actually the hypothesis proposed by Leontiev but it has been specified considerably.

The most important point is that cognitive processes, not having the status of activity as such, were related to actions and emotions are formed immediately from needs.

The general function emotions perform is that they enable a person to set a certain vital task; but this is half the work. The most important thing is that emotions enable a person to decide from the very beginning whether the physical, spiritual and moral means he needs to fulfill the task are available. If they are — the person starts his analytic apparatus to consider the conditions of achieving the goal. If his emotions say, "No, the means are not available," the person refuses to take up the task.

By the way, the majority of investigations in the psychology of thinking somehow obscure this point, namely the grounds on which a person accepts a task and attempts to fulfill it, successfully or not.

The only school in our country that started investigations into emotions and their relationships with thinking was initiated by Oleg Constantinivich Tikhomirov. Those works, besides being interesting enough, are unique.

I have now discussed the activity structure. The second part of my report will be concerned with an activity cell, but I am going to deliver it in the form of theses.

The first component of the activity cell is transformation of reality by a collective subject in the course of collective activity of this subject. I can repeat — transformation of reality by a collective subject, or, to say it in modern way, by a *team*.

It is a cell in the exact meaning of the word. In the organic world a cell is what everything stems from and is reduced to. But I am not going to explain this complicated cell theory along the lines of the logical theory of ascending from the abstract to the concrete.

Or a unit. It is a more general concept, an activity unit, is a certain kind of integrity, which is always present in any activity.

Any collective activity is always realized in various kinds and forms of material and spiritual communication.

The two points — transformation and communication as activity components — were detailed by Marx in his *Philosophical and Economic Manuscripts* from 1844 and in other of his writings.

The above aspects of the issue — that is transformation and communication — were dwelt on at length by Bibler in the book I have already mentioned.

But in the process of communication, either material or spiritual, a basic principle emerges, to which we all are aware but do not attach any essential meaning to — that is collective performance of a certain activity by individuals. Appealing to the other collective members for true cooperation, for control over my individual actions, and for evaluation of those actions. All the things enumerated can be interpreted as other people's potentialities I have realized.

When I appeal to somebody for something it means that I can conceive other people's potentialities. I would not appeal to a stone! Appealing to other people takes place in the frame of collective activity, the activity that is fraught with individual or team problems.

By the way, appeals to others is the basis from which standards in a collective emerge; and the standards are cultural prototypes. That is, one can appeal to other people, if one is weak himself. But the very fact of appealing to others means, as I have hinted at, that an individual as a constituent of a collective subject has an idea of his associates' positions and potentialities. An individual's awareness of all other people's positions and potentialities is what Ilyenkov called the ideal in man. Following Ilyenkov I call it the ideal plane that is present in an individual.

But certain individuals can appeal to others only on reflecting — in certain ways — over their own actions. Their actions could be unsuccessful, or require aid, evaluation or control which is beyond the individuals' possibilities, but could be rendered by others. That is why such a component as appealing, which presupposes an ideal plane, at the same time presupposes the person's reflection, which is directed toward himself, to his actions, to his component of activity within the collective activity.

Ilyenkov in his writings stated directly that imagination is the only thing that enables a person to conceive others' positions and potentialities. It is imagination that enables a person to look at himself through other people's eyes. It is the individual's awareness of others positions and potentialities.

And when we investigate the ideal plane in an individual and the way it functions through imagination, we will approach the opportunity of defining an individual subject, an individual activity bearer.

What do we mean by an individual subject? We mean an individual's initiative in setting collective activity goals and the individual's responsibility for the initiative, and the responsibility to himself and to the others.

The ideal plane, or imagination (what Ilyenkov called human consciousness), follows from important tenets in Marx's theory, and Marx borrowed a considerable part of those tenets from Hegel. The ideal plane that emerges when people appeal to each other is the basis of human culture. Imagination, a function of which is the ideal plane realization, is consciousness according to Ilyenkov.

I am not going to quote Ilyenkov at length but on page 264 of his collected works titled *Philosophy and Culture*, published in 1991, he said that consciousness proper emerges when an individual gets the opportunity to see himself through other people's eyes. That means that an individual should have the idea of "other people's eyes" (to speak figuratively). One can conceive this only on the ideal plane. As Ilyenkov has noted in several parts of his theory of the ideal, the ideal enables a person to perform a very mysterious act when he sees himself through other people's eyes without taking their positions one after the other.

Thus, in my cell of activity, and I can say now — of conscious activity because there can be no other activity than conscious activity — there are the following points.

A unit or a cell of conscious activity includes the collective nature of performing an activity by a collective subject, or a team, as the first point. Or, in other words, what we call businesslike communication, but in the literal meaning of the word and not in the metaphorical sense.

Let me point out once more — the collective activity is performed by a collective subject. Any collective activity can naturally be performed in certain material or spiritual forms, it is business communication, as we call it in everyday life. This is the first point.

The second point is people's appealing to each other, or reflecting over their actions and means, over actions and means of other people.

The third aspect of the cell is comprised of ideal plane and imagination.

The fourth aspect is the individual conscious activity of an individual subject.

The collective activity performed by a collective subject, and the individual subject was analyzed in detail by Vladimir Bibler in a number of his writings. The second and third aspects, about the ideas of activity and the ideal plane and imagination, are expressed vividly in Ilyenkov's work. People's appealing to each other or to themselves is also referred to in many works, but I succeeded in integrating the appealing into the activity cell. It does not mean at all that I am an inventor, but that is the structure as a whole. It is said sometimes: there can be no individual activity, except for the one that has stemmed from the collective one. But we can find collective kinds of activity in which individual activity is demonstrated. That is true. Those are complex kinds of activity, the kinds of collective activity but complex ones. And this is an abstract structure. But any individual activity stems from collective activity, in the ontogenetic perspective, at least. And, I believe, in the historical perspective as well.

That is why a special term and thorough understanding of interiorization is required to specify a unit of conscious activity. Interiorization does not imply anything but the necessity of investigating the transformation process of collective activity into individual activity. This is the interdisciplinary scientific task to be fulfilled.

The next question I am going to dwell on quite briefly.

Where is the psychological point in the cell?

The psychological aspects should be looked for somewhere else. I have outlined — though quite briefly — the nature of this psychological aspect in some experimental works conducted together with my colleagues, but being busy with teaching, in a polydisciplinary manner, by the way, I could not dwell on it at any length.

But the psychic point should be looked for in the transition from animals to human being. Psyche can be found as early as at the animal stage. And the essence of the psychic is, in my view, the attempt to identify what is possible, made both by human beings and animals. I can repeat: The psychic and psyche are of the same nature in animals and human beings, and that is orientation in the world of possibilities and using those for goal achievement.

But this search for what is possible is realized through trying. Trying is what animals do and man does, but in human activity trying is realized when people appeal to each other, when they attempt to fulfill a task on the ideal plane — all this is trying as a way of search.

I cannot maintain that what I am going to name is true regarding animals. But it is undoubtedly characteristic of humans and still more it has been studied closely enough. The initial natural function of the psychic (if it is initial it is supposed to be present in animals though I admit it as a hypothesis) is that there always goes a process of transition from a successive mode of performing certain operations, or actions if man is concerned, to a simultaneous one.

In our country the phenomenon has been thoroughly studied by Lomov's school, by Galperin's disciple Podolsky at the Psychology Department of Moscow State University, and in some experimental works of mine which are published. Those laws were thoroughly studied by V.P. Zinchenko who investigated sensory processes and by Andrei Brushlinsky in his works on thinking processes.

Actually this aspect is studied by the major part of psychologists but some scholars emphasize this aspect while others consider it as a sort of background, however important, but a background.

In all points of the activity cell, that is in searching, trying, transforming the successive into the simultaneous, there is the individual subject proper, which is a pure simultaneity in regard to successiveness of collective subject, or collective activity. What a collective does occasionally in the present case an individual is doing at the definite essential moment. To repeat: I always argue that the problem of activity and the concept of activity are interdisciplinary by nature. There should be specified philosophical, sociological, culturological, psychological and physiological aspects here. That is why the issue of activity is not necessarily connected with psychology as a profession. It is connected at present because in the course of our history activity turned out to be the thing on which our prominent psychologists focused their attention as early as in the Soviet Union days. Things just turned out to be this way.

A scientific inquiry into the nature of the psychic, the nature of searching and trying, the successive and the simultaneous, the psychological proper makes the psychological aspect that can be considered in any activity cell and in activity as a whole.

# 4 Activity Revisited as an Explanatory Principle and as an Object of Study — Old Limits and New Perspectives

*Bernd Fichtner*

*Activity* designates a general way of looking at things, viewing something as an activity, and, at the same time, a concrete process such as playing, learning, working. The Soviet philosopher Eric Grigorievich Yudin (1978) was the first to differentiate between activity as a "perspective" — he calls this an explanatory principle — and as an "object of study." In my view, this differentiation leads to the following consequence: We can only develop a cultural-historical theory of activity further if we study concrete activities on an empirical level by making activities the subject of our investigation. But in order to do this, we require activity as an explanatory principle.

If this principle is to help explain anything, if it is to make a sphere of reality accessible in certain ways, then it is not simply to be equated with a tool. Its methodological potential is not simply, as with a tool, a quality of the term itself, but, quite to the contrary, results from its conceptual context — more precisely, from its connection to fundamental philosophical problems.

Activity as an explanatory principle is not a self-explanatory concept, but is to be developed as a philosophical theory of activity. To this end, it is necessary to generalize the findings of individual sciences, although this is by no means the final step in the process. Philosophy is not a science of science, only concerned with generalizing the data of the individual scientific disciplines. Philosophy is concerned with discovering in which way the concept of activity describes the relationship of human beings to the world and to their knowledge of the world.

Individual sciences such as psychology, history, and sociology deal — in the sense of an approximation — with a predetermined, more or less conceptualized world as Otte (1994) has pointed out in his study about philosophy of mathematics. For philosophy, reality is in a certain way fundamentally indeterminate. In philosophy, a theory deals in an

---

\* Translated from German by Thomas La Presti.

absolute and precise manner with an ideal reality — similar to a work of art. Benjamin (1963) has demonstrated in his preface of *Ursprung des deutschen Trauerspiels* how a work of art is realizing this function by means of representation.

For me, the particular methodological potential of the cultural-historical school lies in the fact that its basic concepts constitute three levels simultaneously: a philosophical level, one of an individual science, and a pedagogical-practical or clinical-therapeutical level. These levels cannot simply be reduced to or deduced from one another; usually, they are sharply opposed to and contradict one another. Each level encompasses its own logic and legitimation.

Especially the often incomplete works of Vygotsky's final creative period demonstrate an entirely unusual productivity of the simultaneity of these three levels. Precisely because of their fragmentary nature, they provide a closer look at the "workshop" (i.e., at the process of the simultaneous work on these three levels). In the very same study, their differences and contradictions remain dynamic and effective.

Philosophy or, rather, the philosophical level does not mean metaphysical speculation, but a form of reflection which Vygotsky (1927/1997) calls dialectics in his book *The Historical Meaning of the Crisis in Psychology*.

Dialectics cover nature, thinking, history — it is the most general, maximally universal science. ... In order to create intermediate theories — methodologies, general sciences — we must reveal the *essence* of the given area of phenomena, the laws of their change, their qualitative and quantitative characteristics, their causality, we must create categories and concepts appropriate to it, in short, we must create our *own das Kapital* (p. 330)

At the same time, Vygotsky criticizes relentlessly any attempts to already discover the basics of such a science in Karl Marx's *Kapital*:

It should be known what one can and must be looked for in Marxism. ... We must find a theory which would help us to know the mind, but by no means the solution of the question of the mind, not a formula which would give the ultimate scientific truth. ... Neither Marx, nor Engels, nor Plekhanov possessed such a truth. ... I do not want to learn what constitutes the mind for free, by picking out a couple of citations, I want to learn from Marx's whole method how to build a science, how to approach the investigation of the mind. (p. 331)

In this sense, philosophy (dialectic or methodology) as the "most general and universal science" is without any prerequisites for Vygotsky. Within the scope of its explorations in the realm of thought, philosophy attempts to apprehend those prerequisites that are hidden in this original beginning without any prerequisites — and precisely for this reason, philosophy is historical. But with this form of reflection we call philosophy — as also with art — historical can never mean that there is any such thing as progress, that Aristotle would be better or more advanced than Plato or that Marx would be more exact and more advanced than Spinoza. Philosophy ignores every possible authority apart from itself. It does not adhere to anything except itself.

One element accounting for the topicality, freshness, and vigor of Vygotsky's thought is surely to be seen in this connection. Whenever he is concerned with the child, the youth, or the relationship between learning and mental development, he always takes an original standpoint regarding these objects. The basic concepts he uses to reflect on these objects are similar to works of art. They are related to an ideal reality (i.e., they are objectively indeterminate). But their relationship to their object itself is, as with a work of art, precise and absolute.

In the studies on the "mental development of personality" from Vygotsky's final productive period, the "seven-year-olds," for example, are introduced by a mention of Charlie Chaplin. Chaplin plays the roles of adults, serious persons, but demonstrates a very childish sort of naiveté and immediacy in his behavior. Here, as with children, external and internal behavior are the same. The most essential characteristic of the "crisis of the seven-year-olds" is the differentiation between internal and external.

At the age level of seven years, we are dealing with the onset of the appearance of a structure of experience in which the child begins to understand what it means when he says: "I'm happy," "I'm unhappy," "I'm angry," "I'm good," "I'm bad," that is, he is developing an intellectual orientation in his own experiences. (Vygotsky, 1933-34/1998, p. 291)

The individual science, in this case psychology, must proceed from certain prerequisites with respect to the seven-year-olds. What a seven-year-old is, is determined by the particular procedures and methods of individual approaches to research within psychology. Here, Vygotsky always goes into a very exact and detailed discussion of the current state of research.

With respect to the pedagogical-practical level, there is a conspicuous absence in Vygotsky's work of any didactics or school pedagogy in the modern sense of the word. There is no methodological discussion of how to act pedagogically, how to instruct, and so on — but there are some studies of a certain diagnostic breadth, primarily related to special education. In my opinion, the pedagogical-practical level of Vygotsky's thought becomes apparent in an exemplary fashion in his "Lectures on Psychology." He delivered these in March and April 1932 at the A.I. Herzen Pedagogical Institute in Leningrad. The topics of the lectures range from "Perception and its Development in Childhood" to "Imagination and its Development in Childhood" and "The Problem of Will and its Development in Childhood." Within the scope of these lectures, Vygotsky (1932/1966) strictly refrains from any direct practical implementation related to teaching. Instead, he traces certain lines of development as perspectives. Here, perspectives are views that are not implemented, but rather views with which one can act. They provide a certain openness for one's own practical experiences and their development.

I will end this sketch here, as it would have to be more concretely and systematically developed on the basis of the work of Métraux (1996), Jantzen (1996), and Lompscher (1996). I consider the problem of the unity of the three levels to be a perspective that can help to oppose the current tendencies of a positivist reduction of the cultural-historical approach to a sociocultural or socio-interactional approach.

Let us return to the theoretical concept of activity. Activity as an object of study and activity as an explanatory principle are complementary; they are mutual prerequisites of their individual development. I would like to point out some issues, problems, and perspectives relevant to this context. First, I wish to inquire into the systemic character of activity. Then, I would like to substantiate a proposal to conceive of development as directedness. Finally, I will formulate a few theses on the communicative or language-like quality of human action and its significance for the concept of activity.

### On the Systemic Character of Activity

Leontiev (1971) devised the concept of activity from the analysis of the most elementary life processes: *"The fundamental 'unit' of the life process is the activity of the organism"* (p. 29). Here, the specific processes a living system engages in are considered as activity, indeed as a systemic formation. This description is related to a concrete phenomenon and is, at the same time, an explanatory principle. Its essential aspects are as follows:

Activity is not what an organism does. Rather, the organism consists in its activity. Activity is the mode of existence by which organisms establish themselves as subjects of their life processes. Equally, in this perspective the object of activity is nothing the individual relates to, it should rather be considered as something the organism constitutes by its activity. Only objects relating to its activities are actually objects for an organism.

Only within and by means of the life process does that which we refer to as subject and object of this process originate. What we call the "subject" and "object" of life processes only comes into being as a result of two different perspectives on a developing system, the system of subject–activity–object.

For the elaboration of his own model, Leontiev draws from the most up-to-date model of the origin of life among his contemporaries, from that proposed by Oparin. Now, my question is: Do current explanations of the origin of life allow or perhaps necessitate a modification of Leontiev's conception?

At present, there are a number of competing models which all explicitly refer to the worldview consequences of their approaches in their initial inquiry: Why did life originate at all? Is life on Earth an extremely amazing and chance phenomenon, or did it originate with some necessity? The current debate reminds one of the worldview conflicts about Darwinism more than a hundred years ago and thus calls to mind the fact that our models for explaining the origin of life always reflect modes of discourse by which society implicitly discusses itself and its praxis.

I will restrict myself to the model put forth by Eigen (1971), who was awarded the Nobel prize for his research on this topic a number of years ago. It is a physical-chemical theory of biogenesis.[1] I will sketch only those aspects that, in my opinion, are relevant to the conception of activity as an explanatory principle.

1. The hypercycle model demonstrates how cycles of macromolecules that reproduce themselves are generated. For the first time, linear chains of cause-and-effect become circular. Effects influence their own causes.

2. The qualitatively new feature of these systems is their functional expedience. Living systems contain a structure that has the purpose of maintaining itself.

3. This expedience is totally directed by information. Whatever is functional (i.e., directed by information) in a living system has a certain *value*.

With this perspective, information originates with the development of life. Information exists only as an aspect, a quality and result of expedient processes (i.e., of those of life). But what exactly is information in this context?

The concept of information was developed by branches of telecommunications interested in the transfer of information. As a consequence, the focus of attention for the original, mathematical theories of information is on measuring the amount of information.

However, with regard to biogenesis, the emphasis is not on the transfer of information, but, rather, on its origin, its function, and, above all, its storage. Here, information is something like a pattern that allows the construction of a pattern. Information has meaning, but only if it is capable of surviving the ongoing processes of generation and deterioration. Thus, not the amount, but rather the value of information for a living system is of the greatest significance.

In this way, the concept of information becomes a "highly-charged" theoretical concept. Such a concept makes it evident that living systems can no longer be adequately described from a causal perspective, as is usually the case in physics or chemistry. Living systems react to certain external conditions, not simply in accordance with chemical or physical laws. Living systems convert external conditions selectively into activity. They achieve their objectives by evaluating something.

---

1. He formulated a mathematical model for this, the main postulates of which can be checked experimentally. So this is not a model of how life actually originated, but, rather, one of how life can originate.

Leontiev described elementary life processes as a nondistinguishable union of activity and reflection. Only on a further level does reflection develop as an activity in its own right, namely, as an internal one in relationship to external activity.

Now, either we can provide a more precise formulation of this stipulation or we may have to correct it. Is not something physical in its original forms necessarily inherent in every life process? What sort of relationship exists between the information and the processes (functions) in which a living system maintains its structure? Is it a relationship between one level and a higher metalevel (Russell)? Is information a pattern that forms a connection (Bateson, 1972/1980)? Which changes result if we structure the union of external and internal activity with the figure of the "connecting pattern?" Why is activity's development a necessary result of the systemic formation of activity?[2] My suggestions will have to be evaluated in light of how much they further our understanding of activity as a system of relationships (and not of characteristics).

## Development as Directedness

Biological evolution, individual development, socialization, and history have been and still are understood as a linear process, as an advancement from the simple to the complex. The tendency from simple to complex, from immature to mature, from asocial to social is considered to be the fundamental mechanism which guides this development. Likewise, the increase in differentiation, complexity, and structure is regarded as the directedness of the development.

Today, this perspective seems to be more and more of a myth which was primarily influenced by the understanding of biological evolution in the 19th century, by bourgeois society's ideology of progress, and by certain variants of a vulgar Marxism.

---

2. Our language is not very well suited to comprehending the dynamics of the *subject–activity–object* system. Our European languages are not very well prepared to describe and represent relations developing in a complementary way. We are accustomed to begin by naming the parts of a relation, for instance, "subject" and "object," and according to this procedure the relations between the parts will surface as predicates that are tagged to one of its parts, rather than connecting the two parts of the relation. Consequently, our language suggests that relations are properties of their parts.

From the perspective of the classical theory of evolution, development has always already taken place. Thus, in order to comprehend this, it is above all necessary to reconstruct development. Discovering its laws means reconstructing the phases, segments, and sequences of development. In phylogenesis, the living organism always develops in the direction of a functional, adaptive form. This form exists as a result and functions as the criterion of the optimum in the reconstruction of the phases and stages of its development.

However, in ontogenesis, development is something that develops at each stage from the immediately preceding stage. Development is brought about by processes that are currently taking place.

On the whole, it seems rather doubtful that a simple reconstruction of phases and stages can already be considered to be a real explanation, an understanding of development. The issue of development has a much wider range of implications than a reconstruction of its sequences and phases.

What differentiates development from a simple course of events, from a simple sequence of conditions which might repeat themselves? Development is a process that for a number of reasons is affected by the impossibility of maintaining the available forms of functioning. Here, the organism is, in a sense, forced to move on to another level of functioning which beforehand was not available or not possible, or rather, forced to develop this new, unfamiliar level in the first place. Exactly the elements of such a process are what is expressed by the directedness of the development.

I see the key to a more precise understanding of directedness and thus of development itself in this impossibility to maintain previous structure and previous life forms. One arrives at a mechanistic idea of development if causes are looked for only in the alteration of external, objective circumstances and conditions. If these are seen exclusively within the organism, then development entails nothing more than self-discovery, the momentary implementation of an internal, preexisting available potential.

This dilemma can be clarified using, as did Hegel, the philosophical category of contradiction as the principle of all self-development. For Hegel, contradiction is not a logical or temporal (i.e., temporary) deviation, but rather a universal relationship applying to all of reality. In the famous concluding chapter of *The Science of Logic*, he describes the process in which differences become opposites and, finally, a contradiction, which is the "inherent pulse" of all self-development and liveliness.[3]

Thus, contradiction is not a source or driving force outside of development and alteration. The specific effects of the contradiction depend upon the intensity of the interaction between the opposites. Their mediation determines to what extent development processes are set in motion. Thus, development consists in setting up and solving contradictions; it is the form of mobility, the realization of the contradiction.

Using the category of contradiction, Hegel radically criticizes the idea of development as a continuous enlargement or reduction, as simply a quantitative decrease or increase. Development is not primarily an alteration, a transformation, but, rather, setting up and solving contradictions, "becoming otherwise" — breaking off gradually formed conditions and becoming qualitatively different in comparison to one's previous existence (cf. Hegel, 1832/1963, 48 ff.). Every qualitatively significant change establishes a "new standard" in comparison to the previous situation.

At this point the question arises: How can the main element of development, its directedness, be formulated more precisely by means of these stipulations (contradiction as a driving force, development as becoming otherwise, as a qualitatively new change)?

I suggest not comprehending directedness as a specific type of sequences, but rather comprehending it as a specific organization of these sequences. In that case, directedness is something like a logical type which is not to be found on the same logical level as the change itself. Directedness is a metalevel that contains the scheme or pattern of the sequence of conditions in a certain way.

I think a position expressed by. Bateson may help to clarify this relationship. He assumes that such metalevels, schemata of processes, or patterns of patterns in extremely diverse forms characterize life as a phenomenon in general. Playing, for instance, is not a particular type of activity, but, rather, a type of organization of activity. A game is a sort of context in which the same activities attain a certain relevance and meaning which they do not have in other contexts. According to Bateson, patterns of patterns, metalevels, represent a unique type of generality which is simultaneously consistent and inconsistent with the indi-

3. "Something is only alive to the extent that it contains a contradiction within itself, and, indeed, this is the power to grasp the contradiction in oneself and endure it" (Hegel, 1832/1963, p. 59).

vidual and just for this reason reminds one of the logical relationships between elements and sets — a set, defined by a certain number of its elements, can never be an element of itself (cf. Bateson, 1972/1980, p. 252ff.).

Accordingly, directedness would not be a general quality, a formal characteristic common to individual qualitative changes, phases, and stages. Rather, it would be a particular way of organizing their sequences — directedness as a temporal context. In this view, directedness does, then, indeed function as a "frame" that includes and excludes by establishing premises, allowing for certain possibilities, and, on the whole, provides the changes, phases, the process of becoming different in development, with coherence, meaning, and relevance. This context is not given as a static frame of conditions for development. The frame is more of a sort of "story" that the living system itself writes as a dialogue with its surroundings.

Development is a context different from the sequence of phases on the same level. The inherent intensification of opposing forces leading up to their contradiction makes it impossible to maintain previous forms of functioning, and forces the individual to move on to another level.

I wish to explain the problem of the directedness of development processes by considering the development of perception during infancy. Here, directedness is traditionally understood as an increasing specification and structuring of the perception system (i.e., as a certain sequence of individual steps). The issue at stake here does not concern the sequence of the steps, but, rather, their organization. So the question is: Which pattern, which context does the organism itself produce in the course of a dialogue with the conditions of its existence?

In a fascinating study written during his final productive period, Vygotsky characterized infancy as a unique and unrepeatable situation in social development in which a fundamental contradiction materializes between a maximum social relationship and minimal communication possibilities. All of the relationships between the infant and the surroundings and the infant's relationship to himself/herself are mediated by an adult who serves as the psychological center of every situation. The first new mental formation that corresponds to this developmental stage is an "elementary collective consciousness" (*Ur-Wir-Bewußtsein*). The child is not able to separate itself, its mental experiences, from the perception of material objects. Mental life is an undifferentiated, unstructured experience, an amalgam of affects, drives, and sensations. Recent research on infants, associated with researchers such as Bruner (this volume), Schaffer, Trevarthen, and above all Stern, has confirmed this perspective and put it into more concrete terms.

Having emerged as a new mental formation from the specific and unique circumstances of the social situation, this elementary collective consciousness (*Ur-Wir-Bewußtsein*) then goes on to alter this social situation, above all with the development of the fascinating pattern of face-to-face interaction. These effects are so diverse and significant that they embrace the entire life of the child. In comparison to other activity systems such as gesturing and motor functions, there are two partners interacting here with approximately the same possibilities for application and control, and of these two, one of them is only three months old.

During the last month of the first half-year a radical change occurs that introduces a process of becoming otherwise within development. With the development of eye-to-hand coordination that is formed within the old context, the previous pattern of interaction between mother and child is fundamentally transformed. It now has three poles and becomes a matter between child, object, and mother. The previous situation in social development disintegrates. The contradiction which had functioned as the motor of the child's development inevitably leads to the destruction of the actual basis of development and creates a new situation in social development.

### The Communicative or Language-Like Structure of Human Action

In Leontiev's conception, activity is of a social character. Activities are literally produced by society. In activity, humans put their social relationship to the world and to themselves into practice. An individual activity is implemented by action which, in turn, is organized by conscious aims.[4]

Within the development of small children, long before language acquisition we encounter phenomena that cannot be integrated readily into this theoretical conception: movements and actions of small chil-

4. Davydov (1991) effectively refuted the assumed opposition between activity and communication: "People's activity is the *only possible method* of their social existence and development" (p. 33). "People's *communication* is a judicial expression of these relations. Communication can only exist in the process of different kinds of activity realization by people" (p. 34).

dren develop a language-like, communicative structure.[5] Correspondingly and simultaneously, a symbolic structure of their perception
originates. Human actions are language-like, not because they are more
or less molded by a social milieu, but, rather, the reason is much more
profoundly related to their structure.

Movements of animals reach a mature stage very early and then
have an absolute and definite motor function. The world they perceive
demonstrates a fixed and stubborn indifference regarding all sorts of
perceptions that are not immediately related to vital functions or drives.
Furthermore, cooperation between eye and hand is unknown to
animals.

The early phase of childhood which we think we have already
understood by labeling it the "sensorimotor period" is actually full of
movements by which the child engages in dialog with the objects surrounding him, treating them in a communicative manner. An object is
seen, touched, felt, tasted, and smelled. By means of this communication, the child experiences heaviness and lightness, hardness and soft-
ness, wetness and dryness, and so on. In these processes the hands
work together with all of the senses, but especially with the eye. This
coordination displays an unbelievable diversity in its abundance of
combinations.

All of this is not directed by any physical needs or desires. The
actions are in no sense purposeful, but neither are they reflexes or
innate. They have a more or less theoretical quality. They stem from the
child's own initiative and seem to be limited solely by physical exhaus-
tion. They are performed in a social and relaxed atmosphere and, with
regard to the amount of activity, are extremely dependent upon the
presence of familiar adults who represent closeness, trust, and security.

All of these communicative movements and actions have a fascinating circular structure; they are circular processes. They do not only deal
with the objects, but also with oneself, with one's own movements and
perceptions. Tactile sensations occur simultaneously when performing
tactile movements. The tactile system of the hand makes movements
possible that are oriented to the active and objective pole (grasping an
object) and, at the same time, to the subjective pole. The movements
themselves can also be felt; they are sensorially reflective. The movements are reflected in an immediate sensory manner. Evidently, these
repercussions provide an impulse to further develop the movements.

5.  Gehlen (1940/1986) was the first to develop this aspect in detail.

With increasing pleasure, the child produces babbling sounds. The child articulates sounds actively; the product of this activity returns effortlessly to the ear and further develops the child's sense of hearing. Apparently, self-awareness of one's own activity directs the further development of this activity.

The eye and the hand cooperate with each other. At the intersection of these two heterogeneous senses a peculiar sort of intimacy establishes itself — an intimacy which constitutes the objectivity of the world that we adults take so much for granted. The production of objectivity is apparently contingent upon its being reflected in self-awareness.

Finally, before actual language acquisition takes place, we encounter a phenomenon with a new quality going beyond that of the activities sketched above concerned with coping with the world in a communicative manner and discovering one's own abilities. We encounter the initial stages of representational behavior. Upon hearing church bells ringing, a child at the age of one or one and a half will begin to mimetically portray the movements of the bells with his upper body.

This is more than simply a superficial imitation. Independently of the given situation, the child portrays the behavior of someone (or something) else and by doing so realizes a particular relationship to himself. If there is no direct relationship to himself, the child discovers himself via the portrayed behavior alien to him.

### New Perspectives

The elements sketched in the previous section can be found in all cultures, manifested in different ways and varying according to the particular fundamental patterns. From these elements, a series of questions that deserve further investigation can be raised.

1. Why have they been developed and to what end?

2. Are their origins to be found in the phylogenesis of the human race?

3. Does the development of the first activity simultaneously include two different types of action that cannot simply be reduced to one another?

4. Can the first type be adequately characterized as the entire ensemble of instrumental, technical actions oriented to changing reality, to effecting, making and producing something?

5. Can the second type be adequately characterized as the entire ensemble of mimetic, representational actions oriented to producing a meaningful context for a society or a community? Then, instrumental, technical actions would be mediated by tools and signs as primary artifacts. Mimetic, representational actions would be mediated *in vivo* and *in materia* by a variety of ritual representational means such as dances and pictures as secondary artifacts (Wartofsky, 1979).

## References

Bateson, G. (1980). *Ökologie des Geistes* (H.G v. Holl, Trans.). Frankfurt: Suhrkamp (Original work published 1972)..

Benjamin, W. (1963) *Ursprung des deutschen Trauerspiels*. Frankfurt: Suhrkamp.

Davydov, V.V. (1991). The content and unsolved problems of activity theory. *Multidisciplinary Newsletter for Activity Theory, 7/8,* 30-35

Eigen, M. (1971). Selforganization of matter and the evolution of biological macromolecules. *Naturwissenschaften, 58,* 465-523.

Gehlen, A. (1986). *Der Mensch. Seine Natur und seine Stellung in der Welt.* Wiesbaden: Aula. (Original work published 1940)

Hegel, G.W.F. (1963). *Wissenschaft der Logik, Teil 2.* (G. Lasson, Ed.; 2nd expanded ed. of 1932). Hamburg: Meiner. (Original work published 1832)

Jantzen, W. (1996). Das spinozanische Programm der Psychologie: Versuch einer Rekonstruktion von Vygotskijs Methodologie des psychologischen Materialismus. In J. Lompscher, (Ed.), *Entwicklung und Lernen aus kulturhistorischer Sicht* (Vol. 1, pp. 51-65). Marburg:: BdWi Verlag.

Leontiev (Leontjew) A.N. (1971). *Probleme der Entwicklung des Psychischen.* Berlin: Volk und Wissen.

Lompscher, J. (1996). Lew Wygotski — nur eine Stimme aus der Vergangenheit? In J. Lompscher, (Ed.), *Entwicklung und Lernen aus kulturhistorischer Sicht.* (Vol. 1, pp. 12-38). Marburg: BdWi Verlag.

Métraux, A. (1996). Das kulturhistorische Forschungsprogramm und was seit Vygotskij vergessen wurde. In J. Lompscher, (Ed.), *Entwicklung und Lernen aus kulturhistorischer Sicht* (Vol. 1, pp. 39-50). Marburg: BdWi Verlag.

Otte, M. (1994). *Das Formale, das Soziale und das Subjektive. Eine Ein-*

*führung in die Philosophie und Didaktik der Mathematik.* Frankfurt: Suhrkamp.

Vygotsky, L.S. (1966). *Vorlesungen über Psychologie.* Marburg, Germany: Verlag Bund demokratischer Wissenschaftler. (Original work written 1932)

Vygotsky, L.S. (1997). The historical meaning of the crisis in psychology: A methodological investigation (R. van der Veer, Trans.). In R.W. Rieber & J. Wollock (Eds.), *The collected works of L.S. Vygotsky: Vol. 3. Problems of the theory and history of psychology* (pp. 233-343). New York: Plenum Press. (Original work written 1927)

Vygotsky, L.S. (1998). The crisis at age seven (M.J. Hall, Trans.). In R.W. Rieber (Ed.), *The collected works of L.S. Vygotsky: Vol. 5. Child psychology* (pp. 289-296). New York: Plenum Press. (Original work written 1933-34)

Wartofsky, M.W. (1979). *Models: Representation and the scientific understanding.* Dordrecht: Reidel.

Yudin, E.G. (1978). *Sistemnyi podchod i princip dejatel'nosti* [The systems approach and the principle of activity]. Moscow: Nauka.

# 5 Activity as Explanatory Principle in Cultural Psychology

*Peeter Tulviste*

## A Personal Introduction

The topic of my presentation could hardly be more abstract. I am going to discuss what it means to use culture to explain the so-called higher, semiotically-mediated mental processes. But permit me to start with a rather personal introduction. The circumstances that bring us to abstract issues often are very concrete.

In the mid-1960s, Alexander R. Luria was writing a book about the results of his two psychological expeditions to Uzbekistan in the then Soviet Central Asia in 1931 and 1932. He looked for a student who would be interested in searching for and reading what had been written in the West on cultural differences and historical changes in mental processes during the decades Luria had been busy with other topics — first of all, with neuropsychology, of course. The expeditions got him into serious political trouble in the 1930s, so I remember him wondering after he had completed the manuscript whether it would not be better to publish it posthumously, as he put it. (Like many people in the former Soviet Union, he survived, among other things, thanks to his sense of humor.) That's how I, an undergraduate at the Faculty of Psychology (which was established at the Lomonosov Moscow State University in 1966), came to read Luria's protocols, which he could not mention for more than 30 years. Those who have read this volume titled *Cognitive Development* (Luria, 1974/1976) can imagine the impression the protocols made on a student more interested in human mind than in higher nervous activity or classical experimental psychology.

* This chapter is based on a keynote lecture presented at the Fourth Congress of the International Society for Cultural Research and Activity Theory. The expansion and rewriting of this lecture was supported by the Swedish Collegium for Advanced Study in the Social Sciences, Uppsala, where the author was a fellow during the autumn semester 1998. The author is grateful to Seth Chaiklin and Professor Yrjö Engeström for discussion. The statements made and the views expressed are solely the responsibility of the author.

Luria's immediate aim in Central Asia was to find out if social and cultural changes cause changes in mental processes. Looking for differences in the so-called higher or specifically human processes in people who had participated to a various extent — or had not participated — in the cultural and social changes that were occurring there at that time, Luria did discover significant differences in their thinking and self-consciousness.

Data about solving "simple" verbal syllogistic tasks by subjects with no formal schooling are no doubt the most striking part of the book. I have protocols of the following kind in mind. This example is not from Luria, but psychologists who have presented tasks of this kind to unschooled subjects in various parts of the world have obtained similar reactions everywhere:

Two men [local names] always drink tea together, the two of them. One of them is drinking tea now. Is the other man drinking tea now or not?

Typical answers are:

— I don't know these men, how could I answer.

— We are here, and we cannot see what these men you are talking about are doing presently.

— The guy who is drinking tea now probably is ill. Otherwise he would be out hunting. When it gets dark, the other man will return from hunting, and join the sick guy in drinking tea.

The problems that arose for me when reading Luria's manuscript, and certainly for many readers of Luria's book, were: How could these results be possible at all, and how were they to be explained? Why is it that adults with no formal schooling produce these kinds of answers? It took a long time before I understood that the real question is: Why is it that people who have been to school — as well as their children who have not attended school yet — solve these tasks in the way the investigator regards as correct?

When one reports these kinds of results, one typically gets two kinds of reactions. Some listeners say that subjects with no schooling are underdeveloped or even stupid. Others say that it is the researcher who is stupid; instead of asking subjects to do things they can do, he asks them to do things they cannot. The first reaction is more common in the former Soviet bloc countries with our long mandatory experience of Marxist evolutionary thinking; the second one is more common in Western Europe and America.

Neither of these reactions seems adequate. The same subjects easily solve other tasks which are much more complicated — whatever *complicated* means — so they are certainly not generally underdeveloped or stupid. And comparative research, by definition, compares subjects who have some capability with those who do not have the same capability. For example, if we are interested in the impact of literacy on memory, we have to compare subjects who can read and write with those who cannot.

The official ideological reaction in the Soviet Union of the 1930s was that Luria had described the builders of socialism in the Soviet East as primitives with a Lévy-Bruhlian prelogical thinking. (To my mind, this is similar to the present-day ideological critique that accuses researchers of eurocentrism. Instead, we should be working toward plausible explanations of the results obtained by researchers in many different cultures in various parts of the world.)

The explanation that Luria provided for his provocative results was not convincing. He related differences in the ways schooled and un-schooled subjects approached and/or solved verbal syllogistic tasks to: (a) differences in their level of social and cultural development, and (b) the fact that unschooled subjects were only involved in practical activities.

The first suggestion is, among other things, too general to serve as an explanation. Luria made no attempt to find out which components of the social and cultural changes were responsible for the changes in mind, and in what way the changes in mind occurred. The second suggestion is wrong. There is no culture where people would be occupied only with practical activities. Whatever functions art, religion, and play may have, they are present in all known cultures, separate from purely practical activities, and they certainly have a lot to do with thinking.

So I looked in the then-emerging cross-cultural psychological litera-ture, as well as in old authors like Lévy-Bruhl and new authors like Lévi-Strauss, for a theory or at least some idea that would make Luria's data seem possible, if not natural or even necessary. And looked in vain. There were no good answers to be found to such general and simple questions as: Should there be cultural differences or historical changes in thinking or not? If yes, why, and what should be different and what should change in thinking (Tulviste, 1988/1991)?

Now we come to the topic mentioned in the title of my presentation: activity as explanatory principle. Happily enough, exactly at the time when I was looking desperately for theories or categories that would permit me to handle the changes in mind described by Luria, Alexei N. Leontiev, then Dean of the Faculty of Psychology at the Lomonosov Moscow State University published his papers on what, in a wisely cautious way, he called an *activity approach*. Whereas activity was presented in these papers mostly as an object of study, there were also suggestions about activity as the factor that permits one to explain the specifically human mind; or, as Vygotsky put it, higher mental functions. From this point of view, when applied to cultural differences and historical changes in thinking, one had to expect that in any culture, these (and only these) higher (semiotically-mediated) processes exist which correspond functionally to the social activities executed in this particular culture. To the extent that activities present in different cultures and, correspondingly, the typical tasks to be solved, vary significantly, one should expect to discover corresponding significant differences in thinking processes as well.

I could also conclude that given that in all cultures people are never involved in only one activity but in many different kinds of activities, however we define and differentiate them, then one has to expect that any human being in any culture has at his disposal as many different ways of thinking as there are significantly different kinds of activities — not just a single one way of thinking (or two of them, as absolutely most existing discriminations or typologies of ways of thinking would have it: abstract vs. concrete, logical vs. prelogical, practical vs. theoretical, etc.). Human thinking in any culture is heterogeneous by nature (Tulviste, 1988/1991; Wertsch, 1991).

So here at last was a theory that made cultural differences and historical changes in thinking look natural. People involved in different kinds of activities, and therefore solving different kinds of tasks, will have different semiotic means or tools provided by the society, and by using different tools, they would think in different ways.

Coming back to Luria's data about syllogistic reasoning, it was easy to see that when presented with these tasks, people from unschooled groups approached them as practical tasks about concrete people and applied the thinking devices any schooled subject would also apply in the practical situation in which it is necessary, say, to actually meet one of the two tea-drinkers. The way of thinking applied by the unschooled people was not at all exotic, as it might appear on a first reading of Luria's book. Rather, it was just common sense, a universal way of thinking, related to practical situations, and activities. Subjects with some schooling, in turn, applied, in this particular situation, a specific way of thinking acquired at school and aimed at solving scholarly tasks. It would be quite unusual, from the point of view of activity theory, if this way of thinking existed in cultures in which there was no science and no schooling.

Also, it was possible to show why solving scholarly tasks, as opposed to practical or everyday tasks, necessarily requires that a new way of thinking was added, usually at school, to the already existing ways of thinking which are good for many things but not for solving these specific tasks.

I will not discuss further details here about explaining historical changes in thinking or describing the various ways of thinking (for a detailed presentation, see Tulviste, 1988/1991). The important thing for now is that Leontiev's theory was the only one that permitted one to explain, *post factum*, Luria's results. (It also showed that an ethno-graphical study of activities, both those present in the traditional Uzbeki culture of Central Asia and those implanted in the course of cultural and social changes, should have preceded or accompanied Luria's psychological studies. This procedure was systematically intro-duced into cross-cultural psychological research in the 1970s by Michael Cole, e.g., Cole, Gay, Glick, & Sharp, 1971.)

We now see it was only natural that Leontiev's theory fit Luria's data. They both worked in the cultural-historical or Vygotskian tradi-tion according to which specifically human mental processes are deter-mined by culture and therefore can only be explained through culture. Luria showed that with change within culture mind also changes, Leontiev pointed out the particular aspect of culture that makes changes in mind a necessity. From this particular point of view, Leontiev's activity theory is a concretization — a remarkable one — of Vygotsky's cultural-historical theory rather than an alternative to it.

## The *Experimentum Crucis* of Cultural-Historical Psychology

Although Luria's research in Central Asia is widely known, it seems that its aim and meaning were not fully understood. It was radically different from the preceding research in remote or exotic cultures where researchers were interested in finding out — by any chance, for whatever reasons — if there were differences in the minds of people belonging to cultures very different from "ours." Luria did not go to Uzbekistan to find out how Uzbekis think. His aim was different and much more ambitious, namely to prove the central point of Vygotsky's cultural-historical theory that could not be proved in Moscow. I think it is no exaggeration to say that Luria's work in Central Asia was planned as the *experimentum crucis* for Vygotskian psychology. If one succeeds in demonstrating that under conditions of rapid social and cultural change, mental processes of people involved in these changes also change, then one has proven the central point of cultural-historical psychology: The so-called higher, specifically human, semiotically-mediated cognitive processes are determined by culture. By the way, here lies the reason why Luria's study was planned as "cross-historical" and not just cross-cultural. In the case of a cross-historical comparison within one culture, all differences must necessarily be of sociocultural origin because it remains genetically the same population.

Luria did find confirmation for the central thesis of cultural-historical theory. From here, a new explanatory principle for the human mind followed: If these processes were determined by culture and not by nature, they had to be explained through culture, not through nature. The invention of this new explanatory principle, I dare to say, is the most important achievement and message of cultural-historical psychology.

Indeed, Luria could have returned from the expedition and told his colleagues: "We now know for sure we were right; let's go on explaining the higher processes via sociocultural factors. Not only can we study higher mental processes, but we can also develop them, because they depend much more than everybody thought on what people learn from culture." Instead, he had to shut up, listen to the ideological watchdogs of his time, and be scared for decades.

Forty years later, at the end of the 1960s and in the 1970s, many cross-cultural psychologists returned from their research expeditions with essentially the same message: The main problem is not that we do not know why adults in some remote culture do not solve, say, Piaget's conservation tasks, or verbal syllogistic tasks; the main problem is that we do not know why anybody ever starts to be able to solve these tasks. We do not know what makes thinking develop in children. What we do know is that culture plays a much more important role in the formation of mind than we ever thought. It is not cultural and historical variation in mind that is to be explained via culture and history; rather, the mind itself, its development and functioning can only be explained if culture and history are employed in the explanation in a new way.

### Activity as Explanation

At the same time, there is no doubt that Luria had no clear idea in the 1930s about which cultural factors had to be involved in the explanation. Most probably, he had in mind, first, social processes in general, such as the violent collectivization of agriculture, and the introduction of school education, and second, symbolic processes as described by Cassirer (1923-29).

We are in a somewhat better position today. Permit me to come back, for a moment, to the issue of the cultural determination of the ways of human thinking. From the point of view of the present knowledge in cultural psychology, one can perhaps say that there is a correspondence between: (a) activities executed in a culture and/or by an individual; (b) tasks posed by these activities; (c) semiotic tools, or mediational means which are a part of culture and are acquired by the individual from the culture and applied by him when solving these tasks; and (d) ways of thinking functionally related to the activities and mediated by the semiotic means.

It is obvious that there are various ways of describing societies and cultures. From the point of view of cultural psychology, two levels of description seem to be particularly important: (a) the activity level (i.e., what people, at various ages, do in various cultures and cultural groups), and (b) tools of communication and/or means of mediating their higher mental functioning (see the thorough analysis of this level provided by Wertsch, 1991).

It is also obvious that activity and mediational means are inter-related, and that a full analysis of the determination and nature of specifically human mental processes has to include both. But only at the activity level does it make sense to look for a causal explanation of higher mental processes and their development. To put it in a different way: One cannot describe or explain mind without taking into account the semiotic systems that serve as means or tools in mental functioning. But when we ask questions like why is mind, why are mental processes there and why are they the way they are, it is obvious that they are not there for the sake of the existence of sign systems but rather, for the sake of the human existence which — as Leontiev (1972/1981) nicely puts it — *consists* of activities (activities as *units of human life*). It is activity that serves as an (if not the) explanatory principle in cultural psychology when we look for answers to questions like:

1. Why do people in general or in particular cultures or professional groups have just these and not other modes of thought, ways of memorizing and re-calling, other cognitive processes?

2. Why do these processes develop in history and in the child the way they do?

3. Why are there differences in these processes between people belonging to different cultures or cultural groups?

No theoretical tradition in psychology has provided good answers to these questions so far. The activity-oriented cultural psychology seems to have better chances here than other theories or schools in present-day psychology.

When applying activity theory to issues of cultural and historical variations in thinking in the way I have tried to describe here, when establishing functional links between activities and ways of thinking, one soon starts to wonder why these relationships were not immediately obvious to us. It looks so perfectly natural. Indeed, why should one ever expect to discover scientific thinking in subjects in a culture where there is no science and no schooling? Or, why should people in a culture without formal schooling be able to define concepts (one of the things Luria asked his subjects to do), if — to the best of our knowledge — science is the only activity in which one has to do it? It would be a disaster if one would try to define concepts in, say, poetry. Indeed, it seems natural that people are able to produce definitions in societies where science plays such an important role that most citizens are trained for twelve years mainly to be able to cope with scientific knowledge. If twelve years of training to think in a very specific direction does not make a difference in thinking, what does? If the presence or absence of concept definition and other cultural tools of scholarly thinking in a particular culture does not make a difference, again — what does?

### Tasks on the Agenda

Within cultural-historical psychology, there are significant differences in the ways the three questions listed above are handled and in the role ascribed to activity. Permit me to move to some general problems of activity as explanatory principle in cultural psychology. I think that in the long run, activity theory and cultural-historical psychology will be taken seriously if we succeed in: (a) moving from the now popular "weak" version of activity theory which makes us study mind in an activity context, to the original "strong" (i.e., Leontiev's) version which makes us explain mind, its origin and development, through activity; (b) moving, together with semiotics of culture, from studying isolated sign systems and particular ways of thinking and remembering toward constructing comprehensive, exhaustive images of both culture and mind;[1] (c) overcoming the present gap between developmental and general psychology.

Looking back at the last decades, we see important achievements in activity-related psychological research both in cross-cultural and "monocultural" settings. Let me mention just two splendid examples here, both belonging to the tradition founded by Michael Cole. I have in mind the classical study of Sylvia Scribner (1984) on mathematical problem solving by dairy workers, combining ethnographic and psychological fieldwork with experimental studies, and the work of Geoffrey Saxe (1991) and his colleagues (e.g., Nunes, Schliemann, & Carraher, 1993) on mathematical thinking in children who sell candy on streets in Brazil. In both cases, it has been demonstrated in a beautiful way how mathematical thinking adapts to tasks posed by certain

---

1. When we study a particular cognitive process which makes use, say, of a certain kind of mathematics, we have to be able to locate the particular kind of mathematics in a general image of culture, and to locate the particular kind of thinking used in a comprehensive image of mind. At the same time, these exhaustive images of both culture and mind have to be well differentiated.

activities — or, to put it in a different way, how people make use of different mathematics (i.e., different semiotic means) for solving different tasks in the course of different activities.

In both these cases, as well as in the work of Michael Cole and his colleagues, activity is used in the role of context rather than as an explanatory principle. It is demonstrated how various ways of thinking are used in various contexts, not asked why and how these ways of thinking come into being, or what is their origin? While these demonstrations, descriptions and analyses are of great value, I do not entirely understand why we should limit ourselves to descriptions and not try to offer explanations. The choice about explanation can be formulated in a weak version and a strong version: Either (a) various ways of thinking come into being independently; culture just decides which ways of thinking are used at all and in which particular situations, or (b) culture, including activity, is responsible for the coming into being of various ways of human thinking functionally related to activities. Leontiev's position in this matter was both the "strong" and the "weak" version (although he did not use this differentiation).

It seems to me that cultural psychology should not limit itself to the mere acceptance of the existence of different ways of thinking. Instead, we should ask — together with disciplines like semiotics and history of culture — why, when, and how these ways of thinking have come into being, and then changed and interacted over time.

It is obvious that most significant cultural differences and historical changes in thinking discovered by Luria and the cross-cultural psychologists of the 1960s and 1970s are related to scientific thinking or, perhaps, a specific kind of scientific thinking, which is found in some cultures and not in others. Here we have the grand possibility to study directly the expansion of an important way of thinking into cultures where it is not yet present, and indirectly, its historical origins and development.

I would like to add that what I have said so far does not mean that a way of thinking functionally related to some kind of activity necessarily comes into being in the course of the activity itself. Rather, the origin of ways of thinking as well as the origin of the semiotic means used in them is much more complicated (Wertsch, 1998).

By no means should the application of activity as explanatory principle be restricted to cognitive processes only. As a matter of fact, Leontiev (1971) offered a beautiful schema for the explanation of the social origins and development of specifically human needs, building on the productivity of human activity. A special case is the explanation of group processes and group development through group activity (Engeström, 1987).

Let me move now to the problem of the necessity of exhaustive images of culture and mind. If higher mental processes correspond functionally to activities and make use of sign systems as tools, it is only natural to ask how many different kinds of activities and how many sign systems there are, or rather how many activities and sign systems should be differentiated for the purpose of studying mental processes. What we need is some exhaustive, complete description of culture(s) on the activity level, as well as on the semiotic level, and a corresponding description of mind based on a functional correspondence between mind and activity, and relations between mind and semiotic processes. In cultural psychology as well as in semiotics of culture, research has so far concentrated on some particular sign systems or cognitive processes. (By the way, preferences have most often been different in these two fields. Semiotics has focused on artistic, mythic, and religious texts and little research has been done on scientific texts, while in psychology it is easier to find studies of scientific thinking and its development than studies of artistic or religious thinking.)

The variety of cultural and mental phenomena is certainly not less than that of plants or animals. Whereas Linnaeus published his *Systema Naturae* in 1735, we still lack a *Systema Culturae* and, correspondingly, a *Systema Animae*. Activity theory and semiotics, with taxonomies of activities and sign systems, should offer the basis for a taxonomy of higher mental processes that would live up to the complexity of the human mind. A catalogue of activities executed in a particular cultural group or by an individual, together with a catalogue of the semiotic means (sign systems) at their disposal, would permit one to build hypotheses about the ways of thinking and remembering used by this individual or in this culture. This would bring us, in the study of culture-determined mental processes, from the realm of general ideas and fragmentary empirical studies into the realm of massive empirical research.

Last but not least, let us consider activity as a bridge from developmental to general psychology. It is hard not to notice the present gap between general and developmental psychology when considering the scope of research, methods of study, and explanatory principles, among other things. Research on the functioning of mind has little to do with research on the development of mind. It is enough to compare the existing research on scientific thinking in adults with research on the development of scientific (or scholastic) concepts in children to see what I mean. For several reasons, cultural-historical psychology was born on the "developmental" side of psychology and, to an important extent, has remained there, even when adults are studied. While (neo)Piagetian psychology certainly is able to expand its conceptual framework beyond the border of developmental psychology, into the field that general psychology regards as its own, there is no reason to expect that this would change the fact that while the beauty and strength of Piagetian psychology lie in descriptions, explanations remain its weakness. Therefore, it is not clear what kind of explanations Piagetian psychology could offer general psychology. Cultural-historical psychology in its turn has (a) awakened some hope in recent decades that it is looking for causal explanations of mind in the right place, and (b) introduced the idea that the semiotic means — the acquisition of which is an important issue in developmental psychology — should not be forgotten when processes that are mediated by these means are studied in adults. After all, adult activities are what cultures prepare their children for by providing them the necessary tools.

The move from cross-cultural to cultural psychology occurred when an understanding arose that what was to be explained through culture was not some aberrations from European-American norms of mental functioning, but human mind par excellence and its development. There are good reasons to believe that the movement in this direction has not ended, but only just started. There will be no need for cultural psychology when it is generally accepted, that higher mental functioning in humans can only be explained through culture and not through nature. Culture will turn into the general explanatory principle for the specifically human mind. And perhaps a presentation will be made one day on "Activity as Explanatory Principle in Psychology."

## References

Cassirer, E. (1923-29). *Philosophie der symbolischen Formen* (Vols. 1-3). Berlin: Bruno Cassirer.

Cole, M., Gay, J., Glick, J., & Sharp, D.W. (1971). *The cultural context of learning and thinking*. New York: Basic Books.

Engeström, Y. (1987). Learning by expanding: An activity-theoretical approach to developmental research. Helsinki: Orienta-Konsultit.

Leontiev, A.N. (1971). *Potrebnosti, motivy i emotsii* [Needs, motives and emotions]. Moscow: Moscow University Press.

Leontiev (Leont'ev), A.N. (1981). The problem of activity in psychology. In J.V. Wertsch (Ed. and Trans.), *The concept of activity in Soviet psychology* (pp. 37-71). Armonk, N.Y.: Sharpe. (Original work published 1972)

Luria, A.R. (1976). *Cognitive development: Its cultural and social foundations* (M. Cole, Ed.; M. Lopez-Morillas & L. Solotaroff, Trans.). Cambridge, Mass.: Harvard University Press. (Original work published 1974)

Nunes, T., Schliemann, A., & Carraher, T. (1993). *Street mathematics and school mathematics*. Cambridge: Cambridge University Press.

Saxe, G.B. (1991). Cultural and cognitive development: Studies in mathematical understanding. Hillsdale, N.J.: Erlbaum.

Scribner, S. (1984). Studying working intelligence. In B. Rogoff & J. Lave (Eds.), *Everyday cognition: Its development in social context* (pp. 9-40). Cambridge, Mass.: Harvard University Press.

Tulviste, P. (1991). *Cultural-historical development of verbal thinking: A psychological study* (M.J. Hall, Trans.). Commack, N.Y.: Nova Science. (Original work published 1988)

Wertsch, J.V. (1991). *Voices of the mind: A sociocultural approach to mediated action*. Cambridge, Mass.: Harvard University Press.

Wertsch, J.V. (1998). *Mind as action*. New York: Oxford University Press.

# 6    Categories in Activity Theory: Marx's Philosophy Just-in-time

*Uffe Juul Jensen*

The relation between scientific concepts and philosophical categories is a perennial philosophical problem. Theories of natural science encompass theoretical concepts that specify mechanisms and structures in nature. The concept of *nature* is not, however, a part of such theories. Biomedicine and the health sciences use a variety of models to account for conditions of disease and health, but the general concepts or categories of *health* and *disease* are not commonly a concern of these sciences (Jensen, 1987). Theoretical concepts in activity theory such as *activity*, *motive*, and *operation* form part of an interrelated theoretical system used in accounting for conscious human life and personality. But how are these theoretical concepts related to corresponding categories, such as activity, which are well-known and well-established within philosophy?

In this chapter I shall argue that categories in the human sciences actually play a different and crucial role in theoretical development than they play in the theoretical development of the natural sciences. I shall try to explain this difference by presenting the idea of a philosophy *just-in-time*. To pave the way to reach this philosophy, and to understand its importance for activity theory, it is first necessary to make some preliminary comments about the status of categories in activity theory and their relation to its scientific practice.

## The Activity Concept in Activity Theory

Davydov (1988) stresses that "the concept of activity is introduced into contemporary science by dialectical logic, which examines — from a particular point of view — the universal structure and universal schemata" (p. 19). According to Leontiev (1975/1978), "Introducing

\* This chapter is a revised version of the lecture that I held in memory of Marx Wartofsky at the ISCRAT Congress. I thank Seth Chaiklin for fruitful comments on previous drafts, just-in-time, as it were.

the concept of activity into psychology changes the whole conceptual system of psychological knowledge" (p. 50). Soviet psychology, according to Leontiev, was "the first to introduce into psychology a series of important categories... Among these the category of activity is of greatest significance" (p. 45).

Leontiev gives full credit to Marx, referring to Marx's first thesis on Feuerbach in which Marx criticizes Feuerbach's mechanical materialism and neglect of human practice. In the introduction to *Activity, Consciousness, and Personality*, Leontiev wrote that the most important thing in the book is the attempt "to comprehend psychologically the categories subjective activity, consciousness of man and the category of personality" (p. 6).

Leontiev, Davydov and other activity theorists distinguish implicitly or explicitly between philosophical categories that are presupposed in one way or another in activity theory from the theoretical concepts that constitute the theory. Similar distinctions are made in the natural sciences where one distinguishes between theoretical concepts in the natural sciences and the general concept *nature*, or between theoretical concepts in biology and the general concept *life*.

There does, however, seem to be a crucial difference between an activity theorist's preoccupation with categories and the natural scientist's interest in general concepts or categories as nature and life. Very few, if any, scientists would claim today that conceptual or philosophical clarification of our concepts of nature or life would contribute to a further development of natural science or theoretical biology. Most philosophers would probably agree. And it is likely that both scientists and philosophers would also agree that theoretical development in the sciences is more important to philosophy than the other way round.

But philosophy is not irrelevant to the sciences and the development of the sciences. It is widely recognized that metaphysical ideas have often inspired scientists, and many scientists would probably agree that critical philosophical thinking can contribute to cleaning science from the influence of obscure, metaphysical ideas. So philosophy can be an initiator, at the psychological level, contributing to a scientist's creativity and at a conceptual level in the analysis of conceptual confusions.

Leontiev, Davydov and other founding fathers of activity theory seem, however, to suggest that analysis of the philosophical categories, such as the category of activity, has a constructive role for the development of a scientific psychology. However, the activity theorists' account of the relation between philosophical categories and scientific concepts often seems unclear. This lack of clarity reflects in a way the current situation in philosophy.

There is no consensus today concerning the role and status of categories. In this chapter, I shall argue that philosophical categories, such as activity, are important to activity theory as Leontiev and Davydov suggested. It is, however, necessary first to show how two important philosophical traditions have interpreted the relation between theoretical concepts in the sciences and philosophical categories, and to suggest why these traditions have been unable to account for the constructive role of categories in the theoretical development of the human sciences.

### A Philosophy Just-In-Time is Needed

In the Platonic, foundationalist tradition of Western philosophy, philosophers have given primacy to philosophical categories in a desire to occupy an Archimedean point outside the turmoil of practice and historical change. From their detached vantage point, they want to assume responsibility for correcting and directing practice and science. With this perspective, philosophers are always *ahead* of the practice and science of their time. In another tradition, philosophy is always *too late* to direct or correct science and practice. Philosophy, in this perspective, is conceived of as primarily a reflexive enterprise. Hegel takes this stance (at least in one interpretation of his difficult work). In the preface to his *Grundlinien der Philosophie des Rechts*, Hegel (1821/1991) addresses the subject of issuing instructions on how the world ought to be and writes that "philosophy at any rate comes too late to perform that function" (p. 23). His view is summarized beautifully in the phrase: "The owl of Minerva begins its flight only with the onset of dusk" (p. 23). In this perspective, philosophy cannot provide categories to direct practice or scientific activity.

In this chapter, I present and defend a third approach to philosophy: a philosophy just-in-time. That is, a philosophy that can simultaneously (or maybe concurrently) play a constructive role in science and practice and be a critical reflection of actual science and practice, a philosophy that changes through its participation in changing science and practice. I shall argue that this approach is fundamentally compatible with activity theory, as well as the marxian philosophy that was an important source for this psychological theory. I shall also argue that an articulation and development of this philosophical stance will make it possible to clarify the relationship between the scientific concepts of activity theory and the philosophical categories that activity theorists presuppose.

### Concepts in Practice

From the standpoint of activity theory, and its implicit philosophy, human consciousness, including human cognition, must be analyzed and understood in the context of human activity. This standpoint also has implications for our understanding of science and philosophy. In most philosophical traditions from antiquity to present-day philosophy, philosophy has been reduced to its products: categorical or metaphysical systems, conceptual structures, strings of arguments, and so forth. Similarly, science has been reduced to its products: hypotheses and systems of hypotheses or theories (see Lektorsky, this volume).

This reduction has had a crucial influence on philosophers' analyses and accounts of the relationship between philosophy and science. Abstract concepts of science and philosophy have been scrutinized in isolation from the complex practices in which they play a role. Hume, for example, tried to illuminate the relationship between the category *causality* and our experiences. He argued that causality is nothing over and above the constant conjunction of events. Similarly, he concluded his analysis of the general concept of *the self* by claiming that the self is nothing over and above a stream of consciousness. But the whole analysis is based on a crucial presupposition: the content or meaning of general ideas or categories, such as causality and self, could be revealed by a "bottom-up" analysis (i.e., by accounting for impressions or experiences we have when using these categories).

Today, when postmodern thought is a common feature of academic institutions, most philosophers and psychologists — not only activity theorists — deny that anything is just given or natural. What appears as immediately given is a result of practices and its appearance is theory- and value-loaded in diverse ways. Hume's foundationalist presupposition misdirects his account of experience. He treats constant conjunctions as something given in experience. But constant conjunctions are established or produced under experimental conditions, which presuppose a closure of open systems in nature (Bhaskar, 1975; Lektorsky, this volume). Hume also misinterpreted philosophical categories which he tried to force into his empiricist straitjacket. Causality can only be understood in the context of complex practices governed by procedures for choosing and justifying objects of intervention. And the self cannot be accounted for in abstraction from concrete practices with procedures for interpersonal recognition as argued (in different ways) by Hegel and Marx.

Positivists and other philosophical foundationalists are not the only philosophers who have tried to characterize the relation between categories and scientific concepts by abstracting from science and philosophy as practice or activity. This neglect of practice can also be found sometimes in the works of marxists (e.g., textbooks that purport to present dialectical materialism by presenting dialectical "laws" that are supposed to justify scientific hypotheses), and in activity theorists. The rise of activity theory and its development as a research tradition shows, however, that it is misleading to present the theory as if it were based upon philosophical categories and principles that would — in some way — guarantee the validity of the theory.

The theoretical concepts of activity theory are not just instances of philosophical categories. That is, the hypotheses and principles of activity theory are not just deduced from general philosophical principles. They are, on the contrary, formulated as part of a scientific discourse: articulated and developed in opposition to other psychological theories (e.g., reflexology, behaviorism, Piagetian psychology) with the aim to solve theoretical, empirical and practical problems and contradictions that could not be solved by the other theories.

The philosophical categories that have played a role in the development of the research tradition of activity were never once-and-for-all, articulated categories; rather they were formulated as part of an ongoing dialogue with other philosophical traditions (e.g., Hegel, Feuerbach) and scientific perspectives and traditions. It is one of the great merits of Marx Wartofsky's "historical epistemology" to have situated the perspectives and categories of a Marxist philosophy in the context of a historical dialogue between scientific approaches and philosophical traditions (e.g., Wartofsky, 1979).

Most of the philosophical positions criticized by Karl Marx were kinds of foundationalism or essentialism that assume that particular categories or concepts represent the eternal structure of reality, the essence of things, our inherent nature and so forth. In the same way activity theory has criticized alternative psychological approaches that postulate a direct or unmediated relation between the acting subject and the object of his or her activity (e.g., Uznadze's and Leontiev's critique of the "postulate of directness" in Leontiev, 1975/1978, p. 47).

Why are activity theorists' account of the relation between philosophical categories and scientific concepts often unclear or even obscure? I believe that one of the reasons is that they have not applied their insight about the situated nature of practice, and the practice-situatedness of concepts reflexively. Only rarely have activity theorists accounted for their own concepts and theories as embedded in activities and practices (see Chaiklin, 1993, 1994, for exceptions).

This chapter is a plea for a situated approach to theoretical concepts, an approach that is reflexively consistent with the theory, and which will deepen the philosophical self-consciousness of activity theorists. This self-consciousness is likely to promote further theoretical progress and stimulate further research in the interplay between scientific and philosophical activity.

### Structure of the Argument

I shall try to pave the way for this situated approach by analyzing a concrete case: Marx himself and the way scientific and philosophical activities were interrelated in his life. I hope to show that Marx not only presented a new system of categories but also a new understanding of categories and their role in thinking and acting.

Categories in the Aristotelian tradition, as well as the Kantian tradition, are conceived of as something absolute. According to Aristotle, categories, such as substance or quality, represent different ways of being. According to Kant, categories are absolute, unchangeable conditions of experience embodied in the knowing subject.

Marx did not abandon categories but he rejected their status as something absolute beyond human practice. Categories, in Marx's view are embodied in forms of practice or in standpoints in practice. To illustrate concretely how categories are embodied in practices, I will discuss the category of *civil society*, and the relation between the standpoint of civil society (a particular practice in which individuals act to ensure their own interest) and the standpoint of — what Marx calls — human society (a practice embodying other norms and standards such as solidarity). If categories are not eternal essences or structures but conditions of acting embodied in particular practices, then there will be important implications for our understanding of the human sciences in general, and activity theory in particular. Subsequent reflections on and development of the activity category will be understood as a necessary part of the scientific task of activity theory.

### How Did Marx Change Philosophy?

Marx developed his theories of political economy significantly between the *Pariser Manuskripten* (1844) and *Das Kapital* (1867). The initial plan for *Das Kapital* was formulated in 1857, followed by almost 10 years at the British Museum in London studying classical economics. This development of Marx's work is interpreted in contradictory ways in two different narratives of Marx's intellectual career.

According to Michael Theunissen, professor in philosophy and a renowned scholar (now emeritus) at Freie Universität Berlin, Marx's studies at the British Museum were a crucial event in the development of modern philosophy (Theunissen, 1989). By this activity, Marx set a new standard for philosophy, namely, philosophy as research. This standard makes it impossible to do serious philosophy in a field without having studied the sciences about which one will philosophize.

In contrast to Theunissen, Alaisdair MacIntyre (1991) interprets Marx's studies and research after Marx's (1845/1994) "Theses on Feuerbach" in quite a different way. He argues that Marx made distinctions and suggested perspectives in his "Theses" that could revolutionize philosophy; but after Marx turned to economics, he never developed his revolutionary philosophy in a satisfactory way.

In the following I shall try to fuse Theunissen's and MacIntyre's perspectives on Marx's philosophy into a coherent narrative that shows the interrelationship between philosophical and scientific activity. Theunissen and MacIntyre do not present contradictory perspectives; rather their views provide mutually supplementary perspectives on Marx developing a new kind of philosophy neither too early nor too late but just-in-time. Marx's decision to spend so much time doing research in economics was, according to Theunissen, motivated by a basic philosophical assumption: Reality does not ever just present itself. Reality is always mediated through cognitive activities and products that precede any philosophy. In our modern age, our relation to the world is primarily mediated by scientific practice and its products.

Theunissen did not discuss Marx's theses on Feuerbach in his account of the Marxian revolution in philosophy, and he did not discuss the extent to which Marx's scientific studies and research are related to his earlier philosophical activity. But it is not difficult to trace the assumption mentioned above to the theses on Feuerbach, especially to the first thesis in which Marx (1845/1994) criticizes "all previous materialism" (p. 116). The chief defect of these materialisms, which encompass what we today would label *realism*, is

that the concrete thing, the real, the perceptible is considered to be an object or (datum of) perception only and not to be perceptible human activity, or praxis; i.e., it is not considered subjectively. (p. 116)

Like so many of Marx's other views, the ideas expressed in the first thesis are now widely accepted far beyond marxist quarters (which by the way are now almost nonexistent). For example, it is almost axiomatic in recent science studies that we live in a world populated by objects produced in techno-scientific practice (e.g., Latour, 1987), or constructed in accordance with procedures of abstraction and idealization of experimental practice. These "fossils" of human practice, which together with our ongoing practices, mediate our relation with the world and our intersubjective relations.

Marx's scientific activity in London, it now appears, is not a break with the philosophy announced or sketched in the "Theses on Feuerbach." Rather it realizes in practice at least some of the perspectives presented in the "Theses." Marx does not express explicitly the view in the "Theses" that Theunissen ascribes to him: that philosophy in our modern age must "reflect through the science" that it is studying. But the perspectives in the theses are, I think, not only compatible with but also imply the view Theunissen ascribes to Marx. For example, in this Marxian perspective, an adequate philosophy of mind or philosophical anthropology must necessarily take into account and reflect through psychological research and its products. Similarly, a philosophy of medicine cannot be developed a priori but must systematically reflect through the health sciences. A philosophy of nature that does not take into account, say, thermodynamics in particular and the biological sciences in general should not be taken seriously. This does not imply, however, that Marx reduces philosophical activity to scientific practice. He never became an advocate of scientism, in the sense of canonizing methods of natural science as universally valid methods of research or reasoning. It is well known that Marx did not accept *tout court* the theories of political economy that he studied in London. On the contrary, he put them through careful criticism, rejecting them as universally valid economic laws, and interpreting them as products of a research practice carried out under specific sociopolitical conditions representing only the appearance of socioeconomic reality.

MacIntyre might agree with this preceding argument, but he would still insist that the theses contain philosophical resources that were never used nor developed by Marx (nor by anybody else). He might respond to Theunissen's glorification of Marx's scientific approach by saying that taking science into account and criticizing ideological misinterpretation of scientific theories are necessary components of any adequate philosophical activity today, but certainly not sufficient. He might even argue that Marx's criticism of mechanical materialism (in the first thesis) implies a philosophical theory that was never developed.

The mechanical materialists that Marx criticized certainly took science into account in a serious way (as scientific realists do today). But Marx criticized them for misrepresenting the sciences, and for not understanding the practical character of cognition (including scientific research). They lacked an adequate philosophical framework for analyzing and understanding scientific concepts and theories. Ignoring the practical character of cognition, they reified the products of scientific practice and interpreted them as something manifest or immediately given — as "data," as we might say today. Marx criticized this but he did not develop the necessary arguments to show why it was wrong.

Marx had, MacIntyre claims, good reasons to reject Hegel and Feuerbach. But according to MacIntyre he made the fatal mistake to reject philosophy as such and

by rejecting philosophy, at a stage at which his philosophical enquiries were still incomplete and were still informed by mistakes inherited from his philosophical predecessors, Marx allowed his later work to be distorted by presuppositions which were in key respects infected by philosophical errors. (pp. 278-279)

I argued that Marx, in his first thesis on Feuerbach, articulated a view of philosophy that was realized later in his own practice as a student of and researcher in economics. In the first thesis, Marx interpreted a particular philosophical perspective (Feuerbach's) and the division be-tween two opposing perspectives in philosophy. Later he set a new standard through his scientific activity, and thereby changed philoso-phy. In the following, I shall argue that the theses when considered in their entirety, rather than the first thesis alone, sketches a philosophical approach that Marx tried to develop and realize through the rest of his life.

### A Basic Problematic: Transcending Civil Society

According to MacIntyre, there were implications in the "Theses on Feuerbach" that Marx never fully developed. To understand Mac-Intyre's point it is necessary to take a fresh look at the theses, and at MacIntyre's critique of Marx's activity after the "Theses on Feuerbach." First, let us review the basic problematic in the theses. The theses were not only, or primarily, a defense of materialism against idealism, or of science against a priori thinking and speculation. Feuerbach was also a materialist. In a way Feuerbach represented the modern standpoint of science, but, according to Marx, it was "the standpoint of the old mate-rialism" (p. 118). This "old" materialism presupposed a standpoint of isolated individuals in bourgeois (or civil) society. The standpoint for the contrasting kind of materialism that Marx wanted to defend, is the standpoint of "human society or social humanity" (10th thesis, p. 118).

MacIntyre rightly focuses on the distinction between the standpoint of civil society and a standpoint beyond this society. This point is crucial for understanding what is at stake in the theses. Civil society, as introduced by Adam Ferguson and adopted by Hegel, refers to the so-cial, economic and judicial relations in which we take part to satisfy our needs. The relations in which individuals participate become the means for individuals to realize their ends. Individual citizens taking part in relations become means for other citizens to achieve their aims. Marx focused on and developed the "sphere of needs" in Hegel's concept, so when Marx refers to the civil society (*Bürgerliche Gesellschaft*), he is thinking, in simple terms of private citizens, families and firms each ensuring their own interests and who all depend upon being able to exchange commodities and services with each other. The standpoint of civil society is the standpoint from which society is nothing over and above individual citizens, families and firms ensuring their own inter-ests.

Currently civil society is glorified worldwide and conceived of as a precondition for a democratic and humane society. So, MacIntyre is very bold in not only reminding us of the Marxian critique of this standpoint, but also in claiming that transcending the standpoint of civil society is still a precondition for a democratic and humane society.

I agree with MacIntyre that the critique of the standpoint of civil society and its built-in individualism is the philosophical cornerstone of the theses on Feuerbach. And I agree that science and practice are conceived of in completely different ways when considered from the standpoint of civil society or from the standpoint of collective or communal practice. In some branches of the marxian tradition, the philosophical importance of the category of communal practice has not always been well understood. Productive practice and science have often been emphasized at the expense of communal interaction; or to put it in Aristotelian terms: production has overshadowed praxis; techne taken precedence over phronesis. This imbalance in the use of crucial categories has probably also had unfortunate effects on activity theory (Davydov, 1988, pp. 27-28). Is it true that Marx never gave a satisfactory account of the distinction between the two different standpoints referred to in the theses?

Marx drew a demarcation line between the two different standpoints. According to MacIntyre, Marx tried "to identify what is involved in transcending the standpoint of civil society" (p. 279). His attempt was partly successful, and partly unsuccessful, MacIntyre claims. To assess this claim it is necessary to examine MacIntyre's arguments in more detail.

Many philosophers and others, both before and after Marx, have criticized the individualism implied by this conception of social life. The "Theses" are, however, philosophically revolutionary in claiming that

the standpoint of civil society cannot be transcended, and its limitations adequately understood and criticized by theory alone, that is by theory divorced from practice, but only by a particular kind of practice, practice informed by a particular kind of theory rooted in that practice. (p. 279)

MacIntyre admits that he ascribes a view to Marx which Marx does not express explicitly. But MacIntyre claims that

if Marx had done the work of spelling out in detail the key distinction which the argument of the Theses on Feuerbach needs, he would have been compelled to articulate it in something very like Aristotelian terms. Hegel's idiom is just not adequate to the task. (p. 281)

The key distinction referred to by MacIntyre is the distinction between activities governed by the norms of civil society and those governed by another kind of practice or activity (objective activity). In the norms of the civil society, there "are no ends except those which are understood to be the goals of some particular individual or individuals, dictated by the desires of those individuals" (p. 280). In this other kind of practice, the ends or goals are "characterizable antecedently to and independently of any characterization of the desires of the particular individuals who happen to engage in it" (p. 280).

MacIntyre's reading of Marx is, in general, very enlightening. But his account of the distinction between civil society and teleologically organized practices is unclear and ambiguous in a philosophically interesting way. By illuminating some ambiguities I shall try to show that Marx did not, as claimed by MacIntyre, leave philosophy after having written the "Theses." On the contrary his activities serve, as noted by Theunissen, as a model of a new kind of philosophy, the philosophy he proclaimed in his theses.

## What is "Transcending the Standpoint of Civil Society?"

MacIntyre uses, I think, civil society as a classificatory or natural-kind term that specifies a kind of society with a specific essence. Members of a civil society act in a specific way. They are characterized by a specific deceptive self-understanding: In civil society individuals are trying to meet their own personal interests. Civil society is "a social order in which human beings are generally deprived of a true understanding of themselves and their relationships" (p. 284). This essentialist understanding of civil society determines what is meant by the phrase "transcending the standpoint of civil society." To transcend the civil society is to be (or become) a participant in a social order that is characterized by a kind of practice that is incompatible with the practice of civil society.

MacIntyre's essentialism implies, it appears, a particular perspective on social transformation or revolution. Transcending civil society implies a kind of jump into a human society characterized by a communal practice. But how is such a transcendence possible? The necessary skills are not acquired, as Left-Hegelians thought, through theoretical critique of the civil society and its contradictions. MacIntyre claims that no philosophical or scientific educators could prepare people for that jump, referring to the third thesis in which Marx stresses that the "educator must himself be educated" (p. 117). Educators — political, scientific, or philosophical — who believe they can promote transcendence of the civil society by enlightening people take themselves "not only to know more, but also to know best ... to know what is genuinely good for others, something that they do not themselves know" (p. 287).

According to MacIntyre's reading of Marx, people will transform themselves by transcending the standpoint of civil society. It remains unclear, however, how this transcendence is at all possible, and how it, so to speak, gets started. The precise meaning of "transcending" in this context is simply unclear.

MacIntyre is probably aware that his account may appear to be an utopian and unrealistic agenda for a political-philosophical alternative to the standpoint of the civil society. For example, he admits that his Aristotelian elucidation of Marx's theses scarcely could be justified if it proved impossible to give just one example of a practice which is both revolutionary in a Marxian sense[1] and is "adequately characterizable only by an Aristotelian reference to the goods internal to it" (p. 287). He finds such an example in Thompson's (1963) *The Making of the English Working Class*. At the end of the eighteenth and the beginning of the nineteenth century hand-loom weavers of Lancashire and Yorkshire "embodied in their practice a particular conception of human good, of virtues, of duties to each other and of the subordinate place of technical skills in human life" (p. 287). A special rhythm of work and leisure allowed the cultivation of gardens, learning of mathematics and reading, and composition of poetry. The weavers had, to the extent it was possible, placed themselves outside civil society. Is this an example of transcending the standpoint of civil society? If yes, what is MacIntyre's point in claiming that we need a philosophical account of transcending the standpoint of civil society? MacIntyre has already used an Aristotelian vocabulary in presenting the example. What more is needed?

---

1. In the sense expressed by Marx (1845/1994) in the third thesis: "The coincidence of the change of circumstances and human activity, or human self-transformation, can be grasped and rationally comprehended only as *revolutionary praxis*" (p. 117).

The weavers, MacIntyre writes, were lacking a theory to articulate what was embodied in their practice. Such a theory

which had successfully articulated their practice and which had been formulated so that its dependence on that practice was evident would have supplied just the kind of example of the relationship of theory to practice which the argument expressed in the theses on Feuerbach so badly needs. (p. 287)

It is not clear what kind of theory MacIntyre imagines here. And it is unclear what role such a theory should play in transcending the standpoint of civil society. According to the first thesis on Feuerbach, as interpreted by MacIntyre, the standpoint of civil society cannot be transcended by theory alone or by theory divorced by practice "but only by a particular kind of practice, practice informed by a particular kind of theory rooted in that same practice" (p.279).

In one sense, a theory is involved in the weaver's practice (as described by MacIntyre). The practice embodies a theory of the good or of something of universal worth. Why is MacIntyre asking for a theory over and above the theory embodied in practice? Perhaps MacIntyre's reading of Marx's famous 11th thesis furnishes a clue for answering these questions. Here Marx criticizes philosophers for having interpreted the world. The point, he claims, is to change it. This has often been understood as a cry for action or activism at the expense of theoretical work. If that was Marx's intention, giving up philosophy would have been a logical consequence of the theses.

MacIntyre, obviously, interprets the 11th thesis in a different way. According to MacIntyre, Marx does not criticize philosophers for trying to interpret or understand. He is complaining, however, that their understanding is not guided by the aim of transforming the natural and social world in the requisite way to "achieve something of universal worth embodied in some particular form of practice through co-operation with other such individuals" (p. 279).

The weavers do not, it now appears, provide a real exemplar of transcending the standpoint of civil society. They lacked a special kind of theory to inform their practice. We begin to understand why MacIntyre complains that Marx did not develop a philosophical theory. If he had not left philosophy, he could, as MacIntyre sees it, have provided the weavers and other revolutionaries with the theory they needed to "articulate what was embodied in their practice" (p. 287). MacIntyre is implicitly criticizing Marx for not having — in theory or philosophy — transcended the standpoint of civil society.

### Revolutionary Activity: Transcendence in Practice

MacIntyre's critique of Marx seems to imply an understanding of the phrase "transcending the standpoint of civil society" that is different from the essentialist interpretation I have ascribed to MacIntyre above. However, MacIntyre does not elucidate this non-essentialist sense of transcending civil society. I shall do so in the following, showing that Marx had his own way to transcend the standpoint of the civil society, which MacIntyre's critique does not appreciate.

In a non-essentialist sense of transcendence, "transcending the standpoint of civil society" means showing the incoherence of the standpoint as embodying a theoretical perspective. That is, one shows the incoherence of the view that we are isolated individuals, only aiming to promote our individual interests, in relation to the view that cognition and science are individual acquisitions. The standpoint of civil society presupposes another standpoint in which we are always communal beings — in our private life as well as in our public life and our scientific activities. Transcending the standpoint of civil society in this sense is not primarily a critical activity detached from practice — as Left-Hegelians, many later critical theorists, and others have thought. It is a theoretical transcendence that is inseparable from a struggle in practice to limit the influence of institutional structures and other power structures that give priority to the standpoint of civil society.

This non-essentialist sense of transcending civil society implies another perspective about revolutionary practice as well as another perspective about philosophical activity than the perspective presented by MacIntyre. As noted before, an essentialist interpretation of civil society specifies a special kind of society in which the members share quite specific characteristics. For example, no other goods are recognized except those involved in the satisfaction of the wants and needs of individuals. Even groups, such as workers, who have an interest in fighting the standpoint of civil society have become absorbed into it. Proletarianization makes it necessary for them to resist, but, according to MacIntyre, proletarianization also deprives "workers of those forms of practice through which they can discover conceptions of a good and virtues adequate to the moral needs of resistance" (p. 288).

Marx opposed essentialism.[2] A term like *civil society* is not a classificatory, natural-kind term. It is a theoretical or analytical concept used to account for certain aspects of human activities and kinds of relationship. It does not specify inner, essential features of a group of individuals, and it leaves open the possibility that other concepts might represent or characterize other aspects of the activities of individuals or groups. In this light, the standpoint of civil society does not specify an ontological entity which completely permeates what we, for short, call "members of civil society." In discussing the standpoint of civil society we specify norms, standards and ideals governing a particular (complex, often contradictory) human practice considered from a particular standpoint.

Understanding how institutions of practices of civil society constrain other communal human practices is not obtained by jumping out of the existing practice. We live our lives in different contexts and move constantly between different practices. As workers, philosophers or physicians, even during shorter periods of time, we take up different standpoints. To transcend one standpoint, say the standpoint of civil society, does not mean that we have to jump out of civil society. It is not even clear what this would mean.

We have the possibility in practice to experience and interpret how some practices may constrain other practices. We transcend particular standpoints (for example the standpoint of civil society) through processes of challenging or changing such constraints. Change-directed activities will contribute to widening the understanding of both the practice of civil society and the more or less oppressed practices in which people act to achieve something of universal worth. I think this encapsulates the idea of revolutionary activity expressed by Marx in the "Theses on Feuerbach."

Revolutionary activity is not a miraculous jump into a practice beyond the complex social practice in which we live; rather it is an ongoing struggle for changing circumstances that undermine our possibilities for developing or sustaining communal practices (or what Marx called "human society"). At one and the same time, this struggle embodies the self-transformation expressed by Marx in the third thesis.

In this perspective Marx did not give up philosophy after having

2.  This anti-essentialism is expressed clearly in the 6th thesis on Feuerbach: "The essence is not an abstraction inhering in isolated individuals. Rather, in its actuality, it is the ensemble of social relations" (Marx, 1845/1994, p. 117).

written the "Theses on Feuerbach." On the contrary: His political and scientific activities were necessary steps on the road forward to a new kind of philosophical practice in a process through which he contributed to radical social change, development of scientific and philosophical practice — and his own self-transformation.

## The Fusion of Science and Philosophy in Social Practice

Categories have, at least since Kant, been interpreted as absolute preconditions of objective knowledge. Kant and several others have anchored categories in the constitution of human consciousness. In that sense Kantian conceptions of categories also represent the standpoint of civil society. Categories as presented in this chapter are also conditions of human knowledge. The conditions are, however, anchored in social practices and the system of norms and standards embodied in such practices. In that light, philosophical activity must necessarily include participation in social practices and reflections on the relation between the standpoints of different practices.

There is no Archimedean point from which the philosopher can draw a map of absolute categories. This does not imply that we are left in the hands of a chaotic postmodernist world of constantly changing practices. We can reflect from diverse standpoints and through the practices we participate in.

The anti-essentialism which is a cornerstone of Marx's theses on Feuerbach is developed in Marx's later scientific and political work. If Marx had thought it was possible to give an essentialist account or definition of philosophical categories (as human nature or civil society), then further scientific research would, from a philosophical standpoint, have been superfluous.

But civil society is not defined by reference to an internal essence in members of a particular society (just as the general biological concept of *species* is not defined by reference to a set of particular properties inherent in the members of the species). Marx's studies and research in political economy aimed at developing a theoretical system or structure to overcome some of the tensions and contradictions created by essentialist interpretations of civil society. In the same way, conceptual development in evolutionary biology has contributed to illuminating and overcoming problems created by essentialist interpretations of species in pre-Darwinian biology and philosophy (see also Tobach, this volume, on integrative levels). A person who contributes to theoretical and conceptual development through scientific research is not giving up philosophy, but enacting a necessary part of an anti-essentialist philosophy.

Scientific research, however, does not only contribute to developing the content of an anti-essentialist philosophy for which the theses on Feuerbach paved the way. By his research, Marx, as argued by Theunissen, also fixed a new standard for philosophical activity. By doing scientific research, and hereby adopting standards of justification and validity developed within scientific communities, the philosopher transcends the standpoint of civil society in practice. Marx's later work is much more than a contribution to economics. *Das Kapital* also contains philosophical reflections on scientific activity, partly developed in the context of Marx's political economy, partly a result of reflecting through scientific practice that Marx participated in himself.

In the third volume of *Das Kapital*, Marx elucidates the concept of science in the context of his economic theory in general and his analysis of the concept *universal labor* in particular. According to Marx, "Universal labor [*Allgemeine Arbeit*] is any scientific work: All discoveries, all inventions" (Marx, 1867/1970a, p. 114). Marx's account of science also has implications for the themes addressed by MacIntyre. According to Marx, scientific activity is a practice which in itself may embody the ideal of universal worth. Marx did not only contribute to transcending the standpoint of civil society by doing scientific research; his political work, or rather his way of doing political work, also exemplifies the idea of transcending civil society in practice.

In the concluding section of his inaugural address to the first International, Marx (1864/1970b) considers ethical perspectives. After having reminded the workers of their enduring task, Marx — contrary to what many critics have claimed — shows his respect for ethical discourse. The workers should continue developing cooperatives and fighting for political power, but as part of this struggle, the workers should confront politicians of the European nations with the cruelties in the world for which the politicians are responsible. Moreover, the workers should do this by appealing to rules or ideals of morality and right that should regulate our relations as private persons. These rules or ideals should be the supreme rules regulating the relations between nations.

Marx is implying here that even in the European nation-states, imbued with norms or standards of the civil society, there is another ethical stance; our private relations are not just reduced to contractual relations which theorists of the civil society claim. To transcend the civil society philosophically, one cannot simply recall forms of community beyond the grasp of civil society, or recall and reflect upon a harmonious past age, before everything fell apart, or give utopian visions of possible future forms of communal life. Philosophical activity was, for Marx, to reflect critically upon the concepts and theories being used in practice and at the same time to take part in practices in order to attempt to overcome limitations and contradictions in practice. Transcending civil society is not partly a conceptual or theoretical matter and partly a practical matter; rather it is theoretical and practical at the same time. Marx's philosophy is an exemplar of a philosophy just-in-time.

## Activity Theory: A Science of Categories

Throughout the history of philosophy the crucial role of categories for our cognition has been widely recognized. Traditionally categories have been thought of as absolute presuppositions for experience and knowledge, independent of practice and history. This has not, in general, had any detrimental effect on the natural sciences. Even natural scientists who have espoused foundationalist ideas have, in their scientific work, taken the standpoint of practice (i.e., implicitly or explicitly recognizing that the world is always approached from a particular standpoint, usually of experimental practice).

The situation is, however, different within the human sciences. These sciences have ourselves and our condition as its object. We can and actually do take different standpoints (e.g., the standpoint of civil society and a standpoint of communal practice transcending the standpoint of civil society.). The human sciences therefore are about humans-taking-different-standpoints and moving between different standpoints. But standpoints embody, as argued above, different categories which implies that sciences of man are — among other things — sciences of categories.

This seems to create a logical problem with serious practical implications: If a science always presupposes general concepts or categories, how could a science at the same time be a reflection on categories — a philosophical and scientific activity at one and the same time?

This problem explains, I think, a tendency to discuss categories in an absolute way.[3] MacIntyre assumes that a theory of man as a communal being should presuppose a general (Aristotelian) categorical or meta-physical framework. Marx presents another approach in his theses on Feuerbach, an approach that he developed in theory and practice for the rest of his life. Categories embodied in this practice, such as the category "objective activity" cannot be articulated a priori. Activity theorists cannot simply select a ready-made category such as "objective activity" from the theses on Feuerbach. The definition of the category has to be done in the process of scientific as well as philosophical activity. My argument implies that activity theorists should be aware of the Marxian categorical framework that is presupposed by the scientific problematic they are addressing when accounting for human personality and consciousness in the context of activity. The categorical framework presented in the theses implies a psychological problematic: how to account for the transition between context or practices (or human self-transformation) from the standpoint of the individual. What Marx did not have and could not have (and what we still are working to develop in an adequate philosophical and scientific way) is a category of the individual subject (see González Rey, this volume). The category of "subject" is different from the category of the individual embodied in the standpoint of civil society, which is still canonized as the real concept of the individual. This was a main concern for Marx in his political and scientific practice for the rest of his life (Gould, 1978). It is largely thanks to the Marxian perspective on transcending the standpoint of civil society and the individualism built into this standpoint that activity theory became a scientific revolution in psychology. As a research tradition, accounting for movements across contexts and standpoints from the perspective of the individual subject who is moving, activity theory will itself contribute to our understanding of categories in change, and so to the revolution in philosophy initiated by Marx.

### References

Bhaskar, R. (1975). *A realist theory of science*. Leeds, England: Books.

Chaiklin, S. (1993). Understanding the social scientific practice of *Understanding Practice*. In S. Chaiklin & J. Lave (Eds.), *Understanding practice* (pp. 377-401). Cambridge: Cambridge University Press.

3.  Another possibility suggested by Seth Chaiklin is that the classical view of concepts, around which our educational systems are usually organized, makes it difficult to acquire a practice of working with concepts in a dialectical way.

Chaiklin, S. (1994). Where is the "historical" in the cultural-historical tradition? In J. Mammen & M. Hedegaard (Eds.), *Virksomhedsteori i udvikling* (Psykologisk Skriftserie, Vol. 19(1), pp. 11-22). Aarhus, Denmark: Aarhus Universitet, Psykologisk Institut.

Davydov, V.V. (1988). Problems of developmental teaching. *Soviet Education, 30*(8).

Gould, C.C. (1978). *Marx's social ontology: Individuality and community in Marx's theory of social reality.* Cambridge, Mass.: MIT Press.

Hegel, G.W.F. (1991). *Elements of the philosophy of right* (A.W. Wood, Ed.; H.B. Nisbet, Trans.). Cambridge: Cambridge University Press. (Original work published 1821)

Jensen, U.J. (1987). *Practice and progress: A theory for the modern health care system:* Oxford: Blackwell Scientific.

Latour, B. (1987). *Science in action.* Cambridge, Mass.: Harvard University Press.

Leontiev, A.N. (1978). *Activity, consciousness, and personality* (M.J. Hall, Trans.). Englewood Cliffs, N.J.: Prentice-Hall. (Original work published 1975)

MacIntyre, A. (1991). The *Theses on Feuerbach*: A road not taken. In C.C. Gould & R.S. Cohen (Eds.), *Artifacts, representations, and social practice* (pp. 277-290). Dordrecht: Kluwer Academic.

Marx, K. (1970a). *Das Kapital, Dritter Band.* (*Marx-Engels Werke*, Vol. 25). Berlin: Dietz Verlag. (Original work published 1864)

Marx, K. (1970b). Inauguraladresse der Internationalen Arbeiter-Association, London. In *Marx-Engels Werke* (Vol. 16, pp. 5-13). Berlin: Dietz Verlag. (Original work written 1864)

Marx, K. (1994). Theses on Feuerbach. In J. O'Malley (Ed. and Trans., with R.A. Davis), *Marx: Early political writings* (pp. 16-18). Cambridge: Cambridge University Press. (Original work written 1845)

Theunissen, M. (1989). Möglichkeiten des Philosophierens heute. *Sozialwissenschafliche Rundschau, 19,* 77-89.

Thompson, E.P. (1963) *The making of the English working class.* London: Gollancz.

Wartofsky, M.W. (1979). *Models, representation and the scientific understanding.* Dordrecht: Reidel.

# 7 Historical Change of the Notion of Activity: Philosophical Presuppositions

*Vladislav A. Lektorsky*

In this chapter I analyze principal changes in the philosophical under-standing of the notion of activity. These changes are connected with dif-ferent conceptions of human sciences, psychology in particular. The main stages in the development of the idea of activity in western philo-sophy are the philosophy of the 17th and 18th centuries, the German idealist philosophy at the beginning of the 19th century, and Marx's philosophy. In my opinion the understanding of activity in the spirit of the philosophy of the 17th and 18th centuries still exists, and continues to be influential. So I will analyze this understanding in detail. Marx's ideas concerning activity have not yet been accepted by some human sciences, although these ideas are very fruitful. At the same time human sciences are facing new problems, the solution of which presupposes the development of some of Marx's ideas concerning activity and cer-tain additions to this conception.

## The Rise of Modern Experimental Science: Cognition as Construction

Modern experimental natural science, which appeared in the 17th century, became possible as a result of some new assumptions about the relations between human beings and nature. These assump-tions can be considered as conditions for the possibility of modern sci-ence. Among them is an idea of nature as a simple resource for human activity, as a plastic material, which admits human intervention that transforms it to human interests. The human being can in principle completely control natural processes and is situated, as a making and cognizing agent, outside the objects of his activity. In the ancient Greek worldview, technical activity, producing artificial objects, did not have any relations to the cognition of natural objects, because natural and artificial processes were considered to be different. The rise of modern science eliminated the principal difference between these processes; nature came to be understood as a huge mechanism. If you wanted to know nature's inner secrets you should dismantle it. In the process of experiment there is a violent influence on natural processes, which enables a scientist to construct phenomena, uncover their hidden parts and produce facts, which are the empirical base of science. Thus a specific feature of modern science, which distinguishes it from the science of antiquity, is that empirical facts are not so much described as produced, constructed in the process of experimental activity. Modern scientific thinking, in contrast to ancient scientific thinking, arose and developed in the framework of a projective-constructive attitude.[1]

There is another important circumstance. The experiment as a way of investigating nature presupposes not only giving up the idea of a principal difference between natural and artificial processes, but also the possibility of isolating closed systems in the natural world[2] which enables an investigator to control factors influencing processes under his study. If you do not hold these assumptions, then you are not likely to conduct scientific experiments, because you would not expect that they would, in the long run, provide comprehensive answers about nature. But if you accept them, then you should also agree with the consequence: the possibility of exact prediction of future events (not factual possibility, which depends on the concrete stage in the development of science, but in-principle possibility). But if we can predict some processes, then we can regulate, control, and possess them.

This attitude influences specific features of scientific thinking. The main aim of a theory in ancient science was understanding natural phenomena with the help of proof, proceeding from such premises the truth of which can be given intuitively.[3] In modern science, theoretical thinking is connected with a certain activity, using specific objects — ideal ones. The work of a theoretician with these objects resembles in some respects the work of a technician with material constructions: Ideal

1. I wish to stress that science did not first arise in the modern period. There are reasons to speak about ancient and medieval sciences, which are distinguished from the modern one in some essential respects, as they developed within other cognitive and value attitudes. Modern science is a product of a definite cultural and historical situation.
2. And maybe the possibility of understanding the entire world as a set of such systems.
3. So a theory in ancient science is understood and practiced as revealing certain content, which is primordially given, which can be contemplated, intuitively comprehended. Hence the original meaning of the word *theoria* as contemplation.

objects are united, separated, transformed, put in unusual conditions, tested in view of their endurance, and so forth. So-called ideal experiments are carried out with the help of ideal constructions. I wish to stress that real experiments presuppose ideal experiments. Only in the ideal experiment can a researcher select a phenomenon under investigation in "a pure form," revealing inner, deeply hidden mechanisms of natural processes. In the real experiment a researcher tries to approximate (as much as possible, although that is impossible in a complete form) the creation of those situations that were first studied by means of ideal constructions. These features of theoretical activity that developed in the framework of modern science are especially apparent when we deal with the emergence of this kind of science (in particular with the work of such founders of experimental natural science as Galileo). Scientific theory as it began to be understood and practiced contains the possibility of producing empirical phenomena in real experiments.[4]

I wish to stress that in the framework of modern experimental science there is a sharp opposition between scientific and ordinary thinking. The main ideas of Aristotelian physics are not significantly different from ordinary knowledge. Aristotle's ideas that every motion stops in a corresponding "natural" place, that a body moves only when an external force acts on it, and so on, are in many respects simple generalizations of ordinary experience. In this case scientific thinking is a continuation and development of a nonscientific one. The situation in modern science is different. The real motion of the Sun is not the same as its apparent one. According to classical mechanics (which was considered as an example of genuine science at that time), characteristic features of moving bodies are contrary to those that one can observe in experience. Science is based on experiment, but the latter is the result of artificial conditions, in which an ordinary person does not live and does not act. The development of experimental scientific thinking meant distrusting everything that is naturally given.

---

4. It does not mean a conception of theory as a record of the results of real experimenting. (It was the idea of operationalism, that the meaning of a scientific notion can be reduced to the set of experimental measuring operations.) The real dependence here is converse: The real experiment presupposes the ideal one, and the latter is not reducible to the first. There is no coincidence between ideal and real experiments. Theoretical thinking does not copy the procedures of the real experiment, but creates possibilities for the latter. The theory does not depict current experimental practice, but expresses possibilities of constructive human activity.

The philosophy of the 17th and 18th centuries (many of its founders were at the same time founders of modern science) explicates the assumptions of modern science, about which I wrote, and made certain philosophical conclusions. Now I will analyze these conclusions.

The position of distrusting all that is naturally given and cannot be controlled, and trusting only those phenomena that can be produced and controlled leads Descartes to radical doubt in the existence of everything, with the exception of the doubting subject himself. If natural phenomena are important first of all from the point of view of human interests, if man is interested in possessing these phenomena, in controlling them, in making them the peculiar continuation of human being, he can be considered as standing in the center of natural processes and at the same time outside of them. To the human being himself, consciousness cannot also be considered as something given, but as something that is constantly reproducible by its own activity (and thus existing beyond any doubts).[5] Thus two interconnected ideas arise: (a) the idea of the self-evident mode of the existence of consciousness and of the doubtful mode of natural things (the sphere of subjectivity is sharply opposed to everything else), and (b) the idea of the possibility and necessity of the complete control of natural processes by human beings.

The latter idea is connected with the understanding of achieving freedom. If freedom is not only choice from existing possibilities, but also the removal of dependence on factors that externally constrain human beings and dictate their mode of activity, then it seems natural to connect this removal with the possessing and controlling of one's surroundings. The latter includes not only natural, but also social phenomena, the human body, and spontaneous mental phenomena, in particular emotional ones (philosophers in Descartes' time wrote a lot on the struggle with passions). The means of controlling the surroundings is first of all science and different instrumental techniques, which can be created with the help of science. With such an understanding, the complete control of one's surroundings and domination over spontaneous natural and social phenomena is the ideal of "rationalization."

But the idea of possession and control can be extended further. Genuine freedom presupposes that "Ego" can control everything else.

5. Descartes considers consciousness as thinking (hence his famous *cogito, ergo sum*). In other words thinking is interpreted in a broad sense, when all acts of consciousness are understood as belonging to thinking.

Scientific thinking is considered possible only when the subject can control both external factors, influencing an experiment, and his own operations (material experimental and ideal ones). I can control my surroundings by means of different technical devices, and I can do the same with my consciousness with the help of some reflective procedures. The idea of gaining full control of the operations of thinking leads to the idea of *method* as a general and universal procedure, by means of which one can produce knowledge. In general the thought of a close connection between a complete self-reflection and the achievement of genuine thinking and freedom is among main ideas of this philosophy.

The interpretation of the sphere of subjectivity as something self-evident, and at the same time the position of doubt in everything that is given to consciousness from outside, has other interesting consequences. If one accepts the thesis, going back to Aristotle, that the knowledge of the essence of a thing presupposes the knowledge of its immediate cause, and if one shares the position that only the sphere of subjectivity is self-evident, then it is possible to make a conclusion that man can only have real knowledge of those things that are made by himself, with the help of his consciousness (because he has inner access to the process of their construction). Knowledge in this case is identified with production and construction. Some thinkers at that time made such a conclusion.[6] But if one considers that only the sphere of consciousness is really given, then, from this point of view, real knowledge is only possible of those things that are constructed with the help of consciousness and at the same time remain in the subjective realm, not going beyond it.

Ideas of "the philosophy of consciousness" about human being, subjectivity and Ego greatly influenced the development of modern philosophy, determining for a long time the mode of defining problems in ontology, epistemology, philosophy of science and in many human sci

6.  Spinoza's (1677/1910) discussion of the essence of a circle is interesting in this respect. He writes that the circle can be defined as a figure with equal radii. This definition, Spinoza says, does not express the essence of the circle, but only one of its properties, which is only derivative and secondary. This definition is only nominal. Real definition must express the immediate cause of a thing, but it is equal according to Spinoza to describing the mode of the construction of a thing. So he thinks that the circle must be defined as a figure that is produced by a line one end of which is fastened and the other is moving (paragraphs 95 and 96).

ences, particularly in psychology (the aim of which was understood as the study of the "inner" world of subjectivity). As a result of this understanding some problems arose that often seemed insoluble: the relation of "I" and the outer world, the possibility of understanding "other minds," and so forth. It is interesting to note that those who tried to explicate philosophical presuppositions of modern science faced these kinds of problems. Modern science, on the one hand, presupposes a realistic epistemological position (which is incompatible with the tradition of "the philosophy of consciousness"). On the other hand, the projective-constructive attitude, which is at the base of modern science, is closely connected with "the philosophy of subjectivity." I think it is not an accident that many outstanding philosophers of science — some of them were at the same time creators of contemporary science — combined two philosophical positions which seem to be incompatible: realism and subjectivism. I mean, in particular, such men as Mach, Bridgman, and Russell.[7] Husserl (1954/1970) was not quite right, when he considered objectivism as the cause of the crisis of European sciences and argued that the way to overcome the crisis was by returning to subjectivity. In reality the objectivist position, understanding cognized objects as something counterposed to the subject, alienated from him, is the reverse side of subjectivist attitude. These are only two projections of the same position.

Such were the consequences of the understanding of activity as the construction of phenomena by a subject who has a direct access to himself but not to outer objects, and who has complete control of the products of his/her activity.

## German Idealist Philosophy: Humans as Self-Creators

The next stage in the development of the idea of activity is connected with the German idealistic philosophy of the end of the 18th and the beginning of the 19th centuries. This philosophy inherited the principal idea of the philosophy of the 17th and 18th centuries: understanding cognition as construction. At the same time the German phi-

---

7. For example, Mach (1906/1908) believed that psychic processes could only be understood as the result of physiological processes. On the other hand, all "physical" processes, including physiological processes are going on between "elements," which can only be interpreted as sensations (see pp. 23-57).

losophers introduced some new important elements in understanding activity.

First of all the subject of activity was conceived not as an empirical individual, but as something lying beyond it. For Kant and Fichte it was Transcendental Subject (not an empirical individual, but a certain "inner essence" of it), for Hegel it was Absolute Spirit, realizing itself, in particular, in the historical development of human spiritual and practical activity.

These philosophers made an important attempt to overcome the dichotomy of the "the inner" and "the outer," the subjective and objective worlds. Fichte and Hegel elaborated the interesting and fruitful idea of the co-occurrence between two processes: the process of changing or transforming the outer object and the process of changing the subject. The only means of changing the subject is the process of objectification, creating new things, new objective situations. But it is not only the process of changing the subject; in a certain sense it is also the process of forming or creating it. Although activity always presupposes the subject, in the beginning of the process the subject exists only as a potentiality, as something undetermined, as Ego in itself, as Absolute in itself. It can realize itself, become a genuine subject, only as the result of historically developing human activity, transforming the natural and the social worlds. The subjective world exists only so much as it expresses itself in objective forms, in the process of creating and transforming these forms. In turn the objective world exists only as the result and the process of activity of the subject (Transcendental Subject of Fichte, Absolute Spirit of Hegel).

So the understanding of a human being as a self-creator, living in the world of man-made things, is something natural for German philosophy. Otherwise activity cannot be understood. At the same time, according to the German idealists, the essence of activity belongs to the sphere of spirit (Transcendental Ego, Absolute Spirit).

Fruitful ideas concerning activity, elaborated in the philosophy of German idealism at the beginning of the 19th century, were not generally accepted by the human sciences. It was Marx who not only inherited these ideas, but also developed them and gave them a form that can be productive for contemporary human sciences.

## Marxian Philosophy: Mediated Practice in Collective Societal Activity

Marx, who was a genuine heir of the German idealist tradition, managed to overcome its subjectivism. The starting point in understanding a human being for Marx is not activity of consciousness (empirical or transcendental, individual or Absolute), but real empirical activity, practice, transforming natural and social surroundings. It is first of all not individual, but collective social activity. Individual activity and individual consciousness are derivative from the collective one. The latter presupposes inter-individual relations, interaction and communication.

But also when I am active *scientifically*, etc. — an activity that I can seldom perform in direct community with others, my activity is *societal*, because I am active as a *human being*. Not only is the material of my activity given to me as a societal product — even the language in which the thinker is active — but my *own* being *is* societal activity, and therefore that which I make of myself, I make of myself for society, with the consciousness of myself as a societal being. (Marx, 1844/1964, p. 137)[8]

Activity cannot exist without a subject. But the initial form of a subject is not ego, but a subject of collective activity (e.g., a group, a community, a team). The individual subjective world, individual consciousness, ego are not something given (as philosophers of the 17th and 18th centuries thought), but the result of the development and transformations of the collective activity or practice.

Marx (1845/1976) developed and changed the idea of the German idealist philosophy concerning the co-occurrence of the change of outer objects and the change of a subject. For him it is "the coincidence of the changing of circumstances and of human activity or self-change" (p. 4). It is not something going on in the sphere of transcendental consciousness, but real human practice, which overcomes the counterposition of the inner and the outer worlds. It means that the only way of creating and changing the inner world of consciousness is real practice, the process of objectification, of externalization, the process of real embodiment of human motives, the process of making a human world.

---

8. This citation and subsequent citations from Marx are sometimes modified slightly from the quoted sources in accordance with the original text.

Marx stressed that a human being, in creating a world of artifacts, doubles himself and so creates the possibility for looking at himself from outside. A human being looks at human-made things and other persons with whom he communicates[9] as if in a mirror, and he sees himself in this mirror. Through this self-reference and self-reflection

nature appears as *his* product and his reality. ... [a human being] duplicates himself, not only as in consciousness, intellectually, but also actively, in reality, and therefore views himself in a world that he has created. (Marx, 1844/1964, p. 114)

As he neither enters into the world possessing a mirror, nor as a Fichtean philosopher who can say "I am I", a person first sees and recognizes himself in another person. Peter only relates to himself as a person through his relation to another person, Paul, in whom he recognizes his likeness. (Marx, 1867/1990, p. 144)

Human-made things, beginning with tools for work and finishing with language signs, mediate all human relations and, in this process of mediation, participate in creating specific human features: consciousness, freedom of choice, psychic processes, and so on.

For not only the five senses, but also the so-called *spiritual* senses, the practical senses (will, love, etc.), in a word, *human* sense, the human nature of the senses, first come to be through *its* object, through *humanized* nature. (Marx, 1844/1964, p. 141)

In this context Marx also elaborated his famous idea of alienation, which I will not consider in this chapter.

## Collective Activity and Communication: New Problems

The marxian idea of activity as presupposing the use of human-made things, mediating relations between human beings, has played an important role in psychology in the 20th century. This influence is seen first of all in the theory of Lev Vygotsky, where it is the central idea in his conception. Vygotsky elaborated the theory of the cultural mediation of higher psychic functions, focusing on communication between the

---

9. The process of communication can also be considered as a process of exteriorization of human subjectivity.

child and the adult using such human-made things as language signs and creating intrapsychic processes. This problem was at the center of the studies of Vygotsky and his many pupils in Russia and other countries.

Vygotsky's ideas have significantly influenced contemporary psychology. The philosopher and theoretician of psychology R. Harré (1984; Harré & Gillett, 1994), elaborating his project of "discursive psychology," wrote that Vygotsky has created a principally new ontology for psychological research, such that one can divide the history of psychology into pre-Vygotskian and Vygotskian stages. I think Harré has serious reasons for expressing such an opinion. Activity theory, which has been successfully elaborated in Russian psychology, is considered to be a continuation of basic Vygotskian ideas. Both Vygotsky and founders of activity theory in Russia (e.g., Leontiev, 1978; Rubinshtein, 1997, Galperin, 1977/1992) stressed that human activity is possible only as a result of appropriation of cultural forms and is a historical phenomenon. Moreover, founders of activity theory such as Leontiev and Galperin were personal pupils of and collaborators with Vygotsky.

At the same time the relations between Vygotsky's theory and activity theory as elaborated in Russia after Vygotsky are not simple and direct. On the one hand, Leontiev, Galperin and other of Vygotsky's pupils elaborated the psychological problems of activity which were not topics in Vygotsky's research: relations between activity, actions, operations, transformations between activity and actions (and correlating them to motives and goals), interiorization of external activity, and so forth. On the other hand, the problems of activity as a collective process, presupposing interactions and communication between different participants were practically not investigated by them. In reality individual activity and individual actions and operations were in the center of their research. Vygotsky understood the importance of the problems of collective activity and stressed the collective character of the primary forms of psychological processes. But he studied mainly the process of communication between adults and children.

But now the problems of joint, collective activity are at the center of research of many psychologists in Russia and abroad. This research uses some principal philosophical ideas of Marx concerning collective activity and some principal psychological ideas of Vygotsky. This research raises some new philosophical problems.

First of all collective activity is not a simple extension of an individual activity, as it presupposes inter-individual relations, not simple activity and actions, but inter-activity and inter-actions. Interactivity and interactions can be understood as communication. It is a very important point. Recent research by Russian psychologists showed the significance of collective forms in such a kind of activity as learning (Davydov, 1996, pp. 204-228). Collective activity presupposes a goal that is common for all participants and cannot be achieved by them separately, but only in interaction. At the same time the ways of achieving this goal can be different. Correspondingly the forms of collective activity can also be different. Participants can interact with each other relatively independently. Collective activity can be distributed. In this case activity consists of a number of different actions, and each participant fulfils his own actions. Collective activity can presuppose constant communication between participants as a necessary condition of its success. This kind of collective activity has turned out to be especially interesting. In the latter case members of activity constantly have to discuss certain problems with each other, to participate in dialogues and "multilogues," to be able to understood the positions of others and to look at themselves with the eyes of others, to be self-reflective. This research has shown in particular that the process of interiorization should be understood not as the result of the transformation of individual activity, but as the form of the individual appropriation of collective forms of activity.

If this kind of activity presupposes first of all interaction between different participants, in particular, communication, then the very notion of activity should be understood in different way. Actions directed to another person are different from actions producing a certain thing or certain changes in an objective situation. The first kind of actions deals with independent actors interacting with each other. The result of such actions cannot be in possession of a subject, cannot be completely controlled and manipulated. Dialogue and discussion cannot be programmed. So this kind of activity is very different from those with which the philosophy of the 17th and 18th centuries and the German idealism of the beginning of the 19th century dealt.

The next important point is that communication is not reducible to language communication. There are facts (some of them found by Russian psychologists) that give evidence concerning the important role of a special kind of infant activity in the development of psychic life at the pre-speech level. These are actions with man-made things. Culture has created modes of actions with these things and with the help of them (a baby is shown concrete examples in order to teach him/her these actions), and these modes have corresponding meanings.[10] So the meanings of these actions can be understood by analogy with the meanings of language expressions, which are their uses according to Wittgenstein (1958). I think that it is possible to speak not only about language games, but also about *practical games* (with correspondent rules) at the pre-speech level of psychic development.

Another problem connected with the development of a communicative approach to psychic development is the following. If all psychic processes are the result of communication, can one claim to have knowledge of them? The point is that the investigation of most of them presupposes communication between an investigator and a person who is investigated. But this communication necessarily influences the results of previous acts of communication, which are psychic structures and processes. It is even possible to say that a researcher (in particular, an experimenter) and a subject under investigation do not discover something that existed entirely before their communication, but in the process of a dialogue jointly create or construct a new social reality. Some contemporary psychologists, including some from Russia, think that as a consequence psychology cannot be a science in a traditional sense (and some deny that it is a science in any sense). According to this view, experiments in a strict sense of the word are impossible in psychology, because objects of psychological investigation are created by the very process of research.[11]

But the results of communication can be interpreted in a different mode. Rules and norms of communication, some attitudes and systems of values, accepted in a certain culture, cannot change as a result of singular acts of communication. Experiments in psychology are possible,

10. Already after six months of life, infants, in collaboration with an adult, form object-manipulative actions, reproducing socially developed ways of acting. A baby appropriates them mainly through imitation, that is direct reproduction of actions that are shown (Davydov, 1996, pp. 106-7; Elkonin, 1978, p. 305). The results of Russian psychologists in educating blind and deaf children (and really in forming their psychic functions) are especially interesting in this respect. This research shows that a baby can only appropriate genuine speech after appropriating social modes of dealing practically with man-made things. And social modes of practical dealing can only be fulfilled through collaboration with an adult. A baby communicates with an adult first through practical actions (see Meshcheryakov, 1974, pp. 72-83).

11. In a roundtable discussion, Golov, Rozin, and Puzyrei expressed views along these lines (Bratus et al., 1993, especially pp. 26-34). See also Rozin (1994), pp. 22-54.

although not in all cases. When it is possible, their implementation is much more complicated than in natural sciences. In this connection I wish to stress that the so-called "developmental experiment," which was practiced and theoretically elaborated by Vygotsky (1960/1978, pp. 72-75; 1960/1981), is a means of studying psychic phenomena in the process of their formation. This is another kind of experiment, different from that with which classical science dealt and which was interpreted in the conception of activity in the philosophy of the 17th and 18th centuries.[12]

So the notion of activity has had different meanings in different stages of its development in the history of western philosophy and science. In the current stage of this development new philosophical problems arise. In my opinion these problems are very important, as their interpretation and mode of solution influence our understanding of the possibilities and character of human sciences, in particular psychology.

### References

Bratus, B.S., Brushlinsky, A.V., Genisaretsky, O.I., Golov, A.A., Kuznetsova, N.I., Ogurtsov, A.P., Puzyrei, A.A., Rozin, V.M., Rozov, M.A., & Zinchenko, V.P. (1993). Psikhologia i novye idealy nauki [Psychology and the new ideals of science] [Roundtable]. *Voprosy filosofii*, no. 5, 3-42.

Davydov, V.V. (1996). *Teoriia razvivajuschego obuchenie* [The theory of developmental teaching]. Moscow: In-tor.

Elkonin, D.B. (1978). *Psikhologii igry* [The psychology of play]. Moscow: Pedagogika.

Galperin, P.I. (1992). The problem of activity in Soviet psychology. *Journal of Russian and East European Psychology, 30* (4), 37-59. (Original work published 1977)

Harré, R. (1984). *Personal being: A theory for individual psychology*. Cambridge, Mass.: Harvard University Press.

Harré, R., & Gillett, G. (1994). *The discursive mind*. London: Sage.

Husserl, E. (1970). *The crisis of European sciences and transcendental phenomenology: An introduction to phenomenological philosophy* (D. Carr,

12. By the way some new ideas in contemporary science, in particular, connected with the conception of self-organizing systems (e.g., Prigogine & Stengers, 1984), are very close to this understanding of experiment and human activity.

Trans.). Evanston, Ill.: Northwestern University Press. (Original work published 1954)

Leontiev, A.N. (1978). *Activity, consciousness, and personality* (M.J. Hall, Trans.). Englewood Cliffs, N.J.: Prentice-Hall.

Mach, E. (1908). *Analiz oschuschenii i otnoshenie fizicheskogo k psikhicheskomu* [Analysis of sensations and the relation of the physical to the psychical] (5th ed.; G. Kotljar, Trans.; with additions by E. Mach). Moscow: Skirmunt. (Original work published 1906)

Marx, K. (1964). *Economic and philosophic manuscripts of 1844* (D.J. Struik, Ed.; M. Milligan, Trans.). New York: International Publishers. (Original work written 1844)

Marx, K. (1976). Theses on Feuerbach. In *Karl Marx-Frederick Engels collected works* (Vol. 5., pp. 3-5). London: Lawrence & Wishart. (Original work written 1845)

Marx, K. (1990). *Capital: Volume 1* (B. Fowkes, Trans.). London: Penguin. (Original work published 1867)

Meshcheryakov, A.I. (1974). *Slepogluhonemye deti: Razvitie psikhii v processe formirovanie povedenija.* [Awakening to life: Forming mind and behavior in deaf-blind children]. Moscow: Pedagogika.

Prigogine, I., & Stengers. I. (1984). *Order out of chaos: Man's new dialogue with nature.* Boulder, Colo.: New Science Library.

Rozin, V.M. (1994). *Psikhologii i kulturnoe razvitie cheloveka* [Psychology and cultural development of man]. Moscow: Russian Open University Publishers.

Rubinshtein, S.L. (1997). *Chelovek i mir* [Man and world]. Moscow: Nauka.

Spinoza, B. (1910). *Treatise on the correction of the understanding* (A. Boyle, Trans.). London: Dent. (Original work published 1677)

Vygotsky, L.S. (1978). Problems of method. In M. Cole, V. John-Steiner, S. Scribner, & E. Souberman (Eds.; M. Cole, Trans.), *Mind in society* (pp. 58-75). Cambridge, Mass.: Harvard University Press. (Original work published 1960)

Vygotsky, L.S. (1981). The instrumental method in psychology. In J.V. Wertsch (Ed. and Trans.), *The concept of activity in Soviet psychology* (pp. 134-143). Armonk, N.Y.: Sharpe. (Original work published 1960).

Wittgenstein, L. (1958). Philosophical investigations (2nd ed., G.E.M. Anscombe, Trans.). New York: Macmillan.

# 8 Activism, Activity and the New Cultural Politics: An Anthropological Perspective

*Terence Turner*

### Introduction: What Are We Fighting For?

Activists must be pragmatists, as well as principled opportunists. What we do as activists will depend on what we think can — and should — be done under the given historical conditions. As an anthropologist working with indigenous peoples in South America, as a member of the Committee for Human Rights of the American Anthropological Association, and as teacher in a university attempting to convey concepts of social and cultural activism to students, I feel it is essential to understand how contemporary economic, political and cultural developments are affecting the situation and prospects of the peoples with whom I, my colleagues and students work, and also how they affect us ourselves — our relations with those with whom we want to work and also our ideas about what we can and should try to do. Like any activist, we must constantly ask: What are we fighting for? What can we hope for? What can we do? With whom and against whom should we do it?

The historical events of the last several decades — the hypertrophy of consumerism and weakening of working-class movements, the antiestablishment movements of the late 1960s and early 1970s, which among other things shattered the identification of the academic social science and political establishments; the end of the Cold War; and above all, the global expansion of capitalism in the form of transnational corporations and globally integrated financial markets, with their closely associated phenomena, the widespread implementation of neoliberal social and economic policies by national governments and the internal political transformations of nation-states, have profoundly affected the social sciences in general and anthropology in particular, both as a theoretical discipline and an activist project (Turner, in press). These effects must be grasped by way of an understanding of the changes in the global system and its constituent nation-states which caused — and are continuing to cause — them. For purposes of focusing this discussion, let me take the issue with which I have been most closely concerned as an activist — that of the situation and struggles of indigenous peoples, and by extension other cultural minorities, as they have been affected by these historical developments.

Not so long ago, applied anthropologists went to the field thinking of themselves as ambassadors of modernity, bringing the possibility of a future to people trapped by their different cultures in a past with no viable entry into the present. Modernization, as the mission of applied anthropology, meant overcoming cultural difference as a necessary condition of bringing those with different cultures into a common temporality with the modern world. The more different or "primitive" the culture, the more self-evident, though perhaps also the more hopeless, this appeared. The anthropologist, in this perspective, for all of his or her "participation" in local activities, remained essentially external to the local reality because the very difference that was his/her reason for being there defined him or her as an emissary of a discontinuous mode of social time, a missionary of history to those who had either failed to enter it or fallen out of it, an observer of a mode of existence with neither continuity nor future as part of the modern world from which he or she had come. This is no longer the case. In the language of scripture, we have all been changed — they, the indigenous peoples, as well as us, the activists.

Over the past three decades, political-economic processes have produced massive quantitative changes at every level of the world system, that have led in turn to qualitative transformations of social relations and political patterns. The material changes involved have led in turn to transformations in the ideological perceptions of the relation of states and dominant national populations to such minorities, extending to the fundamental categories of space and time in which they are framed. Cultural difference, yesterday perceived in the temporal terms of evolutionary progression, has been rearticulated in terms of spatial separation, transmuted into a positive basis of contemporaneous coexistence.

As the evolutionist ideology of progress, which until recently was the established frame of reference for dealing with social and cultural diversity, tends to give way to the pluralist forms of identity politics and multiculturalism, national societies increasingly tend to appear to their citizens more as a plurality of mutually differing but contemporary culturally-differentiated identities than as a culturally homogeneous national community. Cultural and ethnic minorities appear in this context not as survivals of antecedent stages of the process of building homogeneous national communities but as more or less compatible members of plural national societies. This in turn has made it appear natural and commonsensical to regard even radically different cultural groups beyond national boundaries, such as distant indigenous peoples, as coexisting contemporaries in a world system that is no longer seen as composed of socially and culturally undifferentiated nation-states. Cultural and social differences previously classified along a temporal dimension of progressive evolution have thus come to appear as contemporary members of a common social space.

These changes have created new prospects and possibilities for indigenous peoples and other cultural and ethnic minorities, even while they have brought intensifying threats and pressures against them. They have also unavoidably altered the relations of anthropologists, both as researchers and activists, to the same groups.

### Global Political Economy, the Nation-State, and the Transformations of "Culture"

The existence of a transnational system of capitalist operations is of course not new, but over the last few decades, the quantitative increase in the volume and rate of transnational productive, marketing and financial operations that has come to be referred to as *globalization* has reached a point where it has had a number of qualitative effects on the internal economic, social and political conditions of nation-states. Globalization essentially means the construction of a sphere of transnational capitalist economic operations beyond the regulatory control of states. The construction of this global level enables a powerful base of leverage used by transnational corporations to avoid attempts by state regimes to control or regulate them. Globalization, in other words, effectively undermines the power of state governments and political systems to control internal economic processes, and weakens their ability to defend their populations against the effects of external economic processes operating at the global level. Globalization is directly associated with the widespread adoption by state regimes of neoliberal policies. These policies include cuts in the funding for social services; denial of support for groups of persons that do not contribute directly to economic performance; and fiscal and monetary policies that favor capital accumulation by private corporate capital.

The resulting surge in the global expansion of capitalism has created an unprecedented demand for raw materials and resources, intensifying pressure on the last relatively unexploited regions of the earth, such as tropical forests and other remote areas that tend to be the home of indigenous peoples and other politically powerless groups. One result of this expansion has been an exacerbation of the environmental destructiveness of so-called economic development projects, which in turn tend to damage the social and political-economic interests and cultural continuity of local peoples. Another effect (as well as cause) of this process is the pressure for privatization, as governments, international development agencies and multilateral financial institutions have been obliged to turn increasingly to private corporations and non-governmental organizations (NGOs) for the provision of social services and the implementation of public development projects of all kinds. Privatization means, in pragmatic terms, that state agencies tend to exercise less control over the operations of the private corporations engaged in extraction and development operations, and feel less political responsibility for the results. These effects are not mere coincidental byproducts of globalization, but like globalization itself, constitute deliberate effects of the neoliberal policies instituted by elites identified with the interests of socially irresponsible global capital that have risen to power in most economically developed states.

An unintended result of globalization is the projection of the incipient crisis of underconsumption/overproduction of state economies onto a global scale. As the transnational system has grown in complexity to the point where it has become effective for corporations to leverage state economic and regulatory policies, it has also taken on the besetting contradictions of state-level capitalist economies. The chronic crisis of overproduction has emerged as a structural limit of the global system as a whole. As labor becomes ever more productive under the pressure of global competition, relatively fewer workers are required to produce ever greater quantities of commodities, with the result that an ever-increasing proportion of the world's population is effectively excluded from the opportunity to consume the constantly increasing amounts of goods and services. The market for commodities thus tends to shrink as the supply continues to expand (Greider, 1997, pp. 45, 192-223, 233, 421).

This limiting contradiction acts as a feedback loop, reinforcing its own effects at different levels of the system: that of the transnational system as a whole and that of the internal political-economic systems of its component states. The need for national economies to remain competitive under global conditions becomes an effective lever for dismantling welfare-state class compromises at the state level, while relatively more highly-paid workers from the original state populations of successful states are increasingly replaced by cheaper migrant labor from poorer states, and exportable productive operations are moved from successful states to areas of cheaper labor. The result is an intensification of class conflict, increasingly unmediated by social welfare policies at the state level.

At the level of transnational relations the same pattern is replicated by the polarization between more successful capitalist state economies, net exporters of capital, and relatively unsuccessful (uncompetitive) state economies that cannot meet the economic needs of their populations and thus become net exporters of labor, feeding the competitive demands of successful countries for ever cheaper laborers. The massive transnational flows of migrant laborers and productive capital, which have been emphasized by some theorists of the global system, as constitutive forces of a new, postcapitalist, or at least post-statist order fomented by new technologies of transportation and communication, are thus to be understood as byproducts of the intensification of the same old capitalist processes. The massive and effective projection of these processes onto the global level has resulted in a recrudescence of unregulated competition and a replication of forms of internal class conflict at the level of relations between whole states and their peoples.

Another byproduct of this limiting contradiction is the persisting inability of global capitalism to employ or make continuous use of labor and lands of peoples at the margins of the capitalist system, in particular, indigenous minorities occupying marginal areas with simple subsistence economies. Such areas become the targets of extractive enterprises, most commonly mining and logging. These activities, although damaging to the ecology and social fabric of the areas directly involved, normally result in no permanent occupation and employ few, if any, local people. The local people tend to remain outside, or at best only partly engaged in, capitalist wage-labor relations. In this respect, the limiting contradiction of the global capitalist system presents a window of opportunity to indigenous and other peripheral subsistence-based groups to maintain and reproduce their own communities with a measure of local autonomy.

### The Transformation of Nationalism and the Crisis of Sovereignty in the Nation-State

Globalization has clearly undermined the powers of nation-states to make economic policy and to regulate their internal economies. This, however, should not be taken to mean that nation-states are in the process of disappearing or losing all political and economic functions. Rather, the state has assumed new functions and powers as a facilitator and catalyst of its economic participation in the global economy. Meanwhile globalization, and policies that states have adopted in their efforts to come to terms with it, have led to a series of transformations in the social and ideological underpinnings of the state, including most notably nationalism, sovereignty and culture. These changes have profound implications for the fate of indigenous and other cultural minorities, as well as for anthropology, both as a theoretical and an activist project.

The principal social effect of neoliberal policies is the polarization of national populations between the corporate and corporate-oriented elites, which serve as administrators and formulators of state policies that foster globalization and corporate interests, and the rest of the population, increasingly politically disfranchised and economically impoverished by these policies, and by more general effects of globalization. The political effect is to undermine the political effectiveness of representative democratic institutions, which in turn undermines the constitutional principle of popular sovereignty, which has been the legitimating principle of modern states since the early 19th century.

The same process has tended to transform the character of the ideological corollary of popular sovereignty, namely nationalism. *Nationalism*, defined as the shared identification of a population with a state in mutually exclusive opposition to other states, has historically carried the implicit concomitant that the state reciprocally embodies the values and interests of its citizens, who jointly comprise the community of the nation. Nationalism, so defined, was of course from the first an ideological construct (a term I prefer to the more anodyne if popular "imagined community") which served to mask and mystify the many social divisions and inequalities of class, ethnicity, language and region among the citizenry. The original promoters of nationalist ideology were, broadly speaking, representatives of the middle class, who were in the process of seizing state power, and therefore identified their class interests and ¬erspective with those of the state. Nationalism was an effective ideological rubric for recruiting and subsuming other classes and ethnic groups in this essentially bourgeois project. (In the potent formulation of the Sieyès, 1789/1970, foundational to the modern doctrines of popular sovereignty and nationalism alike, the Third Estate *is* the nation.) Together with the principle of popular sovereignty, nationalism thus served to deny the relevance of all received differences of region, ethnicity, language, status or class to the political life of the state, assimilating them, as a matter of political solidarity and loyalty, into the national community. This resulted regularly in repressive discrimination against indigenous, racial and ethnic minorities.

So long as the state could be perceived as opposed to or threatened by other states, and so long as its internal political institutions could be perceived to constitute reasonably effective instruments of popular political participation, nationalism and popular sovereignty continued to serve as effective legitimation of the state, and the ideological denial of the relevance of social differences among groups within the national population as relatively less important than, or subversive of, sovereign egalitarian fraternity of individual citizens comprising the national community.

However, with the end of the Cold War and the hyperdevelopment of economic globalization, accompanied by the adoption of neoliberal policies at the state level, the original premise of nationalist consensus, the idea of the state as the expression of the national community as a unified, culturally homogeneous people, has been eroded. As the state has increasingly reoriented itself from an internal focus on national affairs to an external focus on relations to the global economic system, and as neoliberal policy criteria of economic rationality replace broader social and political commitments, the state has come to appear less as the direct manifestation of the national community and more as its adversary. Concomitantly, the positive content of the nationalist myth of the national community as the social form of a homogeneous national character or culture has tended to be replaced by more negative notions of the way its rightful claims, interests and expectations of the nation are disregarded, marginalized or betrayed by the state. The reorientation of state policy towards participation in regional and global eco nomic systems at the expense of large segments of the population, reinforced by the state's adoption of neoliberal domestic policies disadvantageous to roughly the same groups, have led many of these groups to assert their nationalist identity as grounds for protest against state policies and global processes (such as labor migration) which they perceive as threats to their own interests. Nationalism continues, but now expressed more frequently as a basis for oppositional claims to the state, or to global economic pressures or penetration, rather than a positive expression of national character or culture.

The same causes have paradoxically led many to assert collective identities defined as different from the national norm. In place of the culturally-uniform imagined community of the nation as the primary category of social identity, there has developed a politics based on collective but subnational identities which are defined by their differences from the communal cultural identity of the nation. In this "identity politics," groups identified in terms of ethnic, cultural, gender, regional or other differences confront the state and its jural and ideological principles of egalitarian community with claims that they have been unequally disadvantaged because of their differences. "Difference" becomes, in this context, a potent claim on an egalitarian system perceived as failing to live up to its principles, and the claims of difference are paradoxically legitimized by the values of uniformity, articulated in rhetorics of egalitarianism and national community originally constructed to transcend and submerge difference. The rhetoric of nationalist cultural community is thus retained but turned against itself as a call for genuine inclusion (or at least equal treatment) by those excluded by virtue of their differences.

Despite its loss of control over aspects of economic policy, the state retains indispensable functions and powers in the economic as well as the political sphere. The state alone has the power and organizational resources to establish and enforce the conditions of social peace, legal uniformity, infrastructural resources of transportation and communication, and administrative services necessary to guarantee market access for the whole population of its national territory. Uniform legal and bureaucratic standards are in themselves pragmatic commitments to egalitarian treatment of citizens. A major social function of the uniformitarian administrative and legal apparatuses of the modern state is to enable the equal access of all citizens to markets and participation in the consumption of market commodities. With the atrophy of popular sovereignty and meaningful political participation for the majority of the population, the state's legitimation has come to depend increasingly on its ability to deliver economic benefits of commodity consumption and infrastructural services on uniformly equal and accessible terms to its population. Through this form, the contemporary state both fulfills the needs of the global economy and makes itself indispensable to it. The implicit commitment to homogeneous access to, if not equal economic capacity for, consumption, thus becomes a form of commitment by the modern state to a kind of social equality. Difference in all its cultural, ethnic, regional and gendered forms has thus become a political touchstone in the ideological vacuum left by the evacuation of the positive cultural content of the nationalist myth of community.

## New Meanings of Culture: From *System* to *Difference*

The political and economic changes of globalization have led not only to a reorientation of temporal and spatial categories, but to shifts in the social and ideological meaning of culture itself. From its origins in 19th century Germany through its development as the master-concept of American anthropology in the 20th century, the idea of *culture* was essentially the idea of an inclusive system of ideas, representations, perspectives on the world, values, techniques, etc., attached to, and collectively shared by, a total social group: a people or nation. The natural condition of such a group, once it had attained a sufficient level of social and political development, was in turn thought to be embodiment in a state. The changes in the nationalist vision of the national community and its relation to the state outlined above (from the concept of the state as the positive expression of the culturally homogeneous national community to the oppositional relation of "nation" to "state") has, consistently enough, had as a corollary the decoupling of the idea of culture from that of the nation, and by extension, from any bounded, politically organized social group. Culture, like identity, is now commonly understood to denote, not a total system of ideas, symbols and meanings, but an unordered aggregate of traits, styles or values that mark off subgroups, social movements, identities or categories of persons from one another. The conception of culture as a total system or organic whole was based on its association with a total society or group, prototypically a state. Once this association was severed, the systematicity of culture, along with its singularity as a collective entity, accordingly disappeared. *Structure* and *system* are words no longer applied to cultural phenomena, at least by anthropologists who aspire to a career in the discipline. (One of the few currently acceptable ways to discuss plural configurations or combinations of cultural elements is as hybrid mixtures of elements drawn from different social contexts, with no overall structure, distinctive boundary, or central organizing principle.) The decoupling of *nation* in its positive sense as homogeneous community from *state* thus led to the dissociation of culture as a total system from society as a whole, a step that led directly to the deconstructive shift of focus from culture as singular, total system to the minimal units of culture, difference or distinction. Difference, along with identity, its logical twin, have thus appeared as the new master categories of anthropological discourse on culture.

### Consumerism and the Politics of Difference

At the same time, the hypertrophy of consumerism has led to transformations in culture and social consciousness that have converged in important respects with the deconstructive reconceptualization of national culture as a randomized array of differences and identities. The combination of increased labor productivity and a decreased productive labor force in the metropolitan capitalist countries of the First World, and the great expansion of commodity circulation and consumption have contributed to a displacement of political concerns from class relations rooted in production to individual relations of consumption. The old "master narrative" of social evolution through ever-expanded production, which legitimized the subordination of human workers and nature as productive resources, has given way to the new master antinarrative of a synchronic spectrum of consumption choices, legitimized by its universal accessibility and its supposed ability to promote the quality of life and personal self-realization. This new social consciousness, uncritically severed from its roots in production, has nevertheless become the basis of a variety of critical political (or potentially political) reactions to the consequences of production, in so far as they impinge on the quality of life and the right to personal fulfillment through the creation and realization of individual and cultural "life styles." The recent widespread popularity of causes such as the environment, human rights and the cultural survival of indigenous peoples, owes much to these developments.

The hypertrophy of commodity production, meanwhile, has not resulted in the cultural homogenization of the consumers served by the increasingly diversified commodity market. Instead it has stimulated the development of ever more varied subcultural life styles. Life styles and their close family relations, identities, have been developed by various groups within late capitalist society as emblems of individual and collective differences or distinctions. Through such stylized patterns of consumption, individual consumers participate in the production of personal identity and meaning (such self-production has become the master value of contemporary consumerist culture).

These distinct ethnic, class, regional and generational identities, as currently maintained and expressed, are ultimately rooted in varying modes of access to, or exclusion from, the sources of wealth and political influence in production, a circumstance which is obscured by the consumerist rituals through which the collective identities in question are constituted. The point for present purposes, however, is that the development of late capitalist consumer culture, in contrast to the ideological formations associated with earlier phases of capitalist expansion, no longer depends upon enforcing homogeneous cultural patterns closely identified with the class and political hierarchies of Western society, but on the contrary, promotes the heterogeneity of cultural and subcultural styles, as many different concrete forms of consumer demand. Public opinion shaped by this late capitalist consumerist ideology tends accordingly to relate to indigenous and ethnic minorities of distinct culture, not with the evolutionist and assimilationist assumptions of previous historical formations of capitalist social consciousness, but rather as many different consumption styles, analogous to the life styles or subcultures of metropolitan capitalist society, where all have an equal claim to disport themselves in the general *juissance* of universal consumption. This view de-legitimizes the assimilationist principles of previous capitalist ideological formations, but it also tends to lead to the opposite conclusion, namely that other cultures or ethnic identities assume legitimacy and merit support in direct proportion to their apparent difference and exoticism, as perceived from the standpoint of conventional or hegemonic patterns of Western culture. In comparison peasants or assimilated tribal peoples in societies of Western culture, whose difference appears merely as an impoverished refraction of the dominant culture, attract relatively little interest or support.

Deculturation and assimilation into national states seemed the inevitable course of social adaptation and integration as long as the capitalist world system remained articulated through traditional state hierarchies of political control and economic organization. The hypertrophy of the world market for consumption commodities, together with the concomitant development of international communication and transportation networks, has had the unforeseen effect of legitimizing the social status of ethnic minorities and tribal peoples of distinct culture and also of facilitating their ability to develop direct relations with transnational sources of support (nongovernmental advocacy groups, foreign governmental and financial agencies, and world public opinion) for the assertion and defense of their cultural uniqueness.

### The Appeal to Universals and the New Civil Society

A remarkable feature of the new politics of difference (i.e., identity politics based on ethnicity, gender, sexual orientation, and multiculturalism), however, is that the ethnic, cultural and identity groups engaged in this politics tend to appeal to universal standards of equality, justice and rights for their collective claims against the nation-state, seeking recognition of equal rights and status-honor (perhaps identity-honor would now be the more appropriate tag) that corresponds with those of other groups within the same society. Their assertions of difference from the homogeneous national identity projected by received nationalist ideologies lead paradoxically but inexorably from the assertion of difference to appeals to universal values (e.g., human rights, environmentalism, disarmament) that transcend the state and therefore appear as constraints upon its political power, sovereignty and legitimacy. Such universal values and causes are now felt by many to confer a legitimacy superior to that vested in the conventional institutions and processes of state politics. Differentiation at one level thus begets homogenization at another, and relativistic assertions of difference give rise to appeals to universal principles.

As national civil societies have tended to fragment into subnational identity and ethnic groups, in sum, there has been a complementary tendency for the new groupings into which civil society is becoming increasingly differentiated to appeal beyond the state to a transnational consensus on the rights of minorities, peoples, and categories such as women and children. This represents a reorientation of the conception of rights as norms enforced by the state to a conception of rights as principles supported by global opinion and institutions like the United Nations, which can bring moral and political pressure to bear on states to recognize and enforce the rights in question.

Some of the identity groups and new social movements that champion such universal values have increasingly tended to communicate and collaborate in furthering common political and ethical causes, giving rise to an emergent transnational community of movements and groups that has begun to coalesce as a new, global level of civil society, in contrapuntal opposition to the global civil society comprised of private transnational corporations. Global civil society in this new sense is a latent network intermittently activated in response to events, rather than a political system or "society" in its own right. This global civil society, even in its present embryonic form, challenges both the political limitations of the existing system of nation-states, and the unchecked power of private transnational capital constituting global civil society in the latter sense. It has nevertheless sporadically proved itself capable of mobilizing transnational ad hoc coalitions of movements, groups and opinion in support of the values to which it is committed, that have succeed in frustrating and confounding realist planners and politicians committed to state and global political and development agendas.

The conditions for the effectiveness of global civil society depend on the global extension and penetration of the world capitalist system. This system includes production relations, marketing networks, and commodity consumption patterns (for instance of new media of information and transportation); the legal and bureaucratic infrastructure that support them; and the neoliberal social and political policies that have so vigorously fostered the development of all of the above. If global civil society may in some cases appear as part of the solution to the problems precipitated by globalization and neoliberalism, then, it must be remembered that it is equally part of the problem.

Mention of the important role of the new electronic media of communication brings the analysis back to the shift in spatio-temporal perspectives on cultural difference mentioned at the beginning of the chapter. The shrinkage of time and space (what Harvey, 1989, has called "space-time compression") brought about by new technologies of communication and transportation, has clearly played an important role in

this shift, but they would not by themselves have been enough to produce the revolution in the social meaning of cultural difference and the
reorientation of public opinion concerning the prospects for the survival
and future role of indigenous and other cultural minorities as
contemporary members of modern societies. The successes of indigenous peoples in asserting and defending themselves and their differences against pressures for assimilation and exploitation, and the
remarkable growth in indigenous populations in many countries over
the past three decades, have played an important role here. Another
contributing factor is the failure of global and national capitalist development to employ the populations or colonize the lands of peripheral
regions inhabited by many indigenous groups, to the extent confidently
expected by capitalist corporations and national development planners.
The political-economic transformations involved in globalization and
the associated changes in the state must be regarded, however, as more
fundamental causes of the changes in spatio-temporal representation of
social and cultural difference than the changes in communication and
transportation technologies that have accompanied and facilitated
them.

In the modernist nationalist vision, modernization, conceived as economic and technological progress, was seen as the main force for
effecting the assimilation of ethnically and culturally diverse elements
into the national community. Economic, political and cultural processes
were thus seen as interdependent and mutually supportive. I suggest,
however, that one of the main effects of globalization and neoliberalism
has been the decoupling of economic activity, and the political relations
and policies associated with corporate interests, from any ideological
role as forces for the progressive integration of national society. The reorientation of the state toward providing uniform market access for its
entire citizenry (regardless of cultural or ethnic difference, and without
concern for the leveling or homogenization of class inequalities) has replaced national social integration as a policy goal in the most developed
capitalist states. The considerably narrowed relation of state to civil
society, I have suggested, now legitimates the state in its new role as
facilitator of economic prosperity in collaboration with the global economy (Turner, 1998). The main point for now is that the new relation of
state and civil society polarizes economic and institutional political processes, as the central concerns of the state and the corporate sector,
against the remaining aspects and sectors of civil society including rela-

tions with the environment, education, cultural life, the family, social values like human rights, feminist concerns, minority rights and equal recognition of minority identities and cultures. The result has been to divide civil society into opposing sectors: a political-economic core identified with corporate interests oriented toward the global economy and represented by the state, and a peripheral zone of social and cultural groupings, relations and values increasingly marginalized and disempowered by the power core in connection with the enveloping global economic system. Under these social and political-economic conditions, nationalism, as a commitment to a unified and homogeneous national community, tends to give way to more fragmented forms of social identity based on alternative principles defined in terms of difference from and opposition to the dominant core.

## "Difference" and Anthropological Activism

The deconstructive trajectory of much recent anthropological theorizing about culture has been content to follow the same logic as postmodern political and cultural ideologies that reify difference as a basis for the repudiation of systematic analysis or the search for universal principles. Anthropological activism in areas such as human rights and support for indigenous peoples, however, has converged with the opposing tendency, noted above, of groups seeking to defend social and cultural difference to ground their struggles in universal principles. The result has been a renewed attempt to reconcile concepts of human universals with cultural relativism. As I have already remarked at several points, difference and identity as the abstract essence or common denominators of culture have also emerged as the basic principles and categories of the new social movements, human rights activism and multicultural politics. A case in point is the proposed Declaration on Anthropology and Human Rights promulgated recently by the Committee for Human Rights of the American Anthropological Association (AAA). The proposed Declaration reads in part:

Anthropology as an academic discipline studies the bases and the forms of human diversity and unity; anthropology as a practice seeks to apply this knowledge to the solution of human problems.

As a professional organization of anthropologists, the AAA has long been, and should continue to be, concerned whenever human difference is made the basis for a denial of basic human rights, where "human" is understood in its full range of cultural, social, linguistic, psychological, and biological senses. (Committee for Human Rights, 1997)

In the terms of the document, "human difference" is a criterion of human rights because it comprises the concrete specificity of what humans, individually and collectively, have made of themselves, socially, culturally, and evolutionarily. Difference in this sense presupposes the universal human capacities that enabled their production — in the familiar anthropological phrase, the human "capacity for culture." The capacity for culture is essentially the power to produce social existence and thus to determine its meaning and social form. Difference as a principle of human rights denotes the realization of this capacity or power (Nagengast & Turner, 1997; Turner, 1997; Turner & Nagengast, 1997).

For the authors of the proposed AAA Declaration on Anthropology and Human Rights, the criterion of difference emerged from the need to find a common principle to guide action on the great variety of cases that were constantly being brought before the Committee, and encountered by anthropologists in the field. In contrast to the abstract concept of universal human nature conceived as embodied in self-existing, pre-social individuals, it is a context-sensitive principle, which takes its specific meaning from the pragmatic contexts in which it is applied. At the same time, it gives equal weight to collective and individual differences (both collective and individual difference being equally human). It also attempts to reconcile and integrate a universal concept of the human capacity for culture with a cultural relativist recognition of the fundamental importance of cultural, social, and individual differences. In a sense, the Committee's formulation of the principle of difference converges with the recent deconstructive turn of popular, ideological and anthropological notions of cultural identity and difference — both represent attempts to formulate a minimal common denominator of cultural and social phenomena. In sharp contrast to deconstructive formulations of difference as a principle of justice or rights (e.g., Turner, 1997, pp. 288-290; Young, 1990), which explicitly deny the possibility of universal or unifying principle other than difference itself, the Committee's formulation attempts to ground its principle of difference in a concept of self-productive activity and the realization of the universal human capacity for self-production.

Culture (i.e., cultural difference) has become a by-word of many of the new social and political movements. This has had the serendipitous result of validating the struggles of indigenous peoples to maintain their separate identities and defend their heritage as distinct peoples and cultures. Stimulated in part by this windfall of support from the world system, indigenous peoples around the world have become more aggressive and successful in using their cultural differences as leverage in asserting their rights and interests, as grounds for alliances with non-indigenous groups, and as legitimation for their demands for local autonomy. More militant and politicized forms of anthropological activism in defense of indigenous lands and resources have appeared in support of this growing activism by indigenous people themselves. The great increase in the numbers and political clout of NGOs and new social movements committed to universalistic causes like human rights and environmentalism, beginning in the late 1960s and early 1970s, has helped to stimulate an upsurge of human rights activism on behalf of the rights of indigenous and other minorities, who are exploited or otherwise disadvantaged because of their cultural, ethnic, linguistic or racial differences (Laraña, Johnston, & Gusfield 1994; Offe, 1985). Anthropological activists, partly in response to these developments, have become more concerned than ever before with issues of human rights and local empowerment.

Meanwhile the new social movements and cultural forms of identity politics and multiculturalism have catalyzed the development of new forms of activism in support of indigenous and other minority movements for cultural revitalization and autonomy. Examples include media activism in support of community and indigenous video, bilingual education programs using teaching materials based on local cultural knowledge and traditions in indigenous languages, cooperative promotion of ecotourism, defense of cultural property rights, projects for the sustainable production of wild resources, promotion of travel and communication among previously mutually isolated Fourth World peoples, support for training and use of new technologies for the mapping and surveillance of indigenous territories, and specialized training in new managerial and administrative skills to enable local control of production and marketing. At the same time, older forms of activism, such as efforts to promote local development and community empowerment, have been continued and extended.

Of course, in many respects, the global economy and the shifts in political orientation and economic policy at the state level associated with it, such as privatization, the deregulation of extractive and other development industries like dambuilding, and of course the curtailing of public services like health and education, are actively or potentially destructive of the material interests and cultural identities of indigenous peoples and other groups marked by ethnic or cultural difference. These negative effects of globalization and neoliberal policies clearly pose challenges to anthropological activists. To check or mitigate the destructive effects of these projects and policies, they need to develop effective ways and means of acting within their own societies and governments, as well as working at the global level with, and against, transnational corporations, international institutions like the Organization of American States or the United Nations, and multilateral development banks. Professional anthropological associations like the AAA or its division, Society for Applied Anthropology, can be effective in lobbying for and against governmental policies, projects of private corporations, and actions of multilateral institutions. The Committee for Human Rights of the AAA, for example, has just produced a lengthy report exposing and criticizing the World Bank for its involvement in forcible resettlement and other violations of the rights of the Pehuenche Indians of the BíoBío River in southern Chile, in connection with a series of dams for which it provided original financing. The report has led to a series of actions in support of the Pehuenche, including letters of protest to the President of Chile and other officials of Chile and the World Bank, distribution of the report at the conference of Presidents of the Americas in Santiago, and collaboration with other U.S. and international human rights organizations in a campaign against the resettlement scheme (Johnston & Turner, 1998). Other recent actions by the AAA Committee for Human Rights have included the documentation and condemnation of rights violations by development projects and governments in Brazil, Botswana, and Venezuela (Committee for Human Rights, 1998). These actions have drawn upon the unique professional competencies of anthropologists as ethnographers and analysts of local situations involving intercultural contacts, as well as on the influence and insights of anthropologists in their roles as consultants for development policies and projects.

Anthropological activists have played significant roles in several transnational mobilizations of global civil society in response to crises involving abuses of the rights and environments of indigenous minorities by development projects implemented by state governments or private transnational corporations supported by transnational financial institutions in recent years. In a few of these crises, indigenous groups, the most peripheral elements of the periphery of the world system, have briefly found themselves at the center of transnational conjunctures of global and local forces, as NGOs and other elements of international civil society have taken up their cause. Such conflicted conjunctures (e.g., the Kayapo-led indigenous opposition to the Kararaô dam at Altamira in the Brazilian Amazon, or the resistance by adivasis or tribal peoples to the Sardar Sarovar dam in India) become crucibles in which the forces of the global capitalist economic and state system and those of the emergent global civil society become pitted against each other. The resolution of these confrontations may entail revisions in the balance of forces and operating constraints of states and transnational economic and political institutions in relation to local groups and global civil society. They may thus become fraught with significance for the development of the world system as a whole, far beyond the local conjunctures of events that occasion them.

## Conclusion: Activism and the Struggle for Production

As these examples attest, activism in defense of cultural difference and relative autonomy by indigenous peoples and anthropologists is inseparable from the struggle against political-economic exploitation and class-like oppression as relatively marginal and powerless groups whose resources, environments and lands can be exploited and despoiled with impunity by corporate and state-backed development interests. The struggle for cultural integrity and relative autonomy in such contexts is the struggle for the continued production of collective identity, the self-reproduction of the social group, with its values and forms of personhood. This is a struggle for social production in the broadest sense, not merely cultural politics. I would argue, in contradiction to Laclau and Mouffe (1985) and other theorists of new social movements, for whom the cultural character of these movements is evidence of their removal from social and class issues, that the cultural activism of indigenous peoples and their anthropological supporters, as well as other new social movements, point rather to the opposite conclusion. Social groups marginalized and disempowered by globalization and the neoliberal policies associated with it have turned to cultural forms of political struggle in direct defense of the reproduction of the noneconomic social, personal and natural aspects of their lives, that are threatened by the economic processes and political policies represented by the global corporate economy and state governments. In negative terms, the focus of the new movements on these ostensibly noneconomic and apolitical issues is a reaction to the overwhelming domination of the economy and institutional political processes by corporate interests and the political elites aligned with them. The new movements concentrate on aspects of existence that are not controlled or monopolized by corporate or state power, and remain directly involved in the lives of ordinary people. In positive terms, however, the new social, cultural and indigenous movements, taken together, may be understood as counterposing an alternative vision of production to the narrowly economistic approach to production represented by the global corporate economy: an insistence that the production of human social life and the ecosystem on which it depends must also be counted as production, and as a legitimate interest of society as a whole cannot be left to the determination of corporate executives and neoliberal politicians.

The cultural struggles of contemporary social movements and indigenous peoples are essentially responses to the effects of global political-economic forces, and the changes these forces have brought about in the nation-state, that have tended to disempower or restrict the ability of people and groups not included in the dominant political and economic elites to preserve and reproduce their cultural values, social lives, natural environments and personal identities. That the response of many to this situation has taken cultural forms, like identity politics and the new social movements, should not be allowed to obscure the roots of the new politics of difference in political-economic forces. When the sources of difference politics as forms of protest and resistance against the political-economic effects of globalization are understood, the essential meaning of difference as a cultural and political value, as well as the quality of life issues like environmentalism with which it is often associated, can be recognized as an attempt to defend a more inclusive (and in this sense more global) notion of production, as the total production of human life, society, and the natural environment, against the narrowly economistic notion of production embodied by the global capitalist system and the neoliberal social policies that attempt to implement its social, environmental and ideological implications. Indigenous societies and their cultural forms embody such a totalizing vision of human production, and for this reason, indigenous peoples' struggles, and the cause of indigenous rights, have attracted wide support among large portions of the middle class of the advanced capitalist countries, world public opinion, non-governmental organizations and new social movements previously indifferent to indigenous issues. Anthropological activism in support of indigenous struggles and rights thus converges with the many-faceted world movement to assert and counterpose a global notion of human self-production to the global economism of transnational capitalism. Anthropological activists and indigenous people participate in this struggle as contemporaries, each with as much at stake as the other, namely, the defense of indigenous cultural autonomy converges, in the present world-historical conjuncture, with the many-sided struggle to reassert the powers and values of human self-production against the corrosive effects of globalization and disempowerment by neoliberal state policies.

## References

Committee for Human Rights. (1997). *Declaration on anthropology and human rights.* Washington, D.C.: American Anthropological Association. Retrieved January 20, 1999 from the World Wide Web: http://www.ameranthassn.org/chrdecl.htm

Committee for Human Rights. (1998). *Briefing documents.* Washington, D.C.: American Anthropological Association. Retrieved January 20, 1999 from the World Wide Web: http://www.ameranthassn.org/chrbrief.htm

Greider, W. (1997). *One world, ready or not: The manic logic of global capitalism.* New York: Simon and Schuster.

Laraña, E., Johnston, H., & Gusfield, J.R. (Eds.). (1994). *New social movements: From ideology to identity.* Philadelphia: Temple University Press.

Harvey, D. (1989). *The condition of postmodernity: An enquiry into the origins of cultural change.* Oxford: Blackwell.

Johnston, B., & Turner T. (1998). *The Pehuenche, the World Bank Group and ENDESA S.A.: Violations of human rights in the Pangue and Ralco Dam projects on the BíoBío River, Chile.* Washington, D.C.: American Anthropological Association, Committee for Human Rights. Retrieved

January 20, 1999 from the World Wide Web: http://www.ameranthassn.org/pehuenc.htm

Laclau, E., & Mouffe, C. (1985). *Hegemony and socialist strategy: Towards a radical democratic politics* (W. Moore & P. Cammack, Trans.). London: Verso.

Nagengast, C., & Turner, T. (1997). Introduction: Universal human rights versus cultural relativity. *Journal of Anthropological Research, 53,* 269-272.

Offe, C. (1985). New social movements: challenging the boundaries of institutional politics. *Social Research, 52,* 817-868.

Sieyès, E.-J. (1970). *Qu'est-ce que le tiers état?* (R. Zapperi, Ed.). Geneva: Droz. (Original work published 1789)

Turner, T. (1997). Human rights, human difference: Anthropology's contribution to an emancipatory cultural politics. *Journal of Anthropological Research, 53,* 273-292.

Turner, T. (1998). Globalization, the state and social consciousness in the late twentieth century. Unpublished manuscript, Cornell University, Ithaca, N.Y.

Turner, T. (in press). Anthropological activism, indigenous peoples and globalization. In C. Nagengast & C. Velez-Ibañez (Eds.), *The scholar as activist.* Washington, D.C.: Society for Applied Anthropology.

Turner, T., & Nagengast, C. (Eds.). (1997). Human rights [Special issue]. *Journal of Anthropological Research, 53*(3).

Young, I.M. (1990). *Justice and the politics of difference.* Princeton, N.J.: Princeton University Press.

# 9 Evolution, Genetics and Psychology: The Crisis in Psychology — Vygotsky, Luria, and Leontiev Revisited

*Ethel Tobach*

And again we may ask: which discipline other than general psychology can decide this controversy between animal and man in psychology; for, on this decision will rest nothing more and nothing less than the whole future fate of this science. (Vygotsky, 1927/1997, p. 236)

I chose the problem of the biological and social because there are still views that affirm a fatalistic conditioning of people's psyche by biological inheritance. These views spread ideas in psychology of racial and national discrimination, and the right to genocide and destructive wars. They threaten mankind's peace and security, and they are in flagrant contradiction with the objective findings of scientific psychological research. (Leontiev, 1960/1981a, p. 155)

One of the many characteristics of Vygotsky's work that was important ... was his insistence that psychological research should never be limited to sophisticated speculation and laboratory models divorced from the real world. The central problems of human existence as it is experienced in school, at work, or in the clinic all served as the contexts within which Vygotsky struggled to formulate a new kind of psychology. (Luria, 1979, pp. 52-53)

## World Crisis Reflected in Psychology: U.S.A. as Exemplar

The world in which Vygotsky (1927/1997) was writing the book on the crisis in Soviet psychology was different from the world today. A successful revolution had taken place and academics and intellectuals were being asked to participate in the creation of a new society with goals and aspirations that differed from those of the old regime (Graham, 1987, p. 62). Vygotsky was calling upon psychologists to examine their discipline and the role it would play in that new society, as reflected in Luria's remarks. The quotation from Vygotsky presents an issue that was significant in the necessary revision of the thinking and working of psychologists. The persistence of this issue is seen in Leontiev's remarks. Vygotsky could call upon all psychologists for change as they shared common goals in the pursuit of their profession.

In today's world, many psychologists may profess to pursue common goals, but they are divided by lives that discourage formation of organized, consensual activities that achieve common societal goals based on the kind of consciousness that Vygotsky envisioned. Just as the crisis in Soviet psychology reflected the societal conditions in which psychologists functioned, so do today's psychologists reflect the societal conditions in which they function. Some psychologists are concerned about the dissonance between achieving professed societal goals that would ameliorate the human condition and the activities of organized psychology. Such dissonance reflects the contemporary crisis in psychology. The source of this dissonance lies in philosophical and ideological processes that were present in Vygotsky's time and are present today. These processes are seen in the preceding quotations: obfuscation about the difference between animals and humans; the obsession with genetic processes in understanding behavior; and the division between the lives of people in their worlds and the reductionist laboratory studies carried out by psychologists.

Vygotsky wrote the book on the crisis in psychology in 1927. Reading that book today, one is impressed with the fact that it concerns matters that bedevil contemporary psychology. The situation in psychology in the U.S.A. is an example of the crisis in psychology that exists in all of the most industrialized, free-market countries. As the economies of the world become more and more centralized in transnational monopolies, technological change brought about by those monopolies affect the lives of all nations (Solomon, 1994), and psychologists share in the contemporary crises of that world and in their discipline. Of course, in each country, the symptoms and the etiology of the crisis differ somewhat, but to the extent that psychologists were trained in the psychology of the dominant industrialized countries, they may be said to have much in common.

The crisis in psychology reflects (a) the world economic crisis in which most people live in poverty (Papadimitriou, 1994), while a small portion of the world's population are inordinately rich; (b) the world's natural and human resources are exploited and diminished to obtain those riches; and (c) lives are lost in military attacks against people fighting for equity as well as in small wars that result from the activities of an arms industry that battens on conflicts based on ethnic and religious antipathy. The intensification and extension of the profitable domination by powerful societal groups, led by the U.S.A., affects the health and welfare of the people, and the planet itself.

Biologists, physicists and engineers — experts in the biological, chemical and physical aspects of the struggle for survival — are actively attempting to mitigate those destructive applications of technology (e.g., Natural Resources Defense Council). The science of psychology is in quite a different relationship to that struggle. Psychologists are involved mostly in the mitigation of the effects of those destructive policies seen in the physiological and psychological ill health of people, and in attempting to counter the oppressive educational policies and practices as they relate to poor and societally disadvantaged people. Educational, health, and clinical psychologists are so engaged. Some psychologists are concerned with these issues and are active in making psychology socially responsible (e.g., Psychologists for Social Responsibility, U.S.A.).

*Psychology in the U.S.A.*

In the halls and laboratories of academia, government agencies, military institutions, and pharmaceutical companies, research psychologists are engaged in reductionist experimentation that has been made possible by advances in instrumentation and the handling of large masses of data. The development of such fields as neuroscience and genomics have done much to deepen the traditional division of psychology as either "scientific, basic" or "applied" (Hilgard, 1987, pp. 750-771; Viney, 1993, pp. 449-450). Psychologists who work with the actual living conditions of people — where they work, study, and come to be healed — are separated from the psychologists who work with the tools that reduce psychological life to commodities that are marketable in the genomic, medical, and pharmaceutical industries.

This is one aspect of the contemporary crisis in U.S.A. psychology. The psychological community is specialized and fragmented. As a result of its fragmentation, it is difficult for psychologists to act together in a way that integrates the varied subdivisions of psychology in attempts to solve the many problems each subdivision faces. It becomes impossible for psychologists to struggle successfully against the continuing programs of discrimination and exploitation of various populations, or to work to satisfy the needs and aspirations of people for a

better world and life. It also prevents the development of a consciousness to expose the flawed philosophy that lies at the base of a reductionist science that is manipulated for the satisfaction of greed.

In the U.S.A., psychologists cannot carry out mental-health treatment
programs as they should, because insurance and government agencies
place a higher premium on profit and cost respectively than on people's
health. In the U.S.A., educational psychologists are being channeled
more and more into being trainers of technicians for industrial profit-
making tasks, rather than for the education of all the people in knowing
how to solve problems and obtain knowledge. In the U.S.A., psychologists are coerced into carrying out research that satisfies the agenda prescribed by governmental agencies and industry. These are some of the
symptoms of the crisis in psychology today.

But the most serious development that deepens and exacerbates the
crisis in psychology today is genetic determinism, expressed in the theory of evolutionary psychology and in the practice of genomics. These
are arguably examples of mechanical materialism and reductionism.

### The Contemporary Crisis in U.S.A. Psychology

U.S.A. psychologists — by accepting genetic determinism, which
is used to support discrimination and exploitation of the working class
and poor, expressed in racism and sexism; and by their complicity in
serving industry's needs, without regard for the welfare of people —
have affected their intellectual freedom and economic security, and betrayed the goal of psychology as dedicated to the welfare of the people
(American Psychological Association, 1997, Art. 1). This betrayal has
created an identity crisis for many psychologists who entered the field
because of their desire to help people, the reason given by most people
who elect to major in psychology when they enter the university. The
crisis in psychology, which extends beyond the U.S.A., is the inability of
psychology, because of a flawed philosophy and practice, to fulfill its
societal role.

### Comparison of Contemporary U.S.A. Crisis with Early Soviet Crisis

Given the differences between the historical and socioeconomic
characteristics of the Soviet Union in which Vygotsky was living, and
the U.S.A. today, it is hard to see any relation between the crisis in

U.S.A. psychology and the crisis in Soviet psychology. However, the nondialectical materialist legacy of the prerevolutionary psychologists that was left to the psychologists whom Vygotsky was addressing had the same genetic determinist base within it and the same reductionist approach as U.S.A. psychology then and now. Questions of evolution, specifically, the difference between humans and other animals, and of heredity, were endemic in the Soviet academy. In fact, there was an active eugenics movement in the U.S.S.R. in the 1920s and 1930s (Adams, 1989).

Vygotsky had a vision based on an understanding of dialectical and historical materialism as postulated by Marx, Engels, and Lenin. Similar interest is evident in the writings of Luria and Leontiev as well. Dialectical and historical materialism formulates its tenets with a levels approach, but the concept of integrative levels was not made explicit until the 1930s (Needham, 1937/1943). It is not clear that Vygotsky, Luria or Leontiev were familiar with any explicit discussion of the concept, or whether Luria or Leontiev were aware of the discussion about levels that was sparked by Novikoff in 1945 (Novikoff, 1945a, 1945b; see also Leontiev, 1975/1978, pp. 141-143 on levels).

Making the statement that there are differences between humans and other animals is one stage of understanding integrative levels, even when expressed as the result of sociohistorical processes (e.g., the role of labor, Engels, 1940). When this is the primary consideration of levels in evolution, one may also see this difference between humans and other animals as being derived from Darwinian concepts of heredity, and this may lead, as it did for Vygotsky, to research on twins. Discussion of the relation between heredity and socialization was still in the Mendelian mode of familial characteristics, yet he saw the preeminence of the latter rather than the former in understanding the ways in which children learned and behaved. Nonetheless, through his study of twins, he sought some explanation of the role that inherited characteristics played in how children developed and learned.

Although the biochemical characteristics of heredity were not known in his time, Needham had already indicated that the biochemical level of organization could not explain biological phenomena on what he called "higher" levels of organization, such as social behavior. (Formulating the concept of levels in terms of time is more accurate; thus one might talk not of "higher" levels, but of "later" levels as developmental, historical evolutionary processes.)

In Needham's systematic levels approach, that is, in the explicit analysis of a category such as social behavior (in Vygotsky's twin study, learning behavior would be the category of social behavior), the physiological or anatomical characteristics that were "inherited" as evidenced by the many shared characteristics of twins, would not be seen as offering explanations of the learning processes. Such shared structural and functional characteristics would have to be analyzed and shown to be related to learning activity, or social behavior. In other words, it would not be assumed that because they shared such physiological or anatomical characteristics, one would be able to better understand the similarities or differences in the ways in which so-called identical twins learned, or the ways in which siblings, or so-called fraternal twins learned. The functional and structural characteristics of one level (i.e., physiological/anatomical) do not in and of themselves predict the functional and structural characteristics of succeeding levels.

The science of genetics was undeveloped in Vygotsky's day, and evolutionary theory had not yet integrated Darwinian Mendelian biology with the later sophisticated molecular genetics. Nonetheless, as indicated in the previous quotations from Vygotsky and Leontiev, the new Soviet psychology was in a crisis because of the same mechanical materialist, reductionist thinking about biology expressed in ideas about heredity, and about the relationship between human sociopsychology and evolution.

### Can a Program for Resolving the Contemporary Crisis be Proposed?

If there is a crisis in psychology, what is our responsibility to resolve the crisis? Can psychologists who support activity theory, societal-historical theory, develop and set forth a psychology that will attract and unify psychology to be most constructive in the solution of the problems faced by humanity today? Can we develop a psychology that is theoretically responsive to changing knowledge and applicable to daily problems (cf. Wozniak, 1975)?

Such a program might be developed if the legacy of activity and societal-historical theory left by Vygotsky, Luria, and Leontiev were fused with the concept of integrative levels. This concept can clarify one's thinking of about biology, evolution, heredity and psychology as they are related to each other, and provide some necessary tools for resolution of the crisis in psychology.

## A Societal-Historical Perspective on the Concepts of Evolution and Heredity: A Comparison of the U.S.A. and the U.S.S.R.

*Evolution and Psychology in the U.S.A.*

*Some history.* Darwin, and Romanes, as well as Herbert Spencer, were concerned with the relationships between the behavior of humans and animals as expressions of evolution. The basic concepts of Darwinian evolution are natural selection, the centrality of reproduction, adaptation and heritability. Because Spencer applied Darwinian theory to human society, which became known as Social Darwinism, he is important for this discussion. Psychology had been interested philosophically in human nature, and now was stimulated to consider human nature in a new way. Dewey, Ladd, and Baldwin accepted Darwin's evolutionary theory and focused on the concepts of natural selection and adaptation, with a strong teleological bias, rather than on reproduction and heritability. Galton, McDougall, and G. Stanley Hall were more concerned with heritability and emphasized individual and group differences in humans, as well as instinct. Boring (1950) describes Hall as "a genetic psychologist, that is to say, a psychological evolutionist who was concerned with animal and human development and all the secondary problems of adaptation and development" (p. 522). In other words, Hall was an evolutionary psychologist.

The evolutionary thinking in psychology as seen in the interest of Galton, McDougall, and Hall in the inheritance of behavioral and mental characteristics became the warp and woof of another area of psychology: behavior genetics.

E.O. Wilson (1975) stimulated the more recent changes in the relationship between evolutionary theory and psychology. He proclaimed the unifying virtues of sociobiology through the integration of molecular genetics and evolutionary biology, and predicted that sociobiology would cannibalize comparative psychology, the study of the development and evolution of behavior.

The term *sociobiology*, much acclaimed as a result of Wilson's book, was actually coined by J.P. Scott, a comparative psychologist and a founder of the Animal Behavior Society (U.S.A.). Scott, who was primarily an interactionst, defined sociobiology as the study of the biological basis of social behavior, and based his concepts on the relationship of experience and inheritance (J.P. Scott, personal communication, 1995).

Wilson (1975) also defined sociobiology as the systematic study of the biological basis of all social behavior, but he added

one of the functions of sociobiology, then, is to reformulate the foundations of the social sciences in a way that draws these subjects into the modern synthesis (i.e., the synthesis of evolutionary theory with genetics) ... each phenomenon is weighed for its adaptive significance and then related to the basic principles of population genetics. (p. 4)

During the early post-Darwinian period of these developments in psychology, biologists concerned with evolutionary issues emphasized evolutionary history of species and the process of inheritance. This latter concern resulted in the development not only of population genetics, but of molecular genetics as we know it today. Population genetics and molecular genetics are looked to by many psychologists as providing a foundation for a unified approach to behavior.

Most recently, the old concept of evolutionary psychology has been given a new birth by Cosmides and Tooby (1987). Their evolutionary psychology is derived from Wilsonian sociobiology, which in turn is derived from the work of Hamilton (1964a, 1964b), Trivers (1971) and Dawkins (1976). The fundamental sociobiological concepts are: fitness, that is, the probable genetic contribution of an individual to succeeding generations, and particularly, inclusive fitness as developed by Hamilton: the sum of an individual's own fitness plus all its influence of fitness on its relatives other than direct descendants, hence the total effect of kin selection with reference to an individual. Kin selection refers to the selection of genes due to one or more individuals favoring or disfavoring the survival and reproduction of relatives (other than offspring) who possess the same genes by common descent. This is related to reciprocal altruism, that is, the favoring of individuals on the basis of the extent of shared genes.

The "new" evolutionary psychology of Cosmides and Tooby is worth consideration, because at the present there are more than a dozen doctoral programs in evolutionary psychology in U.S.A. universities.

Cosmides and Tooby propose an evolutionary psychology based on two aspects of genetic function:

1. Nuclear and cytoplasmic genes are in conflict with each other and this conflict is the ultimate expression of differences between females and males (women and men) (Cosmides & Tooby, 1981);

2. Contemporary humans carry the same genome as the hominid species of 2.5
   million years ago (Tooby & Cosmides, 1990).

They say that each type of gene tries to maximize its fitness, producing the conflict. The cytoplasmic genes are primarily maternally
derived (mitochondria) and win out over the male genes except where
the male needs the female genes to survive. Cosmides and Tooby recognize that their theory is based upon an incomplete understanding of
the structure and function of human mitochondria; their discussion is
based primarily on plants, bacteria and fungi. However, because they
believe that the phenomena of altruism, fitness and kin selection are
ubiquitous in all species, they extrapolate from the organelles of those
organisms to humans. Their theory demonstrates the sociobiological
"explanation" for the "conflicting" sociosexual drives of females and
males on the biochemical level, which then is translated into geneti-
cally-driven differences between the behavior of women and men.

   In this analysis and extrapolation from one level to another (biochemical to physiological to behavioral), they also demonstrate the fal-
lacious outcome of theory that not only ignores integrative levels but
becomes a useful tool in the societal exploitation of women.

   The second fundamental aspect of Cosmides and Tooby's evolutionary psychology does the same, that is, confuses levels and categories,
emphasizing the biochemical, without consideration of socio/societal/
historical processes. Although they say they are not genetic determi-
nists, they formulate the existence of developmental "programs," that
is, regulatory processes that control development and are directed by
genes that depend upon the properties of the environment. Evolution
works through the genes and through evolutionary time; there is selec-
tive retention of advantageous variants (Darwinian natural selection).
The genes are the ultimate causal agents.

   What has genomic research taught us about gene function and
structure that demonstrates the dangers of confusion of categories and
lack of consideration of integrative levels of those categories? First,
genes are likely to change more frequently than was thought (Lawrence
& Roth, 1996). The possibility of recombination, loss of parts of the
sequence, cross over from one to another chromosome with consequent
changes in genetic function, take place and do not always have deleteri-
ous effects (Griffiths, Miller, Suzuki, Lewontin, & Gelbert, 1993). In
addition, genomics has confirmed the interdependence of the mito-

chondrion on the nuclear genes, and on proteins in the cell. This may lead more to cooperation between nuclear and cytoplasmic genes than to conflict between them.

Although the validity and reliability of the molecular clock are debatable — and therefore the possibility to give an accurate story, based on this clock, about the time scale of genetic change and speciation — there is reason to believe that in 2.5 million years, some changes may have taken place (Ciochon & Fleagle, 1992). For example, let us consider the many changes that took place in the morphology in the known species between *Homo erectus* and maybe *habilis* at about 2.5 million years ago, and the appearance of *archaic Homo sapiens* and *Neandertal* until finally modern *Homo sapiens* 100,000 years ago. Given the changes in climate and other aspects of the environment at those times, one may hazard that behavior changed as well.

*Contemporary synthesis of evolutionary theory and genetics: Genomics.* Genomics is the science of defining the genetic configuration of an organism; eventually all species, including *homo*, will be so defined.

The history of the human genome project in the U.S.A. starts with Hiroshima and Nagasaki, and continues through our continued testing of atomic and hydrogen bombs (Patrinos, 1997). The Department of Energy was interested in knowing how one could detect the effects of radiation on genes. This interest did not become crystallized as a funded program until 1986. Today the research is being carried out at many sites, and the preponderance of research is on disease, both mental and physiological, such as alcoholism, schizophrenia and, amazingly, homosexuality. In addition, there is much research on economically important organisms, as farm animals and plants.

Although genetic sequences have been defined to a large extent in some species (various invertebrates, mice), and a little more than 2% of human genetic material has been defined, the actual functions of the regions of the chromosome that are called genes are not completely known. The research that seeks to identify the proteins that are produced, their developmental history, and their function at different stages of development remains to be done (Fodor, 1997; Rifkin, 1998, p. 157).

The interplay of the motivations of profit and the search for knowledge is seen in the recent developments in which several companies have been formed to carry out genomic research, and most of these have direct relations with pharmaceutical companies (Wade, 1998). They say they will be able to carry out the human genomic analysis faster than any of the U.S.A. governmentally-supported laboratories.

But, what should their philosophy and research methods be in approaching the functions of genes, and in particular, behavioral processes? To date, the genomists have turned to the behavior geneticists who are positivistic and reductionist in their philosophy and methods of doing research (Plomin, 1990).

Although there is a clear need for a developmental approach to behavior genetics, the preponderance of genetic research in medical, psychiatric and psychological research ignores the activity of the organism as it develops or the social/societal processes which are important in the expression of genetic (biochemical and hormonal) function in behavior (Rifkin, 1998). Consideration of such activity-societal-historical processes would refocus the emphasis on the preventive aspects of mitigating biochemical and hormonal errors. The reductionist, positivistic approach may create policies to "fix" the genetic defects, that is, eugenics, in a "new, scientific" way. Despite the demurs of the behavior geneticists, the response of those who see the need to fix the population in its own image has been to acclaim the finding as the answer to their problems with poor scholastic achievement, addictive behavior, and so forth (Duster, 1997).

The confidence of the genomist that a gene or a group of genes can alone help us understand behavior sufficiently to propose other biochemicals to affect that behavior (medication of schizophrenia, alcoholism) makes the behavior and its treatment into objects that lend themselves to the free-market approach to treatment of individuals. Who will have access to these "designer" gene products?

The easy extrapolation from one level (biochemical, morphological and physiological) of the expressions of genes to the behavioral level, leads to renewed confidence in genetic determinism and exacerbates the crisis in psychology.

*An approach to evolution, genetics and behavior: The concept of integrative levels.* In the Soviet Union, there was much confusion about the relationship of the biochemical, physiological and morphological characteristics that are shared by humans and other animals, as there is today in the U.S.A. The concept of integrative levels is useful in delineating and understanding characteristics that may be considered as continuous or discontinuous within defined categories of structure, function or the integration of structure and function, brought about by, and resulting in, the activity of the organism.

Using the concept of integrative levels in dialectical and historical materialist analysis requires awareness of the question, or topic and how it became worthy of study. This leads to defining the nature and function of categories. In other words, one needs an explicit statement and definition of the category as it is shown to subsume levels in a developmental or historical process necessary for its becoming a category. To this end, I propose the following working definition of category:

1. A category is a unit of thought, reflecting human experience in organizing, changing and planning human relationships with the real world. Categories change with the increasing knowledge and experience of humanity.

2. A category can be defined in terms of its levels of integration and organization; in its relationship to other categories; and its similarities and differences from other categories. (Tobach, 1987)

In other words, a category is defined in terms of the levels of integration it subsumes. For example, consider the attempt to understand differences in scores on IQ tests by studying differences in the rate of neural conduction (Rijsdijk & Boomsma, 1997). Let us assume for the sake of discussion that the question being posed is, are population differences in these two levels related to heritage? Perhaps this has been seen worthy of answering in order to find how different levels of integration (the physiological level and the societal level) produce a particular behavior such as answering questions on an IQ test in a particular fashion. More would have to be known about the history of the question and its place in the category of societal processes. But, can the question be posed so as to clarify the societal process of answering questions on the IQ test and being given a particular score? Can the answers to the question produce new knowledge about the relationship between these two levels?

Applying the concept of integrative levels, certain questions would have to be asked. Which is the appropriate category for analysis? The nervous system is the physiological level in the category of organism. But, the nervous system itself may be seen as a category, that is, subsuming different levels of organization and integration. For example, the earliest level in organismic development of the nervous system (in this case, the human) are the undifferentiated embryonic cells that will become neurons. These become differentiated as a result of their inner contradictions (intracellular processes) that result in migration through other cells and tissues. These other cells and tissues present outer contradictions, which in relation to the inner contradictions, bring about further changes in the neuronal cells (particular new intracellular differentiation, extensions as dendrites or axons, etc.) The integration or resolution of inner and outer contradictions brings about a new level of integration, a particular neural system, such as sensory, motor, spinal, brain, and so forth. At every level of integration, there is both continuity, in the presence of cells (the earliest level), and discontinuity, the differentiated cortical area, in which the structure and function of the neurons are specialized.

To reach the level of integration in the nervous system (the brain and its relation to the subsumed neural levels) that is expressed in the behavior of answering questions on an IQ test would require the detailed study of all the levels of integration in the nervous system that the activity of the organism integrates in the IQ test behavior.

It becomes clear that the category of the nervous system by itself cannot subsume the test taking. Similarly, the organismic category by itself cannot include test taking although it includes the neural (physiological) level. It is in the integration of the organismic category and the category of societal/historical processes, in which test taking might be one level, that the scores on IQ can be understood. On the societal/historical level further analysis would be needed to know what levels of integration are subsumed in the category of test taking.

It is important to recognize that in all the categories, the nervous system, the organismic and the societal/historical, the methods of study are particular to each level in the category. The methods for studying the societal/historical category levels cannot use the instruments with which the nervous system functions; the interview, paper and pencil, and other aspects of the test taking study cannot be used to study the function of the nervous system.

The definition of the category in terms of its levels clarifies its relationship with other categories. By using the integrative levels concept, the confusion of the categories is demonstrated when the question is asked: Are the differences in IQ scores produced by differences in neural conduction rates?

Those who find the concept of integrative levels useful understand that many characteristics can be considered as continuous and discontinuous within defined categories of structure or function. Discontinuities are seen at different levels of integration as they are expressed in different species (humans and other animals) and in different developmental stages. Psychologists should not confuse categories (extrapolating from the biochemical category which includes genes to the psychological category of individual behavior); both the continuities and discontinuities need to be defined and studied (Tobach, 1987, 1995b).

*Brief (Incomplete) Review of the Evolutionary and Genetic Thinking in the U.S.S.R. (1924 to 1979)*

This review is based on texts available in English, which are in many cases fragmentary. As will be evident, the material presented by Graham is most helpful in the discussion.

*General situation of relation between the theorists of the Communist Party of the U.S.S.R., governmental institutions and science (particularly psychology).* It is difficult to interpret the relation between any scientist and the state and economic institutions which monitor education and control the infrastructure which makes research and scholarly writing possible. Through the lens of our own understanding of these constraints, we can cull material from the writing of Vygotsky, Leontiev, and Luria that is significant for the discussion of the crisis in contemporary psychology, and was relevant to the crisis in psychology, as Vygotsky characterized it. Graham (1987) cites Vygotsky aptly:

The crisis stems from the sharp contradiction between the factual material of science and its methodological and theoretical premises, which have long been a subject of dispute between materialistic and idealistic conceptions. (p. 170)

This dispute expressed itself in various ways during the lives of Vygotsky, Luria, and Leontiev, but most significantly, in the theoretical and practical activities of psychology as it wrestled with the problems of evolutionary biology, heredity and societal-historical processes. The clearest expression in the U.S.S.R. and in the U.S.A. of this struggle was, and remains, the role of genetic processes in evolution, and particularly in human evolution and psychology.

It is evident that Vygotsky, Luria, and Leontiev, who were committed to dialectical and materialist theory and practice, had difficulty integrating the biochemical levels of genes and hormones with the psychological structural/functional levels, without employing mechanical materialist (genetic determinist) or idealist concepts (instincts, innateness). In Graham's (1987) review of the period after 1979 (Leontiev's death), the struggle became the typical "nature/nurture" debate (see also Glass, 1993; Shumny, 1989). Even those who argued for the importance of "nurture" were forced to reify "nature" and to become involved in arguments about the quantitative expression of heredity and environment. This is the result of an interactionist approach (nature and nurture are interacting). The pitfall of needing to quantify how much heredity contributes to behavior leads to an acceptance of the gene as the ultimate "limit to potential." The concept of integrative levels, in which the biochemical, or genetic level, is seen to be subsumed in later levels of development and history avoids this pitfall.

The effects of Darwinian concepts of heredity are seen in the formulations of Marx and Engels, and continue in the writings of Vygotsky, Leontiev, and Luria. The dichotomization of "nature" and "nurture" is fertile ground for the acceptance of genetic determinism which developed in the later years of Luria and Leontiev's lives (Graham, 1987, chap. 6). This mechanical materialist approach also was seen in the application of ethological concepts in the study of the evolution of behavior in all the U.S.S.R. (Krushinsky, 1990; "Russian Psychology," 1992; Tobach, 1995a, 1996).

*Discussion of evolution and heredity.* One of the most frequently cited concepts from the writings of Marx and Engels is the distinction they made between humans and other animals, namely, the invention and use of tools, which was central in the evolution of the human species. They believed that the structure of the human brain was completed by the time the modern human species evolved and that with the invention of tools and language, the societal/historical process delineated the further development of the human species (Engels, 1940).

Nonetheless, in discussing other aspects of nonhuman animal activity, they frequently viewed that activity as instinctive, naive, or natural. These are hereditarian concepts. Leontiev (1947/1981b) in his outstandingly well-documented experimental discussion of the evolution of the psyche of animals makes it clear that the activity of the animal is an important process in the evolution of structure, which in turn makes it possible for the animal to make use of the environment for survival. However, he views the activity as "driven" by the needs of the animal, in the usual teleological fashion, with little attention to the developmental and historical processes that elaborate tissue changes into needs. The teleology extends to the adaptive value of the behavior for the species as well. These formulations bring the concept of drives and instinct into congruence. In this respect, the formulation of such a reification of "drive" does not differ from that of most mainstream biologists and psychologists. Commitment to dialectical and historical materialism was not sufficient to avoid such idealist, reification of need and drive as essentialist factors that initiate the activity (see also Leontiev, 1975/1978, pp. 115-119). In discussing evolution of the animal psyche, Leontiev (1959/1981c) writes:

We distinguish experience of two kinds in animals: (a) that accumulated phylogenetically and reinforced by heredity; and (b) individual experience acquired during life. (p. 420)

Animals' ontogenetic development can hence be represented as the accumulation of individual experience mediating the performance of their instinctive activity progressively better in complex, dynamic, external conditions.

Matters are quite different with man. Unlike animals man has experience of yet another kind, viz., the social, historical experience he has acquired. It does not coincide with either species experience, biologically inherited, or individual experience, with which it is often incorrectly confused. (pp. 420-421)

In contrast to the phylogenetic development of animals, whose advances are consolidated in the form of a change in their biological organization itself, and in the evolution of their brain, the advances of men's historical development are consolidated in the material objects and the phenomena of ideas (language, science) that men create. (pp. 421-422)

In these quotations, it would appear that there is a recognition of the differences among phyletic histories. However, the species history (evolutionary process) is seen as one based on the inheritance of behavior, in much the same way that humans inherit their spoken, material, written history. Fundamentally, there is agreement with conventional concepts of the inheritance of behavior, if not the products of the behavior. The reliance on the concept of instinct demonstrates the influence of ethological thinking in the Soviet Union, where Konrad Lorenz's Nazi past and racist formulations were either overlooked or unknown (Lerner, 1992). (See section below on racism.)

How are we to understand the role of genetics or heredity in psychology, when heredity is seen as a material entity? Thus, in Vygotsky's (1935/1994b) discussion of the environment:

[P]aedology approaches heredity from its own special point of view and is not interested in the laws of heredity as such, but in the role heredity plays in child development. ... In exactly the same way as when he studies heredity, a paedologist investigates not just the environment and the laws governing its framework, but the role, meaning and influence of the environment on child development. (p. 338)

In discussing his work with twins, he writes the following:

To begin with, once again we come across the same problem which was facing us when we were investigating heredity ... no all out definition of the influence of heredity on every aspect of development exists or can exist, and that, when we want to study not just the laws of heredity, which are basically uniform in nature, and the influence of heredity on development, then we must differentiate the effects of heredity upon various aspects and development. If you remember, I tried to demonstrate how results obtained from an investigation of twins have disclosed that heredity does not play the same role in relation to higher psychological function as it does in relation to elementary psychological functions. So it follows that one must differentiate the effect of heredity upon various aspects of development. ... it is unlikely that environment carries the same influence and exerts this influence in exactly the same way in relation to all aspects of development. (p. 347)

Vygotsky clearly realized that this split of psychology's phenomena into two spheres that are supposedly subject to fundamentally different regularities — the natural scientific and the cultural-historical one — was very dangerous for psychology and for its future. ... as he wrote more than once, by the confrontation of the "biotropic" (oriented to the natural sciences) and the "sociotropic" (oriented to the world of culture) currents. The problem of the synthesis of these currents was constantly on his mind. (Yaroshevsky & Gurgenidze, 1983/1997, p. 350)

But, the synthesis that would be possible in the concept of integrative levels was not available to him.

In some of the formulations of the relation between what they call variously behavior, nature, phylogeny, heredity, and innateness, and what they call variously activity, experience, environment, sociohistorical processes, etc. they seem to be using a concept of levels. However, their application of dialectical and historical materialism did not develop an integrative levels approach that would encompass the evolutionary history of all life and the historical development of human behavior.

Luria and Leontiev may not have been familiar with the theoretical writing on this subject being done outside the U.S.S.R., by both dialectical and historical materialist psychologists and others. The policies of the theorists and philosophers of the Communist Party of the U.S.S.R. tended to be suspicious of dialectical and historical materialists from bourgeois countries. At the same, the policies of the bourgeois countries was to discourage accessibility to the writings and research of Soviet theorists by the scientists of U.S.A. and other bourgeois countries.

*Vygotsky's philosophical integrity.* Despite these formulations of heredity which may be termed mechanical materialist, or idealist (Selsam & Martel, 1963), Vygotsky was sensitive to the idealist conceptualizations of many of the non-Soviet psychologists with whom he was familiar. He saw that the "old psychology," that is the prerevolutionary psychology, was still imbued with many of these idealist concepts. He wished to place a new psychology at the center of the new life in the Soviet Union, as this nonmaterialism was creating a crisis in psychology. Vygotsky's criticism of these systems in psychology is an application of dialectical and historical materialism, although he was very critical of those psychologists who were writing of a "Marxist" psychology. He believed that the crisis in psychology would not be solved by dogmatic, superficial application of dialectical materialism. He sought a psychology that started out with an emphasis on practice and activity, in which scientifically obtained information would be the basis for the development of a dialectical materialist psychology. This psychology would produce a general psychology in which philosophy and practice would be unified on the basis of dialectical materialism. Vygotsky writes:

Marxism is ... applied in the wrong place (in textbooks instead of a general psychology)... We do not need fortuitous utterances, but a method; not dialectical materialism, but historical materialism. *Das Kapital* must teach us many things — both because a genuine social psychology begins *after Das Kapital* and because psychology nowadays is a psychology *before Das Kapital*. (p. 331)

The psychology which would yield the facts on which the materialism of psychology would be based was the psychology of practice, or applied psychology.

*The main driving force of the crisis in its final phase is the development of applied psy-chology as a whole.* ... We can elucidate this by referring to three aspects. The first is *practice.* ... The importance of the new practical psychology for the *whole* science cannot be exaggerated. ... [T]he second aspect [is] *methodology.* ... The *third aspect*: [applied psychology] instigates a rupture and creates a real psy-chology. (pp. 305-306)

The central role of philosophy is clear in his analysis:

But the nature of psychological material does not allow us to separate the psy-chological propositions from philosophical theories to the extent that other empirical sciences have managed to do that. The psychologist fundamentally deceives himself when he imagines that his laboratory work can lead him to the solution of the basic questions of his science; they belong to philosophy. (p. 308)

[T]he cause of the crisis ... lies in the development of applied psychology, which has led toward the reform of the whole methodology of the science on the basis of the principle of practice, i.e., towards its transformation into a natu-ral science. This principle is pressing psychology heavily and pushing it to split into two sciences. It guarantees the right development of materialistic psychol-ogy in the future. Practice and philosophy are becoming the head stone of the corner. (p. 309)

Vygotsky is calling for the development of a philosophical base for the practice of psychology; only in the actual activity of working as a psychologist in industry, education and the clinic can psychology be-come materialist; only by applying historical materialism can it develop the methodology, the philosophy of practice.

He omits the dialectical materialism which developed out of Engels' analysis of the dialectics of nature, and would be applicable to biologi-cal evolution. Vygotsky and Leontiev only discussed biological evolu-tion in contrast with historical materialism, which they considered as more appropriate for human psychology. Nonetheless, the legacy of biological evolution in the psyche of the human is part of their thinking about general psychology.

*Denunciation of racism based on genetic determinism.* In 1934, Vygotsky (1934/1994a), with a group of Jewish scientists, published a brochure attacking the Nazi racist programs. As indicated in the citation at the beginning of this chapter, Leontiev also understood the significance of genetic determinism and public policy. Similarly, Luria (1979) criticized ethological formulations which supported the concept of a genetic base for wars and aggression.

### The Similarities and Differences Between the Two Crises

The fundamental difference between the political economy of the U.S.S.R. and the U.S.A. is reflected in the emphasis that Vygotsky placed on the practice of psychology as part of the development of the new Soviet man. Vygotsky's crisis differs in that respect from the U.S.A. crisis in psychology: In the U.S.A. the aim is to treat the damaged human and to prepare the human for the exigencies of societal processes. In U.S.A. society, psychology is in a paradoxical situation. On the one hand the bourgeois society expects that psychology will make people available for the work they must do, without causing such problems as drug and alcohol abuse, or violence, and with appropriate training useful in the various aspects of production of surplus value, at a minimum of cost to industry. At the same time, psychologists are supposed to be concerned about the welfare of people. This consideration would call for them to be the sentinels or advocates in society who must warn people about the dangers they face when psychotechnics are used against them.

Despite this fundamental difference between the previous Soviet crisis and the contemporary U.S.A. crisis, it is significant that the issue of the biological and societal processes in the evolution of human psychology was seen as critical by Vygotsky. This issue is critical in the U.S.A. today.

In both countries the ability to be productive was a function of the relationship of the scientist to the power structure. In both situations, there are scientists who are happily committed to their respective governmental institutions. Yet, in the U.S.A. there is a history of psychologists who have attempted to change the philosophy, practice and ethics of the organized psychological community (Psychologists League; Psychologists for Social Action). New developments in the former U.S.S.R. will be interesting to observe (Bereczkei, 1993; Koltsova, Oleinik, Gilgen, & Gilgen, 1996; Tobach, 1996).

An application of dialectical and historical materialist theory and practice using the concept of integrative levels may be useful in bringing about constructive change in psychology today.

## Suggested Program for a Possible Resolution of the World Crisis in Psychology

Psychologists have much to do in pursuing their theory and practice of the discipline, in societies that do not encourage societal responsibility. The development of societal consciousness is a poorly understood process (Tobach, 1998). Suggestions for consideration of some of the issues raised in this chapter are based on the hope that psychologists will become aware of the need to examine their societal consciousness, and its relation to their theory and practice as psychologists.

Some of the theoretical foundations for such an examination rests on dialectical and historical materialism; on the concept of integrative levels; and on activity theory. Given the dominance of genetic theory in much of the behavioral sciences, psychologists need to update their literacy in evolutionary theory and genetics.

This program might lead to the further development of activity and societal-historical theory. More important might be its effect on the elimination of genetic determinism from psychology, and psychology's unwitting exploitation as a support for antihuman policies. To bring that about, psychologists need to be active in the interface between their profession and society, an activity known as political activity.

## References

Adams, M.B. (1989). The politics of human heredity in the USSR, 1920-1940. *Genome, 31,* 879-884.

American Psychological Association. (1997). *By laws.* Washington, D.C.: Author. Retrieved on January 24, 1999 from the World Wide Web: http://www.apa.org/governance/bylaws/art1.html

Bereczkei, T. (1993). An intellectual legacy of the past: The reception of sociobiology in the East-European countries. *Biology & Philosophy, 8,* 399-407.

Boring, E.G. (1950). *A history of experimental psychology* (2nd ed.). New York: Appleton-Century-Crofts.

Ciochon, R.L., & Fleagle, J.G. (1992). *The human evolution source book.* Englewood Cliffs, N.J.: Prentice-Hall.

Cosmides, L.M., & Tooby, J. (1981). Cytoplasmic inheritance and intra-genomic conflict. *Journal of Theoretical Biology, 89,* 83-129.

Cosmides, L.M., & Tooby, J. (1987). From evolution to behavior: Evolutionary psychology as the missing link. In J. Dupre (Ed.), *The latest on the best: Essays on evolution and optimality* (pp. 277-306). Cambridge, Mass.: MIT Press.

Dawkins, R. (1976). *The selfish gene.* New York: Oxford University Press.

Duster, T. (1997). Molecular halos and behavioral glows. In E. Smith & W. Sapp (Eds.), *Plain talk about the human genome project* (pp. 215-222). Tuskegee, Ala.: Tuskegee University.

Engels, F. (1940). *Dialectics of nature.* New York: International Publishers.

Fodor, S.A. (1997, July 18). Massively parallel genomics. *Science, 277,* 393-395.

Glass, B. (1993). Racism and eugenics in international context. *Quarterly Review of Biology, 68,* 61-67

Graham, L.R. (1987). *Science, philosophy and human behavior in the Soviet Union.* New York: Columbia University Press

Griffiths, A.J.F., Miller J.H., Suzuki D.T., Lewontin R.C., & Gelbert, W.M. (1993). *An introduction to genetic analysis* (5th ed.) New York: Freeman.

Hamilton, W.D. (1964a). The genetical evolution of social behavior. I. *Journal of Theoretical Biology, 7,* 1-16.

Hamilton, W.D. (1964b). The genetical evolution of social behavior. II. *Journal of Theoretical Biology, 7,* 17-52.

Hilgard, E.R. (1987). *Psychology in America.* New York: Harcourt Brace Jovanovich.

Koltsova, V.A., Oleinik Y.N., Gilgen A.R., & Gilgen, C.K. (Eds.). (1996). *Post-Soviet perspectives on Russian psychology.* Westport, Conn.: Greenwood Press.

Krushinsky, L.V. (1990). *Experimental studies of elementary reasoning.* New Delhi: Amerind Publishing.

Lawrence, J.G., & Roth, J.R. (1996). Selfish operons: Horizontal transfer may drive the evolution of gene clusters. *Genetics, 143,* 1843-1860.

Leontiev, A.N. (1978). *Activity, consciousness, and personality* (M.J. Hall, Trans.). Englewood, Cliffs, N.J.: Prentice-Hall. (Original work published 1975)

Leontiev (Leontyev), A.N. (1981a). The biological and the social in man's psyche. In *Problems of the development of mind* (pp. 132-155). Moscow: Progress Publishers. (Original work published 1960)

Leontiev (Leontyev), A.N. (1981b). The evolution of the psyche in animals. In *Problems of the development of mind* (pp. 156-203). Moscow: Progress Publishers. (Original work published 1947)

Leontiev (Leontyev), A.N. (1981c). The principles of the child's psychological development and the problem of mental deficiency. In *Problems of the development of mind* (pp. 417-434). Moscow: Progress Publishers. (Original work published 1959)

Lerner, R.M. (1992). *Final solutions: Biology, prejudice, and genocide*. University Park: Pennsylvania State University Press.

Luria, A.R. (1979). *The making of mind: A personal account of Soviet psychology* (M. Cole & S. Cole, Eds.). Cambridge, Mass.: Harvard University Press.

Needham, J. (1943). Integrative levels: A revaluation of the idea of progress. In J. Needham, *Time: The refreshing river*. London: Allen & Unwin. (Original work published 1937)

Novikoff, A.B. (1945a, March 2). The concept of integrative levels and biology. *Science, 101*, 203-215.

Novikoff, A.B. (1945b, October 19). Continuity and discontinuity in evolution. *Science, 102*, 409.

Papadimitriou, D.B. (1994). *Aspects of distribution of wealth and income*. New York: St. Martin's Press.

Patrinos, A. (1997). The human genome project: What is it? In E. Smith & W. Sapp (Eds.), *Plain talk about the human genome project* (pp. 1-7). Tuskegee, Ala.: Tuskegee University.

Plomin, R. (1990, April 13).The role of inheritance in behavior. *Science, 248*, 183-188.

Rifkin, J. (1998). *The biotech century*. New York: Tarcher/Putnam.

Rijsdijk, F.V., & Boomsma, D.I. (1997). Genetic mediation of the correlation between peripheral nerve conduction velocity and IQ. *Behavior Genetics, 27*, 87-98.

Russian Psychology. (1992). [Special issue]. *International Journal of Comparative Psychology, 6*(1).

Selsam, H., & Martel, H. (Eds.). (1963). *Reader in Marxist philosophy, from the writings of Marx, Engels, and Lenin.* New York: International Publishers.

Shumny, V.K. (1989). Development of genetic research in the USSR. *Genome, 31,* 900-904.

Solomon, R. (1994). *The transformation of the world economy, 1980-93.* London: Macmillan.

Tobach, E. (1987). Integrative levels in the comparative psychology of cognition, language and consciousness. In G. Greenberg & E. Tobach (Eds.), *Cognition, language and consciousness: Integrative levels* (pp. 239-267). Hillsdale, N.J.: Erlbaum.

Tobach, E. (1995a). Comments on the present status of comparative psychology. *Polish Psychological Bulletin, 26,* 203-229.

Tobach, E. (1995b). The uniqueness of human labor. In L.M.W. Martin, K. Nelson and E. Tobach (Eds.), *Sociocultural psychology: Theory and practice of doing and knowing* (pp. 43-66). Cambridge: Cambridge University Press.

Tobach, E. (1996). Is there a comparative psychology in the future of the former member nations of the USSR? In V.A. Koltsova, Y.N. Oleinik, A.R. Gilgen, & C.K. Gilgen (Eds.), *Post-Soviet perspectives on Russian psychology* (pp. 297-311). Westport, Conn.: Greenwood Press.

Tobach, E. (1998, September). *The relation between individual integrity and societal responsibility: U.S.A. psychologists after the Civil War.* Paper presented at the annual congress of the Psychological Society of South Africa, Cape Town.

Tooby, J., & Cosmides, L. (1990). On the universality of human nature and the uniqueness of the individual: The role of genetics and adaptation. *Journal of Personality, 58,* 17-67.

Trivers, R.L. (1971). The evolution of reciprocal altruism. *Quarterly Review of Biology, 46,* 35-57.

Viney, W. (1993). *A history of psychology.* Boston: Allyn & Bacon.

Vygotsky, L.S. (1994a). Fascism in psychoneurology. In R. van der Veer & J. Valsiner (Eds.), *The Vygotsky reader* (pp. 327-337). Oxford: Blackwell. (Original work published 1934)

Vygotsky, L.S. (1994b). The problem of the environment. In R. van der Veer & J. Valsiner (Eds.) *The Vygotsky reader* (pp. 338-354). Oxford: Blackwell. (Original work published 1935)

Vygotsky, L.S. (1997). The historical meaning of the crisis in psychology:

A methodological investigation. In R.W. Reiber & J. Wollock (Eds.), *The collected works of L.S. Vygotsky: Vol. 3. Problems of the theory and history of psychology* (pp. 233-343). New York: Plenum Press. (Original work written 1927)

Wade, N. (1998, August 18). New company joins race to sequence human genome. *New York Times*, p. F6.

Wilson, E.O. (1975). *Sociobiology*. Cambridge, Mass.: Harvard University Press.

Wozniak, R.H. (1975). A dialectical paradigm for psychological research: Implications drawn from the history of psychology in the Soviet Union. *Human Development, 18*, 18-34.

Yarosheveky, M.G., & Gurgenidze, G.S. (1997). Epilogue (R. van der Veer, Trans.). In R.W. Rieber & J. Wollock (Eds.) *The collected works of L.S. Vygotsky: Vol. 3. Problems of the theory and history of psychology* (pp. 345-369). New York: Plenum Press. (Original work published 1983)

# 10 Public Philosophy and International Feminism

*Martha C. Nussbaum*

Do you want to know what philosophy offers humanity? Practical guidance. One man is on the verge of death. Another is rubbed down by poverty… These are ill treated by men, those by the gods. Why, then, do you write me these frivolities? There is no time for playing around: you have been retained as lawyer for unhappy humanity. You have promised to bring help to the shipwrecked, the imprisoned, the sick, the poor, to those whose heads are under the poised axe.

Seneca, Moral Epistles

In your joint family, I am known as the second daughter-in-law. All these years I have known myself as no more than that. Today, after fifteen years, as I stand alone by the sea, I know that I have another identity, which is my relationship with the universe and its creator. That gives me the courage to write this letter as myself, not as the second daughter-in-law of your family… I am not one to die easily. That is what I want to say in this letter.

Rabindranath Tagore, "Letter from a Wife" (1914)

### Two Women Trying to Flourish

Ahmedabad, in Gujerat, is the textile mill city where Mahatma Gandhi organized labor in accordance with his principles of nonviolent resistance. Tourists visit it for its textile museum and its Gandhi ashram. But today it attracts attention, too, as the home of another resistance movement: the Self-Employed Women's Association (SEWA), with more than 50,000 members, which for over twenty years has been helping female workers in the informal sector[1] to improve their living conditions through credit, education, and a labor union. On one side of the polluted river that bisects the city is the shabby old building where

---

\* I am grateful to John Deigh, Cass Sunstein, Richard Posner, and two anonymous readers for comments on an earlier draft of this chapter. A version of this chapter was published previously in *Ethics*, 108(4) 1998, pp. 762-96, and reprinted with the kind permission of The University of Chicago Press.

1. In India 92.7% of the labor force works in the informal sector, and 60% of these informal sector workers are women (E. Bhatt, personal communication, March 1997).

SEWA was first established, now used as offices for staff. On the other side are the education offices and the SEWA bank, newly housed in a marble office building. All the customers and all the employees are women. Women like to say, "This bank is like our mother's place" — because, says SEWA's founder Ela Bhatt, a woman's mother takes her seriously, keeps her secrets, and helps her solve her problems (Rose, 1992, pp. 172-174).

Vasanti sits on the floor in the meeting room of the old office building, where SEWA members meet to consult with staff. A tiny dark woman in her early thirties, she wears an attractive electric blue sari, and her long hair is wound neatly into a bun on the top of her head. Soft and round, she seems more comfortable sitting than walking. Her teeth are uneven and discolored, but otherwise she looks in reasonable health. Martha Chen (who has organized the meeting) tells me later she is a Rajput, that is, of good caste; I have never figured out how one would know that. She has come with her older (and lower-caste) friend Kokila, maker of clay pots and a janitor at the local conference hall, a tall fiery community organizer who helps the police identify cases of domestic violence. Vasanti speaks quietly, looking down often as she speaks, but there is animation in her eyes.

Vasanti's husband was a gambler and an alcoholic. He used the household money to get drunk, and when he ran out of that money he got a vasectomy in order to take the cash incentive payment offered by local government. So Vasanti has no children to help her. Eventually, as her husband became more abusive, she could live with him no longer and returned to her own family. Her father, who used to make Singer sewing machine parts, has died, but her brothers run an auto parts business in what used to be his shop. Using a machine that used to be her father's, and living in the shop itself, she earned a small income making eyeholes for the hooks on sari tops. Her brothers got her a lawyer to take her husband to court for maintenance — quite an unusual step in her economic class — but the case has dragged on for years with no conclusion in sight. Meanwhile, her brothers also gave her a loan to get the machine that rolls the edges of the sari; but she did not like being dependent on them, because they are married and have children, and may not want to support her much longer. With the help of SEWA, therefore, she got a bank loan of her own to pay back the brothers, and by now she has paid back almost all of the SEWA loan. She now earns

500 rupees a month, a decent living.[2] She has two savings accounts, and is eager to get more involved in the SEWA union. Usually, she says, women lack unity, and rich women take advantage of poor women. In SEWA, by contrast, she has found a sense of community. She clearly finds pleasure in the company of Kokila, a woman of very different social class and temperament.

By now, Vasanti is animated; she is looking us straight in the eye, and her voice is strong and clear. "Women in India have a lot of pain,"she says. "And I, I have had quite a lot of sorrow in my life. But from the pain, our strength is born. Now that we are doing better ourselves, we want to do some good for other women, to feel that we are good human beings."

Jayamma stands outside her hut in the oven-like heat of a late March day in Trivandrum.[3] The first thing you notice about her is the straightness of her back, and the muscular strength of her movements. Her teeth are falling out, her eyesight seems clouded, and her hair is thin — but she could be a captain of the regiment, ordering her troops into battle. It does not surprise me that her history speaks of fierce quarrels with her children and her neighbors. Her jaw juts out as she chews tobacco. An Ezhava — a lower but not "scheduled" caste — Jayamma loses out two ways, lacking good social standing but ineligible for the affirmative action programs established by government for the lowest castes. She still lives in a squatter's colony on some government land on the outskirts of Trivandrum. Although I am told that I am seeing the worst poverty in all Trivandrum, given Kerala's generally high living standard, it seems remarkably good compared to poor areas in Bombay and in rural areas. The huts in the squat are clean and cool, solidly walled — some with mud, some with brick — decorated with photos and children's artwork; some of them command a stunning view of a lake covered with water hyacinth. Many have toilets, as the result of a local government program; both water and electricity reach the settlement reliably. Although the settlers were originally squatters, by now they have some property rights in the land. The bus stops right outside, on a well-maintained road; there is a hospital not far away; and there is a cheerful primary school in the squat itself. Older children all seem to

2. The amount of maintenance allotted to destitute women under India's Criminal Procedure Code was 180 rupees per month in 1986.
3. Unlike Vasanti, Jayamma has already been studied in the development economics literature (see "Jayamma, the Brick Worker" in Gulati, 1981; also Gulati and Gulati, 1997/1998).

be enrolled in school: clean and proud in their school uniforms, looking healthy and well nourished, they escort visitors around the settlement.

For approximately forty-five years, until her recent retirement, Jayamma went every day to the brick kiln and spent eight hours a day carrying bricks on her head, 500 to 700 bricks per day. (She never earned more than five rupees a day, and employment depends upon weather.) Jayamma balanced a plank on her head, stacked 20 bricks at a time on the plank, and then walked rapidly — balancing the bricks by the strength of her neck — to the kiln, where she then had to unload the bricks without twisting her neck, handing them two by two to the man who loads the kiln. Men in the brick industry typically do this sort of heavy labor for a while, and then graduate to the skilled (but less arduous) tasks of brick molding and kiln loading, which they can continue into middle and advanced ages. Those jobs pay up to twice as much, though they are less dangerous and lighter. Women are never considered for these promotions and are never permitted to learn the skills involved. Like most small businesses in India, the brick kiln is defined as a cottage industry and thus its workers are not protected by any union. All workers are badly paid, but women suffer special disabilities. Jayamma felt she had a bad deal, but she did not see any way of changing it.

Thus in her middle sixties, unable to perform the physically taxing job of brick carrying, Jayamma has no employment to fall back on. She is unwilling to become a domestic servant, because in her community such work is considered shameful and degrading. Jayamma adds a political explanation: "As a servant, your alliance is with a class that is your enemy." A widow, she is unable to collect a widow's pension from the government: the village office told her that she was ineligible because she has able-bodied sons, although her sons refuse to support her. Despite all these reversals (and others), Jayamma is tough, defiant, and healthy. She does not seem interested in talking, but she shows her visitors around, and makes sure that they are offered lime juice and water.

What is a philosopher doing in the slums of Trivandrum? And is there any reason to think that philosophy has anything to contribute, as such, to the amelioration of lives such as those of Vasanti and Jayamma? I shall argue that philosophy does indeed have something to contribute to the guidance of public life, in ways highly relevant to shaping policies that influence these women's lives. Focusing on the role of philosophy in articulating and debating norms of "the quality of life," I shall claim that philosophy provides a badly needed counterweight to simplistic approaches deriving from a certain brand of economic thought. More generally, philosophy has rich resources to offer to any policy maker who wants to think well about distributive justice in connection with women's inequality. But philosophy cannot do its job well unless it is informed by fact and experience: that is why the philosopher, while neither a fieldworker nor a politician, should try to get close to the reality she describes.

In this chapter I shall discuss these issues by narrating, first, the history of the quality of life project in which I was involved through the World Institute for Development Economics Research (WIDER) of the United Nations University. I shall then describe my subsequent work on women and quality of life, particularly in connection with the trip to India during which I met Vasanti and Jayamma. Finally, I shall reflect on the contribution philosophy can make to an international feminism, thinking both about the need that practice has for theory and the need that theory has for practice.

### The WIDER Project

In 1985, a new institute for development economics was founded under the auspices of the United Nations, after consultation with a wide range of specialists, prominently including Albert Hirschman, Paul Streeten, and Amartya Sen. The goal of the institute was to make development economics more interdisciplinary, enriching it with insights drawn from disciplines such as sociology, political theory, and anthropology. Sen, who had opposed the formation of the new institute, was therefore put on its board, so that he could ask skeptical questions and try to ensure that the institute's programs were not (as he had feared) replications of work that was already being done elsewhere. The acronym WIDER, chosen before the name itself, designated both the group's commitment to interdisciplinarity and its preoccupation with issues of undernutrition and poverty (therefore with making human beings "wider" in a very literal sense). A number of countries put in bids to be the location of the new institute, but the proposal by the Finnish government, which promised a small endowment and the use of excellent downtown Helsinki office space, was judged the best.[4] For its director,

4. Throughout its existence, the institute operated largely on soft money. Our project

the new institute chose Lal Jayawardena, a Sri Lankan economist and politician. Jayawardena's wife, Kumari Jayawardena, a leading writer on international feminism (see Jayawardena, 1986, 1995), played a valuable role in shaping the institute, although her political work in Sri Lanka did not permit her to spend long stretches of time there. For this reason and because of Sen's long-standing commitment to feminism, the institute, from the first, put problems of sex equality at the center of its program.

The institute undertook many different types of projects, discussing approaches to macroeconomics, the balance of trade, poverty and nutrition, technology and development, and many other topics.[5] Its general orientation was left-of-center, at least in U.S. terms; its leading economists tended to be neoclassical rather than Marxian, but neoclassical economists who were critical of some prevailing conceptions and models in the field, and who did not believe that free markets could solve all problems of social justice. Although the institute did have some year-round resident scholars,[6] on the whole it functioned by putting scholars who worked elsewhere under year-round contract as "Research Advisors." A Research Advisor was responsible for organizing a project, under the supervision of the director and the board; he or she was expected to spend one month a year at WIDER, but much of the work usually took place elsewhere. Typically he or she organized conferences and research projects involving the participation of many other scholars. In the very first year of the institute's operations, Sen resigned from the board in order to become a Research Advisor, directing the institute's program on Poverty and Nutrition, the program that produced the monumental work *Hunger and Public Action* (Drèze & Sen, 1989) along with three edited volumes of articles on the same topic (Drèze & Sen, 1990-91; Drèze, Sen, & Hussain, 1995). In addition, Drèze and Sen worked more intensively on India, producing the book *India: Economic Development and Social Opportunity* (Drèze & Sen, 1995), accompanied by

was eventually funded primarily by the Swedish Development Agency (SEDA), under the auspices of Karl Tham, now Minister for Education in Sweden's government which is currently led by the Social Democrats.

5. The studies are published in a series from Clarendon Press called WIDER Studies in Development Economics. There is also a series of WIDER Working Papers.

6. Two leading examples were the Bangladeshi nutritional economist Siddiq Osmani — see Osmani (1992), which powerfully criticizes cultural relativism in nutrition science (i.e., the argument that "stunting" is a felicitous adaptation to local conditions) — and Iranian sociologist Valentine Moghadam, who coordinated women's programs (see Moghadam, 1989, 1990, 1993).

a volume of regional studies (Drèze & Sen, 1997), all commissioned by the WIDER project.

I first came to WIDER in the summer of 1986, to participate in a conference on Value and Technology, for which I had coauthored a paper with Sen. The Value-Technology project was codirected by Stephen Marglin, a well-known left-wing economist (e.g., S. A. Marglin, 1984), and his wife Frédérique, an anthropologist who works on women in India.[7] Throughout much of my time at WIDER, the Marglins were Sen's and my major intellectual adversaries. They took the very plausible view that development is a normative concept, and that we should not proceed ahead with "economic development" without asking normative questions; plausibly again, they argued that opulence was not the only relevant aspect of people's quality of life, and that we should ask about the impact of economic growth on the other constituents. Growth, they rightly insisted, does not always mean "development" in the sense of things getting better. However, from that plausible starting point they leapt rather rapidly to the implausible conclusion that no traditional practice ought to be changed, and that economic growth and agricultural modernization should be discouraged on the grounds that they disrupt traditions. From what struck Sen and me as a vantage point of secure distance from the real sufferings of people, they romanticized such traditional practices as menstruation taboos, child temple prostitution, traditional gendered divisions of labor, and even the absence of smallpox vaccine — which, in an extraordinary moment, Frédérique Marglin blamed for having eradicated the cult of Sittala Devi, the goddess to whom one prays in order to avert the disease (F.A. Marglin, 1990).

From the first, Sen objected vehemently to the depiction of this reactionary traditionalism as "Indian culture." Sen comes from the liberal and critical Bengali intelligentsia, which introduced educational reforms for women in the early nineteenth century, in advance of most Western nations. His mother was a student and friend of Rabindranath Tagore, the cosmopolitan humanist thinker, and he grew up in Santiniketan,[8] where Tagore founded his experimental school, which became Vishva-Bharati University (All-the-World University). Far from being a "West

---

7. See F.A. Marglin (1985), a work whose nostalgic and aestheticizing attitude to the practice of child temple prostitution prefigured many of the debates we had with the Marglins at WIDER.
8. Santiniketan is in West Bengal, about three hours by train from Calcutta.

ernized" Indian, Sen is deeply learned in Indian texts and history. Impatient with the tendency of Americans to romanticize India as the mystical "other," he has throughout his career stressed the variety of Indian traditions, and especially the presence from an early date of rationalist and critical schools of thought (Sen, 1997a, 1997b). We discovered that there was a good fit between some things Sen wanted to say about internal debate in India and some things I was thinking about Aristotle's notion of critical refinement of the *endoxa* (reliable beliefs). We therefore decided that Sen's presentation at the Marglins's conference would be a coauthored paper, and we wrote "Internal Criticism and Indian Rationalist Traditions" (Sen & Nussbaum, 1989).

This was a methodological paper, focused on the importance of hearing voices of critique when a tradition is described. But Sen and I had already discovered another convergence in our philosophical interests, between his *capabilities approach* and my interest in Aristotle's ideas of human functioning and capability as a basis for political distribution.[9] The capabilities approach has above all been used as a measure of the quality of life in a nation; we have also used it to articulate a view of the proper goal of politics.[10]

The approach claims that when we ask how people are doing in a nation or region, it is not enough to look at their satisfactions; for satisfactions can be easily deformed by adaptation to a bad state of affairs, or by habits of luxury.[11] Nor is it enough to look at the presence or absence of resources, even when their distribution is taken into account. For individuals differ in their needs for different kinds of resources, and also in their ability to convert resources into valued functionings. For example, people who encounter cultural obstacles to literacy, or working outside the home, will need larger amounts of resources in order to become literate, or capable of working, than people who do not encounter such obstacles. For these reasons, any approach that really wants to know how people are doing needs to look at what they are actually able to do and to be. The approach looks not at actual functioning, since in-

9. Indeed, Sen's capabilities approach, though not directly inspired by a reading of Aristotle, clearly owes a good deal to Marx's reading of Aristotle, which focused on the importance of making "truly human functioning," rather than the distribution of commodities in and of itself, the central political goal (see Nussbaum, 1988/1992b, 1995a).

10. Central statements of the approach by Sen can be found in Sen (1980/1982, 1984, 1985a, 1985b, 1993)

11. This idea, which is prominent in the ancient philosophers, has been developed by Elster (1983), and by Sen in many places (e.g., Sen, 1995).

dividuals in a liberal society may choose not to avail themselves of opportunities to function, but at the opportunities or "capabilities" they have. These, however, are understood not in a merely formal manner, but as involving a set of material preconditions, which must be met before one would be willing to say that the person is genuinely capable of going to school, or taking a job. Our central claim has been that these capabilities of persons are the measure of quality of life, and that a central goal of politics should be to provide all citizens with at least a basic level of these capabilities.[12]

The capabilities approach advances some universal cross-cultural norms that should guide public policy. I have from the beginning been concerned to advance and defend an explicit list of such norms, basing my argument on a notion of "truly human functioning" that has roots in Aristotle and the early Marx.[13] Sen has not committed himself either to such a definite list or to the Aristotelian mode of justification I articulate, but he does commit himself to universal norms of several sorts, in the areas such as bodily well-being, education, and the political liberties. From the first, therefore, Sen and I have been concerned to answer objections from the side of cultural relativism. We do so in part by stressing that the approach is designed to leave a great deal of room for plural specification of the major capabilities; in part by stressing that the goal is capability, not actual functioning (leaving individuals free to choose which functions they will actually perform). I now interpret the list of central capabilities in the spirit of a Rawlsian "political liberalism," as a core of basic goods about which citizens can agree, though they differ about their more comprehensive conceptions of the good (Nussbaum, 1999b, in press-a).[14] But throughout our work, Sen and I have also stressed that our universalism derives support from a complex understanding of cultures as sites of resistance and internal critique. Our paper for the Marglin conference was our first statement of

12. However, Sen has also prominently used the approach as a measure of equality, and I have argued that systematic inequalities reflecting traditional social hierarchies are themselves cases of capability failure.
13. One might also mention Mill's development of an Aristotelian idea of human flourishing in Chapter 3 of *On Liberty*, although Mill's approach is perfectionist, aimed at functioning as a goal, whereas my approach aims at capability as goal in order to construct a type of political liberalism.
14. Sen has not taken a stand on this issue; but see Sen (1994) where he appears to endorse a comprehensive rather than a political form of liberalism.

this methodological point; it thus complemented the substantive work on capabilities that was already in progress.

The Marglin conference combined postmodernist jargon and reactionary politics in an extraordinary way. Western medicine was attacked on the grounds that it presupposed a "binary opposition" between life and death (S.A. Marglin, 1990b). Traditional antifemale taboos were defended on the grounds that they ensured an "embedded way of life," the same values (of sex hierarchy) prevailing in both the home and the workplace (S.A. Marglin, 1990a). We heard that all criticism of tradition is tyrannical, on the grounds that Derrida and Foucault have shown that there is "no privileged place to stand." At one point Eric Hobsbawm (an onlooker) was asked to leave the room, after he had pointed out that the defense of tradition is often constructed by reactionary political forces for their own benefit.[15]

I sat there thinking how terrible it was that this marvelous opportunity to inject good normative ethical argument into the development and policy arena should be thrown away on such intellectually slipshod work. If there was a need to debate about relativism and universalism, fine, but it should be done well, at a high level of philosophical sophistication. Again, if we were going to question reigning economic models of development, fine again, but let it be done with good philosophy rather than trendy sloganeering. I drew up a proposal for a project bringing philosophy together with economics, focusing on the articulation of the concept of the "quality of life." The proposal was accepted, and I became a Research Advisor at WIDER. From 1987 to 1993, I was under year-round contract; I spent a month there every summer. At first, Sen helped organize our conferences; later, as Sen was increasingly involved with the hunger project, the director approved the addition of Jonathan Glover to the team, and Glover served as Research Advisor from 1989 to 1993.

In some ways it was a long leap from working on Aristotle to working on development and the quality of life. One thing I quickly realized was how inadequate my own prior education had been in preparing me to function in an international setting. Everyone I met from Sri Lanka

---

15. For an account of some of these moments, see Nussbaum (1992a, 1995b). Sen's and my paper was refused publication in the Marglins's conference volume, because it did not "fit" with the orientation of the other papers (it certainly did not), and it was later published elsewhere (Sen & Nussbaum, 1989).

and India knew a lot about Aristotle, but I knew virtually nothing about Buddhism, Hinduism, or Islam. I had, and have, a lot of learning to do.[16] In another way, however, my training had prepared me to make a contribution, since Aristotle's ethical and political thought, as I continue to believe, offers rich resources for contemporary political thought, particularly when we try to define norms of life quality. It also soon seemed clear to me that philosophical arguments about relativism and universalism, and about utilitarianism and the critique of utilitarianism, had a valuable contribution to make to the further development and defense of the capabilities approach. Over the years, Sen has continued to focus on the political economy aspects of the approach and on the normative critique of utilitarianism, while I have focused more on the critique of relativism, on issues of justification and basic philosophical motivation (the notion of "truly human functioning"), and on the articulation of the substantive content of the list of capabilities. Although we continue to differ on some important issues, we also agree in allying the approach rather closely with liberalism of a Rawlsian type, and in insisting that it offers a friendly amendment to liberalism, rather than a wholesale replacement (Nussbaum, 1998; Sen, 1994a). We agree in stressing the central role of the political liberties among the human capabilities.[17]

Our first conference, then, addressed the general issue of the quality of life. Its aim was to provide a solid basis for new policies of quality of life measurement and for innovation in other areas of development planning. When policy makers and development professionals compared countries in those days, they used to use gross national product (GNP) per capita as a handy measure of quality of life. This crude measure, of course, does not even ask about the distribution of wealth and income, far less about elements of people's lives that are important but not perfectly correlated with GNP, even when distribution has been weighed in: infant mortality, life expectancy, educational opportunities, the quality of race and gender relations, the presence or absence of political and religious liberty. Even the slightly less crude move of polling people about their satisfactions does not do well enough, because people's satisfaction reports are frequently shaped by lack of information, lack of opportunity, intimidation, and sheer habit. The aim of the

16. This experience led me to focus on the importance of the study of non-Western traditions in undergraduate liberal arts curricula (Nussbaum, 1997a).

17. I have recently allied the approach with political rather than comprehensive liberalism; Sen has not made his view on this question clear. For a clear account of our approaches and their differences, see Crocker (1992, 1995).

first phase of the quality-of-life project was to confront development economists coming out of the narrow economic-utilitarian tradition with the wealth of subtle argument on these questions that philosophy had long been producing. We planned to have debate both about the adequacy of utilitarianism as a normative framework for public choice, and also about the ideas of cultural relativism and universalism that been discussed so unclearly at the Marglin conference. We also planned to focus on two specific issues, health and sex equality, issues that seemed likely to provide valuable tests of the merits of the different approaches.[18]

Why did we think philosophy would help us make progress on these issues? The simplistic aspects of a Marglin-type approach to culture have been criticized from within anthropology and sociology themselves, where scholars now increasingly stress the fact that cultures are not homogeneous but complex, not tranquil but suffused with conflict.[19] The assumptions of development economics have been criticized from within economics (e.g., by feminist economists working on bargaining models of the family, Dasgupta, 1993, chap. 11; Sen, 1991),[20] and also by scholars in political science and sociology. To some extent, then, the shortcomings we found in both groups of opponents might have been addressed simply by bringing in different social scientists. We did use such thinkers in our project.[21] But we gave philosophers a central role from the beginning. One immediate reason for this decision was that the Marglins themselves, like other postmodernist relativists, had used appeals to philosophical authority to underwrite their claims. Without going over any arguments, they had proceeded as if the very names of Derrida and Foucault, could show that these issues had been settled. In gaining a hearing for our universalist proposal, therefore, we needed to

18. Although the 1987 conference group consisted primarily of philosophers and economists, we also included two Scandinavian sociologists who had been using a plural metric of life quality similar to the one we were inclined to support.

19. For just two valuable recent examples of such an approach, see Comaroff and Comaroff (1991, 1997); and Kniss (1997), who shows division and conflict in a community generally imagined as especially peaceful and homogeneous.

20. For other useful examples of bargaining approaches, see Agarwal (1994, 1997); L. Chen, Huq, and D'Souza (1981); Lundberg and Pollak (1996).

21. Sociologists Robert Eriksson, Erik Allardt, Nancy Chodorow and Valentine Moghadam, anthropologist Martha Chen, political theorists Susan Moller Okin and Seyla Benhabib, economists John Roemer, Jean Drèze, Amartya Sen, and (in a related project) Partha Dasgupta, all played a role in our first two conferences. The third conference included, in addition, health policy and medical experts. Other WIDER projects involved still more social scientists from other disciplines.

show the real dimensions and complexity of the philosophical debate and to provide philosophical backing for universalism. But there were two deeper reasons for introducing philosophy into the world of development economics.

The first is that, on foundational issues such as relativism and universalism, or the pros and cons of utilitarianism, philosophers generally produce more rigorous and elaborate arguments than are typically found in the social sciences. There is, of course, no orthodoxy among philosophers on such questions, but debates are typically refined and developed in such a way that real progress is made: the issues are clearly demarcated, many untenable contenders are ruled out, and so forth, until we understand the competing proposals and the arguments that support them with considerable clarity. This happens far less, I believe, in other related fields. There is no shortage of discussion of cultural relativism in the social sciences, for example; but it is usually not as systematic, rigorous, or wide-ranging as the debate in philosophy, which typically draws together considerations from the philosophy of science, the philosophy of language, and the philosophy of mind, using considerations from these areas to illuminate the complex issues of culture. In general, philosophy in our culture has high standards of rigor and refinement in argument; debates on related issues in other professions often seem sloppy by comparison, or lacking in a set of distinctions that has already enabled philosophers to make progress.

Nor is this simply an accident of professional evolution. Philosophers in the Western tradition are the heirs of Socrates. They have a commitment to the critical scrutiny of arguments that makes them good at refining distinctions, detecting fallacies, and doing the kind of work that all thinkers about society — and indeed, at some level all citizens — should be doing, but often do not do.[22] It is not obvious that other disciplines really believe that "the unexamined life is not worth living for a human being," or that rhetoric is inferior to the humble search for correct accounts. Philosophy, while certainly not without its own pockets of dogmatism and blindness, tries hard to live in the spirit of the Socratic ideal, and does so not too badly.[23]

22. For this reason, I argue that, although in principle the abilities of "Socratic self-examination" that citizens need could be imparted through courses in many different disciplines, in practice this will best be done by courses in philosophy (Nussbaum, 1997a).

23. For my understanding of the Socratic elenchus and its contribution see Nussbaum (1997d).

The second reason for making philosophy central to a project on international development can also be traced to the example of Socrates. Philosophers ask the "What is it?" question. Every academic profession has its core concepts, and all make at least some attempt to define them. But philosophy, from its start, has been that irritating gadfly that keeps asking questions about the core concepts — both its own and (irritatingly, but valuably) those of other disciplines and people. Sometimes this function has been understood in too narrow a way: as if, for example, moral philosophy should only engage in conceptual analysis and not in the construction and refinement of theories; or as if conceptual analysis of the most relevant sort did not require attention to empirical facts. But if we have a sufficiently subtle and inclusive understanding of the "What is it?" question, it seems right to think that its pursuit is one of the central tasks of our discipline.

Thus many other disciplines, especially economics, concern themselves with the ideas of utilitarianism; but it falls to philosophy, above all, to ask what this theory is, how it is related to other ethical theories, and how to define each of the core concepts on which it relies. Other disciplines concern themselves with ideas of human flourishing, of "the good life," but it is the special job of philosophy to ask what exactly that obscure notion might be, and how we might adjudicate the debate among different rival specifications of it. Other disciplines (e.g., law and public policy) use notions of freedom and responsibility, and have some working definitions of these notions; but it falls to philosophy to think through the "What is it?" question here too, debating the merits of different ways of conceiving of these obscure and difficult notions, until by now a highly refined set of alternatives has been worked out, of which legal and political academics are usually only dimly aware. Economists and political scientists are all the time talking about preference, choice, and desire. But it is the special job of philosophy to provide a perspicuous investigation of these foundational concepts, distinguishing desire from intention, emotion, impulse, and other psychological items, asking questions about the relationship of each of these to belief and learning, and so forth. By pursuing these inquiries, philosophy has, again, evolved a highly refined account of the alternatives in this area, and its accounts show that many aspects of at least some parts of economics rest on a foundation that is not just crude, but also highly unreliable (Nussbaum, 1997b). Again, thinkers in a variety of fields have shown sympathy with the capabilities approach; but it falls to philosophy to investigate more precisely the all-important distinction between capability and functioning,[24] and related distinctions between different types of human capabilities.[25] Finally, philosophy characteristically, and far more than other fields, turns its own "What is it?" question on its own methods and inquiries, asking, for example, what justification is in political theory, or what judgments, intuitions, or emotions a political argument might reasonably rely on. These questions are rarely asked with comparable pertinacity and subtlety in other disciplines concerned with social life.

These conceptual inquiries are sometimes viewed as examples of obsessive intellectual fussiness; they have, however, important practical consequences, which need to be taken into account in practical political programs. This can be shown in many areas. But to stick to the capabilities approach, the distinction between capabilities and functioning is of the greatest practical importance: a policy that aims at a single desired mode of functioning will often be quite different from one that tries to promote opportunities for citizens to choose that function or not to choose it. Thus, a policy aimed at urging all women to seek employment outside the home will be very different from a policy that aims at giving all women the choice to work outside the home or not to do so. Both policies will need to protect women from discrimination in employment and from intimidation and harassment in the employment process. But the latter, unlike the former, will also need to attend to the social meaning of domestic labor, promoting a sense that a traditional domestic life is worthwhile and consistent with human dignity; it will also need to make such choices economically feasible for women, and not unduly risky, by attending to the economic value of domestic labor

24. Both Sen and I argue that respect for choice should lead us to make capability, rather than functioning, the political goal; by contrast, perfectionist liberalisms such as those of John Stuart Mill and Raz (1986) prefer to construe the goal in terms of functioning.

25. I argue that there are three distinct types of capabilities that need to figure in the approach: *basic capabilities* or the innate equipment of human beings that enables them, with sufficient support and care, to attain higher-level capabilities; *internal capabilities*, or states of the person that would, in suitable circumstances, prove sufficient for the exercise of the relevant functioning; and *combined capabilities*, or the internal state combined with suitable external circumstances for the exercise of the function. For example, a woman who has had some education and training, but who is threatened with physical violence should she leave the house to look for work, has the internal but not the combined capability to seek employment outside the house. Politics should aim at the production of combined capabilities. See Nussbaum (1998) for the most recent statement of this position.

when calculating settlement after divorce. Similarly, it seems very important to distinguish the different types of human capabilities: a policy that aims simply at putting people in the internal state to function well will often be very different from a policy that aims both at creating the internal prerequisites of functioning and at shaping the surrounding material and social environment so that it is favorable for the exercise of choice in the relevant area. If this distinction is not clearly made, the merits of different policy choices will probably not be clearly debated. Thus, a policy aimed at promoting only the internal capability for freedom of expression would only need to educate people; it would not need to construct circumstances in which they can actually speak freely without penalty. A policy aimed at women's internal capability for employment outside the home would need to focus only on education and skills training; a policy aimed at the combined capability would need to focus, as well, on nondiscrimination in hiring, on sexual harassment, and on protecting women from threat and intimidation from members of their own family. The "What is it?" question, in short, is profoundly practical. In its absence, public life will be governed by "what is usually said in a jumbled fashion," as Aristotle so nicely put this point.[26]

Aristotle used this Socratic idea of philosophy to argue that philosophy is an important part of the equipment of every person who aims to take an active role in public life. And for the two reasons I have given here, I believe, with him, that philosophy is an essential part of the training of any citizen who will need to deliberate with other citizens, vote, serve on a jury, or just think clearly, in areas involving debates and concepts such as the ones I have mentioned. I have therefore argued elsewhere that two semesters of philosophy should be part of the undergraduate liberal arts education of every college or university undergraduate (Nussbaum, 1997a, chap. 1). But even those who are not persuaded by that educational proposal should acknowledge, I believe, that philosophers are badly needed in academic deliberations about

---

26. *Eudemian Ethics* 1216a30-39: "For from what is said truly but not clearly, as we advance we will also get clarity, always moving from what is usually said in a jumbled fashion to a more perspicuous view. There is a difference in every inquiry between arguments that are said in a philosophical way and those that are not. Hence we must not think that it is superfluous for the political person to engage in the sort of reflection that makes perspicuous not only the 'that' but also the 'why': for this is the contribution of the philosopher in each area." Aristotle connects understanding the "why" closely to the task of giving definitions and accounts.

public policy, as critical scrutinizers of arguments and as obsessive pur-
suers of the foundational concepts and questions. For here if anywhere,
it is important to seek rigor and conceptual clarity. To perform their role
successfully, however, philosophers will have to overcome two obstacles, one created by the resistance of economics to foundational criticism, the other by philosophy's own professional habits.

Our first conference assembled a distinguished group of philosophers, all of whom did interesting work (Nussbaum & Sen, 1993). But in
two related ways the conference, which was supposed to provide policy
makers and development workers with a new conceptual basis for their
efforts, seemed to me a failure. Both involved the reluctance of specialists to go beyond the models and vocabularies they standardly use in
writing for fellow specialists. First, we more or less failed entirely to get
leading economists to take the philosophical critique of their foundations seriously. The philosophers in our group were deliberately chosen
for diversity of views; they included Utilitarians, Kantians, and neo-
Aristotelians. We wanted, indeed, to highlight arguments that could be
made for and against the capabilities approach. But even the Utilitarian
philosophers had many conceptual and foundational criticisms to make
of economic welfarism; in many respects the type of Utilitarianism
defended by the philosophers who wished to defend it was far closer to
neo-Aristotelianism and Kantianism, as a result of debates that have
unfolded over the decades, than it was to the simpler form of Utilitarianism dominant in neoclassical economics. There was unanimous
agreement among the philosophers that the foundations of economics
need thorough rethinking. Those criticisms, however, had little effect.
With the exception of John Roemer, who has long since been a quasi-
philosopher, nobody seemed to understand that what we were saying
had implications for the ways in which models should henceforth be
built. The general reaction was, "You have a very interesting profession
there," or (still worse), "Sen is now doing philosophy, not economics."
As Roemer observed at the conference, economists are highly committed to their models, which involve a great deal of formal sophistication;
frequently they are selected for success in the profession in accordance
with formal ability. If people just talk ordinary language and do not present them with alternative models, they are not likely to switch over to a
new way of thinking about things, especially if it involves jettisoning
formal work in which a lot has been invested. The philosophical recal-
citrance of economists, and their refusal to admit that their work does

make substantive philosophical commitments that need to be scrutinized, continues to be one of the greatest barriers to philosophy's effective participation in public life. Given the public dominance of economics, any profession that cannot get itself taken seriously by it will have tough going. But economics is extremely self-satisfied, and its tendency to repudiate nonformal and foundational work as irrelevant to its concerns poses a major problem.

The philosophers had an analogous problem. The people in our team did good work; and yet they did not altogether fulfill their assignment. Sen and I commissioned the papers (with very generous stipends), asking people to spend time familiarizing themselves with pertinent pieces of the development literature, so that they could relate their abstract discussions to these debates. We also asked them to address an audience of policy makers and nonspecialists. Nonetheless, people have a marked tendency to present the work that they are doing anyway, and philosophers are in the habit of addressing their peers, rather than the general public. I see no reason why the issues of our conference cannot be discussed, at a high degree of sophistication, in a clear and jargon-free language, with concrete factual or narrative examples.[27] But philosophers need to have more practice in this type of writing if they are to do it effectively. The fact that this type of writing is not rewarded by the profession or encouraged in graduate programs poses an obstacle to philosophy's public influence.

We had already decided that the next conference would focus on women's quality of life. Women's issues, as I said, had been at the center of our concern from the beginning, both for their own sake, as especially urgent issues of justice, and for the clear challenge they posed both to cultural relativism and to normative utilitarianism. Women are especially likely to be the losers if we defer uncritically to local traditions, or, rather, to the voices of powerful men that have usually been permitted to define what a tradition is; they also frequently have preferences that are distorted by absence of information, by intimidation, and by long schooling in self-abnegation. Looking at what a normative theory can say about these problems offers us a good way of assessing that theory.

27. Brock (1993b) is a fine example of such clear writing, and of research specifically responsive to our commission. Taylor (1993) is another extremely lucid and readable paper. It is interesting that both these authors have spent time in practical politics, and therefore know from experience what sort of writing will be effective.

Reflecting on our previous difficulties, I made several decisions. First, persuading the economists could wait, and we would just get on with our work; henceforth, we included only Roemer and Sen on the economic side of our project. Second, we needed a field study so that the philosophers would have something very concrete around which to orient their work. We therefore commissioned Martha Chen to do a field study of women's right to work in India and Bangladesh.[28] We asked her to focus on women's right to work because we felt that this would provide a fertile starting point for discussion of many related human capabilities, such as nutrition and health, bodily integrity, political participation, dignity and self-respect. Third, instead of presenting a menu of different philosophical options, as the first conference had done, we would now try to produce a more coherent philosophical account, focusing on the issue of relativism and universalism. Finally, we would try to integrate into the project philosophers from developing countries who also had some contact with fieldwork and the women's movements in their own countries.[29]

The 1990 conference from which *Women, Culture, and Development* grew was, I believe, our most successful conference. Our aim was to articulate and defend a form of universalism based on the capabilities approach, answering objections from the side of relativism. At the same time, we aimed to develop a more complex conception of cultural tradi-

28. Chen is a highly experienced field worker and social scientist who has spent over half her life in India and is fluent in three modern Indian languages, as well as Sanskrit. She had worked closely with Jean Drèze on a research project involving widows, and was therefore well acquainted with our work at WIDER. Because she understands the philosophical concepts and yet has experience in fieldwork that we lack, she has been and continues to be an invaluable intermediary. She is also an eloquent writer, who has the rare ability to let real women's voices emerge clearly (M.A. Chen, 1983).

29. This was not easy, because philosophy, unlike economics, is not an international profession; it lacks a common language and a common set of paradigms. Nor are the reigning paradigms especially revealing of indigenous thought (e.g., one philosopher from Brazil, who was highly recommended to us, turned out to be a graduate of University of California at Santa Cruz and spoke entirely in the abstract language of French philosophy. We attempted to find people with whom we spoke a sufficiently common philosophical language so that we could communicate reasonably well, and who, at the same time, related their general claims to their own cultural and religious traditions, and who had done practical political work in addition to their philosophical work. In this way, we integrated into the project Roop Rekha Verma, Nkiru Nzegwu, Xiaorong Li, and Margarita Valdés (who had already been a commentator at our previous conference). We were also helped very much by the fine work of Moghadam, who had recently been appointed to reside at WIDER year-round, coordinating women's projects.

tion and intracultural debate than is frequently used in such discussions (a return to the theme of Sen's and my original coauthored paper).

As tends to happen, people defended a universal approach to human functioning in their own characteristic ways, and the contributions were thus heterogeneous in terminology and philosophical orientation.[30] Nonetheless, we converged on many important matters, and it was intellectually fruitful to see how similar arguments against traditionalism and relativism could be made from a variety of distinct philosophical starting points. Especially valuable was Chen's fine field study (accompanied by a film), which provided a solid starting point for our more abstract ruminations. Chen's detailed account of two representative women, secluded widow Metha Bai and women's employment activist Saleha Begum, caught the imaginations of the participants and provided a valuable focal point for discussion of a wide range of human capabilities. Our feminist writers, whether philosophers or not, wrote better for a general public audience, on the whole, than had the writers of the previous volume — perhaps because feminist theory has usually kept its feet squarely planted in the empirical reality of women's lives. Because of our focus on the field study, the papers did not suffer from the remote nonpractical abstractness that often characterized the papers in the earlier volume.

We held one more conference, in 1992. Glover was its primary organizer, and it focused on new reproductive technologies and their relation to women's equality. Its aim was to examine a wide range of new reproductive techniques in the context of women's capabilities and functioning, asking what line an approach such as ours should take about the roles of law and public policy in the area of reproductive choice. For this conference we assembled an unusually broad and internationally diverse group of participants, but the philosophical level of the contributions was uneven, and we are still at work supplementing this material and getting it revised for publication.

We had two further plans. One involved questioning the anthropocentrism of the whole capabilities approach, and trying to figure out what the approach ought to say about the status of other species and the world of nature. The second involved asking about the relationship of

30. Hilary and Ruth Anna Putnam began from Dewey, Seyla Benhabib from Habermas, Jonathan Glover from a type of utilitarianism, Onora O'Neill and Roop Rekha Verma from a type of Kantianism, and quite a few of us from a type of liberal Aristotelianism already familiar from the prior project.

the capabilities approach to various concrete areas of public and civic life. We had planned an ambitious conference — which, among other things, would have brought various religious thinkers to WIDER to talk about the relationship of our universal account of human capabilities to the understandings of the major religious traditions. This is a topic that had been notably absent in our project.[31]

These plans never materialized, because of the abrupt curtailment of research activities at WIDER. It is painful to describe these events, because they show so clearly the pitfalls of trying to do good intellectual work within the United Nations (UN) bureaucracy, which ought to be a tremendous source of support for such work. But the United Nations University, the branch of the UN under which WIDER had been located, is a rather low-level enterprise, run by an agency that does not care a lot (or cares negatively) about good intellectual work. When Jayawardena had completed his two terms as director, UN rules did not permit him to serve again; at this point, the United Nations University hierarchy intervened to ensure that WIDER's future would not involve high-profile research projects such as our own and others that had made WIDER a name in the professions. The difficult sequence of events, during the administration of an acting director handpicked by the bureaucratic agency, included the firing of almost all the year-round researchers, the refusal to accept new proposals by Research Advisors, and a series of false accusations against Jayawardena that caused most of us to wish to have nothing further to do with the future of WIDER.[32] There is now a new director, but he has decided that the future of WIDER will involve standard noninterdisciplinary development projects, which appear to be intellectually unambitious.

Those of us most committed to the work at WIDER now carry it on under other auspices.[33] Sen and his coauthor Jean Drèze have spent the

31. I continue to feel this a major gap, which I am attempting to address in my own current work (e.g., Nussbaum, 1997c; Olyan & Nussbaum, 1998).
32. Further complications involved Finnish politics, because a leading candidate for the presidency of Finland (who eventually won the election) is a close friend of Jayawardena; his political opponents saw blackening WIDER as a way of scoring political points prior to the election.
33. David Crocker does related work at the Center for Philosophy and Public Policy at the University of Maryland; he has focused on the ethics of consumption and global stewardship (see Crocker & Linden, 1998, which includes several WIDER colleagues as contributors). Glover has recently become Director of the Institute for Law and Medical Ethics at King's College, London; Valentine Moghadam is Director of Women's Studies at Illinois State University, where she continues her work on women and modernization.

past few years completing the ambitious WIDER project on India that has generated the book *India: Economic Development and Social Opportunity*, as well as a companion volume of regional field studies (Drèze & Sen, 1995, 1997). Although much of his current research lies in social choice theory, his other primary area of expertise, Sen regularly writes on development issues, such as women's hunger, global population, and India's rationalist traditions (Sen, 1990, 1994b, 1996, 1997a, 1997b).

A particularly important practical project growing out of the WIDER work can be found in the *Human Development Reports*, issued annually since 1991 by the United Nations Development Programme (UNDP) in New York. The *Reports* use a theoretical approach designed by Sen, Sudhir Anand, and other economists sympathetic to the capabilities approach, most of whom worked at WIDER. It is one thing to grouse about the use of GNP to measure quality of life; it is another to propose an alternative measure.

The *Reports* use a variety of aggregative measures to rank nations. Since 1991, the *Reports* have ranked countries in accordance with the Human Development Index (HDI), a measure that includes three components: longevity, knowledge and income, and a complex weighting process described in the 1991 *Report*. The *Reports* list countries in the order of their HDI rank, thus attempting to provide governments with incentives to compete for better rankings along these parameters. Such a measure as HDI needs to be somewhat cruder than would be ideal, because it must use existing data from the 173 countries that are ranked.[34] But even if the measure is not ideal, just getting richer comparisons out there in quantitative form is one big step forward. And despite imperfections, the *Human Development Reports* continues to provide an important contribution of theory to practice.

### Indian Women and Feminist Internationalism

After the breakup of WIDER, I continued working on women's quality of life, using my own research funds. Because I felt that at this point I needed to see and learn more about how poor women were really thinking about their lives, I went to India in the spring of 1997 for a field trip, visiting various women's development projects, especially

---

34. My own normative proposal, including, as it does, such hard-to-measure items as emotional capacities and the preservation of human dignity, is not a good basis for a measure that the UNDP can go out and use right now.

those connected with credit and employment. I had decided that it would be best for me to focus on a single country that I could hope to get to know in some depth, rather than (as often happens) to cull examples from dozens of countries where one could not possibly appreciate their social context. I chose India because I had spent time there before, because I have contacts there, because it is a democracy where one can hear what people really think, and because I love the country. Martha Chen was my invaluable guide, translator, and coordinator. During my previous visit to India in 1988, I had spent my time primarily in Delhi, Calcutta, and Santiniketan, and had learned a lot about the Bengali renaissance from spending time with the noted Bengali writer Amita Sen both in Santiniketan itself and on many other occasions in Britain and the United States. But I had never pursued my own intellectual projects in the field, and I felt I needed to do this before writing any further.

The project in connection with which I took the trip is a series of lectures developing my version of the capabilities approach as a basis for an international feminism. I defend a substantive account of the central capabilities as a basis for a political-liberal consensus about some core aspects of basic social justice. I argue that people should have these capabilities, whatever else they also have and pursue. In the process, I develop a framework for justifying the list of capabilities, in connection with an Aristotelian/Marxian idea of truly human functioning; I also relate my substantive-good approach to various informed-desire and procedural approaches. Finally, I address several topics that the WIDER project on women did not address: in particular religion, and distributive justice within the family. The capabilities approach is, of course, not restricted to women, but I focus on these problems because of their urgency and centrality. Moreover, the general merit of the approach becomes especially evident when we see that it gives us better ways to handle these problems than do other prominent approaches to thinking about the quality of life.

I told everyone I met that I was a feminist political theorist writing on the quality of life and developing a universal cross-cultural account of that issue with a particular focus on women. I said that I wanted my account to be not remote from reality, but responsive to what people were really thinking about their lives. And I asked lots of questions about how people saw their lives: what were the central constituents of life quality that one might focus on for purposes of formal and informal social planning. I shall focus here on just three portions of the trip that are exemplary of ways in which it influenced the development of my ideas.[35]

Toward the beginning of my trip, I joined Martha Chen in Ahmedabad, Gujerat, where she had been working for some months gathering data for a project on the lives of widows in rural India. With her I spent time at SEWA. I met with SEWA's current director, its heads of child care and education, various officers of the SEWA women's bank, and a variety of the women who participate in SEWA projects, among them Vasanti. One of the highlights of my trip was a meeting with SEWA's founder, Ela Bhatt, one of the world's most influential women's activists, who now organizes informal sector workers worldwide. A woman of electric intelligence and deeply moving simplicity, she organized SEWA around Gandhian principles of self-rule. Just as, for Gandhi, India could only achieve self-rule and dignity if it first established economic independence from Britain, so, Bhatt argues, women need to focus on economic independence from men, if they are to achieve the appropriate level of autonomy and dignity. As I shall later describe, Bhatt's observations about the importance of credit, property rights, and self-sufficiency have been especially influential in leading me to revise some of my views.[36]

35. The trip also included many meetings with scholars and activists, who were in various ways of great help to me. These included Muslim political theorist Zoya Hasan, who writes about internal diversity within Islamic culture; economist Bina Agarwal, who writes on gender and land rights, developing a bargaining model of the family; feminist lawyer Indira Jaising, who runs The Lawyers Cooperative, a group that takes on sex equality and sexual harassment cases and publishes a journal devoted to issues of sex equality in the law; anthropologist Veena Das, who writes about resistance to the dominant culture, from a viewpoint sympathetic to cultural relativism; publisher Ritu Menon, director of the feminist press Kali, who later organized a lecture for me to present my ideas, at the end of my trip; Romila Thapar, a distinguished historian of India; Patricia Uberoi, a sociologist who works on the Indian family; Devaki Jain, an activist and scholar affiliated with the government women's association; Renana Jhabvala of SEWA. Antara Dev Sen, a journalist with the *Hindustan Times*, who reports on women's issues; Abha Bhaiya, director of Jagori, a project that works with domestic violence in the slums. I note that women in India do extremely well in the academy, better than in any other nation I know, in terms of occupying top positions in a variety of field. On the other hand, philosophy is an underdeveloped and low-prestige field, and none of my feminist contacts was a philosopher.

36. I also visited a very similar program in Bombay, the Annapurna Mahila Mandel. Directed by Prema Purao, a former freedom fighter from Goa, the program organizes women who make a living cooking for male laborers who have come to the city leaving their families behind. The project sells them wholesale grain, grants credit, and operates a variety of social programs, including one that gives job training to

Jayamma's life has obviously been a tough one; but it has also been much improved by government action. My ideas about the scope and potential for government action promoting human capabilities were very much influenced by the time I spent in Trivandrum, the major city of the province of Kerala, at the southern tip of India. Kerala has frequently been studied for its contrasts to other regions. Although it is a relatively poor province, there is a high level of literacy and health care, and the position of women is markedly better than in many other regions. Female literacy, 39% in India as a whole, is 86% in Kerala, and close to 100% among adolescents. The female-male ratio, 92:100 in India generally, is 104:100, a figure comparable to those of Europe and North America (Drèze & Sen, 1995, pp. 64, 140-178).[37] Among the factors that make Kerala different are its traditions of matrilineal inheritance, plural female marriages, and matrilocal residence, which date from the eleventh century; the complex influence of Christian missionaries, who influenced this region far more than the rest of India; and the presence of a Communist regional government (which has done poorly on economic growth, but very well in health and education). In Kerala, our primary hosts were Iqbal Gulati, chief economic advisor to the government, and Leela Gulati, a leading researcher in the Center for Development Studies, author of an important book on female poverty.[38]

With Leela Gulati (who is fluent in Malayalam, a Dravidian language that Martha Chen does not speak), we visited Jayamma and her family in the squat that Leela has studied over a period of more than twenty years, talking to family members and neighbors, and gathering an enthusiastic following of little girls, who trooped behind us everywhere in their crisp school uniforms. We went to the primary school in the squatter settlement, where we found quite an upbeat situation; indeed, among the places we visited in the 40° C heat, the squat, with its lake covered with water hyacinth,[39] was far from the least pleasant. Kerala gives a feminist thinker a great deal to reflect about; in particular, one

daughters of prostitutes, so that they may have the choice to avoid their mothers' occupation.

37. Drèze and Sen (1995) note that the sex ratio is influenced by male out-migration, but even adjusted when for this, the ratio is still above unity (p. 142).

38. We were also helped greatly by Sardamoni, an eminent historian of Kerala, who spent a lot of time with us discussing why women's position is different there.

39. This lovely plant, introduced by foreign visitors, has, however, overgrown and snarled up the local waterways. Jayamma's husband, a boatman, had to retire early because it got too hard to propel the boat through the tangles.

observes the impact of government programs promoting both literacy and property rights on the lives of poor women and girls.

In Andhra Pradesh, a chaotic and troubled province, I saw another side of the issue of government action, observing the way in which a national government project, focused on consciousness-raising, could enhance women's sense of their rights as citizens and inspire efforts to extract better material and educational services from local government. Here I was also dramatically exposed to the power of women's collectives in raising women's self-esteem and coordinating efforts for change. As I shall later describe, this experience had philosophical relevance, altering some aspects of my thinking.

My host, Yedla Padmavathi, is the Andhra Pradesh director of a national government program, the Mahila Samakhya ("Women's Collectives") Project. Andhra Pradesh is an especially corrupt and anarchic state; the city of Hyderabad is booming economically, but rural areas frequently lack essential services, such as water, buses, electricity, and schools. The point of the project (given that the national government has little money to improve services on its own) is to enhance women's awareness of their rights and to encourage them to mobilize to demand basic services from the local government. The program is therefore quite unpopular with the local government. Padma told me in matter-of-fact tones that she fully expected assassination attempts — a common style of politics in Andhra Pradesh. With Padma and two coworkers I was driven three hours from Hyderabad to the small city of Mahabubnagar, where we spent some time at the local project field station. As usual, I asked questions about life quality: What are you working for? What do you think important? and so forth. Padma wanted me to visit an extremely poor area that had been in the project only a short time, so I would see how the program grapples with extreme poverty; so we made our way in a jeep for another hour and a half into the desert, to a village that lacked electricity, bus service, and a reliable water supply. Here was the worst poverty that I had observed; and yet, as before, women's attitudes seemed astonishingly hopeful. We sat and talked about hopes, aims, the program, life conditions. The women sang me a traditional song whose lyrics used to be "Women, why are you crying?" — and then the woman would tell all the bad things in a woman's lot. Now it has been rewritten so that it says, "Women, why are you crying? Your tears should become your thoughts." They then asked me to sing an American feminist song. Thinking rapidly, I came up with "We Shall

Overcome." They smiled, for they already knew that song. By the second verse, they were singing along in Telugu.

As Strether says in Henry James's novel *The Ambassadors*, "There's all the indescribable: what one gets only on the spot." How Vasanti's eyes look up and look down, the muscles of Jayamma's neck, the electrifying simplicity of Ela Bhatt, how each poor woman does her daily accounting, how the air around her smells and tastes — these things have a bearing on a theory of gender justice. The feminist dictum that we must "start from women's experience" does not seem to me altogether correct. We will not learn much from what we see if we do not bring to our fieldwork such theories of justice and human good as we have managed to work out until then, and one thing good theory tells us is the extent to which deprivation, ignorance, and intimidation corrupt experience itself, making it a very incomplete guide to what ought to be done. Nonetheless, it is also plain that most philosophers know little about the lives of impoverished women, especially in developing countries, and cannot even imagine those lives without seeing and learning a lot more than philosophers typically do. Even the debate between cultural relativism and universalism has an empirical component. Our answers will properly be influenced by answers to empirical questions such as: How much internal debate and plurality do traditional cultures contain? What common needs and strivings do we find when we look at the lives of people in many parts of the world? And what do women say about their lives, when they are in a setting characterized by freedom from fear and freedom from hierarchical authority? The fact that we look for those answers rather than the answers they give when they are in fear, or cowed by authority shows that we are proceeding with a prima facie theory as we work; nonetheless, these provisional fixed points might themselves be called into question, as a result of what we discover.

We would, then, need experience even if we already knew the right questions to ask. But experience is also often required to get the right questions onto the table. Theories of justice have standardly avoided the thorny question of the distribution of resources and opportunities within the family (Okin, 1989); some have treated the family as a private sphere of love and care into which the state should not meddle. Sex-specific issues such as domestic violence and marital rape have not always been on the table — although Mill is a distinguished exception to this claim. We should insist that theories of justice come to grips with the problems women face in the family and in the larger society, and should make recommendations for their solution. Philosophers need Vasanti and Jayamma, then, to goad them to ask some central questions that have not always been asked.

Feminist philosophy, of course, has tackled such women's issues. And yet it has frequently stopped well short of the international women's movement itself, by focusing above all on the problems of women in America, rather than on the urgent needs and interests of poor women in the developing world. A more international focus will not require feminist philosophy to turn away from its traditional themes, such as employment discrimination, domestic violence, sexual harassment, and the reform of rape law, which these are all as central to women in developing countries as to Western women. But feminism will have to add new topics to its agenda if it is to approach the developing world in a productive way. Among these topics are hunger and nutrition, literacy, land rights, the right to seek employment outside the home, child marriage, and child labor. These topics raise philosophical questions. To deal with them well, we need to think about how care and love of various forms play a role in women's lives, about the diverse forms of affective ties that form the structure of societies of various types; about the relationship between property and self-respect. And thinking about these practical issues also shapes what we shall want to say about the more abstract topics. But to approach these issues well, feminist philosophers will have to learn a lot more than most Americans know about the variety of religious and cultural traditions, and about the political, legal, and economic structures of nations in which large numbers of poor women dwell. (For example, in my experience almost all philosophers and legal thinkers are astounded to discover that India does not have a uniform code of civil law, and that the various religious systems of personal law manage things in the domain of property and inheritance, as well as marriage, divorce, custody, and maintenance. But if they do not know this, they can hardly begin to conceive of the problems women in India face, or to frame the interesting philosophical issues of sex equality and religious free exercise in a relevant manner.) In short, even feminist philosophers, whose theories have been unusually responsive to and shaped by practice, need to look at Vasanti and Jayamma, and to consider the challenge their lives pose to thought.

In my own case, several major changes were brought about by my confrontation with these lives. The first was that I now stress far more than I had done previously the importance of property rights, access to credit, and opportunities to seek employment outside the home, as capabilities valuable in themselves, and strongly linked to others, such as the ability to preserve one's bodily integrity and the ability to think and plan for oneself. Perhaps because I have been teaching in Chicago, where one hears so much about property rights every day, often in a manner that shows little compassion for the poor, I had tended to underrate the importance of property rights in poor women's lives. Everywhere I went, however, I heard women saying that having equal land rights (as women do not currently under the Hindu legal code), and having access to credit, are crucial determinants of their life quality. Bhatt powerfully linked this issue with the Gandhian conception of self-sufficiency in an anticolonial struggle. Indeed, I learned to value the concept of self-sufficiency itself more than I had previously. In defending liberal individualism against feminist objections, I had insisted, somewhat defensively, that an interest in promoting the dignity and opportunities of each person did not entail valuing self-sufficiency as a normative goal (Nussbaum, 1997/1999a). I now understand the value this norm can have, when one is accustomed to a life in which one's survival itself depends on the goodwill of others. Access to employment had been important in my approach since Chen's field study for our project; but seeing the importance of employment opportunities in lives on the edge of starvation made their importance far more vivid.

A second important change was a greater emphasis on the Kantian ideas of dignity and nonhumiliation, which had been implicit in the notion of practical reason I developed in the capabilities account, but which I had insufficiently stressed. My Aristotelian starting point was helpful for the way in which it fostered attention to a variety of meaningful forms of affiliation and friendship, especially forms based on equality. The importance of friendship was amply confirmed by my experiences in women's collectives, where it is hard to convey the delight of women who join with other women in groups based on equality, rather than families based on hierarchy and fear. However, one would be missing something of great importance if one did not add that a crucial constituent of these friendships is a shared interest in dignity and in avoiding situations of humiliation.[40] Thinking about this is essential to thinking well about how women can be integrated into a previously all-male workplace, and about the political capabilities.

40. See, for example, the valuable treatment of these notions in Margalit (1996).

Finally, to return to friendship, my experience in India showed me the great political importance of groups of affiliation among women, as sources of self-respect, friendship, and delight. Relatively few Western women, even women who derive great support from consciousness-raising groups and from the women's movement, have lives in which the primary affective tie is to a group of women as such. Such ties are a common reality in developing countries: of long standing in Sub-Saharan Africa (Nzegwu, 1995), more recent but extremely powerful in India. For most of us, by contrast, the hold of traditions concerning the nuclear family is such that our primary affective ties are usually to a far smaller unit, focused on the home. For many Western women, an especially deep part of the search for the meaning of life is played by romantic love, whether of a woman or of a man; this tie, and the search for this tie, to some extent pull against women's solidarity with other women in groups. Everywhere I went in India, by contrast, women related to the group as to their primary community and source of emotional sustenance; the Western woman's focus on romance and (in many cases) on men is regarded as somewhat strange, and not necessarily conducive to women's functioning. In general, deep affection and trust are more separated from sexuality than they tend to be in our lives; and Western women are thought to emphasize the sexual tie more than is good for their social lives.

These are difficult issues for Western feminists to ponder, for they lie very deep in many people's emotions. But I believe we should be more agnostic than liberal theory currently is about what fundamental affective ties the "basic structure of society" should include, and in what form. The debate in liberal theory usually takes the form of asking how far law is involved in the construction of the family, and how far, and in what ways, it should be involved. But the centrality of something like the heterosexual nuclear family with children (perhaps with suitable extensions to recognize same-sex couples and groups of relatives) is usually taken for granted, and it is this family institution that usually gets special support as part of society's basic structure. I believe this emphasis needs rethinking. Any workable account of quality of life should surely make room for these women's collectives as one valuable specification of general goods of affiliation, and it is not clear to me that the state ought to give priority to the Western-style nuclear family over such groupings in allocating benefits and privileges. By creating the

Mahila Samakhya project, the government of India took a different line, I believe wisely.

### Theory and Practice

But why does practice need theory? What might philosophy offer to lives such as those of Vasanti and Jayamma? The first thing we must say here is that theory is in those lives already, frequently in a bad way. International development economics has a tremendous impact on people's lives, because its theories have great influence on development practice and on the formation of public policy. More generally, economics has influence the world over, not only as a source of prediction but, frequently, as a source of normative guidance as well. It is very common for economists to slide over from the explanatory/predictive mode into a normative mode, although nothing in their training or argumentative practice really equips them to justify norms for public policy. Thus, when we see wealth maximization proposed as the goal of a good legal system (e.g., Posner, 1981), when we see the maximization of satisfaction used as a goal in the selection of public policy on education or population; when we see GNP per capita used as an index of "the quality of life" — economists are playing the role of normative theoretical guide, a role that they typically do not play with great subtlety. Even their predictive work is sometimes marred by conceptual crudeness or questionable motivational assumptions, in ways that can at times affect the models' predictive value (see Nussbaum, 1997b, for a more extensive treatment). They typically take philosophical positions on a variety of contested issues, though usually without realizing that they are doing so, or providing arguments for the position taken.

As I have suggested, economists are not readily receptive to philosophical critique; but this is all the more reason why philosophers need to enter the public arena and make these points themselves to policy makers, legal thinkers, and development workers. We need to get people thinking about the adequacy or inadequacy of utilitarian criteria of well-being, the commensurability or incommensurability of values, the relationship between well-being and agency, the structure of political liberalism and the role of ideas of the good in a liberalism of this type, the relationship between resources and human functioning, cultural relativism and its critique, and much more. Policy makers, leaders of non-governmental organizations, development workers — all these people, like the students we teach, can join in philosophical debates about these issues, if they are presented in a clear and accessible way. In this way, philosophers can try to shape development practice even without converting the economists.

The *Human Development Reports* offer one device through which philosophy is already influencing practice in a good way. The *Report* is useful because it offers a concrete set of tools for measurement and ranking. But, even where it performs its function as well as possible, it is also crude. It does not offer much in the way of justification, and it does not really delve into philosophical distinctions that are ultimately very relevant to practice, such as the distinction between well-being and agency, or even, really, the distinction between functioning and capability. Therefore practice also needs more extensive and analytical discussions. One may hope to reach an audience not only of philosophers and social scientists, but also of policy makers and development workers, showing them the arguments that lie behind the approach, and its substantive content. It is not easy to do this, and frequently one must work on several different levels, presenting material in one way for an audience that would like to know exactly how the approach is related to Rawls's political liberalism, another way for an audience that just wants to see the approach itself in its general outlines. But there is no reason why a philosopher cannot reach a broad audience, if enough attention is devoted to writing. In the past, philosophers such as John Stuart Mill and William James were also distinguished writers for a general educated public. These are good examples for our profession to emulate. If we do not, many public debates will go on without philosophical input.

This emphatically does not mean that philosophers should stop doing systematic philosophy and become essayists or politicians. Of course they may do this, in this area and in others. Some philosophers, for example Bertrand Russell, have in effect had two careers, the philosophical work being quite far removed from the public political contribution. But there is a different contribution to political practice that philosophy can only make by remaining itself, that is, concerned with conceptual subtleties and the clear articulation of distinctions, concerned with systematic argument and theory construction. It is precisely because philosophers have thought with such subtlety and rigor about the nature of well-being and the foundations of human action that they are equipped to make the criticisms of the foundations of economics that they cogently make. When Seneca said that the philosopher should be a "lawyer for humanity," he meant that highly abstract ideas about the nature of anger, the social origins of greed, and so on, needed to be brought to bear on the real-world political scene (Nussbaum, 1995c). But these ideas would only enrich the political scene, giving it something it did not have already, if they were presented with the cogent and patient arguments characteristic of philosophy. Philosophy that moves to the practical "bottom line" too quickly will fail to deliver its characteristic practical benefits. These benefits require systematizing intuitions, sorting for consistency and fit, and articulating clearly the outlines of concepts that are usually employed in a muddy fashion.

Political people often get impatient with philosophers because of their interest in patient argumentation and systematic theory building. They want a quick move to the "bottom line," and if they cannot see an immediate relation to the practical, they tend to assume that one cannot be found. Philosophers find this response painful. They do not like to be treated as ivory tower elitists who have nothing useful to offer. They are therefore sorely tempted either to withdraw, or to stop doing real philosophy, in order to accede to the demand for something immediately useful. Marx's (1841/1975) doctoral dissertation (about the Hellenistic philosophers) contains an eloquent warning about this state of affairs:

When philosophy turns itself as will against the world of appearance, then ... it has become one aspect of the world which opposes another. Its relationship to the world is that of reflection. Inspired by the urge to realize itself, it enters into tension against the other. The inner self-containment and completeness has been broken. What was inner light has become consuming flame turning outwards. The result is that as the world becomes philosophical, philosophy also becomes worldly, that its realisation is also its loss, that what it struggles against on the outside is its own inner deficiency. (p. 85)

In other words, to the extent that the philosopher engages in political action, she risks losing the unworldly qualities of precision, self-containment, and reflectiveness that inform her own characteristic mode of activity.

I agree with Marx to this extent: when we enter into politics, we do run some risk of losing the characteristic philosophical virtues. (I believe that Cicero and Seneca sometimes, though certainly not always, show such defects.) But there is no reason why this must happen. We need to keep reminding ourselves that philosophers are not especially likely to be good politicians. Cicero, Seneca, Marcus Aurelius, and Karl Marx offer distinguished examples of the combination. But the fact that Cicero could write both *In Catilinam* and *De Officiis* is a remarkable coincidence, and it is even a little surprising that someone so interested in philosophy would be willing to get so immersed in rather shady rhetoric. More often, the professional training of the philosopher makes people ill-suited to a world of political action. They get too interested in how things really are, and not enough in how they will sound; they would rather make the distinction that can survive scrutiny, rather than the one that will bring about a politically valuable result (Brock, 1993a). Philosophers charged with uselessness, then, had better not jettison philosophy and take up political speechmaking, unless they think they have a special talent for that, to some extent independent of their philosophical ability. More often, we should conclude that what we do best by training is also the best thing we have to offer to practice: systematic accounts that convey an overall understanding of a domain of human affairs, in such a way that intuitions are brought to bear on a practical problem in a new manner.

The Hellenistic philosophers make a valuable point in this regard. Whether in law or medicine or politics, they say, if you give a lot of prescriptions at an intermediate level of generality, you will not necessarily understand the rationale behind the prescriptions and you will be at a loss to prescribe for a new case of some complexity. You will tend to be rigid, afraid to depart from the rule. If, on the other hand, you seek a deeper and more general understanding of what generates the concrete prescriptions — if you really understand the concepts involved and can connect them in a systematic way — you will be in a far better position to face the new case, especially where the existing prescriptions are ambiguous or incomplete. That, I think, is how we should understand philosophy's potential contribution to the law, to medicine, to development policy: it provides the type of foundational and systematic understanding that can guide prescriptions and laws. Philosophy has to be grounded in experience and concerned with practice, or it will rightly be dismissed as irrelevant. Vasanti and Jayamma were not in my mind before I met them, and to that extent my mind was ill-prepared for its theoretical task. But the commitment to reality does not entail that philosophy should not also be abstract, theoretical, and concerned with conceptual distinctions. Only by retaining these concerns can it make a distinctive practical contribution (Rawls, 1996, p. lxii; also Nussbaum, in press-b).

Kant observed that it is very difficult, looking at the evil in the world, to sustain the hopes for human progress that are probably necessary to sustain us in work that is aimed at practical change. But he also argues that we may adopt some optimistic beliefs as "practical postulates," precisely in order to support our continued engagement with humanity:

History may well give rise to endless doubts about my hopes, and if these doubts could be proved, they might persuade me to desist from an apparently futile task. But so long as they do not have the force of certainty, I cannot exchange my duty ... for a rule of expediency which says that I ought not to attempt the impracticable... And however uncertain I may be and may remain as to whether we can hope for anything better for mankind, this uncertainty cannot detract from the maxim I have adopted, or from the necessity of assuming for practical purposes that human progress is possible.

This hope for better times to come, without which an earnest desire to do something useful for the common good would never have inspired the human heart, has always influenced the activities of right-thinking people.[41] (Kant, 1793/1989, p. 89)

Feminist philosophers have special difficulty taking up Kant's practical postulate, because in all cultures throughout history, the inequality of women has been an established fact of life. And despite the impressive progress women have made in this century, there is still no country in which women do as well as men on the measures proposed by the *Human Development Reports*. As the lives of Vasanti and Jayamma illustrate, women continue to suffer pervasive discrimination with respect to all the major human capabilities, including life itself. So a feminist philosopher might not unreasonably judge that "history" does indeed "give rise to endless doubts about [her] hopes," and that the task that she attempts is indeed futile.

But it seems to me that Kant is right. The large-scale practical task is too important not to be attempted. And so long as there is no certainty that it will prove futile, it is morally valuable to entertain those hopeful thoughts about human goodness that will sustain us in our work.

---

41. I have altered the final word of the translation, substituting *people* for *men*. The German version has a substantivized adjective, "the right-thinking ones."

## References

Agarwal, B. (1994). *A field of one's own: Gender and land rights in South Asia.* Cambridge: Cambridge University Press.

Agarwal, B. (1997). "Bargaining" and gender relations: Within and beyond the household. *Feminist Economics, 3,* 1-51.

Brock, D.W. (1993a). *Life and death: Philosophical essays in biomedical ethics.* Cambridge: Cambridge University Press.

Brock, D.W. (1993b). Quality of life measures in health care and medical ethics. In M. Nussbaum & A. Sen (Eds.), *The quality of life* (pp. 95-132). Oxford: Clarendon Press.

Chen, L., Huq, E., & D'Souza, S. (1981). Sex bias in the family allocation of food and health care in rural Bangladesh. *Population and Development Review, 7,* 55-70.

Chen, M.A. (1983). *A quiet revolution: Women in transition in rural Bangladesh.* Cambridge, Mass.: Schenkman.

Comaroff, J., & Comaroff, J. (1991). *Of revelation and revolution: Vol. 1. Christianity, colonialism, and consciousness in South Africa.* Chicago: University of Chicago Press.

Comaroff, J., & Comaroff, J. (1997). *Of revelation and revolution: Vol. 2. The dialectics of modernity on a South African frontier.* Chicago: University of Chicago Press.

Crocker, D.A. (1992). Functioning and capability: The foundations of Sen's and Nussbaum's development ethic, Part I. *Political Theory, 20,* 584-612.

Crocker, D.A. (1995). Functioning and capability: The foundations of Sen's and Nussbaum's development ethic, Part II. In M. Nussbaum & J. Glover (Eds.), *Women, culture, and development* (pp. 153-198). Oxford: Clarendon Press.

Crocker, D.A., & Linden, T. (Eds.). (1998). *Ethics of consumption: The good life, justice, and global stewardship* Lanham, Md.: Rowman and Littlefield.

Dasgupta, P. (1993). *An inquiry into well-being and destitution.* Oxford: Clarendon Press.

Drèze, J., & Sen, A. (1989). *Hunger and public action.* Oxford: Clarendon Press.

Drèze, J., & Sen, A. (Eds.). (1990-91). *The political economy of hunger* (Vols. 1-3). Oxford: Clarendon Press.

Drèze, J., & Sen, A. (1995). *India: Economic development and social opportunity*. Oxford: Clarendon Press.

Drèze, J., & Sen, A. (Eds.). (1997). *Indian development: Selected regional perspectives*. Oxford: Clarendon Press.

Drèze, J., Sen, A., & Hussain, A. (Eds.). (1995). *The political economy of hunger: Selected essays*. Oxford: Clarendon Press.

Elster, J. (1983). *Sour grapes: Studies in the subversion of rationality*. Cambridge: Cambridge University Press.

Gulati, L. (1981). *Profiles in female poverty: A study of five poor working women in Kerala*. Delhi: Hindustan Publishing.

Gulati, L., & Gulati, M. (1998). Female labour in the unorganised sector: The brick worker revisited. In M.A. Chen (Ed.), *Widows in India: Social neglect and public action*. New Delhi: Sage. (Reprinted from *Economic and Political Weekly*, pp. 968-971, May 3, 1997)

Jayawardena, K. (1986). *Feminism and nationalism in the third world*. London: Zed Books.

Jayawardena, K. (1995). *The white woman's other burden: Western women and South Asia during British colonial rule*. New York: Routledge.

Kant, I. (1989). On the common saying: "This may be true in theory, but it does not apply in practice." In H. Reiss (Ed.), *Kant: Political writings* (H.B. Nisbet, Trans.; 2nd ed.). Cambridge: Cambridge University Press. (Original work published 1793)

Kniss, F. (1997). *Disquiet in the land: Cultural conflict in American Mennonite communities*. New Brunswick, N.J.: Rutgers University Press.

Lundberg, S., & Pollak, R.A. (1996). Bargaining and distribution in marriage. *Journal of Economic Perspectives, 10,* 139-158.

Margalit, A. (1996). *The decent society* (N. Goldblum, Trans.). Cambridge, Mass.: Harvard University Press.

Marglin, F.A. (1985). *Wives of the god-king: The rituals of the devadasis of Puri*. Delhi: Oxford University Press.

Marglin, F.A. (1990). Smallpox in two systems of knowledge. In F.A. Marglin & S.A. Marglin (Eds.), *Dominating knowledge: Development, culture, and resistance* (pp. 102-144). Oxford: Clarendon Press.

Marglin, S.A. (1984). *Growth, distribution, and prices*. Cambridge, Mass.: Harvard University Press.

Marglin, S.A., (1990a). Losing touch: The cultural conditions of worker accommodation and resistance. In F.A. Marglin & S.A. Marglin (Eds.), *Dominating knowledge: Development, culture, and resistance* (pp. 217-282). Oxford: Clarendon Press.

Marglin, S.A. (1990b). Toward the decolonization of the mind. In F.A. Marglin & S.A. Marglin (Eds.), *Dominating knowledge: Development, culture, and resistance* (pp. 1-28). Oxford: Clarendon Press.

Marx, K. (1975). Doctoral dissertation: Difference between the Democritean and Epicurean philosophy of nature. In *Karl Marx-Frederick Engels collected works* (Vol. 1., pp. 25-107). London: Lawrence & Wishart. (Original work written 1841)

Moghadam, V.M. (1989). Against eurocentrism and nativism: A review essay on Samir Amin's eurocentrism and other texts. *Socialism and Democracy, 9,* 81-104.

Moghadam, V.M. (1990). *Gender, development, and policy: Toward equity and empowerment.* Helsinki: United Nations University, World Institute for Developmental Economics Research.

Moghadam, V.M. (1993). *Modernizing women: Gender and social change in the Middle East.* Boulder, Colo.: Rienner.

Nussbaum, M.C. (1992a). Human functioning and social justice: In defense of Aristotelian essentialism. *Political Theory, 20,* 202-246.

Nussbaum, M.C. (1992b). Nature, function, and capability: Aristotle on political distribution. In G.E. McCarthy (Ed.), *Marx and Aristotle: Nineteenth-century German social theory and classical antiquity* (pp. 175-212). Savage, Md.: Rowman and Littlefield. (Reprinted from *Oxford Studies in Ancient Philosophy,* Suppl. Vol. 1, 145-184, 1988)

Nussbaum, M.C. (1995a). Aristotle on human nature and the foundations of ethics. In J.E.J. Altham & R. Harrison (Eds.), *World, mind, and ethics: Essays on the ethical philosophy of Bernard Williams* (pp. 86-131). Cambridge: Cambridge University Press.

Nussbaum, M.C. (1995b). Human capabilities, female human beings. In M. Nussbaum & J. Glover (Eds.), *Women, culture, and development* (pp. 61-104). Oxford: Clarendon Press.

Nussbaum, M.C. (1995c). "Lawyer for humanity:" Theory and practice in ancient political thought. *Nomos, 37,* 181-215.

Nussbaum, M.C. (1997a). *Cultivating humanity: A classical defense of reform in liberal education.* Cambridge, Mass.: Harvard University Press.

Nussbaum, M.C. (1997b). Flawed foundations: The philosophical critique of (a particular type of) economics. *University of Chicago Law Review, 64,* 1197-1214.

Nussbaum, M.C. (1997c). Religion and women's human rights. In P.J. Weithman (Ed.), *Religion and contemporary liberalism* (pp. 93-137). Notre Dame, Ind.: University of Notre Dame Press.

Nussbaum, M.C. (1997d). Gregory Vlastos, *Socratic studies* [Review essay]. *Journal of Philosophy, 94*, 27-45.

Nussbaum, M.C. (1998). The good as discipline, the good as freedom. In D.A. Crocker & T. Linden (Eds.), *Ethics of consumption: The good life, justice, and global stewardship* (pp. 312-341). Lanham, Md.: Rowman and Littlefield.

Nussbaum, M.C. (1999a). The feminist critique of liberalism. In *Sex and social justice*. New York: Oxford University Press. (Reprinted from Lindley Lecture, University of Kansas, Department of Philosophy, 1997)

Nussbaum, M.C. (1999b). Women and cultural universals. In *Sex and social justice*. New York: Oxford University Press.

Nussbaum, M.C. (in press-a). *Feminist internationalism*. Cambridge: Cambridge University Press.

Nussbaum, M.C. (in press-b). Why practice needs ethical theory: Particularism, principle, and bad behavior. In S. Burton, (Ed.), *The path of the law in the twentieth century*. Cambridge: Cambridge University Press.

Nzegwu, N. (1995). Recovering Igbo tradition: A case for indigenous women's organizations in development. In M.C. Nussbaum & J. Glover (Eds.), *Women, culture, and development* (pp. 444-466). Oxford: Clarendon Press.

Okin, S.M. (1989). *Justice, gender, and the family*. New York: Basic Books.

Olyan, S.M., & Nussbaum, M.C. (Eds.). (1998). *Sexual orientation and human rights in American religious discourse*. New York: Oxford University Press.

Osmani, S.R. (1992). On some controversies in the measurement of under-nutrition. In S.R. Osmani (Ed.), *Nutrition and poverty* (pp. 121-161). Oxford: Clarendon Press.

Posner, R.A. (1981). *The economics of justice*. Cambridge, Mass.: Harvard University Press.

Rawls, J. (1996). *Political liberalism* (paperback ed.). New York: Columbia University Press.

Raz, J. (1986). *The morality of freedom.* Oxford: Clarendon Press.

Rose, K. (1992). *Where women are leaders: The SEWA movement in India.* London: Zed Books.

Sen, A. (1982). Equality of what? In A. Sen, *Choice, welfare, and measurement* (pp. 353-369). Oxford: Basil Blackwell. (Reprinted from *Tanner lectures on human values* by S.M. McMurrin, Ed., 1980, Salt Lake City: University of Utah Press)

Sen, A. (1984). *Resources, values, and development.* Oxford: Blackwell.

Sen, A. (1985a). *Commodities and capabilities.* Amsterdam: North-Holland.

Sen, A. (1985b). Well-being, agency, and freedom: The Dewey lectures 1984. *Journal of Philosophy 82,* 169-221.

Sen, A. (1990, December 20). More than 100 million women are missing. *New York Review of Books, 37*(20), 61-66.

Sen, A. (1991). Gender and cooperative conflicts. In I. Tinker (Ed.)., *Persistent inequalities* (pp. 123-149). New York: Oxford University Press.

Sen, A. (1993). Capability and well-being. In M. Nussbaum & A. Sen (Eds.), *The quality of life* (pp. 30-53). Oxford: Clarendon Press.

Sen, A. (1994a, January 10). Freedoms and needs: An argument for the primacy of political rights. *The New Republic, 210*(2 & 3), 31-37.

Sen, A. (1994b, September 22). Population: Delusion and reality. *New York Review of Books, 41*(15), 62-71.

Sen, A. (1995). Gender inequality and theories of justice. In M.C. Nussbaum & J. Glover (Eds.), *Women, culture, and development* (pp. 259-273). Oxford: Clarendon Press.

Sen, A. (1996). Fertility and coercion. *University of Chicago Law Review, 63,* 1035-1061.

Sen, A. (1997a, July 14). Human rights and Asian values: What Kee Kuan Yew and Le Peng don't understand about Asia. *The New Republic, 217*(2 & 3), 33-40.

Sen, A. (1997b, June 26). Tagore and his India. *The New York Review of Books,* 44(11) 55-63.

Sen, A., & Nussbaum, M.C. (1989). Internal criticism and Indian rationalist traditions. In M. Krausz (Ed.), *Relativism: Interpretation and confrontation* (pp. 299-325). Notre Dame, Ind.: University of Notre Dame Press.

Taylor, C. (1993). Explanation and practical reason. In M. Nussbaum & A. Sen (Eds.), *The quality of life* (pp. 208-241). Oxford: Clarendon Press.

# 11 Sociocultural and Feminist Theory: Mutuality and Relevance

*Vera John-Steiner*

The study of human activities, beliefs, minds and emotions goes back to antiquity, as Nussbaum (1998) reminds us. But it is only in the 20th century that the psychological domain became a major field of systematic inquiry. It is shaped by the theoretical endeavors of Freud, Piaget, Vygotsky, Bruner, among many others, as well as the methodological structures of American experimentalists. It is a contentious field, deeply divided between those searching for universal features of the mind, and those who see human activity grounded in historical and cultural experience. In these closing years of the century, we are faced with a new challenge: that of the contradiction between models of human agency, which reflect the strong pressures of the global market, and that of the realities of the workplace. Economic models encourage beliefs in humans as lone, competitive actors, engaged in economic choices of the so-called rational man. In contrast, sociologists tell us of the increasing chains of interdependence in areas of social welfare and reform (Ferge, 1997). And in a surprising new development, management specialists advocate participatory forms of planning with working teams within their organizations. They consider these internal cooperative structures effective in global competition (Katzenback & Smith, 1994).

These competing conceptions about human nature — individualism versus social interdependence — are widespread within the human sciences. Wertsch (1998) writes of this contrast as an unproductive autonomy. He adds that in most contemporary discourse, analytical primacy is given to individuals as agents. Feminist and cultural-historical theories, in contrast, recognize the importance of going beyond the individual when exploring human development and action. These traditions share an emphasis on the roles of *context* and *interdependence*. While approaching the social sources of development in somewhat different ways, scholars representing both groups play an important role in

* I would like to thank Mariane Hedegaard for inviting me to make the keynote lecture that resulted in this chapter, and for the support of her ISCRAT colleagues in giving me the opportunity to address these critical issues in a general meeting.

providing alternatives to traditional narratives of individualism. There is an important philosophical affinity between cultural-historical and feminist theories, but, surprisingly, the awareness of this affinity has been largely absent in most scholarly work within the cultural-historical activity theory tradition. Even in my own case, although I have been deeply involved with both for many years, my knowledge has been developed in parallel lines of inquiry and study. Now new insights reflect my integration of cultural-historical and feminist theories in novel and, I hope, cogent ways.

The cultural-historical theory I stress in this chapter is Vygotsky's, with its focus on the dynamic interdependence of social and individual processes, and its strong emphasis on development, co-construction, synthesis, knowledge transformation, and semiotic mediation. These themes provide an important connection between feminist and Vygotskian theories. The approach to gender that I will present is akin to that of the philosopher Harding (1996), who wrote: "gender is now understood to be a *relationship* between women and men ... not a property that women and men have apart from the other gender" (p. 435).

We psychologists are shaped by our experiences, part of which is the predominance of male theorists in our disciplines. Feminist scholars have confronted this reality and have searched for ways to broaden this asymmetry. They have included women's voices in their inquiries and have explored the implications of the changing roles of women inside and outside the academy (Miller, 1986). They ask: How are we women to be defined? By our reproductive roles? By our economic contributions? By our political struggles? By our partnerships with each other and with men? They have debated the difficulties of gendered discourse and the dangers of being misunderstood as espousing essentialist positions.

Obviously, I will not address all these questions. What I will argue is that feminist and cultural-historical theory have some crucial contributions for each other. Central is the notion that humans come into being and into maturity in relationship to others. Through interdependence we achieve competence as well as connection. This stance contrasts with the classical, Western view that we are driven by powerful intrapsychic forces to individuate, and to become successful, autonomous beings.

A recognition of the generative power of interdependence is shared by feminist and Vygotskian scholars. In the cultural-historical tradition, emphasis has been on interdependence in the learning/cognitive do main. For instance, van der Veer and Valsiner (1991) write of Vygotsky's *intellectual interdependence* with his collaborators and with many scholars he studied and translated. This close collaboration included Luria and Leontiev, and in addition to them, his women coworkers, Natalia Morozova, Josefina Shif, Roza Levina, Lidija Bozhovich, and Lija Slavina (G. Vygotskaya, personal communication, June 4, 1998). Feminist psychologists address relational sources of development, many of them in the emotional domain. Scholars in both groups seek to overcome the dichotomy between thought and feeling. My objective in this chapter is to propose a working synthesis of ideas from cultural-historical and feminist sources and to make the family resemblances between them more visible.

These resemblances have been noted by some previous authors. Tarule (1996), one of the coauthors of *Women's Ways of Knowing* (WWK) wrote:

Vygotsky's emphasis, as in connected knowing [one of the epistemological stances presented in WWK], is on how thinking and knowledge are mediated through interaction with others. ... [Vygotsky's approach] values a dialogue that relies on relationships as one enters meaningful conversations that connect one's ideas with others'. (p. 277)

Tarule points out links between the two traditions, but does not elaborate on them. These links include recognition of the social sources of thought and of the role of language in maintaining and developing meaningful connections.

In this chapter, where the formulation of these theoretical links is my objective, I begin with human connections as formulated by Belenky and her coauthors (Belenky, Clinchy, Goldberger, & Tarule, 1986) and by other feminist authors. I then turn to a discussion of the interrelationship between their work and cultural-historical theories. I will end with a discussion of *collaboration*, the current focus of our research in New Mexico. I ask whether there are differences in how men and women envision sustained artistic or scientific partnership. The issues I am presenting are challenging both theoretically and personally. They have already been raised by some participants in our virtual thought community (e.g., Bryson & de Castell, 1996; and during the 1998 ISCRAT Congress by Lemke, 1998; Nussbaum, this volume; Star, 1998; Wagner, 1998). But on the whole, concerns with gender have received limited and sporadic attention in our decades-long interactions.

## Interdependence and Development

The recent writings of American feminist psychologists, including Miller's (1986) *Toward a New Psychology of Women*; Gilligan's (1982)
*In a Different Voice*; Belenky et al. (1986) *Women's Ways of Knowing* all
emphasize relational dynamics in human development. These authors
have listened to women's personal narratives, to their accounts in clinical sessions, and studied the development of adolescent girls. They
examine the consequences of historically- and culturally-patterned
experiences and their impact upon women.

Among historical factors relevant to psychological development are
women's traditional exclusion from schools and colleges. In spite of
remarkable changes in educational opportunities in developed countries during the 20th century, there are still twice as many illiterate
women as men throughout the world. Life span has also changed in this
century. Women are living longer, having fewer children, and spending
many years by themselves without major family responsibilities. However, women still earn less than men, because their jobs are concentrated
in low-paying service fields (Lerner, 1997).

There is a striking correspondence between women's traditional
responsibilities for infant survival and family duties — what the psychologist Dinnerstein (1976) refers to as "the hand that rocks the cradle"
(p. 28) — and the jobs outside the home that are deemed appropriate for
women. Most women are in jobs that require relational skills.

Feminists are addressing the central relational activities in women's
lives through detailed, nuanced studies. They use interviews, therapeu-
tic materials, and present moral problems to participants. Their works
are widely read and cited. But when they report gender differences in
moral values, relational attitudes, or epistemologies, they are criticized
as leaning toward essentialism. Some see them as supporting biological
determinism: a view in which women are "fundamentally all alike, a
homogeneous group with common life opportunities and experiences
already 'known' to us before we actually see them or hear from them"
(Harding, 1996, p. 432).

The charge of essentialism is a misrepresentation of the way these
authors see gender differences. Goldberger (1996b) recently described
their intent: "In the mid-1980s, women-only studies were seen (by us
and others) as correctives to psychology's historical neglect of women's
experience" (p. 7). The work of the women psychologists who followed
Miller's and Gilligan's lead was aimed at overcoming this historical

neglect. They independently reached conclusions that supported each other. One example of concurrence about relational themes came from studies of children's literacy. Dyson (1997) collected and analyzed stories written over a two-year period by children in a single classroom in the San Fransisco Bay area in the United States. She found that 49% of writings by girls centered on relationships with family and friends, and three quarters of their narratives included specific, named emotions. Only 14% of boys addressed such themes. Most of their stories were about superheroes from the media, a theme hardly occurring among girls.

In the research literature on gender differences we encounter a complex picture. There is rapid change in some areas, conflict and resistance to change in others. Individually identified gender differences are few. Two of them are higher mathematical skills in males, and higher verbal skills in females (Maccoby & Jacklin, 1974). However, these differences are culture-specific, linked to socializing and educational practices. Recent meta-analyses show a decrease in male-female differences on standard measures (Hyde, Fennema, & Lamon, 1990). These are welcome findings for those engaged in intervention programs and in the struggle for new opportunities for women. But in discussing these findings, Bookman (1997) writes

that this should not be read as a linear narrative of progress since other gender specific phenomena continue to present themselves across time. The explosion of anorexia-bulimia among women in the late twentieth century provides a dramatic example. (p. 5)

This explosion warns that the increasing participation by females in formerly male domains may trigger anxiety and self-doubt among some.

Following Maccoby's (1990) analysis, Bookman also mentions gender asymmetries which surface when behavior is assessed in *social contexts* rather than observed or tested individually. In summarizing several studies of children's interactional styles, Maccoby found that girls tend to withdraw from groups in which boys exercise power-assertive behaviors. They prefer modes of interaction which "restore or maintain group functioning" (p. 516). She further suggests that the preference for membership in same-sex groups during childhood has long-term consequences for males and females. In adult task-performing groups, females engage in more maintenance or socioemotional behaviors, while males generate more ideas (Aries, 1996). Studies in group dynamics also reveal that men are more dominant in problem-solving groups than women, a finding Maccoby interprets "that it is especially the monitoring by other *men* that inhibits men from entering into reciprocal influence with partners" (p. 518).

These are interesting differences, but they are not universal. As Deaux and Major (1987) have shown, situations differ in the strong or weak pressures they bring to bear on participants who display gender-stereotypic behavior. The greatest sex differences are to be found in those settings in which gender stereotypes are activated (Aries, 1996). These findings support the importance of contextual factors in male/female behavior. A common emphasis upon context emerges both from feminist and cultural-historical writings. Cole (1996) works with the idea of context "as that which weaves together" (p. 135). It is not simply the surroundings of an act, but a dynamic movement between systems of activities, and the culturally and historically constituted contexts in which they take place. Although the issues of concern to feminist scholars — for instance, the development of identity — are different from those of Vygotskian scholars who study cognitive development, they both give context a central place in their theoretical positions. Scholars in both groups have rejected an historical-methodological approach relying upon standardized, static procedures.

One of the most influential developmental studies tracing changes in gendered behavior is the work of Brown and Gilligan (1992) and their coworkers. Their longitudinal studies document the crises girls experience when struggling with the psychological costs of competence versus connection. They write of an impasse where authentic relationships come into tension with conventional relationships. They trace the muting of girls' voices, the high incidence of depression, of eating disorders, and of suicide attempts when girls reach adolescence (Gilligan, Lyons, & Hanmer, 1990). This contrasts with the exuberance and self-confidence of preadolescent girls.

For many developmentalists, relational dynamics first appear in the infant's dependence for survival on her/his caregivers. But in the interpretation of children's development past the period of infancy, theoretical differences emerge in how interdependence is interpreted. Surrey (1991) summarizes the mainstream theorists' approach which emphasize

the importance of the separation from the mother at early stages of childhood development (Mahler, 1972), from the family at adolescence (Erikson, 1963), and from teachers and mentors in adulthood (Levinson, 1978) in order for the individual to form a distinct separate identity. High value is placed on autonomy, self reliance, independence, self-actualization, listening to and following one's own unique dream. (pp. 52-53)

Differing from that view of development, the Stone Center group (of which Surrey is a member) argues that relational competence is an important objective of development. They reason that people are most likely to achieve their individual objectives when they are sustained by caregivers and partners, and are in turn able to support others.

I, too, claim that mutuality and interdependence are basic and necessary forms of human life, but that they are not biologically linked to one gender or another. The practice of interconnectedness is not a universal female responsibility in all societies. Primary reliance on females as caregivers in the home became widespread in modern, industrializing societies, where work and home are separate geographically and conceptually (de Beauvoir, 1949/1989). In developed countries, with most women part of the work force today, the private/public separation of many women's lives in the 19th and early 20th century has to be and is being rethought. These historic trends have contributed to the widespread discussions of women's changing roles in contemporary life, and have provided some of the impetus for the development of a new psychology of women.

### Theoretical Connections

In a recent study, the Danish anthropologist Hasse (1998) relied on participatory fieldwork to study women entering physics careers. She was struck by the low number of women who chose academic careers, even though they made up 23% of the students in this field. Hasse shows that although women do well on examinations, they drop from university and research programs in physics in large numbers. This situation is not restricted to Danish women; it is characteristic of many universities in Western industrialized countries (Barinaga, 1994).

There are many answers that have been proposed to ameliorate this situation: They include creating a new paradigm for female socialization, the sharing of childcare responsibilities, and the elimination of sexist teaching techniques. Hasse does not ignore any of these, but she believes that additional answers might emerge from a participatory mode of study. She enrolled as a first-year student at the Niels Bohr

Institute of Physics at the University of Copenhagen. Her study is informed by activity theory as well as by feminist writings, both of which include ethnographic modes of research. She found some interesting gender differences through her participatory method: one of these is the role of play in physics learning. Males engage in playful exploration of concepts through invented activities (like jumping up and down in an elevator to test gravitational forces). While these playful activities were at times disruptive to other, primarily female, students focusing on their work, most instructors did little to interfere. Occasionally, these modes of exploration led to new understandings, and they created particular kinds of connections between the male students engaged in play.

There is an interesting link between Hasse's findings and Maccoby's interpretation of childhood interactional patterns of males and females. As described earlier, Maccoby suggests that the play activities of boys are more physical and boisterous than that of girls. Boys also rely on jokes and suspenseful stories in entertaining each other. Hasse found that male physics students engaged in more joking than did the women and that for some of them, their interest in physics was fueled by space narratives, and science-fiction stories. The women did not share these interests. Hasse frames her findings by using activity theory. She conceptualizes the gender differences as related to different objects within the activity system — one of these is *education*: solving problems, passing exams, studying textbooks. There is also a related but somewhat different object: *science preparation*, which is fed by these more innovative activities. "In play, male students often transform the purpose and goal of the textbook exercises by making up their own experiments" (Hasse, 1998, p. 12).

The approach used by Hasse and by many other cultural-historical researchers places social and individual practices as central to their work. According to Charles Taylor, human "social reality is composed of social practices, which provide the intersubjective medium for mind" (Cole, 1996, p. 138). In a similar vein, the feminist philosopher of science, Harding (1996), comments on historically changing differences in ways of knowing by stressing the importance of activities and practices. There are differences in theories of knowledge that arise from the substantive cultural and historical differences in people's lives. To the extent that women and men are assigned different activities and engage in different practices, these will lead to alternative resources and limitations for developing knowledge. Harding (1996) argues that:

Since our theories of knowledge tend to vary according to the kinds of knowledge projects in which we engage, it should not surprise us that parenting, juggling work and family obligations, or experiencing family violence or little opportunity for play or dialogue should affect the theories of knowledge of those who have such experiences. (p. 448)

Harding's comments also highlight the issue of "positionality." None of us carry a fixed "essence" or individual identity. We develop amid multiple relationships, practices and responsibilities, changing within and across historical times, and individual life trajectories. We are not "simply individuals, but differentially placed members of an unequal social order" (Maher & Tetreault, 1996, p. 163). Positionality also refers to race, class, sexual orientation, geographic location, age and work, all which affect gender identities.

A central metaphor in the writings of the women I have quoted is *voice*; they emphasize the way humans construct and reconstruct themselves through language. Tarule (1996) quotes women they interviewed who mentioned "speaking up," "speaking out," "being silenced," and "really talking" (p. 275). As these writers moved from emphasis on individuals to communities, their focus shifted from voice to dialogue. It is through discourse and dialogue that meaning is interpreted, negotiated and contested.

For some, speaking or not speaking is "wrapped up in identity and racism," a description Goldberger (1996a, p. 344) quotes from a highly educated Native American woman. The empowerment of those silenced by violence and marginality raises the issues of language, social practices, and the relevance of Vygotsky and Bakhtin in these analyses. In *Mind as Action*, Wertsch (1998) quotes Bakhtin:

To *be* means to be for the other, and through him, [or her] for oneself. Man [and I will add woman] has no internal sovereign territory, [s]he is all and always on the boundary, looking in the *eyes of the other and through the eyes of the other* ... I cannot do without the other; I cannot become myself without the other; I must find myself in the other, finding the other in me (in mutual reflection and perception). (p. 116)

These words resonate with feminist accounts of "self-in-relation." Debold, Tolman, and Brown (1996) write of identity, or what they refer to as the "selfing" process and emphasize the importance of language (and of Vygotsky's and Bakhtin's analyses): "I ... is developed within and by the complex social interaction and experience of language" (p.

92). Thus, in examining the commonalities across feminist and cultural-historical theory, four shared themes can be identified: (a) the social sources of development; (b) the importance of culturally-patterned practices and power relations; (c) issues of language and voice; and (d) the mutually constituting roles of self and community. If these similarities already exist, how can these two approaches further broaden or complement each other? I suggest by a more two-sided exchange of ideas because, at present, there is little acknowledgment and appropriation from the writings of feminist scholars on the part of cultural-historical theorists.

As discussed before, I ascribe some of this asymmetry to differences in focus. Starting with Vygotsky, our concerns have been primarily with language, literacy, cognition and schooling. To date, we have made limited progress in developing a cultural-historical synthesis between cognition and motivation. The importance of human interdependence in Vygotskian theory implies both cognitive and emotional contexts for development. Similarly, in Cole's (1996) discussion of "prolepsis," which refers to parents' projection of a probable future for their child, emotion and cognition cannot be separated. Parents reveal some of their feelings and hopes for their newborns in the way in which their expectations are shaped by their own pasts, and by their cultural and linguistic practices. These expectations, in turn affect powerfully their children's development. Such an analysis expands our theories beyond purely social-cognitive emphases. Litowitz (1993) directly addresses motivation from a Vygotskian perspective in her paper "Deconstruction in the Zone of Proximal Development." She suggests that the standard accounts of learning in the zone of proximal development omit two important factors: identification and resistance. The former refers to the child's desire to be like the adult, "or to be the one the adult wants him [or her] to be" (p. 187). Litowitz uses a Freudian characterization of identification, which implies innate sources of motivation. I think identification can be rethought in relational terms. If we recognize that human survival requires effective interdependence, particularly in infancy, then trajectories of mutuality can be constructed without relying on instinct. The needs to be given to and to depend on, are crucial for the infant. Dependency and helplessness in infancy are necessary. They call forth caregiving behavior by adults and older siblings. Moreover, young children are also capable of mutuality for and caring about parents and other children, if they participate in healthy, reciprocal relationships.

The psychologist Jordan (1991) writes of early empathic responsiveness on the part of the infant.

A beginning of an analysis of motivation from a cultural-historical perspective may be a developmental one with an emphasis on caregiving practices. These, when seen from a cultural perspective, reveal interesting variations. In some societies, they are the primary responsibility of parents (or their carefully chosen substitutes), while in other societies, both adults as well as female and male siblings are engaged in child care. Identification in the latter settings is linked to multiple interactions across generations. In these contexts the child's desire and processes of identification includes a number of people, or aspects of them.

Issues of motivation are raised by Litowitz through the window of the identification process. She makes us ask: Why do we cooperate, co-construct or resist? When she quotes from the concluding passages of Vygotsky's (1934/1986) *Thought and Language*, she reminds us that Vygotsky recognized the importance of motives:

To understand another's speech, it is not sufficient to understand his [or her] words — we must understand his thought. But even that is not enough — we must also know its motivation. No psychological analysis of an utterance is complete until that plane is reached. (p. 253)

Vygotsky was never able to expand this area of his thinking, and his writings on emotion are not as fully developed as his work on cognition. For example, Vygotsky's (1932/1987) lecture entitled "Emotions and their Development in Childhood" is primarily an historical analysis of extant theories. Work by Vygotsky's followers built on other, more fully developed themes in his writings. I believe that by relying upon feminist works, we can make progress in constructing a fuller cultural-historical theory in which a synthesis between thought and emotion is possible.

In addition to theory, methodology is another area where feminist and cultural-historical scholars share similar approaches. Researchers in both groups use interviews, observational and ethnographic studies, and occasionally, longitudinal studies revealing changes in the behavior of a cohort of participants. Some examples of long-term research are the work by Cole (1997, 1998) on the sustainability of innovative programs, and the studies of Finnish researchers on collaborative patterns at different work sites (Engeström, 1990, 1995, 1998; Saari, 1996, 1998). Among feminists, Gilligan has conducted longitudinal studies of preadolescents and teenagers, which yielded the challenging findings I described earlier.

## Studies of Collaboration

Longitudinal studies usually require collaboration. Sociocultural theory provides a basis for examining interdependence in partnership. It specifies some of the connections between co-construction and appropriation, that is, the incorporation of jointly constructed ideas into one's own being. Through *mutual appropriation* partners expand their skills, knowledge, and vision. A recent, beautiful, example of such mutual appropriation was demonstrated by the American public television series, *Yo-Yo Ma Inspired by Bach* (Rhombus Media, 1998). The series presented a sequence of multiple collaborations between Mr. Ma and choreographers, a filmmaker, a Kabuki dancer, a garden designer and others. Ma and his partners brought the 18th-century music of Bach into our own lives, and added many unexpected layers of cognizance to it.

Only through collaboration can we tackle big questions like the effects of violence, drug abuse, and environmental challenges. These concerns can not be solved successfully by individuals working alone. They require the coordinated efforts of groups of researchers who share a common vision. Again, it is in such endeavors, through mutual appropriation, that participants expand their skills, knowledge and vision. But while the practice of collaboration has become widespread, the processes of collaboration have not yet been widely studied.

Researchers in the cultural-historical tradition have addressed intellectual and work collaboration, but have not developed a shared approach. This lack of a shared approach reflects the complexity of this diverse research community, in which different groups have chosen differing types of collaboration, and somewhat varying conceptual approaches.

Scribner's research with her coworkers in New York focused on knowledge acquisition at the workplace (e.g., Scribner, DiBello, Kindred, & Zazanis, 1992). The tradition she established continues to this day. Glick (1992), DiBello (1996), and Kindred (1998) at the City University of New York study the cognitive practices of workers, particularly during periods of rapid technological change. Research in Finland, at the Center for Activity Theory and Developmental Work Research (Engeström, 1995; Kärkkäinen, 1996; Miettinen, 1995) also concentrates on working adults. They study medical, legal, educational, and scientific research situations. Their work is based on Engeström's expansion of activity theory (Engeström, 1996). It focuses on organizational changes, disturbances and conflicts, and the restructuring of joint processes. A number of Finnish researchers have examined innovations, and the way that workers at universities and technological sites reorganize their activity when new artifacts are introduced into their communities of practice.

A third important strand in research on collaboration is the "social practice theory" of Lave and Wenger (1991). Starting with Lave's (1988) studies of everyday cognition and apprenticeship learning in Liberia, and subsequently among midwives, butchers, and alcoholics, they developed an influential theory on changing participation patterns among communities of learners. In a related vein, Rogoff (1990) and her collaborators (Rogoff, Matusov, & White, 1996) have examined apprenticeships and learners' participation in diverse cultural contexts. While Lave and Wenger focused on adults, Rogoff's research teams included children's learning activities, both in formal and informal settings.

Two collaborative programs in the southwestern United States further illustrate cultural-historical approaches to joint activities in classroom and in afterschool activities. One of these is Moll and Whitmore's (1993) work in bilingual schools in which the teachers assume multiple roles (including those of guides, participants, and facilitators), and the students have considerable control over reading and writing topics. Another program focusing on afterschool activities, known as Fifth Dimension, was developed by Cole and Griffin, and has been further refined by Vásquez, Gallego, and their coworkers throughout California and in other sites in the U.S.A. and abroad. It brings together children and adolescents, college students and university researchers in varied community institutions.

It relies upon computer technology, collaborative learning, play, and imagination "within the framework of a shared and voluntarily accepted system of impersonal rules." (Nicolopoulou & Cole, 1993, p. 293)

In this program, Cole (1996, chap. 10) and his colleagues extended Vygotskian analyses of learning beyond the dyadic and small-group level to include different institutional sites and activities. The success of Fifth Dimension is based, in part, on the character of the collaboration, which includes a fluidity across ages and areas of expertise (John-Steiner & Mahn, 1996).

The practice of joint activities varies among these different groups, although they share a common commitment to the exploration of a culture of collaborative learning (Nicolopoulou & Cole, 1993). Its development, strengths and weaknesses in different settings, and the ways in which groups cope with discord, "knots," and conflict resolution are quite specific to the varying sites.

At the University of New Mexico my collaborators and I have been studying creative dyads as well as large collaborative groups. Our research team is composed of Michele Minnis, Teresa Meehan, Holbrook Mahn, and Robert Weber, among others. The aspects of joint activities we focus on include working methods, roles, value tensions, and conflict resolution. Our work first started with the study of dyads, particularly creative partners (John-Steiner, 1999). This interest dates back to the late 1980s, and grew out of my recognition, while writing *Notebooks of the Mind* (John-Steiner, 1997), that the traditional image of the solitary creator is inadequate when depicting the creative process. My own insights corresponded to major shifts occurring in cognitive studies toward social and distributed models of thought (Resnick, Levine, & Teasley, 1991). These shifts also included creativity researchers, such as Amabile (1990); Csikszentmihalyi (1996); and Feldman, Csikszentmihalyi, and Gardner (1994), who moved from purely person-centered approaches to include the dynamics and social aspects of creative cognition.

While examining the creative complementarity between collaborators such as Picasso and Braque, the physicists: Feynman and Dyson, Einstein and his mathematician friend and collaborator Grossmann, and the choreographers: Graham and Hawkins, I came to realize that my cultural-historical framework, while rich in cognitive concepts, was not inclusive enough to describe motivations of creative work (John-Steiner, 1998).

The research revealed that the long, hard effort to produce something new requires trust in oneself. Such trust is nourished and sustained in effective working and living partnerships. When scientists or artists reexamine old theories that conflict with new discoveries, insights, and perspectives, they find thinking together particularly productive. Thinking and working collaboratively is especially promising in constructing a new framework.

This recognition led my collaborators and myself to expand our studies to include large, interdisciplinary collaboratives. Our definition of collaboration is as follows:

The participants in a collaboration represent complementary domains of expertise. As collaborators, they not only plan, decide and act jointly, they also think together, combining independent conceptual schemes to create original frameworks... In an effective working collaboration, there is a commitment to share resources, power, and talent; no single viewpoint predominates, although roles may differ among the participants. There is an effort to establish authority for decisions and actions within the group, and work products reflect a blend of all participants' contributions. We recognize that collaborative groups differ in their conformance to this profile and that any single group may exhibit some of the features only episodically or only after long association. (John-Steiner, Minnis, & Weber, in press)

In examining collaborative co-construction, we built on Vygotsky's sociogenetic notions. But when we tried to represent the relational dynamics of co-construction, and issues of collaborative values, we found our language was limited. We are relying on our interviews and on the rapidly growing literature on collaboration (Johnston, 1997) to help us describe the emotional issues of trust, uncertainty, rupture, distance and reconnection.

Intense, integrative collaborations between men and women require a long period before equality is achieved. The commitment of time and emotional effort to achieve such a goal is more common in dyadic collaboration than in large groups. Both in the biographical literature (Chadwick & de Courtivron, 1993) and in our own interviews, we find extensive depictions of collaboration both among partners who share life and work, as Marie and Pierre Curie did, and others who work closely together without sharing their intimate lives (John-Steiner, 1999).

In attempting to explore both the cognitive and emotional aspects of intense collaboration in groups, I found women's accounts more detailed than that which has been written by and about men. Women confront the complex dynamics of co-construction, competition, intellectual ownership, gender socialization, and joint authorship with daunting honesty (John-Steiner, 1999).

Some of these themes appeared in my interviews with the four authors of *Women's Ways of Knowing* and in their introduction to the anniversary edition of their influential book (Belenky, Clinchy, Goldber ger, & Tarule, 1997). In one conversation Belenky and Clinchy (personal communication, July 10, 1996) told me:

At the beginning we each talked about what we longed to do in a very open way ... and very quickly we discovered that we were close enough that we could pull something together.

The first resolution of the tension between individual interests and common commitments came as a breakthrough insight: "[Women] learn in relationships, by juggling life demands, by dealing with crises in families and communities" (Belenkey et al., 1997, p. xi).

Integrative collaborators, such as these authors, aim at a shared vision. They write in their introduction how they strove to achieve a single voice:

[This was] an exercise that was difficult but in the end successful, we thought. Throughout the writing, we kept in mind the metaphor of a chorus of voices that was to sing the story we wanted to tell; there were to be no solos. (Goldberger, 1996c, p. xi)

They forged the concept of "we" because of the high level of trust they developed during the decade of their shared endeavor.

In our own data we are finding some interesting gender differences. One of the instruments we use is a Q-sort, a set of 50 statements that the participants are asked to sort into a bell-shaped distribution. At one end of the sort, they place statements most characteristic of their collaboration and at the other end, they place those least characteristic of it. While we administer the sort, the participants comment on their evaluation of the meaning and relevance of a particular item. In analyzing 62 sorts, we found that the most widely agreed upon item was: "In a good collaborative environment, one's ideas can be made explicit through questioning and dialogue." There were no male/female differences related to this item. But the statement: "Among my collaborators there is a sense of mission to establish a community in which we can participate" was rated significantly higher by women than by men. It is also an item that the authors of *Women's Ways of Knowing* ranked as very true of their partnership.

A somewhat different perspective on collaboration is offered by the authors of *Organizing Genius*, Biederman and Bennis (1997). They write about predominantly-male "Great Groups," ranging from the Manhattan Project and the Disney studios to the Palo Alto Research Center (Xerox PARC). They describe these participants as "thinkers, playful and verging in their enthusiasm on adolescent subculture" (p. 14). The contrast between the male groups as described by Biederman and Bennis and the way female groups describe themselves is challenging. The members of the Stone Center and the authors of *Women's Ways of Knowing* emphasize their commitment to build a community in which they argue, play, and bond. The very fact that the women describe themselves, while the men are described by others is of interest. Biederman and Bennis attempt to explain the absence of women from these influential groups as follows: "Although sexism surely kept women out of some Great Groups, there may be something in the group dynamic itself that has discouraged participation by women" (p. 15). Men who participate in these groups possess great self-confidence already at the time they first join. Women are less sure of themselves at the start of their collaborative projects, but they are quite successful in bolstering each other's beliefs in themselves.

These differences in collaborative interaction patterns are quite consistent with Maccoby's (1990) analyses of gender and relationships referred to earlier. She writes of research findings which suggest that women are more successful in tasks that require discussion and negotiation, and men are more assertive and argumentative in groups. In the course of the men's intense engagement many ideas are generated. These trends are further confirmed by Hasse's findings quoted before in which she emphasizes the playful, even manic, quality of male physics students working on challenging problems.

Maccoby's position is that gender-linked interactional patterns reflect socialization practices. But these are not fixed patterns; they change as situational demands shift and as child-rearing practices change. These changes may be responsible for the results in recent meta-analyses (Hyde & McKinley, 1997) which reveal a decrease in male-female differences in the cognitive domain. Thus both contextual and historical factors affect the way in which men and women develop, acquire knowledge, and relate to each other.

Long-term collaboration produces its own dynamics. Conflicts can arise in a group, regardless of its gender composition, and as Engeström (1994; Engeström, Engeström, & Vähäaho, this volume) suggests, conflicts, or "knots" can be quite productive in moving groups beyond the practiced and the known. But some disagreements can be painful. Under the tension of a deadline, or the pain of unequal status in the broader world of material rewards and professional prestige, fault lines may emerge. Hirsh and Keller (1990) coedited a book entitled *Conflicts in Feminism*. Rather than blunt their differing opinions, they wrote two sets of conclusions in parallel columns at the end of the book. A somewhat different approach was taken by Jill Tarule and her coauthors. She recalled in the 1997 preface of WWK:

We had wonderful insights, and agonizing disagreements, some still unresolved. As the theory began to emerge from the mist, we each held a different relationship to it, and struggled over issues of ownership, the individual versus the group identity. (p. xvi)

Thus, it is in collaborative endeavors, that some of the most poignant consequences of human alienation are manifested. We struggle to establish egalitarian relationships against the backdrop of an identity achieved through competition, but as we develop shared objectives and a joint vision, we learn to build on our partners' strengths and explore our complementarity. As yet, these courageous efforts are lacking a comprehensive theoretical framework.

## Conclusions

In the beginning of this chapter, I suggested that traditional psychological and economic models of human agents as lone, competitive actors are losing influence. Increasingly, interdependence between persons is recognized as central to individual and societal functioning. Both cultural-historical and feminist theorists place the social sources of development, or "self-in-relation," as central within their framework. There are shared themes and complementarity, as well as different emphases across these two groups of theorists. Feminists' concerns with developmental and relational dynamics are not explicitly shared by scholars studying mind, culture and activity. However, in looking for areas of commonality, we broaden our ways of knowing, and, in the process, may construct a new synthesis between thought and motive, and cognition and emotion.

## References

Amabile, T.M. (1990). Within you, without you: The social psychology of creativity, and beyond. In M.A. Runco & R.S. Albert (Eds.), *Theories of creativity* (pp. 61-91). Newbury Park, Calif.: Sage Publications.

Aries, E. (1996). Men and women in interaction: Reconsidering the differences. New York: Oxford University Press.

Barinaga, M. (1994, March 11). Surprises across the cultural divide. *Science, 263*, 1468-1472.

Belenky, M.F., Clinchy, B.M., Goldberger, N.R., & Tarule, J. (1986). *Women's ways of knowing: The development of self, voice, and mind*. New York: Basic Books.

Belenky, M.F., Clinchy, B.M., Goldberger, N.R., & Tarule, J. (1997). *Women's ways of knowing: The development of self, voice, and mind* (10th anniversary ed.). New York: BasicBooks.

Biederman, P.W., & Bennis, W.G. (1997). *Organizing genius: The secrets of creative collaboration*. Reading, Mass.: Addison-Wesley.

Bookman, M. (1997). Phantoms slain: Reading Gilligan as a radical text. Unpublished manuscript, University of Colorado at Denver.

Brown, L.M., & Gilligan, C. (1992). *Meeting at the crossroads: Women's psychology and girls' development*. Cambridge, Mass.: Harvard University Press.

Bryson, M., & de Castell, S. (1996). Learning to make a difference: Gender, new technologies, and in/equity. *Mind, Culture, and Activity, 3*, 119-135.

Chadwick, W., & de Courtivron, I. (Eds.). (1993). *Significant others: Creativity and intimate partnership*. London: Thames and Hudson.

Cole, M. (1996). *Cultural psychology: A once and future discipline*. Cambridge, Mass.: Harvard University Press.

Cole, M. (1997). From the creation of settings to the sustaining of institutions. *Mind, Culture, and Activity, 4*, 183-190.

Cole, M. (1998). Sustainability as a utopian anchor point in cultural-historical activity research. *Abstracts of the Fourth Congress of the International Society for Cultural Research and Activity Theory*, 24.

Csikszentmihalyi, M. (1996). Creativity: Flow and the psychology of discovery and invention. New York: HarperCollins.

Deaux, K., & Major, B. (1987). Putting gender into context: An interactive model of gender-related behavior. *Psychological Bulletin, 94*, 369-389.

de Beauvoir, S. (1989). *The second sex*. (H.M. Parshley, Trans.). New York: Vintage Books. (Original work published 1949)

DiBello, L. (1996). Providing multiple "ways in" to expertise for learners with different backgrounds: When it works and what it suggests about adult cognitive development. *Journal of Experimental and Theoretical Artificial Intelligence, 8,* 229-241.

Debold, E., Tolman, D., & Brown, L.M. (1996). Embodying knowledge, knowing desire. In N.R. Goldberger, J.M. Tarule, B.M. Clinchy, & M.F. Belenky (Eds.), *Knowledge, difference, and power: Essays inspired by Women's Ways of Knowing* (pp. 85-125). New York: BasicBooks.

Dinnerstein, D. (1976). The mermaid and the minotaur: Sexual arrangements and human malaise. New York: Harper & Row.

Dyson, A.H. (1997). Writing superheroes: Contemporary childhood, popular culture, and classroom literacy. New York: Teachers College Press.

Engeström, Y. (1990). Learning, working, and imagining: Twelve studies in activity theory. Helsinki: Orienta-Konsultit.

Engeström, Y. (1994). Teachers as collaborative thinkers: Activity-theoretical study of an innovative teacher team. In I. Carlgren, G. Handal, & S. Vaage (Eds.), *Teachers' minds and actions: Research on teachers' thinking and practice* (pp. 43-61). London: Falmer Press.

Engeström, Y. (1995). Innovative organizational learning in medical and legal settings. In L.M.W. Martin, K. Nelson, & E. Tobach (Eds.), *Sociocultural psychology: Theory and practice of doing and knowing* (pp. 326-356). Cambridge: Cambridge University Press.

Engeström, Y. (1996, April). *Innovative learning in work teams: Analyzing cycles of knowledge creation in practice.* Paper presented at the annual meeting of the American Educational Research Association, New York.

Engeström, Y. (1998). Expanding dual stimulation: Developmental work research as a kitchen door methodology. *Abstracts of the Fourth Congress of the International Society for Cultural Research and Activity Theory,* 25.

Erikson, E. (1963). *Childhood and society.* New York: Norton.

Feldman, D.H., Csikszentmihalyi, M., & Gardner, H. (1994). *Changing the world: A framework for the study of creativity.* Westport, Conn.: Praeger.

Ferge, S. (1997, August). *And what if the state fades away? The civilizing process and the state.* Paper presented at the annual meeting of the European Sociological Association, Essex University, U.K.

Gilligan, C. (1982). *In a different voice: Psychological theory and women's development.* Cambridge, Mass.: Harvard University Press.

Gilligan, C., Lyons, N.P., & Hanmer, T.J. (Eds.). (1990). *Making connections: The relational worlds of adolescent girls at Emma Willard School.* Cambridge, Mass.: Harvard University Press.

Glick, J. (1992). Steps in the long march: From principles to practices. *Quarterly Newsletter of the Laboratory of Comparative Human Cognition, 14,* 117-118.

Goldberger, N.R. (1996a). Cultural imperatives and diversity in ways of knowing. In N.R. Goldberger, J.M. Tarule, B.M. Clinchy, & M.F. Belenky (Eds.), *Knowledge, difference, and power: Essays inspired by* Women's Ways of Knowing (pp. 335-371). New York: BasicBooks.

Goldberger, N.R. (1996b). Introduction: Looking backward, looking forward. In N.R. Goldberger, J.M. Tarule, B.M. Clinchy, & M.F. Belenky (Eds.), *Knowledge, difference, and power: Essays inspired by* Women's Ways of Knowing (pp. 1-21). New York: BasicBooks.

Goldberger, N.R. (1996c). Preface: The beginning of the story: Collaboration and separation. In N.R. Goldberger, J.M. Tarule, B.M. Clinchy, & M.F. Belenky (Eds.), *Knowledge, difference, and power: Essays inspired by* Women's Ways of Knowing (pp. xi-xii). New York: BasicBooks.

Harding, S. (1996). Gendered ways of knowing and the "epistemological crisis" of the West. In N.R. Goldberger, J.M. Tarule, B.M. Clinchy, & M.F. Belenky (Eds.), *Knowledge, difference, and power: Essays inspired by* Women's Ways of Knowing (pp. 431-454). New York: BasicBooks.

Hasse, C. (1998, May). Gender diversity in play in physics. Paper presented at the Nordic-Baltic Research Course on Activity Theory, Tartu, Estonia.

Hirsh, M., & Keller, E.F. (Eds.). (1990). *Conflicts in feminism.* New York: Routledge.

Hyde, J.S., Fennema, E., & Lamon, S.J. (1990). Gender differences in mathematics performance: A meta-analysis. *Psychological Bulletin, 107,* 139-155.

Hyde, J.S. & McKinley, N.M. (1997). Gender differences in cognition: Results from meta-analyses. In P.J. Kaplan, M. Crawford, J.S. Hyde, & J.T.E. Richardson (Eds.), *Gender differences in human cognition.* New York: Oxford University Press.

John-Steiner, V. (1997). *Notebooks of the mind: Explorations of thinking* (rev. ed.). New York: Oxford University Press.

John-Steiner, V. (1998, April 28). Creativity and collaboration: A sociocultural approach. The University of New Mexico Annual Research Lecture, Albuquerque.

John-Steiner, V. (1999). *Thought communities: Dynamics of collaboration.* New York: Oxford University Press.

John-Steiner, V., & Mahn, H. (1996). Sociocultural approaches to learning and development: A Vygotskian framework. *Educational Psychologist, 31,* 191-206.

John-Steiner, V., Minnis, M., & Weber, R. (in press). The challenge of studying collaboration. *American Educational Research Journal.*

Johnston, M. (1997). Contradictions in collaboration: New thinking on school/university partnerships. New York: Teachers College Press.

Jordan, J.V. (1991). The meaning of mutuality. In J.V. Jordan, A.G. Kaplan, J.B. Miller, J.L. Surrey, & I.P. Stiver (Eds.), *Women's growth in connection: Writings from the Stone Center* (pp. 81-96). New York: Guilford Press.

Kärkkäinen, M. (1997). Change of discourse in organizational change: A longitudinal study of elementary school teacher teams. *Working Papers of the First Nordic-Baltic Conference on Activity Theory, 1,* 38-53.

Katzenback, J.R., & Smith, D.K. (1994). *The wisdom of teams: Creating the high-performance organisation.* New York: HarperBusiness.

Kindred, J. (1998). Authorship and technology in the workplace. *Abstracts of the Fourth Congress of the International Society for Cultural Research and Activity Theory,* 436.

Lave, J. (1988). *Cognition in practice.* Cambridge: Cambridge University Press.

Lave, J., & Wenger, E. (1991). *Situated learning: Legitimate peripheral participation.* Cambridge: Cambridge University Press.

Lemke, J. (1998). The theme of masculinization of the discourse and activities of natural science and academic professions. *Abstracts of the Fourth Congress of the International Society for Cultural Research and Activity Theory,* 33.

Lerner, G. (1997). *Why history matters: Life and thought.* New York: Oxford University Press.

Levinson, D.J. (1978). *The seasons of a man's life.* New York: Knopf.

Litowitz, B.E. (1993). Deconstruction in the zone of proximal development. In E.A. Forman, N. Minick, & C.A. Stone (Eds.), *Contexts for learning: Sociocultural dynamics in children's development* (pp. 184-196). New York: Oxford University Press.

Maccoby, E.E. (1990). Gender and relationships: A developmental account. *American Psychologist, 45,* 513-520.

Maccoby, E.E., & Jacklin, C.N. (1974). *The psychology of sex differences.* Stanford, Calif.: Stanford University Press.

Maher, F.A., & Tetreault, M.K. (1996). Women's ways of knowing in women's studies, feminist pedagogies, and feminist theory. In N.R. Goldberger, J.M. Tarule, B.M. Clinchy, & M.F. Belenky (Eds.), *Knowledge, difference, and power: Essays inspired by* Women's Ways of Knowing (pp. 148-174). New York: BasicBooks.

Mahler, M. (1972). On the first three subphases of the separation-individuation process. *International Journal of Psychoanalysis, 53,* 333-338.

Miller, J.B. (1986). *Toward a new psychology of women* (2nd ed.). Boston: Beacon Press.

Miettinen, R. (1995). From research to innovation: The case of biotechnical pulp bleaching. Unpublished manuscript, University of Helsinki, Finland.

Moll, L.C., & Whitmore, K.F. (1993). Vygotsky in classroom practice: Moving from individual transmission to social transaction. In E.A. Forman, N. Minick, & C.A. Stone, (Eds.), *Contexts for learning: Sociocultural dynamics of children's development* (pp. 19-42). New York: Oxford University Press.

Nicolopoulou, A., & Cole, M. (1993). Generation and transmission of shared knowledge in the culture of collaborative learning: The Fifth Dimension, its play-world, and its institutional contexts. In E.A. Forman, N. Minick, & C.A. Stone, (Eds.), *Contexts for learning: Sociocultural dynamics of children's development* (pp. 283-314). New York: Oxford University Press.

Nussbaum, M. (1998). Emotions as judgment of value. *Abstracts of the Fourth Congress of the International Society for Cultural Research and Activity Theory,* 89.

Resnick, L.B., Levine, J.M., & Teasley, S.D. (Eds.). (1991). *Perspectives on socially shared cognition.* Washington, D.C.: American Psychological Association.

Rhombus Media (Producer). (1998). *Yo-Yo Ma inspired by Bach.* Ontario and New York: TVOntario/Thirteen and WNET New York.

Rogoff, B. (1990). Apprenticeship in thinking: Cognitive development in social context. New York: Oxford University Press.

Rogoff, B., Matusov, E., & White, C. (1996). Models of teaching and learning: Participation in a community of learners. In D.R. Olson & N. Torrance (Eds.), *The handbook of education and human development* (pp. 388-413). Cambridge, Mass.: Blackwell.

Saari, E. (1996). What makes a research team work? The development of object, collaboration and networks of a Finnish and an American aerosol research team. University of Helsinki, Center for Activity Theory and Developmental Work Research, Finland.

Saari, E. (1998). The changing collaboration between a Finnish and an American research group — Closing the doors in the discussion. *Abstracts of the Fourth Congress of the International Society for Cultural Research and Activity Theory*, 437.

Scribner, S., DiBello, L., Kindred, J., & Zazanis, E. (1992). *Coordinating two knowledge systems: A case study*. City University of New York, Laboratory for the Cognitive Study of Work.

Star, S.L. (1998). The ways in which gender is materially mediated (both male and female) and how seemingly non-material (or traditionally cognitive) aspects of gender order also mediate as tools. *Abstracts of the Fourth Congress of the International Society for Cultural Research and Activity Theory*, 32-33.

Surrey, J.L. (1991). The "self-in-relation": A theory of women's development. In J.V. Jordan, A.G. Kaplan, J.B. Miller, J.L. Surrey, & I.P. Stiver (Eds.), *Women's growth in connection: Writings from the Stone Center* (pp. 51-66). New York: Guilford Press.

Tarule, J.M. (1996). Voices in dialogue: Collaborative ways of knowing. In N.R. Goldberger, J.M. Tarule, B.M. Clinchy, & M.F. Belenky (Eds.), *Knowledge, difference, and power: Essays inspired by* Women's Ways of Knowing (pp. 274-304). New York: BasicBooks.

van der Veer, R., & Valsiner, J. (1991). *Understanding Vygotsky: A quest for synthesis*. Oxford: Blackwell.

Vygotsky, L.S. (1986). *Thought and language*. (A. Kozulin, Ed. and Trans.). Cambridge, Mass.: MIT Press. (Original work published 1934)

Vygotsky, L.S. (1987). Emotions and their development in childhood (N. Minick, Trans.). In R.W. Rieber & A.S. Carton (Eds.), *The collected works of L.S. Vygotsky: Vol. 1. Problems of general psychology* (pp. 325-337). New York: Plenum Press. (Original work printed 1932)

Wagner, I. (1998). Gender, visual cultures, and work. *Abstracts of the Fourth Congress of the International Society for Cultural Research and Activity Theory*, 32-33.

Wertsch, J.V. (1998). *Mind as action*. New York: Oxford University Press.

# 12  Infancy and Culture: A Story

*Jerome Bruner*

Never mind the long, long history of ideas about infancy. Philippe Ariès (1962) has told us enough to make us fully aware that *any* story we tell about human infancy grows as much out of ideological convictions and cultural beliefs as out of observation — whether, for example, it is original sin to be redeemed as in the Christian version of infancy, or innate rationality that is destined to be saved from superstition as in the Enlightenment, or primary process to be saved by the reality principle as in Freudian theory. What I have to say will, doubtless, also have to be examined for ideological presuppositions — submitted to close scrutiny, to use a severe term from Anglo-Saxon jurisprudence. And that is as it should be, even though I will cite buckets of experimental evidence to make my points! So here goes: the story of early infancy that has grown over the last couple of decades — or at least my version of it and, as such, inevitably a reflection of our contemporary cultural scene of which I am an inevitable part. For how can anybody escape that!

## II

I shall give my account, tell my story of infancy in terms of crucial research landmarks. And the opening chapter begins with the research of Bill Kessen (1965) and his group working on infant attention: infants deploying their attention *selectively* and under their own control, not just as push-me-pull-you creatures of the environment. The prototypical experiment is an actual one by Kessen (1963), showing that the older the infants, the more often and the longer they choose to look at more informationally pregnant, asymmetric or irregular checkerboard patterns. What emerged from the study was that human information processing capacity not only increases with age, which is old hat, but that infants *select* pieces of the world to attend to that fit their capacity limits and then work within those limits. In a word, human beings dislike dull banality from the start, but they also dislike the confusion of overload as well and from the start work to avoid both. Now, in those distant days of the 1960s, this finding was, so to say, so *proactively* agentive, so downright *cognitive* as to upset the applecart about infancy as a "blooming buzzing confusion" with which we'd been saddled by our forebears. I was so bowled over, indeed, that I hopped right on the train to New Haven to have a look! Could it be that young infants were like *other* human beings! Not altogether so, obviously, but enough so to make us rethink our view of the passive infant.

Then came the discovery that infants were capable not only of monitoring their own attention, but quite capable as well of acting instrumentally to *alter* the stimulus world around them to make it fit their attentional requirements. All they needed was the means. Hanus Papousek (1961) duly demonstrated just that. His young infants easily mastered the trick of turning their heads twice in a row to one side in order to cause exciting jazzy lights to flash over their cribs for a few seconds. Only operant conditioning? But what kind of a reinforcer is a jazzy light bank? Infants, it turned out, were interested in a little visual excitement, and quickly got skilled in knowing how to get it — and possibly to control it or use it to their advantage. Hmmm.

Aren't cultural Zeitgeists curious! Just about that time, studies by Krech and Rosenzweig (Rosenzweig, 1966) began demonstrating that young rats raised in a Luna Park environment that was full of engaging sensorimotor temptations grew up much smarter than their litter mates raised in duller settings. Sure enough, for Gig Levine (Levine & Alpert, 1959), intending to raise animals germ-free and stress-free to see if that affected their later immune reactions, found that animals raised in dull aseptic peacefulness grew up much stupider (and more disease prone at that) than their *louche*, communally cage-dwelling littermate controls. Hmmm, again.

We all began having second thoughts about the older folk psychology's claims about passive infants in a world of "blooming, buzzing confusion." How had such an idea ever got started? If young kids started life passively in a self-made, featureless *Ganzfeld* of nothingness, how did they ever get out of it? How do you ever get something from nothing? Logic dictates *nihil ex nihilo*. A baby has got to have enough structure to provide some working standard of clarity if she's to attend selectively to the world. Without it, she'd be lost. Babies simply could not be without some conception of structure, simplicity, order.

That thought led my then research assistant, Ilse Kalnins, and I to devise an experiment that, we thought, would put the matter to the test (Kalnins & Bruner, 1973). It did not take much. We devised a pacifier nipple, sucking on which would generate an electrical current by compressing a four-legged strain gauge, the more sucking, the more current. God bless piezo-electricity! The current could then be used to control various features of the world — in this case, to control the focus of a picture of a motherly, smiling woman's face projected on a screen at the infant's eye level. In one condition, sucking on the nipple brought the motherly face from out of focus into focus, the picture drifting out of focus when the baby stopped sucking. In the other condition, an in-focus picture was driven out of focus by sucking, the picture moving automatically back into focus when sucking stopped. The long and short of it was that babies sucked briskly to produce a clear picture, but would desist from sucking when it caused the picture to blur (and desisting is not easy when you're a six-month-old performing for a mad psychologist in a clean-smelling, unfamiliar room). So much for blooming buzzing confusion! (I recall a visiting New Delhi pediatrician who was observing one of our subjects through a one-way screen. "That's impossible," she said on emerging, "a baby's world is a buzzing blooming confusion.") *Sic transit gloria mundi.*

By now, of course, we are well into the 1960s, into America's New Frontier under the restless President Johnson, into Head Start and into newspaper articles about the unique place of infancy and early childhood in shaping life — like one in a series of three written by John Davies in *The Times of London* on changing views of human nature. He singled out the "new idea of competence in infancy" as among the most revolutionary. I mention this here to remind you that where the original nature of humankind is concerned, knowledge and culture quickly begin walking hand in hand. Something deep was happening in Western culture (of which more later), and research was changing with it — whether leading it or following it, we cannot know.

The next chapter in the story takes a fascinating turn: it is about *intersubjectivity*, how we read each others' minds and when and how this process starts. It's a topic that began engaging us as a result of new efforts to understand the blight of childhood autism, but it quickly grew to encompass matters as diverse as the evolution of higher primates and the very nature of human enculturation. I and my gang of irrepressible graduate students and postdocs at Oxford were up to our ears in it — Alison Gopnik, the two Andys, Meltzoff and Whiten, Alan Leslie, Mike Scaife, Paul Harris, George Butterworth, to mention only some of their boisterous number. And if we ever tired of the subject, there was always

Colwyn Trevarthen on a quick visit from Edinburgh to get us back into it. We spent hours debating about it, convinced that culture-using human beings could not possibly have entered a culture unless they were able to "read the minds" of those around them.

The experiment that served as the trope was one that Mike Scaife and I (Scaife & Bruner, 1975) did: infants, we soon discovered, follow an adult's line of regard in search of what the adult is attending to. Yes, they are interested in the world, but *particularly* interested in those aspects of the world that are shared with others. In the twinkling of an eye, the old philosophical problem of Other Minds got transferred (to be parochial Oxford) from Merton Street to South Parks Road, from the philosopher's study to the psychologist's lab — and soon it was to go beyond there. Within a decade, a thriving cottage industry of baby labs took it over and "theories of mind" became the great growth stock of developmental research.[1]

The emphasis had shifted from the competent *solo* infant mastering the natural world virtually on her own to a concern with how infants (and all of us!) ever come to understand each other's minds sufficiently well to live in a human culture. And it is still shifting in that direction. In some ways, this was not altogether a new concern. The post-World War II *culture-and-personality* craze moved in this direction. But it was so enchanted and enslaved by the previous primary-process dogma regarding infancy that it squandered its attention on bowel training, weaning rituals, and never got around to the intersubjectivity issue.

Cognitive research on autism reopened the gate, the wedge study surely being Alan Leslie's (1991) on the symptomatic absence of pretend play in young autists. Why were autistic children so deficient in pretending? His powerful claim was that autism so seriously destroyed an infant's or child's grasp of other minds, that it was impossible for sufferers even to *pretend* to be an Other. This work was followed by a flood of research elaborating the many particulars of his claim (see Baron-Cohen, Tager-Flusberg, & Cohen, 1993; Happe, 1994; and Sigman & Capps, 1997, for a sampling of this fascinating literature).

The work on "theory of mind," as it soon came to be called, had an impact far beyond the pathogenesis of autism. It reawakened specula-

1. For a thoughtful overview of this outpouring at mid-voyage, see Feldman (1992). Among the major books on the subject are several "overview" volumes, ranging from Astington's (1993) book on the then state of the art, through Perner (1991) to Wellman (1990).

tion in many less specialized fields, particularly in primatology where
there had already been some challenging exploratory work on the subject — by Chance and Jolly (1970), by Menzel (1974), by Premack and
Woodruff (1978). Take as an example Menzel's (1974) early work,
showing that young primates in a one-acre field anticipated the line of
*travel* of one of their number known by them to know where food had
been hidden in the field. They did it by monitoring the know-it-all's
*gaze* direction and anticipating where he might be going. Or take the
work on the use of *deliberate deceit* in primate social interaction (Byrne &
Whiten, 1991): How could higher primates *deliberately* deceive a con-
specific unless they had some notion of other minds?

But the real explosion surely began with Sue Savage-Rumbaugh's
study on the *enculturation* of the now famous young bonobo, Kanzi
(Savage-Rumbaugh et al., 1993). To make a long and incomplete story
short and much too conclusive, what has been found is that Kanzi had
not only mastered Von Glasersfeld's "chip" language (which extended
his communicative range enormously) but, equally to the point, he had
been brought by his human handlers to a new level of appreciation of
their "intentional states:" their intentions, desires, expectations, beliefs.
Kanzi had, in the *gemütlich* human intersubjectivity of the Georgia State
Language Center, taken a giant step toward *enculturation*. To get a crea-
ture to that state, in a word, requires "treating somebody like a human
in a human setting," which means treating them as if they had mental
states and as if they knew that *you* had mental states you expected *them*
to understand, to paraphrase a letter I received from Michael Tomasello
(personal communication, 1992) in the midst of this work. It also means
appreciating that intentional states mediate what we *do*. To be encultu-
rated, to put it grandly, means to come to share the folk psychology of
your culture.

And that places some odd and seemingly incidental observations in
a new light, like, for example, Meltzoff and Gopnik's (1993) report that
new parents take especial delight in "discovering" that their young
babies, in their words, "have minds, just like us." Whether they do or
they don't at the outset, parents seem to know intuitively just the right
thing to do to get them there, to promote enculturation. And believe me,
there are plenty of data that should convince you that you'd better act
as if your baby has something in mind! For, if you act otherwise, say by
staying "poker faced" in response to your young baby's changing
expressions (which itself is difficult to do), you will quickly produce

tears and distress, as Stechler and Latz (1966) showed many years ago. Even Kanzi eventually got frustrated by his "natural-raised" sister's lack of intersubjective responsiveness — just like a "real kid" (Savage-Rumbaugh et. al., 1993). For let us not forget that Kanzi shares enough of the humanoid genome to make him more than a little sensitive to our human way of enculturation — but *only* if he has been exposed to distinctively human upbringing.

Now to the final but incomplete chapter of our story. We humans seem geared from the start to deal with each others' intentions, at least to be enormously sensitive to them in their various guises. Positivist philosophers, like Dan Dennett (1991), may be embarrassed by human intentional states, deep-freezing them as an "intentional stance," but eighteen-month-olds are not the least so. I refer again to a Meltzoff (1995) finding. Infants imitate the *intended* behavior of an Other and not its surface properties. In brief, if the outcome of an adult's act is thwarted or blocked, infants of eighteen months will imitate it *as if it had been carried through right to its goal*. Human infants do easily and naturally (and to the delight of their caregivers) what Kanzi does stumblingly, and only if he has the luck of being raised by that gang of very human and dedicated graduate students and postdocs at the Georgia State Language Lab.

Now in a fundamental way, culture requires a sensitivity not simply to what others do, but what they *intend* to do, not to what they say but what they *mean* — how they intend their utterance to be taken. It is crucial, then, that at the start infants be sensitive to intention and intentionality.[2] If they were not, they could not find their way into the complex network of canonical mutual expectancies that characterizes human culture. Or, at least, that is how it seems to us from our contemporary perspective on how the world works.

### III

That is the gist of the story I want to tell — still very much unfinished, but definitely getting there. Our cultural historian friends *love* it, of course. In it, they see the "discovery" of the informationally active, socially interactive infant mind as reflecting our departure from the Industrial Age with its machine models, and they also see in it our entry

---

2. I shall leave out of the discussion the issue of *intentionality* — what things and signs are intended to *stand for*. For a discussion of this broader issue see Bruner (1998).

into the new Information Age where cognition, symbol use, and social networking are crucial. No doubt they're right and perhaps that's why it's so easy to tell the story in French! Je veux dire, tout simplement, que telle l'histoire soit presque irrésistible. Et surement, c'est vrai dans un certain sens. Le bebé passive et sans aucun esprit actif a devenu demodé dans le climat culturel d'aujourd'hui. Mais ...

But I suspect there's another moral to the story too. I suspect that when one enters into a new revolutionary period, as we surely have, a sure sign is that we look afresh at what we mean by the original nature of man and how that nature expresses itself from the start. Infancy research has become (yet again) the new arena for battling out *the* classic and enduring issues of the changing culture — human agency, the nature of interdependence, the limits of responsibility, the scope of human meaning making, the interaction of genes and the environment. So it was in the seed-days of Soviet communisms — the battles over consciousness, reflection, language. But one scarcely needs modern examples to make the point. But so it has always been. Think of the elaborate eschatology of Christianity about Man's original sin, or recall Marcel Mauss on the functions of *rites de passage* in primitive societies.

No surprise, then, that there is something uniquely consciousness-raising and even politically compelling about reflection and research on immaturity and its potentials. It seems able to move mountains, even political ones. I still can't believe what happened when Urie Bronfenbrenner and I first proposed Head Start to the White House Office of Economic Opportunity. "Impossible, hadn't we ever read the Constitution on who controls schools?" Today it is political suicide for a Congressman to suggest cutting it back.

How does psychology enter the ideological issues that are constantly being generated by the dialectical nature of all cultures?[3] I do not mean pop or partisan psychology, but honest-to-god, hardworking psychology of the kind we do and of the kind I've been talking about. Does it just naturally arise out of what we in the West like to call "scientific curiosity" so that it just happens to be there, as it were, right in the nick of time? I deeply doubt that. Scientific curiosity does not just feed on itself. It lives as well on background presuppositions, inevitably religious-metaphysical in origin, about the nature of nature and the nature of man. At the heart of every coherent system of cultural beliefs, there lies

3. For a fuller discussion of the "dialectic of culture" and its capacity to generate ideological conflict, see Amsterdam and Bruner (in press).

a conception of man, of his perfectibility and weakness and what conditions limit or promote these. Living in a culture predisposes us to search for and even to find *empirical* confirmations of these deep beliefs. We just get clever in how we design our studies and set up our experiments, *clever* not dishonest. But culture, as I have argued elsewhere, is not a mould into which thought is poured. It is a dialectic between the canonical expectable and the imaginatively possible. The Fugitive Slave Law of 1793, for all the cruelty it spawned in antebellum America, also spawned the imaginative possibilities of Harriet Beecher Stowe's *Uncle Tom's Cabin*. Monarchical devotion to the canonical Divine Rights of Kings bred John Locke's *Treatise on Government* — and eventually the United States Constitution.

And so it is with honest psychology. Of course, given the authoritarian structure of the family, the newborn is passive. But as the culture changes, and with it the family, there are other ways of conceiving of infancy as well. Indeed, there even arises a temptation to look at infancy again. And see what happened?

So, just as great novels and great philosophical formulations can change a culture, often more swiftly than we think, so can new and powerful insights into the humanly human possible change our views what society is and what it could be. That is the dialectic of culture, and that is why cultural growth is sometimes saltatory rather than glacial in speed. We can never be quite sure about how delicately balanced are those two elements in a culture: the canonical, the expected, the normative, on the one hand, and imagined possible worlds on the other. And I am not the least daunted, let me note, that the story of early infancy that I've just told you partakes of an imagined possible world — despite all the $t$ tests and $p$ values at greater than .001.

What I am arguing is almost too self-evident to be contestable. Psychology is *not* outside of or *au dela de la culture*. It is a part of it. In that deep sense, it both reflects the culture and changes it. It is neither honest nor even coy to claim that all that drives us is The Truth. For the opposites of great truths, as that prescient Danish thinker Niels Bohr taught us, are often also true. Psychologists, like everybody else, are participants in their culture. We tell our stories *salve veritatis*, but *veritas* is rarely singular or, rather, never for long. For psychology too grows out of the life and the conditions of the culture. So, despite our $t$ tests, we are in the midst of it — just like the historians who shape the past in order to presage the future or to justify the present, and just like all those other scholars who explore the possibilities inherent in being human.

So please take my story for what it is. Hear it both as real psychology and as a voice in the dialectic of culture.

## References

Amsterdam, A.G., & Bruner, J. (in press). *Law, culture, mind*. Cambridge, Mass.: Harvard University Press.

Ariès, P. (1962). *Centuries of childhood: A social history of family life*. New York: Knopf.

Astington, J. (1993). *The child's discovery of the mind*. Cambridge, Mass.: Harvard University Press.

Baron-Cohen, S., Tager-Flusberg, H., & Cohen, D.J. (Eds.). (1993). *Understanding other minds: Perspectives from autism*. New York: Oxford University Press.

Bruner, J. (1998). Routes to reference. *Pragmatics and Cognition, 6*, 209-227.

Byrne, R.W., & Whiten, A. (1991). Computation and mindreading in primate tactical deception. In A. Whiten (Ed.), *Natural theories of mind: Evolution, development, and simulation of everyday mindreading* (pp. 127-141). Oxford: Blackwell.

Chance, M.R.A., & Jolly, C.J. (1970). *Social groups of monkeys, apes, and men*. New York: Dutton

Dennett, D.C. (1991). *Consciousness explained*. Boston: Little-Brown.

Feldman, C. (1992). The new theory of theory of mind. *Human Development, 35*, 107-117.

Happé, F. (1994). *Autism: An introduction to psychological theory*. London: University College Press.

Kalnins, I., & Bruner, J. (1973). The coordination of visual observation and instrumental behavior in early infancy. *Perception, 2*, 307-314.

Kessen, W. (1963). Research on the psychological development of infants: An overview. *Merrill-Palmer Quarterly, 9*, 83-94.

Kessen, W. (1965). *The child*. New York: Wiley.

Leslie, A. (1991). The theory of mind impairment in autism: evidence for a modular mechanism of development. In A. Whiten (Ed.), *Natural theories of mind: Evolution, development, and simulation of everyday mindreading* (pp. 63-78). Oxford: Blackwell.

Levine, S., & Alpert, M. (1959). Differential maturation of the central nervous system. *Archives of General Psychiatry, 1,* 403-405.

Meltzoff, A.N., & Gopnik, A. (1993). The role of imitation in understanding persons and developing a theory of mind. In S. Baron-Cohen, H. Tager-Flusberg, & D.J. Cohen (Eds.), *Understanding other minds: Perspectives from autism* (pp. 335-366). New York: Oxford University Press.

Meltzoff, A.N. (1995). Understanding the intentions of others: Re-enactment of intended acts by 18-month-old children. *Developmental Psychology, 31,* 938-950.

Menzel, E. (1974). A group of young chimpanzees in a one-acre field. In M. Schrier & F. Stolnitz (Eds.). *Behavior of non-human primates* (Vol 5, pp. 83-153). New York: Academic Press.

Papousek, H. (1961). Conditioned head rotation reflexes in infants in the first months of life. *Acta Pædiatrica, 50,* 565-576.

Perner, J. (1991). *Understanding the representational mind.* Cambridge, Mass.: MIT Press.

Premack, D., & Woodruff, G. (1978). Does the chimpanzee have a theory of mind? *Brain and Behavioral Sciences, 1,* 515-526.

Rosenzweig, M.R. (1966). Environmental complexity, cerebral change, and behavior. *American Psychologist, 21,* 321-332.

Savage-Rumbaugh, E.S., Murphy, J., Sevcik, R.A., Brakke, K.E., Williams, S.L., & Rumbaugh, D.L. (1993). Language comprehension in ape and child. *Monographs of the Society for Research in Child Development, 58*(3-4, Serial No. 233).

Scaife, M., & Bruner, J.S. (1975). The capacity for joint visual attention in the infant. *Nature, 253,* 265-266.

Sigman, M., & Capps, L. (1997). *Children with autism: A developmental perspective.* Cambridge, Mass.: Harvard University Press.

Stechler, G., & Latz, E. (1966). Some observations on attention and arousal in the human infant. *Journal of the American Academy of Child Psychiatry, 5,* 517-525.

Wellman, H. (1990). *The child's theory of mind.* Cambridge, Mass: MIT Press.

# 13 Social Interaction, Cultural Tools and the Zone of Proximal Development: In Search of a Synthesis

*Anna P. Stetsenko*

One of the most heuristic ideas in Vygotsky's theory of child development was his idea that learning can lead developmental processes. This idea was reflected in three concepts in the Vygotskian framework: (a) social (e.g., child-adult) interaction as the main source of mental processes; (b) cultural tools as mediating components of psychological functioning and (c) the zone of proximal development as the main "portal" through which development proceeds. However, the internal universal relationship between these three concepts (i.e., the germ cell idea that lies behind each of them and unites them) has not been articulated by Vygotsky, thus leaving unanswered a broad spectrum of questions, including a crucial question about how and why learning can lead human development. I will attempt to show that the germ cell of intra- and interpsychological processes is transformations of goal-directed human activities extended and mediated by culturally-generated and socially-transmitted activities crystallized in cultural tools. The main goal of this chapter is to explicate this idea and to explore its importance. Specifically, this idea allows one to understand cultural tools as being indispensable components of developmental processes and consequently to understand a child's learning as being constitutive of development.

## Child-Adult Interactions, Cultural Tools and the Zone of Proximal Development: The Vygotskian Framework

Vygotsky laid important foundations for a new, potentially revolutionary understanding of the relationship between learning and development by proposing a set of concepts that entailed that learning plays a leading role in development, defining and shaping its ultimate course. Three interrelated concepts deserve special attention when addressing the issue of development and learning. These concepts and related ideas are often viewed as separate logical entities, but in fact, the meaning of each one is intimately related to the meaning of the other two, and can only be fully appreciated in the context of their interconnections. This interrelation exists because the same idea underlies each of these concepts, making their genuine synthesis possible. Only this synthesis — as a whole — imparts the meaning to each of its constitutive parts.

First, Vygotsky gave a new meaning to the concept of *social interaction*, as might be found between a child and an adult, by asserting that such interaction is the main source of mental processes and that it developmentally underlies all higher functions and their relationships. Specifically, according to Vygotsky, each cognitive function appears first as an interaction between the child and an adult and then gradually gets internalized by the child, thus becoming an essential characteristic of the child's own mind (cf. so-called "genetic law" of the emergence and development of psychological functions, Vygotsky, 1960/1978, p. 57). However, in such a general formulation, this description of mental development entails very different interpretations that indeed have been explicated by various followers of Vygotsky. For example, this general regularity of human development has often been portrayed as an indication of specific sources of development in the sense that the human mind originates *in* and *from* socially-shared interactions between children and adults. Child-adult interaction is viewed as playing an important role in the development of mental processes, but this role is quite limited. Social interaction is viewed as a prerequisite for development, but social interaction itself is not viewed as an integral component of what is being developed.

The second and related concept is that of *cultural tools*. Vygotsky asserted that there are artificial means that enable individuals to master their own psychological processes. Such artificial means (also termed psychological or cultural tools) allow for the mastery of psychological processes just as technical tools allow for the mastery of labor. Examples of cultural tools, and the complex systems that are formed by them, include different kinds of numbering and counting, mnemotechnical aids, algebraic symbols, art works, writing, schemes, diagrams, maps, drawings, and all sorts of signs. To quote Vygotsky (1930/1981):

Mastery of a psychological tool and, through it, mastery of a natural psychological function always raises the particular function to a higher level, increases and widens its activity, and recreates its structure and mechanism. (p. 142)

Cultural tools, according to Vygotsky, are in fact indispensable elements in the structure of any complex psychological process. Certainly, it has been widely accepted that the acquisition of culture by the child is not simply an addition of new devices or new means to existing psychological processes. These devices and means, once acquired, create totally new functional psychological systems that operate according to new rules and develop according to new laws. Nevertheless, the acquisition of cultural tools has often been portrayed as just one mediating component — albeit an important one — of the overall structure of psychological processes. Moreover, cultural tools are often viewed as a somewhat external element that comes to be acquired by the child in addition to a more general psychological development.

The third and related concept is the *zone of proximal development* (ZPD). The most common understanding of this concept is that the child, in collaboration with an adult or more experienced peer, is able to solve problems on a more advanced level than when acting alone. This understanding of the zone of proximal development, when taken in abstraction from the idea of cultural tools and socially-shared interaction, can entail the view that the adult's help (without specification of the exact content of help) is what makes an impact on a child's development. It is as if the adult's expertise and knowledge or help and cooperation, by being "added" to a cooperative problem-solving situation, is causing the increase of the child's abilities and cognitive potential.

In the Vygotskian framework, the internal links among the three just-described concepts have not been explicated sufficiently. These concepts remain de facto isolated from one another and, as such, their full potential remains to be revealed. Perhaps not accidentally, the concepts of social interaction, cultural tools and ZPD have served, and continue to serve, as the foundations for several distinct research traditions within the sociocultural approach that has developed after Vygotsky. These research traditions have made important contributions to the Vygotskian insights regarding learning and development, but there are only a few efforts to synthesize them (e.g., Hedegaard, 1995, 1998; Karpov & Haywood, 1998; Lompscher, 1984; Stetsenko & Arievitch, 1996). I believe this synthesis can be achieved if the universal germ cell idea underlying these concepts is explicated and its implications are revealed. In what follows, I first describe (in a somewhat simplified manner in order to bring my argument to the fore) three post-Vygotskian research traditions that each bear relevance primarily to one of the three concepts outlined above, and then suggest a general framework in which the synthesis of these traditions can be achieved through the grounding assumptions of the activity principle.

### Focus on Social Interaction

One line of post-Vygotskian studies, represented by the socio-cultural research tradition in the United States, concentrated on socio-cultural models of teaching and learning with an emphasis on shared activity and social interaction (Cole, 1985; Lave, 1991; Rogoff, 1994; Rogoff & Lave, 1984). The focus of analysis in this approach is on socio-cultural practices, "socially assembled situations" (Laboratory for Comparative Human Cognition, 1983) within which individual cognitive development occurs. The concept of the co-construction of meaning (shared understanding) is central to such a view. The work of Rogoff on learning in apprenticeship is most characteristic in this respect (e.g., Rogoff, 1990, 1995). Rogoff conceptualizes learning that results in the child's cognitive development as the process of the child's guided participation in culturally-organized activity with a more skilled partner. The central idea is that children's cognitive development is inseparable from their social environment and is actually an interpsychological process. According to Rogoff, children's cognitive development occurs in the context of guided participation in social activity with more experienced partners who support and enhance a child's understanding and skills in using cultural tools. The processes of guided participation — such as shared problem solving, structuring and supporting the novices' efforts, and transferring responsibility for handling skills — define the direction and organization of a child's cognitive development.

Rogoff, as well as other scholars working in this line of research (e.g., Lave, 1991), make an important contribution to our understanding of developmental processes in their relationship to learning. For example, their work extends the concept of social interaction by stressing the mutual complementarity of the roles of children and their caregivers within guided participation. This perspective also stresses the developmental importance of routine activities as children observe and participate with the others in culturally-organized practices. Rogoff's elaboration is consistent with Galperin's line of research (discussed in the next section) in its general understanding of the relationship between learning and development, but her work has not emphasized the concrete characteristics of cultural tools as such, and how individuals internalize these tools in the course of guided participation. The communicative processes and social activity are the "endpoint" of analysis, whereas individual acquisition of skills and knowledge as well as individual development are dropped in favor of the interpsychological dynamic of the relative contributions of individuals to shared activities.

Can references to communicative processes and social activity exhaustively explain a child's mastery of a new activity? Shared social activity is necessary but only as a starting point in a child's gradual appropriation of new knowledge and skills, serving as a pole in the gradual process of subjectivization (personalization) of a new activity by the child. The strong (and much needed) focus on the communicative aspect of teaching-learning — an aspect that is explicitly present and even dominant in the first stages of acquiring an activity — creates a situation in which other aspects of activity subjectivization recede to the background in the research by Rogoff and her colleagues. As a consequence, neither the operational content of new activity forms that have to be mastered by the child, nor the transformations of this activity's psychological structure are analyzed. The psychological mechanisms of the formation of new cognitive processes, which then regulate the child's actions, remain unspecified. Paradoxically enough, the exclusive concentration on intersubjectivity results in neglecting the process of subjectivization of new activities in the processes of teaching-learning. The focus on interdependency, while highlighting an important dimension of the co-construction of developmental processes, stops short of explaining how a competent, self-efficacious, independent subject emerges in shared activities.

### Focus on Cultural Tools

A second post-Vygotskian line of research focuses on the concept of cultural tools and their functional role in a child's development. This line of research is articulated most explicitly in the works of Galperin (1969, 1989a, 1992), Davydov (1988), Elkonin and Davydov (1966) (see

Arievitch & Stetsenko, 1998; Karpov & Haywood, 1998) and is primarily concerned with the processes of how new cultural tools are acquired by children through specially organized teaching-learning procedures. According to this approach, it is the character and quality of the cultural tools that directly determines the particular features and resulting quality of a child's mental activity (Galperin, 1989b; Davydov, 1988; Zaporozhets & Elkonin, 1964/1971). It is important to note both the significant continuity between Vygotsky's works and those by Galperin and his followers, as well as the qualitative advancements made by Galperin and his colleagues.

Concerning the continuity, it can be argued that Vygotsky was aware that the quality of cultural tools was crucial for understanding both developmental processes and their links to learning. His empirical studies on scientific and everyday concepts was one specific way to illustrate and examine how cultural tools of different quality can differentially shape the development of a child's mind. In this case, Vygotsky showed how differences in learning these two types of concepts in their instrumental function as a "tool" — that is, learning how to employ them in the processes of acting and thinking — can lead to two types of developmental outcomes.

Vygotsky defined everyday concepts as concepts that children form and acquire based on unstructured and fragmented everyday interactions with other people and the world and which reflect the vicissitudes of such interactions. The developmental outcomes of acquiring everyday concepts (i.e., levels of conceptual understanding) are fragmented, subject to chance and often difficult to trace. On the other hand, scientific concepts are learned in specially organized and structured interactions with adults (e.g., at school) that concern studying new ways to solve problems and that aim to introduce children to scientifically sound definitions of diverse phenomena. Through learning scientific concepts, a child can be brought efficiently to new developmental levels. In this sense, it is only this type of learning, based on "high-quality" cultural tools such as scientific concepts, that actually induces, shapes and directs development.

Vygotsky focused so much attention on differentiating between these two types of concepts because they illustrate how learning may affect development. This was not a matter of mere educational significance: Vygotsky aimed at revealing the very essence of developmental proc esses as being contingent upon ways of learning new cultural tools. However, these studies needed to be continued and many theoretical implications of this approach remained to be spelled out.

Galperin's unique contribution to the understanding of learning and development is his explication and empirical study of the mechanisms by which the concrete content of cultural tools being transmitted to the child in the course of teaching/learning lead to developmental processes. Galperin was the first to single out and describe in detail the core distinctive features of the cultural tools and respective instructional procedures that defined the leading role of learning in a child's development and, ultimately, the very course and most fundamental regularities of this development (see Arievitch & Stetsenko, 1998). Galperin scrutinized existing traditional methods and types of instruction and came to a conclusion that they all usually fail to provide the child with the most appropriate cultural tools to deal with specific classes of problems. Even in school, children are faced with fragmented phenomena, and poorly generalized ways of dealing with them; they are supposed to learn by memorizing mosaics of unrelated facts.

Galperin described a whole set of conditions that drew a demarcating line between traditional instruction and instruction based on the utilization of efficient cultural tools. In brief, efficient cultural tools are learning materials (i.e., concepts, theories, ideas) that (a) embody and reify the most efficient cultural practices of the previous generations, in that (b) they express, in a condensed, generalized form, the essence of certain classes of problems or phenomena by (c) representing the genesis of these problems or phenomena and hence the logic — the templates of action and the contexts where these actions can be applied — necessary for dealing with them. A somewhat simplified but illustrative example concerns the geometrical concept of a circle. Usually, this concept is introduced to children with its definition as a curved line on which every point is equally distant from one fixed point inside the curve (i.e., a figure with equal radii). The alternative definition is based on describing the procedure of producing a circle with a stick, where one end is fixed, or by a pair of compasses. Thus, the initial operation underlying the concept of a circle (the operation discovered in human history and reified in such cultural tool as a pair of compasses) is presented to the students, helping to reveal the otherwise concealed genesis (and hence the essence) of this geometrical form. Only in this case does it become clear to the students why all the radii of the circle are (and have to be) equal — namely, because it is actually the same radius revolving around one fixed point (see Davydov, 1988).

Another example concerns the concept of *number* and the concept of *unit* (i.e., "one"). In traditional instruction, the concept of unit is often introduced empirically as a single discrete object. Children are taught that one (object) is one, not two or more, and that this is just something to memorize and accept. The genesis of a unit, that is, the way a unit (and any number) is produced, is not revealed to the child. The more general concept of number is also introduced as the extension of the idea about discrete objects. As a rule, this leads to the formation of empirical concepts in which a unit is erroneously identified with discreteness of objects, and mathematical numbers are confused with discrete objects (Galperin, 1989c). In contrast, with a type of instruction based on Galperin's theory, children learn to understand the kernel idea of number as an expression and reification of the operation of measurement (e.g., Georgiev, 1960). In other words, children are taught to use measurement as an analytical tool to derive fundamental concepts in elementary mathematics. More specifically, children first learn to discriminate between different properties of an object and choose an appropriate measure for each property. As a next step, children learn to apply the measure in order to compare different objects by certain properties (length, weight, etc.). Finally, the concept of unit (something equal to a chosen measure) and of number (the ratio of some quantity to another quantity that is used as the unit of measurement) are introduced (see Galperin, 1989c).

These and similar types of innovative programs of developmental teaching and instructional procedures (e.g., Davydov, 1988), based on elaborated cultural tools, proved to have a true impact on a child's development in several ways. For example, the knowledge acquired by students was characterized by a high level of mastery and maintenance, broad transfer, and intentional reflective use (see Arievitch & Stetsenko, 1998; Karpov & Haywood, 1998).

## Focus on ZPD and Assisted Learning within ZPD

The third research line has focused on the zone of proximal development and implications of this concept for a theory of teaching/learning. The main assumption here is that the adult can assist the child in solving certain types of tasks and thus promote the child's cognitive growth and advance development to new horizons. This assisted performance has been described as scaffolding (Wood, Bruner, & Ross, 1976). Scaffolding implies graduated assistance from the adult/expert (Greenfield, 1984). It also rightfully ascribes an active role to the child in interactions with adults. For example, the child's active involvement is seen as one side of a collaborative process embracing both the child and her partner. The adult structures and models the appropriate solution to the problem, engaging the child in this solution, while monitoring the child's current level of skill, and then supporting or scaffolding the child's extension of current skills and knowledge to a higher level of competence (Wertsch, 1979; Wood, 1980; see also Rogoff & Gardener, 1984, p. 97). However, the concept of scaffolding is related only loosely, if at all, to the concept of cultural tools and implies too strongly that the quantity rather than quality (i.e., content) of the adult's help is the decisive influence on a child's development. Also the content of child-adult interaction, revolving around acquisition of particular cultural tools, remains beyond the scope of attention. Tharp and Gallimore (1988) put it succinctly:

Scaffolding is a concept that has been of unusual importance to the study of child development. However appealing this metaphor may be, the field has advanced to the point that a more differentiated concept can be developed. For example, scaffolding suggest that the principal variations in adult actions are matters of quantity — how high the scaffold stands, how many levels it supports, how long it is kept in place. But many of the acts of the adult in assisting the child are qualitatively different from one another. (pp. 33-34)

The important task of defining the quality of processes of child-adult interaction in the ZPD was pursued recently by several researchers (Brown & Campione, 1994; Griffin & Cole, 1984). Various strategies characteristic of an adult's assistance and the resulting qualities of a child's cognitive operations have been described. For example, attention has been paid to such means of assisting students' performance as modeling, contingency managing, feedback, instructing, questioning, and cognitive structuring (Tharp & Gallimore, 1988). This is an important line of research, which substantially advances our understanding of what exactly goes on within the ZPD and how learning can affect the development of the mind. However, for all the importance of analyzing these means of adults' assistance notwithstanding, this analysis draws on the quality of adult-child (or teacher-student) interactions and not on the quality of the cultural tools involved as integral parts in such interactions. In other words, the question of the content of what is being taught to the students is not considered as important and is not pursued (in clear contrast to Galperin's line of research).

### Activity as the Germ Cell Process

As I attempted to show in the preceding discussion, the concepts of social interaction, of cultural tools and of the ZPD have served as the grounding principle for relatively independent lines of research. It seems however that although each research line makes reference to and uses a variety of sociocultural concepts, only one concept is especially brought to the fore, serving as the grounding principle that typifies that research.

As a result, the full heuristic potential of the concepts of social interaction, cultural tools, and ZPD remains to be explored. This can be done, I believe, by exploring the internal links among the three concepts in a way that exposes the grounding dynamics of human development without compartmentalizing them into separate processes of guided participation, acquisition of cultural tools, and individual development within ZPD. This is the task of revealing the germ cell idea that underpins each of the described concepts and this task cannot be achieved through abstract definitions, but only through finding and describing the concrete germ cell process that underlies human development in its different aspects.

Activity constitutes and is constituted by social interaction, acquisition of cultural tools, and the formation of new skills and abilities within the ZPD. The germ cell process, in my view, is the transformations of activity, which is goal-directed and object-oriented (*predmetnoj*). By adding the facet of transformation of activity as the content of interpsychological processes to the activity principle, it becomes possible to make a synthesis between various dimensions of human development and avoid its compartmentalization. Specifically, much progress has been made recently in arguing for activity as a unit of analysis for sociocultural endeavors and events (e.g., Rogoff, 1995), and in arguing for individual mental processes as arising in and from goal-oriented activity (Martin, 1995; Scribner, 1984). However, these are only two facets of the activity principle, which should be complemented with this additional important facet. It is not enough to note that intra-psychological processes originate from broader human activity, nor emphasize that interpsychological development is placed in a society or presuppose society as its source. By including transformations of activity, we have a way to understand the inseparable interconnection between intra- and interpsychological processes (see Tulviste, this volume).

In this elaborated form, the activity principle suggests that all inter- and intrapersonal psychological processes, including those of individual skill and knowledge acquisition, are nothing but different facets of human goal-oriented activity. In the case of intrapersonal processes, it is especially important to realize that activity can undergo certain transformations (e.g., internalization, generalization, conversion, automation, and integration of its parts as well as mediation of its structure with culturally-invented means), while remaining — in content and hence in its ultimate reality — the same culturally-constituted and socially-embedded human activity.

Galperin (1967) made important contributions to understanding this facet of activity principle (Arievitch & van der Veer, 1995; Stetsenko & Arievitch, 1997). He characterized all human activity through object-related parameters and demonstrated the identity of the objective operational content of activity in the course of its transformation into a mental, intrapsychological form. In Galperin's view, the external, object-related status of mental activity constitutes the genuine "essence" of mind. That was his way to eliminate the Cartesian dualism in characterizing mental actions and the external/internal dichotomy. *Internal* refers to the subject's ability to perform a certain action without the immediately present problem situation "in the mind," and to act with both sensory characteristics and nonsensory properties of the objects. There is no intended meaning of "within the individual" or "in the brain." Mental actions are performed on the basis of mental representation, that is, independently of the physical presence of things. They are a kind of ideal action, but only in a sense that they do not materially transform the situation. In other words, the relationship between inter- and intrapsychological processes is explained as the transition from a material *object-dependent* activity (such as in the actual counting of physical objects by pointing at them with a finger in the initial stages of acquiring the counting operation) to a material *object-independent* activity (when a child comes to be able to count the objects without necessarily touching them or even seeing them).

According to Galperin, the products of psychological development, the intrapersonal forms of mental processes, should be viewed as crystallized and transformed (often highly generalized, automatized and converted) types of activity. These transformations and modifications of activity often go unnoticed — both for the subject in introspection and for the researcher. Even in the works of A.N. Leontiev — activity theory's "founding father" — this idea has often been blurred by an unfortunate selection of concepts to describe the relations between internal and external forms of activities (see Stetsenko, 1995). For example, the main emphasis in activity theory was placed on exploring the *connection* between consciousness (mind) and activity as if these were two different realities (e.g., Leontiev, 1983, p. 105). As a result, the equivalence of mind and activity began to be regarded as the equivalence of their origin and structure, but not as a genuine ontological unity of both types of processes. In the search for principles that connect mind and activity, the idea that the human mind does not have its own structure and its own logic of development, distinct from the structure of object-related activity, has been lost. Even in the theory of activity (works of A.N. Leontiev and his immediate followers), a certain "fetishism" of mental processes has emerged, for example, stating that mental images not only have their structure and properties but also their own ontology and even agency (e.g., Smirnov, 1985; Zinchenko, 1988). In general, it continues to be the case — also within the sociocultural approach — that mind and human activity are conceived to be different, though related, realities (e.g., as product and source, respectively).

This facet of the activity principle as formulated by Galperin must be combined with the other facets, namely, an understanding of activity as a unit of analysis for sociocultural endeavors and events (e.g., Rogoff, 1995; Rogoff, Radziszewska, & Masiello, 1995), and as a unit of analysis for the processes involved in the acquisition of cultural tools. With regard to the latter, it is important to realize that cultural tools can also be conceived of as types of activities (Stetsenko, 1993). Specifically, these tools can and should be viewed not merely as objects (things), but as embodiments of certain cultural practices, crystallized templates of action, schematized representations of certain ways of doing things in human communities. Cultural tools are in this sense embodiments of the function and meaning of things as discovered in cultural practices, they are "objects-that-can-be-used-for-a-certain-purpose" in the human community. As such, they only can be appropriated by a child through acting upon and with them in the course of actively reconstructing their meaning and function. Initially, these reconstructions of cultural tools are possible only in the process of cooperation and interaction with other people who already possess the knowledge (or the meaning) of a given cultural tool. In this perspective, cultural tools are never simply added from outside into the child's mind; nor are they just structural characteristics of the developing mind, which may or may not be present at different stages in development. Rather, their acquisition by a child is an integral part of developmental processes, the pathway that defines the very essence of human development and constitutes its content.

### Learning and Development: Implications of the Activity Principle

If we consider the activity principle in its various facets as just described, then the relationship among the concepts of social interaction, cultural tools, and ZPD becomes clear. All three concepts can be viewed as expressions of different facets of the same process of goal-directed and object-oriented human activity. In other words, the processes underlying each of these concepts are not compartmentalized paths that human development can follow (or take the form of); rather they are aspects of one and the same basic process — a process that includes shared social activity on one pole and individual social activity on the other, with both types of activity being constituted by and constitutive of the use of cultural tools in the ongoing active interactions between child and adult.

The necessary internal links among the concepts of social interaction, cultural tools, and ZPD now become obvious. The child makes progress under the guidance of an adult because the latter, as a representative of human culture, provides the child with new, more efficient cultural tools. These cultural tools, mostly signs and symbols, have to be introduced first on the external, interpersonal level (i.e., in the child-adult shared interaction), because these tools are not static entities, but activities that have to be actively played out and reproduced in the course of interaction in order for the child to acquire them. In the course of such interactions, an adult introduces and reveals the meaning and function of new cultural tools to the child, as well as ways to operate with the help of these tools. Gradually, the actions that can be performed with these cultural tools, according to their meaning and function, get internalized by the child, thus constituting the child's advanced cognitive functioning. By virtue of mastering new efficient cognitive tools in which essential characteristics of cultural practices are embodied in a schematized and abbreviated form, the child becomes able to progress to a new stage of development and, for example, to independently perform more complex tasks.

When one looks at the links that bridge social interaction, cultural tools, and ZPD then — and only then — does it become possible to understand why learning plays a leading role in development, why it constitutes the very essence of development rather than merely following or supporting development. Learning leads development because it is through learning that the child comes to be able to master — through and within interactions with an adult — the new cultural tools; this mastery constitutes the very cornerstone of mental functioning and human development.

The synthesis of the concepts of social interaction, cultural tools, and ZPD, and the research traditions associated with each of them is an important task for the future; only initial steps have been made in this direction. The attempts at achieving this synthesis should not be based on simple comparisons of isolated findings and definitions, but instead on articulating and analyzing the dialectical concrete "objective interconnectedness" (see Falmagné, 1995, p. 209) of the grounding processes involved. As I aimed to show, such analyses bring us back to fundamental principles of activity theory and they potentially advance our understanding of human development, especially in its relationship to learning.

### References

Arievitch, I.M., & Stetsenko, A. (1998). Development through learning: Galperin's contribution. Unpublished manuscript, University of Berne, Switzerland.

Arievitch, I.M., & Van der Veer, R. (1995). Furthering the internalization debate: Galperin's contribution. *Human Development, 38*, 113-126.

Brown, A.L., & Campione, J.C. (1994). Guided discovery in a community of learners. In K.M. McGilly (Ed.), *Classroom lessons: Integrating cognitive theory and classroom practice* (pp. 229-270). Cambridge, Mass.: MIT Press.

Cole, M. (1985). The zone of proximal development: Where culture and cognition create each other. In J.V. Wertsch (Ed.), *Culture, communication, and cognition* (pp. 146-161). Cambridge: Cambridge University Press.

Davydov, V.V. (1988). The concept of theoretical generalization and problems of educational psychology. *Studies in Soviet Thought, 36,* 169-202.

Elkonin, D.B., & Davydov, V.V. (1966). (Eds.). *Vozrastnie vozmozhnosti usvoeniia znanii* [The age-related potential for knowledge acquisition]. Moscow: Prosveshenije Press.

Falmagné, R.J. (1995). The abstract and the concrete. In L.M.W. Martin, K. Nelson, & E. Tobach (Eds.), *Sociocultural psychology: Theory and practice of knowing and doing* (pp. 205-228). Cambridge: Cambridge University Press.

Galperin, P.I. (1967). On the notion of internalization. *Soviet Psychology, 5* (3), 28-33.

Galperin, P.I. (1969). Stages in the development of mental acts. In M. Cole & I. Maltzman (Eds.), *A handbook of contemporary Soviet psychology* (pp. 34-61). New York: Basic Books.

Galperin, P.I. (1989a). Mental actions as basis for the formation of thoughts and images. *Soviet Psychology, 27* (3), 45-65.

Galperin, P.I. (1989b). Organization of mental activity and the effectiveness of learning. *Soviet Psychology, 27* (3), 65-82.

Galperin, P.I. (1989c). Study of the intellectual development of the child. *Soviet Psychology, 27* (3), 26-44.

Galperin, P.I. (1992). Stage-by-stage formation as a method of psychological investigation. *Journal of Russian and East European Psychology, 30* (4), 60-80.

Georgiev, L.S. (1960). Formirovanije nachalnikh matematicheskih ponjatij u detej. [Formation of elementary mathematical concepts in children]. Unpublished doctoral dissertation, Moscow State University.

Greenfield, P.M. (1984). A theory of the teacher in the learning activities of everyday life. In B. Rogoff & J. Lave (Eds.), *Everyday cognition: Its development in social contexts* (pp. 117-138). Cambridge, Mass.: Harvard University Press.

Griffin, P., & Cole, M. (1984). Current activity for the future: The Zo-ped. In B. Rogoff & J.V. Wertsch (Eds.), *Children's learning in the "zone of proximal development"* (pp. 45-64). San Francisco: Jossey-Bass.

Hedegaard, M. (1995). The qualitative analysis of the development of a child's theoretical knowledge and thinking. In L.M.W. Martin, K. Nelson, & E. Tobach (Eds.), *Sociocultural psychology: Theory and practice of knowing and doing* (pp. 293-325). Cambridge: Cambridge University Press.

Hedegaard, M. (1998). Situated learning and cognition: Theoretical learning and cognition. *Mind, Culture, and Activity, 5,* 114-126.

Karpov, Y.V., & Haywood, H.C. (1998). Two ways to elaborate Vygotsky's concept of mediation. Implications for instruction. *American Psychologist, 53,* 27-36.

Laboratory for Comparative Human Cognition. (1983). Culture and cognitive development. In W. Kessen (Ed.), *Mussen's handbook of child psychology: Vol. 1. History, theory, and method* (4th ed., pp. 295-356). New York: Wiley.

Lave, J. (1991). Situating learning in communities of practice. In L.B. Resnick, J. Levine & S.D. Teasley (Eds.), *Perspectives on socially shared cognition* (pp. 41-62). Washington, D.C.: American Psychological Association.

Leontiev, A.N. (1983). *Izbrannije psihologicheskije trudy* (Vol. 1) [Selected psychological works]. Moscow: Pedagogika Publishers.

Lompscher, J. (1984). Problems and results of experimental research on the formation of theoretical thinking through instruction. In M. Hedegaard, P. Hakkarainen, & Y. Engeström (Eds.), *Learning and teaching on a scientific basis* (pp. 293-358). Risskov, Denmark: University of Aarhus, Department of Psychology.

Martin, L.M.W. (1995). Linking thought and setting in the study of workplace learning. In L.M.W. Martin, K. Nelson, & E. Tobach (Eds.), *Sociocultural psychology: Theory and practice of knowing and doing* (pp. 150-167). Cambridge: Cambridge University Press.

Rogoff, B. (1990). Apprenticeship in thinking: Cognitive development in social context. New York: Oxford University Press.

Rogoff, B. (1994). Developing understanding of the idea of communities of learners. *Mind, Culture, and Activity, 1,* 209-229.

Rogoff, B. (1995). Observing sociocultural activity on three planes: Participatory appropriation, guided participation, apprenticeship. In A. Álvarez, P. del Rio, & J.V. Wertsch (Eds.), *Perspectives on sociocultural research* (pp. 139-164). Cambridge: Cambridge University Press.

Rogoff, B., & Gardener, W. (1984). Adult guidance of cognitive development. In B. Rogoff & J. Lave (Eds.), *Everyday cognition: Its development in social contexts* (pp. 95-116). Cambridge, Mass.: Harvard University Press.

Rogoff, B., & Lave, J. (Eds.). (1984). *Everyday cognition: Its development in social contexts*. Cambridge, Mass.: Harvard University Press.

Rogoff, B., Radziszewska, B., & Masiello, T. (1995). Analysis of developmental processes in sociocultural activity. In L.M.W. Martin, K. Nelson, & E. Tobach (Eds.), *Sociocultural psychology: Theory and practice of knowing and doing* (pp. 125-149). Cambridge: Cambridge University Press.

Scribner, S. (Ed.). (1984). Cognitive studies of work [Special issue]. *Quarterly Newsletter of the Laboratory of Comparative Human Cognition, 6* (1&2).

Smirnov, S.D. (1985). *Psikhologiia obraza* [The psychology of the image]. Moscow: Moscow University Publishers.

Stetsenko, A. (1993). Vygotsky: Reflections on the reception and further development of his thoughts. *Multidisciplinary Newsletter for Activity Theory, 13/14*, 38-45.

Stetsenko, A. (1995). The principle of object-relatedness in the theory of activity. *Journal of Russian and East European Psychology, 33*, 54-69.

Stetsenko, A., & Arievitch, I. (1996). The zone of proximal development. In J. Lompscher (Ed.), *Entwicklung und Lernen aus kulturhistorischer Sicht* (Vol. 1, pp. 81-92). Marburg: BdWi Verlag.

Stetsenko, A.P., & Arievitch, I.M. (1997). Constructing and deconstructing the self: Comparing post-Vygotskian and discourse-based versions of social constructivism. *Mind, Culture, and Activity, 4*, 160-173.

Tharp, R.G., & Gallimore, R. (1988). *Rousing minds to life: Teaching, learning, and schooling in social context*. Cambridge: Cambridge University Press.

Vygotsky L.S. (1981). The instrumental method in psychology. In J.V. Wertsch (Ed. and Trans.), *The concept of activity in Soviet psychology*. Armonk, N.Y.: Sharpe. (Original work published 1930)

Vygotsky, L.S. (1978). *Mind in society. The development of higher psychological functions* (M. Cole, V. John-Steiner, S. Scribner, & E. Souberman, Eds.; M. Cole & M. Lopez-Morillas, Trans.). Cambridge, Mass.: Harvard University Press.

Wertsch, J.V. (1979). From social interaction to higher psychological processes: A clarification and application of Vygotsky's theory. *Human Development, 22*, 1-22.

Wood, D.J. (1980). Teaching the young child: Some relationships between social interaction, language, and thought. In D.R. Olson (Ed.), *The social foundations of language and thought* (pp. 280-296). New York: Norton.

Wood, D.J., Bruner, J.S., & Ross, G. (1976). The role of tutoring in problem solving. *Journal of Child Psychology and Psychiatry, 17*, 89-100.

Zaporozhets A.V., & Elkonin D.B. (Eds.). (1971). *The psychology of preschool children* (J. Shybut & S. Simon, Trans.). Cambridge, Mass.: MIT Press. (Original work published 1964)

Zinchenko, V.P. (1988). Problema edinits analiza v teorii dejatelnosti [The problem of units of analysis in the theory of activity]. *Vestnik Moskovskogo Universiteta Serija 14: Psikhologii, 3*, 15-26.

# 14 Personality, Subject and Human Development: The Subjective Character of Human Activity

*Fernando L. González Rey*

The problem of personality has been treated insufficiently by different followers of the cultural-historical approach (A.N. Leontiev, P.I. Galperin, D.B. Elkonin, among others), and more recently by some of the more important followers of the so-called sociocultural approach, who also have not paid sufficient attention to personality. However, personality was one of the most important topics in the work of the pioneers of the cultural-historical perspective in psychology (e.g., S.L. Rubinshtein and L.S. Vygotsky). This topic has continued to be the focus in the works of their followers in the former Soviet Union, including Abul'khanova-Slavskaia (1973), Antsyferova (1981), and Bozhovich (1966, 1976, 1977, 1979, 1980a, 1980b), among others.

Despite the fact that Vygotsky himself did not center his attention on the question of personality, he referred explicitly to the topic in his works. Rubinshtein (1959) focused on personality as one of the more important questions for psychological theory. Research on personality has been developed particularly by the followers of Bozhovich (e.g., Chudnovskii, 1981; Neimark, 1976), as well as other researchers, who practically never appear in western references, such as Lomov (1975), Menchinskaia (1977), Miasishchev (1960), and Nepomnichaia (1977). Among the researchers who have paid attention to the issue of personality following the sociocultural approach in some of its concerns, it is necessary to mention Valsiner, who has devoted many works to this topic (e.g., Valsiner, 1989).

After Vygotsky's death in 1934, activity theory, as proposed by A.N. Leontiev, was progressively turned into a kind of official psychology in the former Soviet Union. To become official was only possible through the complete acceptance of the rules of the dominant Marxist interpretation. At that time official Marxism was influenced strongly by positivism and structuralism and rejected the topics of subjectivity and individuality in the social sciences. If we take this fact into account, it is possible to explain the effort of Leontiev in the development of an objective, experimental approach to the study of the psyche, which led, in my opinion, to a de-psychologization of psychology.

Leontiev defines the identity between external and internal activities by their structure, which leads to an identification of both moments of human activity. In fact, he attributed a primary and dominant character to the external. The relationship between the external and the internal was understood through a linear determinism, in which the internal was considered as a reflex of the external. Considering activity as the way by which something external becomes internal seems to be more of a mechanical than a dialectical comprehension of this complex relationship.

This mechanical identification between external and internal is present in many different moments of Leontiev's work. Regarding personality, he wrote:

The concept of the subject of activity is another matter. In the first place, that is, before the more important moments that form the process of activity are explained, the subject remains as if beyond the limits of investigation. He appears only as a prerequisite for activity, one of its conditions. Only further analysis of the movement of activity and the forms of psychic reflection elicited by it makes it necessary to introduce the concept of the concrete subject, of the personality as of an internal moment of activity. The category of activity is now disclosed in all of its actual fullness as encompassing both poles, the pole of the object and the pole of the subject. (Leontiev, 1975/1978, p. 97)

To consider personality as nothing but an internal moment of activity not only presupposes a complete identification between the external and the internal, but it also ignores the historical character of personality, which is not a moment of activity, but a moment in the history of the subject. The emphasis on the external leads to an object-based activity definition (i.e., to a one-sided definition of activity on the basis of its object), completely ignoring its subjective constitution and its complex social character. In this way the category of the social is reduced to that of object and the role of communication is considered secondary.

Communication was explicitly or implicitly viewed by Leontiev and his followers as one specific kind of object-based activity, and they came to the extreme position of presenting communication within the narrow scheme of the activity category. In this framework one of the partici pants in communication, the listener, is considered as an object (cf. Lisina, 1978). This framework led to a very strong polemic in the 1970s about the place of the category of communication in psychology, which, in my view, had an important influence on the development of social and educational psychologies in the former Soviet Union.

In educational psychology the monopoly of the category *activity* led to a one-sided conception of human development, taking the concept of *leading activity* as the cornerstone of human development. This conception found its most accurate form of expression in the periodization theory of Elkonin (1971/1972), which postulated that each stage of development could be characterized by one particular fundamental activity. This theory ignored the complex network of elements that in very different ways are involved in the development of each concrete subject. Both subjectivity and the concrete subject were completely ignored by these researchers in their conception of development (González Rey, 1996a; González Rey & Mitjans, 1989).

Another psychologist, Chudnovskii (1976), who observed well the limitations of the concept of fundamental activity, wrote:

However, it is not only fundamental activity, but the total way of life of preschool children, their daily communication with their peers and with adults, their activity regarding behavioral rules and the decisive moments that they face in daily life, they all gradually lead to radical modifications in their motivational sphere. (p. 49) [my translation]

Important categories introduced by Vygotsky (1998) in the analysis of human development, such as the *social situation of development* and *zone of proximal development*, were completely forgotten by Leontiev's followers, who emphasized the processes directly involved in immediate activity.

### Towards a Conceptualization of Personality from a Cultural-Historical Perspective

In my opinion, the traditional understanding of personality must be reconsidered. What is needed is a cultural and historical reconceptualization that not only brings back the social and historical dimensions but which treats them an essential condition for understanding the subjective constitution of personality. During the history of psychology, many psychologists from different schools understood personality as an internal, subjective, intrapsychic entity, in opposition to the social, which was considered as external and objective.

The positivistic tradition in psychology has been one of the main historical roots that defines the traditional place of personality in our science. This positivistic influence has appeared in different ways, for example, as the quantitative, objective and atomist conceptualization of personality, which results from the methodological requirements of a positivistic methodology. Another way that positivism has influenced the traditional meaning of personality in psychology has been its tendency to split the subject under study, which has led to considering the personality as a closed entity outside of the complex network of facts within which personality continuously reconstitutes itself.

In the positivist perspective, personality is considered to be a specific psychological field with its own problems and techniques, and not a general category directly involved in the different problems belonging to all spheres of psychological inquiry. If we want to consider personality as a subjectively-constituted phenomenon, we need to take the following principles into account:

1. Personality is not a pregiven essence that characterizes the internal psychological processes of the individual without implications for the social network in which the individual lives. Personality is historically constituted in the course of human development; it is through development that the social becomes historical and acquires its subjective constitution. Subjectivity is not a copy or a reflex of the social, because it is not simply the external turned into internal. Subjectivity is simultaneously internal and external, it exists continuously as it is re-enacted and reconstituted within everyday social interactions. This does not mean that personality should be considered as a linear consequence of these interactions; rather it is embedded in a system of social interactions. Personality takes part in this system as a subjective constituent moment of the whole system, which also changes as personality itself changes.

2. In its subjective definition, personality is far from being considered as a linear cause of human behavior. Any individual expression results from a complex network of dynamic factors, within which different personality configurations acquire subjective sense. This depends on and varies with the quality of the network of dynamic elements in which the subject is involved along the process of development. Both

the personality and the current interactive moments of the subject take subjective sense and meaning and are integrated in different ways in the course of the subjective configuration of the subject's action.

3. The third assumption has to do with the fact that the constitution of personality takes place in the individual. The singular case study is the source of theoretical construction in the study of personality. This is not only a theoretical assumption, but also an epistemological one, because it goes beyond the traditional view in which the only way of making generalizations is through interindividual comparisons (González Rey, 1997). This view leads to supraindividual conclusions in which the general and essential traits of personality are apparently contained. This has been the pretension of the so-called nomothetical approach, which was criticized seriously by Allport (1937) long ago.

Personality, from a cultural-historical point of view, does not and cannot exist in an abstract way. It belongs to the experiential world of the concrete subject. By its contents, personality is deeply singular, because no person has an identical social trajectory to another person. Therefore, generalization will never appear as a result of any given conclusion of some concrete techniques, as has been so popular in the study of personality. Generalization in the study of subjective phenomena always results from a theoretical construction.

Personality here is considered as a theory of individual subjectivity. Subjectivity is seen as something different from experience. It is the complex system of meanings and subjective senses which are configured in many different ways throughout human development. In this system the different facts of our experience have to be subjectively constituted in the same terms of our current subjective development. Personality is a complex system within which current social and historical experiences are permanently in tension in the subject. In effect, this view asserts that the core concern of personality psychology is subjective.

We prefer to use the term *constitution* to refer to any new acquisition of development. Terms like internalization lead to the view of a one-sided, deterministic causality from the external to the internal, and to considering the transit of the external to the internal as the essential way of psychological development. This contributes to perpetuate the mechanical separation between the two different and yet interrelated sides of subjective development.

A comprehension of subjectivity as a key category and the ground for the development of a different approach to personality, is not only compatible with, but essential for, a cultural-historical framework. To understand the development of personality from a subjective point of view presupposes that one overcomes several dichotomies that still plague psychology, such as social vs. individual; intrapsychic vs. interactive; conscious vs. unconscious; and cognitive vs. affective. Personality has a social genesis; it develops simultaneously in social and historical subjective individual space. Personality is intertwined with a subject's current interactions throughout human development.

Subjectivization of social space is an expression of the complex social networks within which any social space exists. Therefore, the subjective character of a social space is not only the expression of the current interactions of its members. Indeed the subjective character of any social space is constituted simultaneously by the ongoing interactions of the persons who are part of that social space in the present time and by those subjective trends that historically have configured it as a moment in its own history and at the same as a particular moment of society. I have called this level of the subjective phenomenon *social subjectivity* (González Rey, 1996b).

The subjective constitution of social phenomena does not mean that one should ignore its objective side. Subjective is another side of the objective world; it cannot be identified as nonobjective. It means that subjectivity should be considered as having its own ontological status that is distinct from objective phenomena, which are known by their observable, concrete and stable attributes. Phenomena are generated in the social subjectivity that go beyond the intention of individuals who configure themselves within that social space.

The concept of social subjectivity is quite different from the position of social constructionism, which has ignored the complex and heterogeneous character of the social reality through the identification of the social with discursive practices. I agree completely with Jovchelovitch (1996) that:

The social is subjective *and* objective at one and the same time. On the one hand, it engenders in its dynamics historical, political and economic elements which constrain and narrow the possibilities of human action. In this sense, the social is a space of institutional boundaries and limits. Yet these limits are not absolute. For, on the other hand, the social is also a space where new possibilities are proposed, a space of communication, a space where self and other meet, explore each others' identities, construct symbols and express affects (pp. 122-123)

Any subjective phenomenon is always a synthesis of many different objective social facts and situations. Objective social influences become subjective through their impact on social and individual, yet constituted, histories, like personality and social subjectivity.

The topic of conscious and unconscious is closely related to the complexity of sociohistorical processes of subjective development. Personality as the subjective scene of individual psychological constitution is the scenario of unconscious processes, because the complex relations and alternatives that characterize the course of emotional and symbolic experiences, which are linked in many ways with each other, are impossible to be organized by the subject's consciousness. We look at the unconscious as a functionally constituted level of human psyche, which is present in the current subjective configurations of personality beyond any symbolic capacity of the individual. It leads directly to complex questions about the relation between the symbolic and emotional and of the cognitive and affective constitution of human experience.

## The Question of Meaning in Light of a Theory of Personality

It is possible to consider the category of meaning as having a central place in current sociocultural approaches (Bruner, Cole, Valsiner, Wertsch and so on). The category of meaning represented an important moment in overcoming the dominant role given to the information-processing paradigm in cognitive psychology. Meaning is not an abstract term; it involves experiential processes, and is produced through the different processes of human communication and continuously produced in social interactions.

However, when sociocultural psychologists took meaning as a central concept, they overemphasized semiotic mediation as a subject of psychological research, coming to a new universal principle of psychological organization that led many of their followers to reject the individual in the name of social. When social processes are understood only in terms of discursive practices, then other important constituent processes of social reality are ignored or overlooked. Moreover the consideration of social reality as discursive practice tends to lead to a new extreme in the mechanical separation between the social and individual, replacing the central place given to the individual in traditional intrapsychical approaches of personality theories with the discursive practices. This leads one to consider the individual subject as a simple voice or negotiator within different social practices. In this scenario, psychology in the name of culture throws away an essential side of cultural-historical phenomenom: the individual.

In my opinion, Vygotskian thinking was oriented to a concrete psychological subject, to a whole comprehension of psyche, articulating dialectically the dichotomy between external and internal, but keeping a focus on the ontological status of psychological subject. Social constructionism, on the other hand, focused on discourse and social practices as the only possible locus of inquiry.

Vygotsky in different parts of his work called for the integration of psychology. For example:

While we do not have a generally accepted system, able to integrate all available psychological knowledge, any important discovery of reality will unavoidably lead to the creation of a new theory able to integrate the recently observed facts. (Vygotsky, 1934/1967, p. 76) [My translation]

What has happened in current sociocultural approaches is similar to what Vygotsky warned us to be careful about. The recognition and construction of discourse as a relevant moment of the psychological subject has monopolized the attention of psychologists within this framework. As a result, they have lost the historical root of the psyche, which has to be found beyond current discursive practices, either in the psychological subject, in his/her personality, or in different phenomena of social subjectivity. From my point of view both concepts open alternatives for the integration of different fields in psychological construction.

### Meaning and Emotion

Another complex topic on which I want to focus is the relationship between meaning and emotions. Meanings are always symbolic entities. This means implicitly that emotions only appear after symbolic processes have been encoded in one way or another in individual experience.

Emotions, in my view, are a cornerstone in the constitution of personality. They are not secondary to symbolic process, or a consequence of them. Emotions and feelings, as Vygotsky (1965) recognized in *Psychology of Art*, continue to be one of the darker chapters in current psychology. Emotions have been treated historically in psychology from their different constituent sides: biological and social — but there has been little effort to work on their subjective side. Emotions have been insufficiently developed in the sociocultural approach where they appear as a consequence of semiotic mediational processes.

This question has also been perceived within the sociocultural approach:

By accrediting a paradigmatical status to language or discourse, discursive psychology focused on meaning insofar as it can be articulated or explicated. The aforementioned research of emotions, for example, is almost exclusively restricted to the study of emotion words, emotion scripts and scenarios, indigenous theories of emotion etc. ... Apparently, our emotions acquire their social meaning only after they have been interpreted by means of shared vocabularies and shared modes of conversation. (Baerveldt, 1997, p. 12)

For a long time emotions have been treated in psychology on the basis of their psychophysiological nature, without any attention to their subjective constitution. Emotions simultaneously are part of two different and closely interrelated systems: subjectivity and neurophysiological self-regulation. Emotions appear as an expression of biological drives, among which it is possible to identify animal survival instincts.

### Needs and Their Relation to Emotions

The process of cultural enrichment presupposes that individuals develop new and different needs, directly involved with the human cultural condition. These needs are clearly associated with new demands that individuals experience as a result of their sociocultural condition. They do not emerge necessarily through any kind of semiotic mediation, but are the result of those qualities of human relationships that acquire emotional sense for the subject. This emotional sense is a consequence of the complex encounter of already subjectively configured individual needs and the emotions that appear during the subject's ongoing interactions.

For example, when entering a new social situation, a person feels different emotions related to previous needs resulting from his/her prior experience. A child, who first starts to attend school, feels worry, anxiety, happiness, hopes, fear, or other emotions, depending on familiar and prior social experience. These emotions are present as a moment in the subjective meaning of the child's relation, but they interact in many ways with the emotions generated during the new interaction, leading in many cases to new needs, which change the subjective sense of the new social space. These dynamic interactions integrate with each other in complex emotional wholes which we call *configurations*. Configurations are a result of the process of subjectivization of social and cultural life. These configurations are dynamic elements involved in the subjective sense that characterizes different kinds of human expressions. Any human activity is constituted as a subjective configuration of personality. The configurations are permanently involved in the constitution of new needs.

On the basis of needs already configured in personality, the subject is involved emotionally in a complex network of social relationships, within which he/she generates new emotions as a result of singular involvement in such relationships. Emotions are an indicator of the quality of the human relationships in relation to the subject's needs. They are not a kind of discursive code. Emotions have a semiotic function, but they do not only result from a semiotic mediation. For example, an experience produces emotions, not from the needs of the subject involved in it, but from the complex network of emotional patterns involved in the situation.

Needs are a complex combination of current requirements of human activities and the exigencies of self-organizing psychological functions, many of which are defined during the development of personality. We do not consider needs within a static and pregiven taxonomy of different stable, dynamic drives of individuals, as they were considered for a long time in the history of psychology. Needs are not a priori, static elements that precede human action; they are dynamic elements involved in the subjective sense that characterizes different kinds of human expressions.

### The Role of Emotions in Personality

The configurations of personality result from the different emotions that are simultaneously present in any human activity. Because those interrelated states are integrated into a configuration, they no longer act as independent states, but as a part of a new qualitative state — as configuration.

The subjective senses define a relatively stable group of emotions experienced by subjects in their different activities and relations. The expressions of personality through a subject's activities lead to continuous processes of reconstitution of personality configurations in different situations faced by the subject in different moments of social life.

Despite the fact that subjective configurations of personality are a permanent source of emotions, the individual as subject should not only be understood in those attributes directly involved with actions, but also in his/her active character in the production of emotions. Emotional tension is a quality of individual involvement in any activity. This involvement represents the first step in the development of those needs that would appear in the course of individual activity. The topic of human needs has particular relevance in many fields of psychology, such as health psychology, couples therapy, and human development.

Emotions involve many different kinds of dynamic processes, which cannot be classified simply as positive or negative. Understanding the qualities of different kinds of emotions and the ways by which they influence somatic systems is a great challenge for psychological research. Cultural diversification implies a wide emotional diversification. For example, in my inquiries regarding human distress, I am currently investigating this theoretical construction in relation to an interesting phenomenon: some persons with somatic disorders cannot identify any emotional trouble in their lives, but they show different indicators of emotional discomfort. In my research I have found persons who have marital conflicts, without being aware of them. These people do not refer to any kind of trouble with their partner, but they cannot overcome a permanent feeling of discomfort that in some cases led to the search for new partners. In view of these facts, I am trying to describe the kind of emotions that are the basis of this phenomenon, but it is too early to present any specific hypotheses.

This research has led me to suppose that these emotions result from the subject's incapacity to experience new needs that appear throughout daily life. This incapacity constrains the subject's expressions in different spheres of life, producing emotions that are able to modify certain somato-physiological functions in some respects. Presently I am trying to identify how these emotions are produced in daily life, and ways to help persons who are in such situations. The cases I have studied have led me to consider the "liturgies" that are rigidly produced by certain ways of functioning in different institutions, from marriage to work, and which sometimes constrain the individual expressions of their members.

Ignorance of these kinds of needs by persons who are permanently under the pressures of daily life is responsible, in my opinion, for the generation of some kinds of emotions that are directly involved in somatic disorders, and which could be one source of human stress. These emotions lead to changes in those subjective configurations related to activities or relations in which the emotions appear. These kinds of emotions are frequently the basis of different human conflicts.

### Comprehension of the Individual Subject in a Cultural-Historical Definition of Personality

The cultural-historical character of subjectivity allows us to integrate the complex dialectical process of personality with social context. Subjectivity is an alternative to the concept of human nature. It is oriented towards the comprehension of the human psychological constitution within a cultural world. Subjectivity is a complex system that constantly reconfigures itself throughout its own development, in an endless process that simultaneously involves the historical and the current social conditions in which the subject is immersed. At the same time, the social conditions that configure the immediate social climate of the subject are part of the complex network of social subjectivity. It is necessary to understand the subject in the light of a dialectical, complex approach to personality.

Historically, most theories of personality have not explicitly considered the topic of the individual as a subject. It seems sometimes that the psychology of personality replaces the individual with personality, particularly in quantitative approaches to personality diagnosis and research, in which the individual disappears into a standard profile. The individual subject does not appear explicitly in Freudian psychoanalysis. The concept of ego in Freud's work is more of an adaptative instance than an active one.

More recently, in postmodern views, the death of the subject is claimed. The subject is replaced by discourse, which is understood as a supraindividual entity. History is not considered anymore as a constitutive moment in the current stage of development of the society and individuals. The forms adopted by social life would completely depend on those discursive constructions that result from dominant patterns of social exchanges. The social reality is constructed. It does not have any prior constituent definition, only social forms of exchange that characterize its current situation. The individual is viewed as being in a vacuum, which underestimates the psychological processes and the mind itself. These researchers consider discourses and social practices as the only focus of attention of social sciences.

We consider the subject as the concrete psychological individual, whose existence takes place in daily life (González Rey, 1992; González Rey & Mitjans, 1989). From our criteria it is impossible to consider a cultural-historical construction of personality without the category of subject, because the subject represents the scenario in which all the psychological processes of individual daily life take place. A subject perceives, thinks, feels and acts in many different directions of his/her social life.

A subject is constituted psychologically by personality, but the subject is not reduced to personality. The subject's position is active in the development of personality. He/she generates new emotions and symbolic productions that influence personality development. Development is not an intentional process, but any subject's intentions influences the developmental course. The subject is interactive, conscious, volitional and always part of any current context within his/her social network. As was mentioned before the subject not only represents a cognitive personal expression, but also is an important source of different needs that appear throughout his/her action.

The subject is essentially active as a result of anticipatory and constructive capacities. As Kelly (1955) pointed out, the subject is constantly constructing his/her experience in terms of personal representations. These representations are not merely cognitive; they are complex dynamic units full of subjective sense. The subject's representations are not defined only by intentions; their subjective constitution is also influenced by emotions proceeding from those configurations of personality that in one way or another deal with the contents of the representation. These emotional substrata appear rarely in the conscious core of representation.

Between the subject's intention and the constituent configurations of personality appears a "zone of tension" that characterizes the whole development of both instances: the subject and the personality, which constantly interweave with each other, defining the general quality of personality development. The subject regularly feels emotions that he/she cannot consciously identify, but on the basis of these emotions the subject constructs hypotheses, develops a system of beliefs, and is constantly engaged in a process of personal production. This personal production is simultaneouly cognitive and affective, conscious and unconscious, interactive and personal. That is, the subject's production is a complex, multidimensional subjective process that integrates different aspects of subjective human constitution within social subjectivity.

The subject's production also takes place in the intersubjective field within which he/she exists. Current social interactions are an important source of emotions and reflections that continually influence personality development and at the same time are influenced by the current personality constitution, which acts in different ways upon the subject.

The subject represents a living and open expression of personality, which constantly generates reflections, emotions and complex clusters of emotions and ideas in process, which enter in contradiction with the current configuration of personality. This contradictory meeting is an important developmental force.

The subject assumes different important functions throughout daily life, which also have an important impact on personality development. The subject's functions identified in my research are the following: decision-making processes, constructions of personal projects, and facing contradictions. The study of these complex functions has been fragmented in psychology, which usually focuses on such functions as separated processes, ignoring the role played by such functions within the complex dynamic of the subject-personality whole.

Some of my concrete inquiries are oriented towards the construction of complex links between moral and professional motives in adolescents and young adults. These inquiries are centered on the complex constructions about ideals and projects and the different ways in which the subjects face their daily life. Ideals and projects are a complex motivational process that rests on a configuration of dynamic states of personality, and are constructed by the subject through an active intellectual elaboration. For example, an adolescent male makes an ideal construction about his father, which is not simply a reflection or imitation of his father, but is truly a construction made through an identification with his father. This ideal construction is a complex process involving both an intellectual side and an emotional side. Adolescents give meaning to their new states of needs through ideals. In this sense, ideals play an important role as a subjective unit of personality development during this age, enabling adolescents to organize many of their conflicts and needs in beliefs, projects and behavior through which they develop new subjective resources and meanings about life and about themselves.

The professional project is similar in its psychological nature. Motivations, organized by personal representation, play an important role in the intentional course of young people towards their professional plans. Both of them are different kinds of motivational formations.

Such inquiries were later enriched by looking at health as a relevant quality of human development. This led me to consider the complexity of the emotional configurations that appear in students as a result of their experiences in school. Those works provided many empirical references for our current constructions on the topics of subject and personality, and also extended our "zones of dialogue" with the studied phenomenon itself.

### Implications of Using the Concepts of Personality and Subject in a Theory of Human Development

Cognitive approaches and a tendency to split development processes into different areas and problems have prevailed in theories of human development. For this reason it is not coincidental that most literature devoted to development, rarely takes into account such topics as health, social and institutional subjectivity, and even the topic of personality. What prevails instead is a narrow approach to processes or contents that have historically monopolized the literature on human development: such as sensory acquisition, learning, internalization of moral values, and socialization. Each psychological process is usually taken by itself, without any effort to connect them.

In such an account of human development, different psychological processes such as learning and internalization of moral values are isolated from the subject and from the complex social context within which development takes place. This view on the study of human functions has led to a one-sided and mechanical comprehension of human development, ignoring the complex network of elements that are the bases of the development of those processses. For example, learning is a complex subjective process, which is configured as a moment of personality development throughout human life, but simultaneously it is also a complex social process that integrates the quality of many different social agencies.

Vygotsky introduced some revolutionary categories which have been useful for a new comprehension of human development. In particular, I would like to emphasize the categories of *zone of proximal development* and *social situation of development*. Both of them were understood by Vygotsky (1998) as processual, open and dynamic. These categories led to a comprehension of development as an open, endless, differentiated process in which the personal attainment of new states of development are always in a complex interplay with qualities of current social relationships. These categories enable a completely different view of development in relation to the view oriented toward a regular, gradual and unidirectional periodization of human development.

Taking these categories into account, one can reconsider the place of the singular in human development. However, despite elaborating theoretical principles, which were oriented toward a new understanding of the processes of human development, it was impossible for Vygotsky to conceptualize development as a singular, nonrepeatable process. This was very clear in his paper "The Problem of Age" where he attempted to establish criteria for the periodization of development on the basis of age.

Some years later, Wallon (1971) defined the individual as the scenario of human development, understanding development as a dialectical and differentiated process. In Wallon's view, development does not follow any standard rule that leads to regular transitions from one stage to another according to an age criterion. The differentiating character of development meant the uniqueness of this process for each subject.

The emphasis on the singular in the comprehension of development is not only a theoretical question, but also an epistemological one. Singularity of development means that this process occurs in different ways involving different subjective structures throughout the course of the subject's action. In addition, the very comprehension of the individual as a subject leads one to consider the subject's decisions and options as relevant in the definition of developmental alternatives. The epistemological implications of Wallon's assumption about the singular character of development have not been appreciated sufficiently among researchers.

The configuration as a category allows one to integrate the singular as an important moment in the theoretical construction of human development. Subjective units of development are subjective constituent configurations of personality, which take particular relevance in any stage of development. This relevance is not inherent to any particular stage; on the contrary, it results from the particular social situation of development within with a person acts (Bozhovich, 1966/1976, p. 143). Therefore, there are no general standardized subjective unities of development that can be taken as universal and undifferentiated for all individuals at similar stages of development (as has happened, for example, with the concept of leading activity). Rather unities appear as a result of the uniqueness of development for each concrete subject. This uniqueness should not be considered as an exception but as an important moment of any generalization about personality development.

To consider these configurations as a unit of human development implies that one should understand the current social conditions of the subject's life and the subjectively-constituted historical experiences in different configurations of personality as part of the same dynamic process of personality development. Current social and historical configurations of personality continually interweave as a part of new configurations. Configurations are not pregiven entities that take part in human development as completely defined structures of sense leading to pre-fixed results. They are open, self-regulated systems that are permanently involved as units of meaning and sense in the different subjects' experiences.

Configurations are processes that are simultaneously structured and structuring. Structured configurations are bound to their own history within the subject's personality. Structuring configurations are an expression of the agency of individual subjects who engage, think, feel, talk and take part in the process of construction of the reality in which their development takes place. Configurations are variable and flexible in their sense throughout human development. The configurations that become relevant for one child or adolescent, are not the same for all their peers, even in the case where the same concrete configuration became relevant for different persons, the subjective sense within the whole constitution of their personalities would be different for each of them.

In an effort addressed to the theoretical construction of human development, I have studied three processes in which the subject and the personality are closely interrelated with each another. At first I studied some kinds of personality configurations that play an important role in the attainment of new states of development in different stages of this process. These configurations result from the process of subjectivization of some activities or relationships, which involve some specific needs related to the socialization of individuals in certain stages of development.

For example, reading is an important acquisition of development in Latin American cultures during the ages of 4 to 6 years, but reading is almost always considered to be a skill rather than an important way to develop personality. Most of the learning contents are mainly considered from their cognitive rather than from their emotional relevance. However, reading may become a very important activity for the development of personality.

Reading, as any other human activity, is involved in the process of subjectivization. During reading development the child is part of a social network within which he/she would experience many different emotions. In this process the subject would also produce beliefs and reflections related to him/herself, which will affect his/her whole development. The subject's construction could play an important role in the subjective configuration of reading. For some children, reading becomes an important way for them to develop self-esteem and self-confidence, as well as extend their socialization, creativity and so on. In these cases reading becomes a subjective unit for their psychological development.

Another example comes from my investigations among adolescents for whom sport is a subjective unit of development. For these adolescents, different conflicts and needs integrate into a unit of development in which sport plays a key role. The subjective sense of those needs and conflicts was mediated by the needs engendered during the practice of sports. Subjective configuration of sport becomes a relevant element of subjective sense for almost all the social expressions of these adolescents. In this regard, the subjective sense of their age is mediated by the subjective configuration of the sport.

The congruence of those emotions, feelings and reflections of the person toward him/herself is closely related with the development of personal identity. Identity is not simply a process of constructing the self-image; it is a complex cognitive-emotional process, in which emotional congruence plays an important role in the development of identity as a whole.

### The Role of Contradictions and Communication in Development

Two other processes that characterize human development are contradictions and communication. The separation of subjective units of development from these two processes is made for expository purposes rather than expressing a view about how human development proceeds. It is impossible to separate subjective units of development from the continuous flux of the subject's emotions and constructions which result from his/her involvement in different social networks.

Contradictions are important constituent moments of any reality, either from the point of view of a marxian dialectic or from the epistemology of complexity. The relationship between subject and personality as an important process in the definition of individual subjectivity is essentially contradictory, so contradictions are an important process in human development. One interesting contradiction of human development is that which occurs between the current system of a subject's personal representations and those emotions that appear in contradiction with the contents of representation. These contradictions could lead, as any contradiction, to new stages of development or to regression of the system, which may have manifold consequences.

The process of personality-configuration development may be very contradictory in cases in which such configurations result from the dynamic integration of contradictory affective states. In general, contradictions are at one and the same time conscious and unconscious phenomena, and it is important how subjects cope with them. In those cases in which contradictions are structured in terms of personality organization, without the conscious involvement of the subject, contradictions can become a source of anxiety and distress. However, when the subject is aware of the situation, and actively takes part in constructing different alternatives to face the problem, the conflict may turn into an important force for personality development.

Development cannot be understood as a process without a subject, as the literature has been pointing out for a long time. Sometimes, development is considered as a result of some determinants external to the developmental process. A subject's actions should be considered as a permanent process of making sense and meaning throughout human development. The subject takes an active part of his/her own trajectory throughout development.

In the complex dialectical process that takes place between social reality, subject and personality, the subject is an open and generative stance, and not a consequence of external influences. The subject is an active and productive agent, whose actions can transform the social context. Communication is an example of one of the more complex processes in which the subject is permanently involved. Communication is an essential process in the constitution of intersubjectivity within which the subject defines his/her interactive condition.

Communication is a constant path to human development. All the processes mentioned before occur in communication scenarios. However, not all relevant situations that take place during communication turn into subjective unities of development. It does not mean, however, that those moments do not have any influence on development. Sometimes a casual conversation may have a particular significance for one person, but this does not necessarily imply that the relationship with that specific partner will become a subjective unity of development.

Communication is an important source for the development of new emotions and meanings. Frequently, a subject is not reflectively conscious of these emotions and meanings, but they contribute to the formation of the subject's intentions, which in turn influence the subject's development.

I will finish by quoting from Gonçalves de Lima's (1997) interesting paper:

We seem to be faced again and again with the questions of how to focus on symbolic production without leading to an idealistic, de-politcized and decontextualized analysis; or alternatively how to avoid mechanical causalities of culture or activity contexts "moulding" passive consciousness. (p. 208)

Both challenges are expressions of real dangers in the development of the current sociocultural trends. I want to prevent any reductionism that could lead to either of the tendencies mentioned by Lima, which are so present in the current "ghosts" that treat the future development of this approach.

### References

Abul'khanova-Slavskaia, K.A. (1973). *Subjekte psikhicheskoi deiatel'nosti* [The subject of psychological activity]. Moscow: Nauka.

Allport, G.W. (1937). *Personality: A psychological interpretation*. New York: Holt.

Antsyferova, L.I. (Ed.) (1981). *Psikhologiia formirovaniia i razvitiia lichnosti* [The psychology of personality formation and development]. Moscow: Nauka.

Baerveldt, C. (1997, October). Cultural psychology as the study of meaning: Some epistemological considerations. In *Unidades de análisis en la psicología cultural*. Symposium conducted at the 17th Coloquio de Investigación, Universidad Nacional Autónoma de México, Escuela Nacional de Estudios Profesionales Iztacala, Mexico City.

Bozhovich, L.I. (1976). *La personalidad y su formación en la edad infantil* (C. Toste Muñiz, Trans.). Havana: Editora Pueblo y Educación. (Original work published 1966)

Bozhovich, L.I. (1977). The concept of cultural-historical development of the mind and its prospects. *Soviet Psychology, 16*(1), 5-22.

Bozhovich, L.I. (1979). Stages in the formation of the personality in ontogeny. *Soviet Psychology, 17*(3), 3-24.

Bozhovich, L.I. (1980a). Stages in the formation of the personality in ontogeny. *Soviet Psychology, 18*(3), 36-52.

Bozhovich, L.I. (1980b). Stages in the formation of the personality in ontogeny. *Soviet Psychology, 19*(2), 61-79.

Chudnovskii, V.E. (1976). O vozrastnom podjodii problemy formirobaniya lichnosti u schkolnikob. [About the aging approach to the problem of the formation of personality of students]. *Voprosy Psikhologii*, No. 4, 41-54.

Chudnovskii, V.E. (1981). *Nravstvennaia ustoichivost' lichnosti: Psikhologicheskoe issledovanie* [The moral stability of the personality: Psychological studies] Moscow: Pedagogika.

Elkonin, D.B. (1972). Toward the problem of stages in the mental development of the child. *Soviet Psychology, 10*, 225-251. (Original work published 1971)

González Rey, F.L. (1985). *Psicología de la personalidad*. Havana: Editora Pueblo y Educación.

González Rey, F.L. (1992). Personalidad, sujeto y psicología social. In M. Montero (Ed.), *Construcción y crítica de la psicología social* (pp. 149-176). Barcelona: Anthropos.

González Rey, F.L. (1996a). *Personalidad, comunicación y desarrollo*. Havana: Editorial Pueblo y Educación.

González Rey, F.L. (1996b). *Problemas epistemológicos de la psicología.* Havana: Editorial Academia.

González Rey, F.L. (1997). *Epistemología cualitativa y subjetividad.* San Pablo, Brazil: Editora PUC.

González Rey, F.L., & Mitjans, A. (1989). *La personalidad: Su educación y desarrollo.* Havana: Editora Pueblo y Educación.

Gonçalves de Lima, S. (1997). Will adding halves make a whole? Comments on Ratner's "Activity as a Key Concept for Cultural Psychology." *Culture & Psychology, 3,* 195-210.

Jovchelovitch, S. (1996). In defence of representations. *Journal for the Theory of Social Behaviour, 26,* 121-135.

Kelly, G.A. (1955). *The psychology of personal constructs.* New York: Norton.

Leontiev, A.N. (1978). *Activity, conciousness and personality* (M.J. Hall, Trans.). Englewood Cliffs, N.J.: Prentice-Hall. (Original work published 1975)

Lisina, M.I. (1978). Obcheniei u padrostkob i diet v pierviye ziemi goddi yistnii [The communication between adults and children in the first seven years of age]. In L.I. Bozhovich (Ed.), *Problemy obcheniya, vozrastnoi i pedagogicheskoi psikhologii* (pp. 232-244). Moscow: Pedagogika.

Lomov, B.F. (1975). Obchenie kak problema obchei psikhologii [Communication as a general problem of psychology]. In E.V. Shorokhova (Ed.), *Metodologicheskie problemy sotsial'noi psikhologii* (pp. 124-135). Moscow: Nauka.

Menchinskaia, N.A. (1977). Osbovotditciya vliyaniya operacionalizma [To get free from the influence of operationalism]. In N.A. Menchinskaia & Z.A. Farapanova (Eds.), *Problemy deiatel'nost v sovietskoi psikhologii* (pp. 40-52). Moscow: USSR Academy of Pedagogical Sciences

Miasishchev, V.N. (1960). *Lichnost i nevrozy* [Personality and neuroses]. Leningrad: Leningrad State University Press.

Neimark, M.S. (1976). *Personality orientation* (J. Ispa, A. Stone, & A. Nakhimovsky, Trans.). Englewood Cliffs, N.J.: Educational Technology Publications.

Nepomnichaia, N.I. (1977). Deiatel'nost coznanie, lichnost [Activity, consciousness, personality]. In N.A. Menchinskaia & Z.A. Farapanova (Eds.), *Problemy deiatel'nost v sovietskoi psikhologii* (pp. 63-75). Moscow: USSR Academy of Pedagogical Sciences

Rubinshtein, S.L. (1959) *Principii i puti razvitiia psikhologi.* [Principles and means in the development of psychology]. Moscow: Nauka.

Valsiner, J. (1989). *Human development and culture: The social nature of personality and its study.* Lexington, Mass.: Lexington Books.

Vygotsky, L.S. (1965). *Iskusstva psikhologiia* [Psychology of art]. Moscow: Iskusstva.

Vygotsky, L.S. (1967). *Pensamiento y lenguaje* (M.M. Rotger, Trans.). Havana: Edición Revolucionaria. (Original work published 1934)

Vygotsky, L.S. (1998). The problem of age (M.J. Hall, Trans.). In R.W. Reiber (Ed.), *The collected works of L.S. Vygotsky: Vol. 5. Child psychology* (pp. 187-205). New York: Plenum Press.

Wallon, H. (1971). Psychologie et materialisme dialectique. *Enfance, 24,* 293-296.

# 15 Institutional Practices, Cultural Positions, and Personal Motives: Immigrant Turkish Parents' Conceptions about their Children's School Life

*Mariane Hedegaard*

## Introduction

The theoretical discussions and empirical analyses presented here are part of a general research goal to analyze attitudes and practices in the two main institutions in which a schoolchild participates — home and school — in order to conceptualize how knowledge learned at home can be related to school learning. My special interest is to study the contradictory and sometimes conflictual life world that arises for schoolchildren when practice traditions and values in home are not consistent with practice traditions and values in school and how these conflicts influences the children's conditions for learning and development. The study of schooling for immigrant children can highlight the contradiction for children between home and community practice, and school practice, hence my motive for studying Turkish children in the Danish school system, together with a genuine interest in creating possibilities for development in Danish schools for children from cultural minority families.

The objective of school education should be to develop the child as a whole person, so that what the child learns in school is useful and meaningful for the child in his or her life outside of school. For children who meet major differences in values and cultural practice between home and school, the problem of combining what they learn in school with everyday life is more demanding than for children from the majority culture.

The goal of my research is to provide a foundation for making interventions into school practices, so that these interventions support the development of minority as well as majority children. Among other things this could contribute to a school policy about how to relate to children from ethnic minority homes. There have been different conceptual models that have guided educational researchers' and school administrators' strategies for integrating ethnic minorities into a school system. None of them, in my view, have been able to formulate a conception of teaching for pupils from cultural minority homes that acknowledges their differences, without simultaneously locking them into a stereotype.

In the study presented in this chapter, my aim has been to analyze Turkish parents conceptions, attitudes and expectations to their children's schooling and future. Research about Turkish immigrants in Denmark has explored adult life forms (Hjarnø, 1988a, 1988b; Schierup, 1993) and children's and young persons' meanings about life in Denmark and school (Mortensen, 1989; Mørch, 1998; L. Pedersen & Selmer, 1992; Rahbek, 1987; Røgild, 1995; Sahl & Skjelmose, 1987). However parents' views and expectations of their children's school and future have not been explored in Danish research. In the U.S.A., Ogbu (1987, 1993) has discussed how differences in parents' positions influence their expectations for their children's school results and future. The differences he analyzed are related to being voluntary immigrants or forced immigrants (as when a minority group is an indigenous people or has a colonized relation to the host country such as Blacks and Puerto Ricans in the U.S.A.). Ogbu's research indicates that the cultural characteristics in themselves are not critical; rather the positions that ethnic groups have in society influence children's success in school.

I want to go beyond just describing parents' attitudes by constructing a method of interpretation that can illuminate conflicts between the parents' public meanings and their personal motivation for confronting problems in their children's school attendance. The method of interpretation builds on a theoretical discussion and a conceptual model that maps a parent's public meanings and private motivations into related categories. By using the conceptual relations depicted in this model it is possible to analyze some of the main conflicts in which pupils from cultural minority families can be caught.

## Models of Integration Dominating the Danish School System

The debate about ethnic or cultural minorities in the Danish society and in school has been dominated by two different models of interaction and integration: the assimilation model and the multicultural model.

Since work force immigration started in Denmark in the late 1960s the main idea has been to assimilate children from immigrant families into the Danish school system. The teaching model that guided this idea has been the assimilation model. The concern implied by this model is the language deficit of immigrants. Special teaching in Danish has been the "treatment" where teaching in mother tongue has also became a right[1] and a possibility for most children from cultural minority families. This concern has been based upon the theory of "double half-language competence" (B.R. Pedersen & Skutnabb-Kangas, 1983; Skutnabb-Kangas, 1981), which states that if children from immigrant families do not become competent in their mother tongue, they cannot acquire full competence in a second language.

Gradually in the early 1980s the idea of multicultural classroom teaching grew as a critique of the assimilation model. Multicultural teaching has been discussed as a model for school practice, but it has never become an accepted practice in the Danish school system. Experiments with double-language classes (half Danish, half Turkish) have been tried (e.g., Clausen et al., 1986; Engelbrecht, Iversen, & Engel, 1989-90), but it has never been established as a permanent model of teaching. Possible barriers include: no success in children's subject matter learning, lack of funds for implementing the project further, lack of educated teachers who can teach in both languages, and so on (Moldenhawer, 1994). Multicultural teaching has therefore remained mainly as a set of ideals: one should take the children's background into consideration, and become conscious of the right of immigrant and refugee children to learn about their own culture. In practice, the multicultural model has been "passive tolerance" of immigrant children in the Danish school system, many times with the effect that the instructional tasks and performance expectations are simpler and lower than for Danish children. I observed this passive tolerance in four different schools, where teachers with a grant from a national fund for school research, were developing strategies for integration of children from cultural minority families. As a result of this passive-tolerance strategy, many immigrant and refugee children do not proceed through the last grades in school as well as

---

1.  Stated by law in 1976, if there were 6 or more pupils with a common first language, then teaching should be provided in that language each week, outside the ordinary school hours.

Danish children. This has now been raised as a problem by immigrant organizations and they demand that immigrant children get better education.[2]

The initial positive attitude in the educational debate about multi-cultural teaching of children from immigrant and refugee families has changed into a critique of this approach. Different researchers start to question the idea of multiculturalism in society (Necef, 1996; Schierup, 1995). In U.S.A., this critique has been formulated in relation to school practice for some time (Gibson, 1976, 1993; Ogbu, 1987, 1993).

Necef (1994), a Danish sociologist and political refugee from Turkey, pointed to the negative consequences of Danish intellectuals in their well-meaning acceptance of other cultures' way of doing things. He argued that the focus on immigrants' right to be different, in the long run, will stigmatize immigrants and refugees and thereby exclude them from becoming equal partners in different institutional practices and in the democratic decisions being made in these institutions. Schierup (1993) discusses the problem of equal rights for immigrants in Danish institutions as a balance between the shared democratic rights and the right to be different, where multiculturalism focuses too much on the right to be different at the expense of social rights in society. Well-meaning respect for the difference of cultural minority groups can create ethnic groups as closed entities, which results in cultural racism (Malik, 1996).

Over 20 years ago, Gibson (1976) discussed and criticized different models of multiculturalism in school teaching for stigmatizing children from cultural minority groups. But no real alternative has been pointed out yet. It is impossible to return to a model of cultural assimilation, where researchers ignore the cultural differences of everyday practices and life forms among different groups of society, and the meaning of these differences for the life of schoolchildren.

A first step toward making an analysis that can lead to culturally-sensitive instruction is to focus on differences in practices between pri-

2. There are not many immigrant children in Denmark, but the policy of social housing by the local counties has resulted in a concentration of immigrants in some areas in the main cities of Denmark. Many immigrants also prefer to live in a neighborhood near other persons who have the same way of life and language, and with whom they can have close contact. These two factors have created concentrations of some groups of immigrants. In one primary school in Aarhus, the concentration of immigrant and refugee families living in the same neighborhood has resulted in one school where 98% of the pupils have Danish as their second (or third) language.

vate institutions (i.e., home and informal communities) and public institutions, how these respective practices have evolved historically, and what they mean for the involved persons.

In what follows I develop a model of these practices that moves toward solving the dilemma between (a) neglecting cultural differences in social practices between families from different ethnic groups and (b) restricting children to a practice where their capacities are conceptualized as limited by cultural and social heritage.

## Cultural Identity and Teaching

Questions such as: "Who am I?" and "What are my roots?" are important for persons belonging to a minority group. A teacher's problem is how to conceptualize these questions so that a person is not locked in a cultural or ethnic identity that he has difficulty transcending both from a personal and societal perspective. Barth (1969) argued that ethnic groups can be seen as a form of social organization. He supports this view by demonstrating empirically that cultural characteristics of an ethnic group change over time and ethnic identity is a creation conditioned by a group's self-deception as well as the deception of other surrounding "ethnic" groups.

A conception of a certain ethnic, cultural or class identity can lock a person into a special life form, and hinder social relations that are important for his or her development. A clear demonstration is found in Willis's (1977) analyses of British schoolboys' conceptions of their future identity as workers.

Teaching children from cultural minority families in majority schools demands both integrating the children into the majority society, while respecting the children's cultural family background. Conditions for children's school learning and development are created in part by the conceptions and attitudes of the significant persons in the children's life world (e.g., teachers, parents, relatives). This is not an opposition between ethnic or cultural identity and national identity.

An example of how cultural and national identity in itself does not predict a child's progress in school comes from a research report about children from Finnish immigrant families in Sweden and Australia (Ogbu, 1987). In Sweden, where Finns are evaluated negatively, Finnish children perform poorly in school and have low self-esteem. In Australia, where being Finnish is neutrally evaluated, the opposite was found.

The task is to move between Scylla and Charybdis: to take cultural practice seriously and at the same time not make culture the main explanatory principle for personal development. My suggestion for a solution is to focus on practice within different institutions and the conditions these practices give for a person's development. This conception transcends the notion of practice as mediating directly between society and the single person; the mediation has to be located in the different institutions in society. Different institutions even of the same type vary in social practice (i.e., the practice varies in different families, as well as in different schools). When social practice in an institution changes, then new conditions are created for the development of persons who participate in the practice of these institutions (see Tulviste, this volume).

### Institutional Practice and Development

Children develop through participation in institutionalized forms of practice that are characterized by communication and shared activities. These forms of practice initiate but also restrict the children's activities and thereby become conditions for their development. A child's participation in an activity contributes to the concrete realization of this activity, which contributes to the conditions for his or her own development.

Different phases in children's development can be found through qualitative changes in institutional practice (Elkonin, 1972), which take place when the child enters new institutions and becomes part of their activities (e.g., when a child enters kindergarten or starts school).

Vygotsky's (1978) theory of the *zone of proximal development* can be used to conceptualize how an interaction between a child and other persons in institutionalized activities can become developmental for the child. If an activity in an institutional context like the school is to be developmental, it has to relate to and challenge the child's capacity. Learning takes place in social interaction with other more competent persons in this institution. But the child is also learning at home in his or her interaction with more competent adults. What the child learns at home is usually different from the other topics and themes that the school provides. Learning within the zone of proximal development contributes both to the child's knowledge about the world and about himself (i.e., about his or her cultural identity and position in the world,

Berger & Luckmann, 1966). Through shared activities (social practice) in home and school, the child learns to combine needs with objects and thereby acquire new motives (Leontiev, 1975/1978). Learning in these two institutions are not always coordinated, and the child can, through different activities in school and home, meet meaning systems that are in opposition or conflict.

## Social Practice, Meaning and Sense

Through participating in different practices a child's sense of these practices develops together with his or her acquisition of connected meaning systems. To give a more nuanced conceptualization of these relations, I will draw upon Leontiev's (1975/1978) differentiation between *societal meaning* and *personal sense*.

Leontiev characterizes the relation between societal meaning and personal sense as mingled during the early stages of the child's development of consciousness. Later, a differentiation gradually becomes more obvious, and becomes part of a person's developing consciousness. This characterization of the relation between meaning and sense, and how they are connected to a person's positions and motives is especially relevant here. They provide a foundation for elaborating the field of conflicts that characterizes everyday life for children of cultural minority parents. Leontiev (1975/1978) wrote:

As distinct from meaning, personal sense, like the sensory fabric of consciousness, does not have its own "supraindividual," "nonpsychological" existence. If in the consciousness of the subject external sensitivity connects meanings with the reality of the objective world, then the personal sense connects them with the reality of his own life in this world, with its motives. (pp. 92-93)

Sense captures the personal and motivational aspects of activity, but it can only be expressed through a shared meaning system. The cultural traditions of home and school and their meaning systems are the public or shared field of practice that a child enters into in these institutions. There can be overlap between the meaning system, and to a lesser extent between the practices of these two institutions. Often the overlap is small and insignificant, as in the biannual contact from the Danish school system where parents can be oriented about how their child is doing in school. For parents, who have not experienced the Danish school system, as well as for teachers, who have not experienced the everyday practice in a Turkish family, it is not surprising there can sometimes be problems in achieving joint understanding based on communication. For the immigrant parents, where the language and meaning system is connected to the Danish society, they can have difficulty to express their motives and personal sense adequately. Therefore when there are conflicts between what parents imagine are the activities in the school and what their own children or the teachers communicate about the actual activities, then the imagined activities tend to be given more credence. The same can happen for teachers where imagined activities about immigrant home practice are trusted more than the objective knowledge that they have, if there is conflicts. Leontiev (1975/1978) described this type of conflict as follows:

In its most naked forms the process about which we are speaking appears in conditions of class society and struggle for ideology. Under these conditions personal meanings reflecting motives engendered by actions of life relationships of man may not adequately embody their objective meanings, and then they begin to live as if in someone else's garments. It is necessary to imagine the major contradiction that gives rise to this phenomenon. As is known, as distinct from the life of society, the life of the individual does not "speak for itself," that is, the individual does not have his own language with meanings developed within it; perception by him of phenomena of reality may take place only through his assimilation of externally "ready" meanings — meanings, perceptions, views that he obtains from contact with one or another form of individual or mass communication. This makes it possible to introduce into the individual's consciousness and impose on him distorted or fantastic representations and ideas, including such as have no basis in his real practical life experience. Deprived of this basis they find their real weakness in the consciousness of man; and turning into *stereotypes*, like any stereotypes, they are so resistant that only serious real life confrontations can dispel them. But even dispelling them does not lead to averting disintegration of consciousness or its inadequacy; in itself it creates only a devastation capable of turning into a psychological catastrophe. It is necessary in addition that in the consciousness of the individual there take place a reshaping of subjective personal meanings into other more adequate meanings. (pp. 93-94)

Senses are created through a person's real relations in his or her life, and reflect the motives in these activities. In class society or for minorities in a majority society, the personal sense cannot always be expressed through a shared meaning system, so that the person's motives can be communicated. As Leontiev wrote, a person does not choose the meanings; if he has to choose, he chooses between colliding social positions, that are expressed and recognized through these meanings, and which are connected to a shared practice tradition. Meanings are therefore difficult to change.

### Social Practice and Positions

The concept of social practice is connected to traditions for activities in institutions. Diversity of practice in institutions such as family or school can be conceptualized within different traditions and be seen as connected to different positions in society.

Conflicts between the positions of home and school can create motive conflicts for children and influence their activities in school. Willis's (1978) study of young British lads shows that a group of boys in the last years of their school attendance change their attitude to school practice and their way of participating in school activities. This change is explained as a result of the boys' associations with positions of the working-class family, where the meaning system differs from the middle-class teachers and school authorities.

To elaborate on these types of conflicts I draw on Bourdieu's (1979/1984) concepts of positions, field, and life forms to formulate the relation between different institutional practice traditions as organized into a system of meaning positions. Different positions create a shared area in the social field. The positions are organized in the social field into changeable systems that are characterized as life forms. In Bourdieu's theory of distinctions of taste, the key to understanding the social field is through the life form of the upper class. Their positions and meaning systems of taste dominate the taste of the other classes, who either imitate or oppose the upper-class positions and meaning systems. Related positions within the societal field will be used to refer to the concept of an idealized life form.

I extended these ideas to analyze Turkish immigrant families' positions and meaning systems about their children's schooling. It is important to note that meaning systems and positions for these families relate to practice traditions associated to two imagined life forms: the "Danish life form" and the "Turkish life form." These two practice traditions are connected to two imagined societies (Anderson, 1991), where the practice traditions are based more on imagination than on the everyday

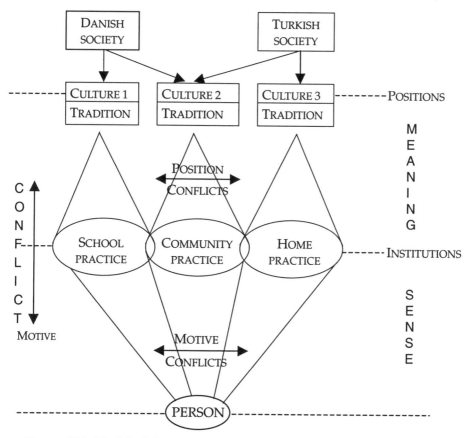

Figure 15.1. Model of the relations between practice, positions and motives.

practices of the Turkish immigrant community in Denmark. The Turkish immigrant families have created their own lived community practice, which distinguishes their life form from the imagined Danish life form and from the imagined Turkish life form in Turkey.

Both for class and minority groups, life form analyses could be used to understand the positions that characterize these groups and how these positions have evolved in relation to the production system of society.[3] But this approach tends to describe ethnic minority groups as homogeneous. I prefer to analyze the practice connected to the institu-

3. Højrup (1983) explored differences in life forms among Danish West Coast inhabitants. Through analyzing a community and its different types of production, Højrup describes four qualitatively different life forms characterized by different forms of daily practice at home and different values.

tion, for example the Turkish immigrant family, and analyze their positions in relation to other institutions (work, school, community).

Positions are associated to a certain practice tradition, such as family tradition, school tradition or work tradition. Turkish immigrant families in Denmark have positions in relation to institutions in Turkey, primarily the family, that are based on direct participation in this practice tradition. At the same time the Turkish immigrant families also participate in practice traditions within Danish institutions, such as work, school, and social welfare. Within the same family, expectations for their children's activities, both in home and school, can be motivated from associations to positions connected to different practice traditions. These multiple associations can create conflict in a family. For example, in school these can be conflicts in the parents' conceptions and expectations both for social interaction (such as overnight camps, playing with Danish children or children from other minority groups) and school subjects (such as physical education, history and religion).

Figure 15.1 depicts a model of the relations between different social practices within different institutions, such as home, community clubs, and school. These relations can be seen as reflecting different cultural traditions connected to different positions. As indicated in the model, one can look for conflicts between different positions as expressed in inconsistencies in a person's meaning system. It is also possible to look for conflicts between a person's motives. A third type of conflict can be found in a disparity between expressed motives and positions.

The categories distinguished in Figure 15.1 are used in the analyses of the interviews about Turkish parents' conceptions and attitudes about school education in Denmark, about their children's integration into the Danish society, about the Danish language and mother tongue teaching, and about knowledge of their own culture and the Danish culture. I want to distinguish possible meaning systems that create Turkish parents' positions in relation to their children's school activities and future education, and point to possible oppositions and conflicts in single families' positions and motives about these themes.

The relation between motives and positions are the core concepts of my empirical analysis. The focus is on a parent's relation to practice in different institutions and how differences in practice can create oppositions between different positions, conflicts between a person's different motives, and problems to find an adequate way to express motives in meanings (that fit into the positions to which a person associates).

### Immigrant Turkish Parents' Conceptions about their Children's School Life and Future in Denmark

The parent interviews are part of a larger project, about different perspectives on Turkish children's school life. This larger project contains (a) interviews with key persons in the Danish public school system and in the Turkish immigrant community, as well as with Turkish parents, with young people who have attended the Danish public school system, and university students; and (b) participant observations of class teaching and teacher planning meetings.

I am currently analyzing the relation between parents and school from the parent's perspective. How do Turkish immigrant parents interact with the Danish school system and with the child about school topics that are relevant to their children's school activity (in a way that creates conditions for their children's learning and development), and what do they expect for their children's further education.

In this chapter I present inconsistencies and contradictions in Turkish immigrant parents' positions and motives about children's school attendance and school activities so that different types of categories that are relevant for analyzing conditions for their children's learning and development in school can be formulated.

### *Immigration Background of Turks in Denmark*

Turkish migration to Denmark started with a request for workers in the late 1960s and the early 1970s. This was mostly a chain migration, so that several families from the same village migrated and are living together in the same neighborhoods in Denmark (Hjarnø, 1988a). Law stopped this work immigration in 1973.

Most Turkish immigrants in Denmark came from an agricultural area and have lived in small villages where the relations between inhabitants are characterized by strong family bonds, intermarriage, and sharp differentiation of work between men and women. Schooling for most people in this area ends with the five-year public school, and some women have no schooling at all (Delaney, 1991).

The intermarriage pattern has continued with the immigrants to Denmark, so many Turkish young people in Denmark marry a person from the village or county where their parents or grandparents were born. This has resulted in a constant renewal of Turkish immigrants in

Denmark, because Danish immigration law allows a person to bring her husband or wife from Turkey to Denmark.[4]

The communities of Turks in Denmark have developed their own practice traditions which relate both to the Danish context of their lives and to the imagined context of their traditions in Turkey. The Turkish immigrant families draw both on the practice of their home community in Turkey, where their grandparents or relatives still live, and on the practice of Danish public institutions such as kindergartens, schools, workplaces, social offices, and hospitals. There are great differences between the cultural traditions connected to the practice in these different institutions, so immigrant children need to develop capacities to act in relation to the different practice traditions, according to the situation.

### Characteristics of the Interviewed Parents

The material presented here is based on interviews[5] with seven pairs of Turkish immigrant parents, chosen so that they have a minimum of eight years experience with the Danish school system. This means that their children have been through the elementary school system (including a kindergarten class), and attended the last grades of this system (7th-10th grade).

The seven families in the interview have children in five different schools. The intention was to get parents whose children go to different schools, so that the parents' conceptions are not only reflecting the effect of the practice of one school. The families live in two different neighborhoods in the same city; both neighborhoods have a high concentration of Turks living there. Each family came from the same village district in Turkey located in Anatolia. Their families were farmers. In Denmark they have become unskilled workers, kiosk owners, and one woman teaches Danish to adults in immigrant courses.

---

4. Immigrants and refugees in Denmark (including Europeans) is currently 4.7% of the total population (or 7.5%, if people who have acquired Danish citizenship are included). Turks are the largest immigrant group in Denmark. There are 45,008 Turks in a total population in Denmark of 5,311,234 (Larsen, 1999).

5. A female, Turkish university student, who lives in one of the big housing areas for Turks, conducted the interviews in the Turkish parents' own homes. The interviews were conducted in Turkish, and structured with a series of questions about school experiences and expectations. The interviews were tape-recorded and transcribed into Danish.

Conceptions and attitudes about school practices
    Teacher consultation meetings
    The content of the teaching
        History instruction
        Religious instruction
    Social events
        Overnight camps
        Relations with classmates

Conceptions of how the child manages in school
    With subject matters
    In social relations

Aims and possibilities to help/support the child
    Homework
    Seeing school friends
    Leisure activities

Wishes and intentions
    For the child's future

Characteristics of the child's problems in school and home
    In subject matter instruction
    Socially
    Culturally

Attitudes toward religion and culture as factors of importance for schoolchildren's development
    Attitudes toward the Danish culture and religion
    Mother-tongue teaching
    The meaning of one's own culture and religion

Figure 15.2. Categories for situated interpretations of Turkish parents' conceptions about their children's school life and future in Denmark.

Only 4 of the 14 parents say that they speak Danish well, even though they have all been in Denmark from 14-30 years. Six others say they speak Danish, but not so well, and give this as reason for not attending or not speaking up at parent meetings at the school, and four say they cannot speak Danish.

## Results

The interpretation of the interviews is a three-step process with three different levels of interpretation. The first level is a situated interpretation, which results in descriptions of Turkish immigrant parents' conceptions of and attitudes about their children's school activity and expectations they have for their children's future education. The second level is an identification of shared positions connected to the tradition for practice with Turkish-immigrant life. The third level is an interpretation of conflicts between different public positions, different personal motives, as well as tensions and conflicts between public position and personal motive.

### Situated Interpretations

The categories and main results will be presented here, as a foundation for the second level of analyses. The categories were found by reading through the transcripts several times and identifying and marking themes. The results of this analysis are presented in Figure 15.2.

All parents express their satisfaction with the school system, and they all want their children to have an academic education in Denmark. Differences appear in their attitude to being in Denmark, and this influences the conditions they give for their children to develop.

Three families (I, V, and VII) have a positive attitude to the Danish society and their children's possibilities in Denmark. One family (VI) can be characterized as neutral in their expectations. Three families (II, III, and IV) have negative expectations to Danish society and their children's future possibilities, but they still view that their children's school attendance and the Danish education are important. The children with the most obvious difficulties in school come from the three families with the negative attitude. None of these families admit directly that their children have troubles going to school (but see the following section on conflicts between motives connected to different practices).

One of the parents (family V) with a positive attitude says that she thinks it is important that she help her daughter in school, even though the parent has only attended school in Turkey for 5 years and does not speak Danish fluently. She says that she tries to do her best, mostly by showing interest in reading her daughter's written homework. This wo-

1. To attend the Danish school is important for my child so he can get a better job than us (the parents).

2. To speak Danish is a precondition to be able to proceed in the Danish society.

3. To go to school with Danish children and to play with them are important for learning the Danish language.

4. Further study is a privilege that children should use.

5. Children should decide themselves if they want to study.

6. If there are no complaints about my child, then everything is going well in school.

7. One's child should not be treated as a foreigner in the Danish school.

8. To go to school with too many foreign students has a negative effect on my child's education.

9. It is important that Turkish children learn and keep their Turkish culture.

10. Turkish children should not participate in religious instruction in school.

11. Upbringing should be disciplined/planned.

Figure 15.3. Shared positions in the Turkish families in their relation to the Danish school.

man can be contrasted with another woman (family VI) who has a high-school degree from Turkey and who can speak Danish. She does not express any wish to help her child with his homework, and gives as a reason that her experience with school is too different from the Danish school tradition.

These two woman also have a different attitude to being in Denmark, where the first mother expresses that he and her husband have really discussed moving back but that they have decided to stay in Denmark because this is where they want their children to have a future. The other family has a house in "their village" in Turkey, and the mother is unsure about where they wish their children's future.

### Shared Positions

The relation between the situated analyses of conceptions, attitudes and wishes is the background for the formulation of positions. The positions can be seen as formulations of what is meaningful for Turkish immigrant parents in relation to their children's education in the Danish school system. The 11 meaning positions I have found are shown in Figure 15.3.

### Conflicts

Three types of conflicts can be found (see Figure 15.1). These are between (a) positions associated to practice in different institutions or to imagined life forms (the Danish life form and the Turkish life form), (b) motives connected to different forms of practice, and (c) public positions and personal motives.

*Conflicts between different positions.* The conflicts in meaning positions expressed in the parent interviews are:

Conflicts between the position that my child should not be looked upon as a foreigner in the Danish school and the position that my child should keep the Turkish culture (positions 7 and 9).

Conflicts between the position that it is good for my children to play with Danish children so they can learn Danish and the position that Danish children are undisciplined so my children should not become close friends with Danish children (positions 3 and 11).

These two conflicts can be illustrated with Family I: The mother expresses that she is very happy for the class teacher and that they have a very good contact. She appreciates that the class teacher does not treat them as foreigners. Both parents express that their children should learn the Danish culture in school, and here they evaluate the culture as positive. Both parents mention several times, the importance of their daughter's contact with other Danish children, and that she only has Danish friends (in school).

At the same time the father expresses that he still feels that he is a foreigner even though he has lived in Denmark since he was 15 years old [for 24 years]. Both parents are critical towards Danish culture and religion. The father said he does not know what it stands for, and that the Danes do not believe in anything. The mother says the Danes have no family ties, they have no culture.

Both parents want to keep a distance between their daughter and other Danish children, even though they think it is important that she has Danish friends. They do not find Danish young people disciplined, so they want to have control over their daughter when she is seeing friends.

> Conflict between the position that there should not be too many foreigners in the school and the position of keeping one's own culture. One can find parents that express that even children from their own culture are negative company in school because they hinder their own children from learning Danish (positions 1, 7, 8).

Family V: The mother prefers a school with less foreignness. At the same time, she expresses that it does not matter with whom her daughter plays. The parents say that they chose their children's school so that there would be few foreigners. The mother tells that their daughter is seldom together with Turkish children. She is seeing Danish children. "I do not think it really matters for her who she is together with."

> Conflict between the position that their children should study in Denmark and the position that their children should keep their Turkish culture (positions 1 and 8).

Family VI: The mother says, "It can well be that we live in Denmark but we act as we live in Turkey. As we are in Turkey. We try to give our children norms from there. It should not be like that. Our children are here. They are going to school here. If we thought about it, we would realize that it is here they shall stay."

*Conflicts between motives connected to different practices.* Motive-conflicts are created through situations where different opposing motives are at stake. The motive-conflict is personal but some general aspects in the different conflicts can be recognized.

> One kind of motive conflict is connected with the position that if there are no complaints about my child, then everything is perfect, and the realization that there can be problems even though there are no official complaints (position 6).

Family II: The father says, "In the parent consultation meetings about my son we have not received any complaints from the teachers. They tell us that our children behave well, that they do their homework. There has only been one dissatisfaction from the teacher, that our son is very reluctant to put his hand up when the teacher asks questions, but now S. [he is in the 7th grade] has nearly overcome that problem." The father does not mention that S. stammers, and his statement contrasts with the mother who says that S. has difficulties answering the teacher in class. She says "S. is afraid that his classmates will laugh at him if he says anything wrong."

The conflict between the motive that there is no problem with my children and the acceptance that there can be problems takes different forms but this conflict characterizes five of the families (II, III, IV, VI, VII).

> Another type of motive conflict is the strong value placed on educa-
> tion manifested in the parents' wish that their children go on to fur-
> ther studies and at the same time their attitude that children have a
> right to choose what kind of education/job they want (positions 4
> and 5). All seven families express this conflict.

Family VII: The father expresses that he wishes that his children get an education with a title. "That they do not become unskilled workers. That's what we expect nothing else." But then he says that he wants his son to have an education with the computer, he wants him to go to the university. But then he adds that it depends on what his son wants.

> *Conflicts between public positions and the personal motive.* A type of
> conflict comes from inconsistency between a shared meaning position
> and the related personal motive. This is a mismatch that results in, as
> Leontiev noted, distorted and inconsistent meanings.

> To go to school with Danish children and to play with them is im-
> portant but it also implies adaptation to norms that a Turkish family
> does not want to accept (position 3).

Family III: The father says that it starts in the racist families, that they educate their children to become racist. "A Danish child at 6-7 years old does not know what racism is, but when the child's mother asks who he had played with in school, and the child says Ahmet, then she screams, 'why have you played with foreigners?'" The father does not mean that all parents act this way, but they do in Risskov [an upper middle-class neighborhood].

The father's view about the separatist nature of Danish families can be contrasted with following views from the same father and his wife about the goals of the Danish culture:

Father:    In the Danish culture they wish to assimilate immigrant children.
Mother:    They want us to look like them.
Father:    They will melt a Turkish child into their culture. This is when a child is 16, without any boundaries, and he is together with his father and does everything, smoke, drink and call his father bad names.

Upbringing should be disciplined and this conflicts with the wish that the child should have freedom to play (position 11).

Family II: The mother says that her son has many friends but they do not come to their home. She thinks that her son should plan his day and be disciplined and at the same time he should be free and play. The mother express that children should learn to plan their life; she thinks that the activities in their current life at home are not planned enough. She wants to write down plans so the children can eat at a certain time, go to bed at a certain time, and she tells that she has started to write down her plans. At the same time she wants her child to play and says that her son develops through play. But asked what he plays, she says he plays with his computer and watches football on TV. She thinks that her son has so much to do, but when asked what he does, it is very little she actually describes. She says he goes to football Saturday, and Koran teaching Sunday. The rest of the days she says he does not want to go out.

A distortion of the position: Turkish children should learn and keep their own culture, for which the Danish state should be responsible (position 9).

Family VI: The mother says, "The Turkish young people find themselves in an empty space. When we go home to our country they call us Almanci (which means Turkish European) and in Denmark they call us foreigners. We can neither find a permanent place there or here." Further she expresses that, "Denmark does not live up to its responsibility in relation to young Turks, because they [the politicians] do not take care of bringing the right kind of teachers to teach mother tongue." She wants mother-tongue teachers [imans] who come from Turkey and are stationed in Denmark for a four-year period. She says, "How can a person grown up in Denmark teach Turkish?" At the same time the father expresses that, "The teacher in the Danish school is the second important person in a child's life, he comes just after the parents."

## Discussion

The analyses of the parents' interviews resulted in a system of categories that could reveal the parents concepts and attitudes to their children's school life. These analyses also revealed that immigrant families even if they have a similar ethnic background and come from the same community with the same working class background can have different attitudes to the Danish society and their children's possibilities in Denmark. Even though there are clear differences in their attitudes and expectations, it was also possible to identify 11 shared positions of how Turkish parents relate to the Danish school.

Through analyzing parents' conceptions, three different types of conflicts were identified. The first type was conflicts between positions. Here four conflicts were identified. These four conflicts are all conflicts between a parent's positions about learning and developing in a Danish school tradition and keeping the Turkish culture. In particular, these conflicts were between the conception that school education is important and concerns about how contact with Danish or other foreign children could result in their children's loss of their own tradition's values and culture. This type of conflict reveals that the parents have difficulty recognizing the importance of supporting their children in developing capacities to act appropriately in different contexts (i.e., within practice traditions of different institutions in society).

The second type of identified conflicts was between parents' different motives for their children's school practice. Two were found: (a) the conflict between the possibility or actuality that a child's school competencies are criticizable and wanting to help the child with problems, and (b) the conflict between a wish to decide that a child studies further after public school and accepting the child's right to choose the kind of education he or she wants.

The third type of conflicts is between parents' motives and positions. Here three conflicts were identified: (a) to play with Danish children is unacceptable for both Danish parents and Turkish immigrant parents, (b) play is preferable because it is developmental but it interferes with disciplined upbringing, (c) Turkish children should learn and keep their own culture, for which the Danish state should be responsible.

The first two types of conflicts have the possibility to become educational or developmental if they are recognized and supported from the school. The first type of conflicts between parents positions connected to different practice traditions can be addressed by establishing better communication between teachers and parents, which leads to greater awareness and sensitivity towards practice traditions. As a result, parents and teachers may better support children to develop this awareness and sensitivity and the demands of different practice situations and to develop capacities to act in different contexts.

The second type of conflict between parents' motives can also through parent and teacher communication lead to increased awareness. If these concerns are communicated to the children, the the children can experience their parents' positive interest in their problems and future.

Research has been started in Denmark, that works with the creation of conditions for communication between school and parents, which results in cooperation between parents and teachers in shared problem-solving of school matters (e.g., Kristjánsdóttir, 1995).

The third type of conflicts between position and motives is the most difficult to analyze and tackle educationally. This type of conflict between meaning positions and motives is expressed by the three families that have a general negative expectation to the Danish society and their children's future possibilities.

In the conflict — to go to school with Danish children and to play with them is important but it also implies adaptation to norms that a Turkish family does not want to accept — the father in the example expressed dissatisfaction about how Danish parents react to Turkish children. But he did not give any examples from his experience to illustrate his dissatisfaction; instead, he formulated a constructed general example. This illustrates Leontiev's point that meanings, that do not have a real relation to experience from participating in practice, turn into stereotypes.

This third type of conflict is difficult to handle in teachers' interactions with parents, because these conflicts do not disappear by discussing the matters with the parents, and they can become a condition of obstruction for children's school activities and learning. Leontiev (1975/1978) writes that stereotypes are so resistant that only serious real life confrontations can dispel them:

A more intense analysis of such reshaping of personal meaning into adequate (more adequate) meanings indicates that it takes place under conditions of the struggle in society for the consciousness of people. Here I want to say that the individual does not simply "stand" before a certain "window" displaying meanings among which he has but to make a choice, that these meanings — representations, concepts, ideas — do not passively wait for his choice but energetically dig themselves into his connections with people forming the circle of his real contacts. If the individual in given life circumstances is forced to make a choice, then that choice is not between meanings but between colliding social positions that are expressed and recognized through these meanings. (p. 94)

For the Turkish families that have negative expectations to the Danish society, their negative attitude is not found in relation to the school institution and to learning subject matter. The negative attitude is toward the social relations in which the child participates when going to school. Because subject-matter teaching and social relations in school are interwoven, my suggestion is to introduce immigrant parents — both those with a positive attitude to school practice and those who have a negative attitude to their children's school practice — by bringing them into activities that contribute to subject-matter teaching.[6]

A general educational strategy can be through subject-matter teaching to introduce the children to knowledge about society and history of both their parents' original and current societies. Social science teaching which includes the immigration history of Turks can be a way to work with knowledge that transcends stereotypes (see Hedegaard, 1996, Hedegaard & Chaiklin, 1995).

### References

Anderson, B. (1991). *Imagined communities: Reflections on the origin and spread of nationalism* (rev. ed.). London: Verso.

Barth, F. (1969). Introduction. In F. Barth (Ed.), *Ethnic groups and boundaries. The social organization of culture differences* (pp. 9-38). Bergen, Norwegian: Universities Press.

Berger, P.L., & Luckmann, T. (1966). *The social construction of reality*. Garden City, N.Y.: Doubleday.

Bourdieu, P. (1984). *Distinction: A social critique of the judgement of taste* (R. Nice, Trans.). Cambridge, Mass.: Harvard University Press. (Original work published 1979)

6. One positive example was a research project in several public schools in Tucson, Arizona where parents of Mexican minority schoolchildren were used in the classroom as part of subject-matter teaching in English (Moll & Greenberg, 1990).

Clausen, I., Rasmussen, V., Andersen, A.-M., Dogan, N., Tanriverdi, G., Saed, A., Ørts, I., Brix, R., Hansen, A.T., & Schalburg, K. (1986). *To-kulturel skolestart Enghøjskolen 1985-86* (Report No. 3) [Bicultural school beginning, Enghøj School]. Hvidovre, Denmark: Hvidovre Pædagogiske Central.

Delaney, C. (1991). *The seed and the soil: Gender and cosmology in Turkish village society*. Berkeley: University of California Press.

Elkonin, D.B. (1972). Toward the problem of stages in the mental development of the child. *Soviet Psychology* , *10*, 225-251.

Engelbrecht, M., Iversen, K.A., & Engel, M. (1989-90). *Danskundervisningen i de to-kulturelle klasser i Høje-Taastrup. En undersøgelse af de tyrkiske børns kunne på dansk* [Danish teaching in bicultural classes in Høje-Taastrup. A study of Turkish children's competence in the Danish language]. Høje-Taastrup, Denmark: Høje-Taastrup Kommune.

Gibson, M. (1976). Approaches to multicultural education in the United States: Some concepts and assumptions. *Anthropology and Education Quarterly, 7,* 7-18.

Gibson, M. (1993). The school performance of immigrant minorities. In E. Jacob & C. Jordan (Eds.), *Minority education: Anthropological perspectives* (pp. 113-128). Norwood, N.J.: Ablex.

Hedegaard, M. (1996). Ændring af skolepraksis: Et kommunalt projekt med statsløse palæstinensiske børn [Change in school practice: A local authority project with stateless Palestinian children]. In M. Hedegaard (Ed.), *Praksisformers forandring — Personlig udvikling* (pp. 71-96). Aarhus, Denmark: Aarhus University Press.

Hedegaard, M., & Chaiklin, S. (1995). Building cultural identity of minority children through social studies. In J. Hjarnø (Ed.), *Multiculturalism in the Nordic societies* (pp. 231-242). Copenhagen: Nordic Council of Ministers.

Hjarnø, J. (1988a). *Indvandrer fra Tyrkiet i Stockholm og København* [Immigrants from Turkey in Stockholm and Copenhagen]. Esbjerg, Denmark: South Jutland University Press.

Hjarnø, J. (1988b). *Socialt arbejde blandt flygtninge og indvandrere* [Social work among refugees and immigrants]. Copenhagen: Billesø & Baltzer.

Højrup, T. (1983). *Det glemte folk. Livsformer og centraldirigering* [The forgotten people. Life forms and central direction]. Copenhagen: Institut for Europæisk Folkelivsforskning.

Kristjánsdóttir, B.S. (1995). Samarbejde med forældre på tværs af sprog og kultur [Cooperation with parents across language and cultures]. In P. Arneberg & B. Ravn (Eds.), *Mellem hjem og skole. Et spørgsmål om magt og tillid.* Copenhagen: Unge Pædagoger.

Larsen, K.T. (1999). *Statistik om etniske minoriteter i Danmark* [Statistics on ethnic minorities in Denmark]. Copenhagen: Mellemfolkeligt Samvirke.

Leontiev, A.N. (1978). *Activity, consciousness, and personality* (M.J. Hall, Trans.). Englewood Cliffs, N. J.: Prentice-Hall. (Original work published 1975)

Malik, K. (1996). *The meaning of race: Race, history and culture in Western society.* New York: New York University Press.

Moldenhawer, B. (1994). Etnicitet, minoriteter, kultur og skolegang [Ethnicity, minority, culture and schooling]. Unpublished doctoral dissertation, University of Copenhagen, Denmark.

Moll, L.C., & Greenberg, J.B. (1990). Creating zones of possibilities: Combining social contexts for instruction. In L.C. Moll (Ed.), *Vygotsky and education: Instructional implications and applications of sociohistorical psychology* (pp. 319-348). Cambridge: Cambridge University Press.

Mortensen, L.B. (1989). *Tyrkisk ungdom i København og Ankara* [Turkish youth in Copenhagen and Ankara]. Copenhagen: Akademisk Forlag.

Necef, M.Ü. (1994). *Jeg vil ikke være en simpel fremmedarbejder som min far* [I do not want to be a simple foreign worker like my father]. Odense, Denmark: Odense University Press.

Ogbu, J.U. (1987). Variability in minority responses to schooling: Non-immigrant vs. immigrants. In G. Spindler & L. Spindler (Eds.), *Interpretative ethnography of education: At home and abroad* (pp. 255-278). Hillsdale, N.J.: Erlbaum.

Ogbu, J.U. (1993). Variability in minority school performance: A problem in search and explanation. In E. Jacob & C. Jordan (Eds.), *Minority education: Anthropological perspectives* (pp. 83-112). Norwood, N.J.: Ablex.

Pedersen, B.R., & Skutnabb-Kangas, T. (1983). *God, bedre, dansk — Om indvandrerbørns integration i Danmark* [Good, better Danish — About immigrant children's integration in Denmark]. Copenhagen: Børn og Unge.

Pedersen, L., & Selmer, B. (1992). *Muslimsk indvandrerungdom* [Muslim immigrant youth]. Aarhus, Denmark: Aarhus University Press.

Rahbek, B. (1987). *Børn mellem to kulturer* [Children between two cultures]. Copenhagen: Hans Reitzel.

Røgild, F. (1995). *Stemmer i et grænseland. En bro mellem unge indvandrere og danskerne* [Voices in a border district. A bridge between young immigrants and Danes]. Copenhagen: Politisk Revy.

Sahl, F., & Skjelmose, C. (1987). *Fremmed i skolen* [Strangers in the school]. Høje-Taastrup, Denmark: Høje-Taastrup Kommune, Pædagogisk-Psykologisk Rådgivning.

Schierup, C.-U. (1993). *På kulturens slagmark — Mindretal og størretal taler om Danmark* [On the battlefield of culture — Minority and majority talk about Denmark]. Esbjerg: South Jutland University Press.

Schierup, C.-U. (1995). Multiculturalism, neo-racism and vicissitudes of contemporary democracy. In J. Hjarnø (Ed.), *Multiculturalism in the Nordic societies* (pp. 10-29). Copenhagen: Nordic Councils of Ministers.

Skutnabb-Kangas, T. (1981). *Tvåspråkighet* [Bilingualism]. Lund, Sweden: Liber Läromedel.

Vygotsky, L.S. (1978). *Mind in society* (M. Cole, V. John-Steiner, S. Scribner, & E. Souberman, Eds.; M. Cole & M. Lopez-Morillas, Trans.). Cambridge, Mass.: Harvard University Press.

Willis, P.E. (1977). *Learning to labor: How working class kids get working class jobs*. Farnborough, U.K.: Saxon House.

# 16 Cultural Mind and Cultural Identity: Projects for Life in Body and Spirit

*Amelia Álvarez and Pablo del Río*

Among all the disciplines that have tried to explain or analyze the constitution and development of cultural identity, psychology retains the dubious honor of having avoided this topic in its research program, at least explicitly or in its most direct terms. Insofar as cultural-historical psychology holds that psychological development is culturally constructed and must be analyzed and explained in the settings where such construction takes place (i.e., in settings where cultural-historical development models are embedded and serve as true guidelines for the behavior of the community's members), then the problem of cultural identity must be confronted, because it is part of the theory's foundations.

Our research program is aimed at developing an analysis of cultural identity in terms of cultural-historical psychology. As part of this work, we are using ideas from *la generación del 98*, a generation of Spanish theoreticians who, from the beginning of the 20th century, deeply analyzed the motives of human action rooted in one culture. Our long-term interest is to integrate these ideas into a cultural-historical approach to psychology, in an attempt to advance a psycho-cultural functional model. As part of concretizing this model, we focus on the methodological requirements for dealing with the dialectics between situated-symbolic processes in the constitution of identity. Our current and ongoing research attempts to use this dialectic for analyzing a particular

* Most of the ideas in this chapter were developed in a research project carried out under contract SE-95-1252 from Comisión Interministerial de Ciencia y Tecnología del Ministerio de Educación y Cultura. The theoretical/methodological ground is indebted to the Human Futures Project, a long-term research sponsored by the Fundación Infancia y Aprendizaje. Some of the results are being used in the Centro Tecnológico de Diseño Cultural of Salamanca University, supported by Interreg II, Project IV of the European Commission. We are indebted to Miguel del Río for his help in translating the Spanish text into readable English draft, and to Seth Chaiklin for his invaluable editorial work and keen remarks on many unclear ideas in the draft. Nevertheless, anything that remains unexplained or inaccurate is the authors' responsibility.

cultural construction of human psyche that is undermined by thrusts of past history and threatened by recent history: Castilian identity.

In this chapter, we introduce briefly some of the theoretical assumptions in the cultural-historical tradition that we use for conceptualizing cultural identity, followed a presentation of some of the thought of *la generación del 98*, and its implications for analyzing Castilian identity, together with some examples of how we are trying to incorporate these ideas in our concrete research program.

## Cultural Architectures for Making Humankind

### *The Question of Identity in the Cultural-Historical Approach to Functional Systems*

The evolutionary functional tradition (see Appendix) holds that the psychological functional system is based and shaped around action. From a sociocultural perspective, we prefer to say around a cultural directivity-activity system in which the development of the child-person-individual takes place, going through several planes of human biological-psychical action, all of them intertwined in complex networks of cultural mediations (see del Río & Álvarez, 1995b). The central organ of this functional system is a social-cultural consciousness system (Vygotsky, 1989).

The body of consciousness is situated mediated activity. Vygotsky (1983) said that the first construction of consciousness is unconscious: Processes and functions are used, but not seen, as long as they are shared and distributed in social and cultural space. The symbolic mediations are not, in turn, mediated, but are transparent. The embodied and embedded nature of consciousness in a culture system allows us to develop human, higher functions, and social and personal identities at a first level, but these are experienced through a sort of "extended present." A second level of consciousness, that which enables us to see the unconsciousness of the first level is, for example, something like a dream. The mediation of first-level mediations (through novels, science, myths) allows us to go further in our life projects.

Vygotsky's analysis can be applied to describe the constitution of personal identity as proceeding through at least two levels of consciousness, both of them culturally mediated: situated identity and symbolic identity.

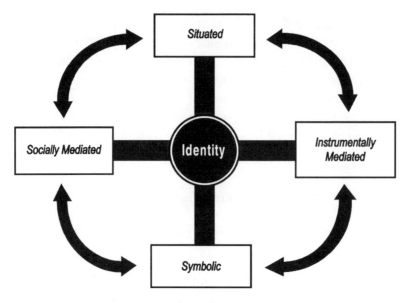

Figure 16.1. The functional system of identity.

*Situated identity.* The concepts to be analyzed here are: (a) external brain (del Río, 1994a, 1994b); (b) syncretic zone of representation (del Río, 1990) or cultural shells (Álvarez, 1996); and (c) symbiotic conscious-ness — socially and culturally distributed identity. Situated identity merges in real contexts or scenarios with the activity system, using the activity system and being used by it. When the culturally-mediated con-sciousness at this first level becomes mediated, then a second level is reached.

*Symbolic identity.* Usually the form of personal identity is structured hermeneutically in stories, narratives, or conceptual categories. The biographies and sociobiographies — life, cosmos (myths) and homeland stories in Unamuno's three levels of novel (discussed later) are distributed and may be analyzed through explicit records found in cultural mass-media contents or produced in scientific investigations (e.g., questionnaires). The functional system is therefore socially dis-tributed among diverse individuals and social subjects, and culturally, in the operators and activity's instrumental mediation systems articu-lated in cultural scenarios (see Figure 16.1).

Starting from this culturally-rooted conception of personal identity, we have advanced a definition of cultural identity for guiding our research into the historical ways that Castilian people and the Castilian nation have used to define its identity along with other cultural identities in Spain.[1] The question of cultural identities is understood to be a fundamental problem within the cultural-historical perspective.

### Defining and Framing Cultural Identity

We conceive of *identity* as a unit of relation and recognition, of reacting and projecting, implicit or explicit, based in belonging and participation, situated in and mediated by specific cultural spaces and times. The words that comprise this definition have the following meanings:

*Unit.* We adopt a Vygotskian-Wallonian conception of identity, in which the functional units of human agency, feeling and recognition are shared, from the starting symbiotic dyad of mother-child, to the different consciousness groups or social-functional identities (family, peers, etc.) or wider, fully-integrated communities (a little village), and collectivities shared in physical or symbolic space. The personal unit would be a dialogical and systemic incorporation of these different distributed units. The units are more or less integrated according to the cultural system and personal life.

*Relation and recognition.* Identity is felt, experienced and formed through interacting and relating, be it real interactions or postural, such as participating in symbolic experiences, like those of spectator.[2] Recognition is a deeper reflexive process of accepting identity concerning a symbiotic unit or oneself (relation with ourselves).

*Reacting and projecting.* Identity may be active-situated or active-symbolic. In a situated, embedded system of identity one can live a strong situated and distributed identity without projecting. One can, so to speak, "write" his/her own life without ever thinking of it as a

---

1. Our research group in Salamanca participates in a nationally-coordinated research project involving five different teams. Each team studies a regional identity (Andalucía, Castilla-León, Cataluña, País Vasco or Madrid) and national Spanish identity. Each of these regions (out of a total of 17 regions in Spain) is a *Comunidad Autónoma* (autonomous region), with its own regional parliament and government. Furthermore, some of them have a constitutional designation as *Comunidades Históricas* (meaning they have historical reasons and rights for their autonomous claims). *Comunidades Históricas* confers a special status in relation to the Spanish state, and in some cases (Cataluña, País Vasco) there is a strong nationalist flavor expressed in both moderate and strong independentist movements.
2. See the theory of postural participation in literature and cinema by Vygotsky-Zaporozhets and Wallon-Zazzo (Vygotsky, 1916/1987; Wallon, 1942; Zaporozhets, 1977; Zazzo, 1954).

novel.[3] If one connects different levels of situated and symbolic identities one must necessarily share novels and projects. In the personal acting of a project, one comes to write new personal novels or even propose communitarian novels for others.

*Implicit or explicit*. Relating, recognizing, reacting and projecting can be more or less conscious. Unconscious or implicit identity benefits from situated, shared functions, while conscious identity is explicit.

*Based in belonging and participation*. The unity of feeling, acting, recognizing, projecting is based in the real or postural participation and belongs to the symbiotic, cultural unit. Belonging is not so much an interrelation as an intrarelation in terms of psychological functioning.

*Situated in and mediated by specific cultural spaces and times*. Following Luria, the neurological-representational networks of the functional system are distributed in three blocks (del Río & Álvarez, 1995a, 1995b; Luria, 1978/1983). The first manages activation, the second (mainly perceptual) manages situation and simultaneous representations, and the third manages action and sequencing. All three have developed extra-cortical (cultural) extensions embedded in human cultural settings. These mediations allow for inserting actions into the here and now; the there and past and future planes; in memories of the past and plans or memories for the future. At the same time, these mediations can be either simple cultural operators inserted in the present physical space and scenario of activity, or systemic operators that insert whole settings and scenes (symbolic contexts and narratives). The postural system facilitates to re-act from the three blocks both in basic systems (e.g., praying in front of a cross, or acting from a note on the refrigerator) and in the more complex ones (as watching a film or television program, or reading a newspaper or a novel

This definition allows us to conceive personal or cultural identity as a characteristic functional system in the way that Vygotsky and Leontiev defined personality. The system does not change bit by bit; rather it

3. In what follows, we adopt the term of *novel* in Unamuno's sense, to refer to the personal construction of the individual life-story, intertwined with the cultural humanity's History. In Spanish, the word for *story* and *history* is the same: *historia*. Life-story is *historia de vida* and history is *historia de la humanidad*, but at the same time, a story (*una historia*) is also understood as a tale, and *una historia* that is constructed literarily will become *una novela*. Unamuno proposes that life is a novel, and the person writes or conceives his/her story in the same way that professional writers conceive their novels. Unamuno used to employ such word-games for communicating the profound philosophical/psychological sense in words to the reader.

is an integrated whole, a way of acting and being conscious in the human sociocultural environment. Identity is a sociocultural mechanism through which the system protects its integrity and identifies itself. It is not just an identification label or a way to distinguish beings separately from their functional system. Thus, if the main task of cultural-historical psychology is the diagnosis of historically- and culturally-constructed functional systems (see end of the Appendix), then one needs to make specific analyses of different "cultural ways of being."

Vygotsky assumed that the sociocultural system of natural functions is rebuilt in ontogenesis and in historiogenesis, giving birth to a new functional system (higher functions). But if these new functions emerge from a distributed functional cultural system (i.e., from a culture organized on consciousness and activity systems), then changes in cultural and historical systems will cause changes in the functional personal system. Thus, the functional system's diagnosis of a culture (and not simply the diagnosis of a particular step in history) becomes the main task for contemporary cultural-historical psychologists. This is the long-standing problem of folk psychology recomposed within the frame of a biological and cultural functionalism.

The central role attributed in the Vygotskian approach to identities as cultural-historical constructions is not unique. This same concern appears explicitly in the thought and work of *la generación del 98* — Spanish writers, philosophers, artists, and social scientists who worked during a crucial moment in the historical constitution of the idea of Spain as a nation.

### Identity and Cultural Architectures: The 98 Debate in Spain

At the end of the 19th century an intense scientific-cultural debate took place concerning the entity of Spain itself, of the Spanish people and, linked to it, of humanity in general.[4] The weaknesses and virtues, accomplishments and faults, pride and shame of Spaniards

4.  1898 marked a turning point for the Spaniards' cosmological view. The progressive decline of the Spanish role in the international arena, starting in 18th and 19th centuries, was marked decisively by the defeat of the Spanish fleet in Cuba by the U.S.A., which led to the loss of the last American possessions of the Spanish Empire, and the loss of the Philippines in Asia. This defeat constituted more than a simple material loss. It meant a strong sense of identity loss along with a deep and urgent need to define "Spain" from a new and non-power-based status. There was also a need to question what traits of being Spanish had led to such a disaster.

were analyzed by *la generación del 98*, and compared to the other countries in the world. The aim was to establish if there was something specific to being Spanish and if so, what it was, so that specific and valued achievements could be preserved, while allowing for needed changes to overcome undesired handicaps (Altamira, 1902/1997; Ganivet, 1897/1996). Castilian (and, by extension, Spanish) cultural psychological architecture was conceptualized as *casta* (Unamuno, 1895/1996).

One of the debates in Spain during this period was about rationalism and the universality of the concept of subjectivity from which it came. This debate is significant for cultural-historical researchers in Spain for two reasons. First, does our history and culture have an identity, a way of being that is to be preserved? What part of it? Second, *la generación del 98* intellectuals[5] are a substantial part of the process of forming Spanish identity and not only raw data sources to be interpreted.

### The Identity of Castilla and the Identities of the Castilians

Some of the intellectuals focused on Castilian and Spanish culture, others on history and narratives. Identity as narrative gave way to the historical consciousness debate, first as *historical account* introduced at the end of the 19th century by historians such as Menéndez Pidal, Menéndez y Pelayo and continued in the 20th century by Sánchez-Albornoz.

The question of Castilian identity is a problem of historical identity but somehow, also, of epistemics and psychocultural thinking on identity. The process of developing the historical consciousness of Castilian spirit and culture is fused with the process of conceptualizing and defining national and cultural identities in Spain. Spain is frequently seen as arising from what today are intranational communities: Aragón, Castilla and the other cultural-political communities in the Iberian peninsula.

Different stories/histories of Spain interpret this outgrowth as leadership, domination, or merging. Sánchez-Albornoz said that Castilla gave cultural-historical content (i.e., a way of being, a projecting to Spain), and in doing so, Castilla emptied itself, physically and psychically, by pouring out or handing over its resources and identity, while remaining economically depressed, without its own distinctive defini-

---

5. The term *intellectual* is a creation of *la generación del 98*, and not French as commonly thought.

tion. These characteristics are reflected by the fact that some Castilian and Leonese provinces are among those with the highest poverty index in Spain today.

Of course there are other less "pro-Castilian" versions of Spanish identity. What is common to all versions is that historical accounts are made that render coherent images with actual, present accounts and future projections. There is a lot of interpretation and hermeneutic fiction in past and present accounts, but these are the essential components for the future projections.

In this sense, there are competing historical accounts of Castilian identity that received more or less political support, with the roots situated in the beginning of the 16th century, when the imperial version of Carlos I (Charles the First), was confronted with the *Comuneros* version — and not only with a figurative meaning.[6] Those versions still remain in the Spanish-Castilian soul, reincorporated in the flow of scientific and folk communication and mass media (films, music, novels), and even in political commemorations (e.g., the anniversary of the defeat of *Comuneros* by imperial forces became the "national day" when the political entity (*Comunidad*) of Castilla y León was constituted in 1979).

The intellectual movement claiming the importance of historical consciousness generated a flourishing of historical studies, and stimulated the emergence of a trend emphasizing *narrative account* (Unamuno, Ortega y Gasset, Azorín, Machado), a way of thinking of identities as narratives, as novels, as personal-cultural projects articulated in a dialectic between fiction and reality.

*La generación del 98* marks in this sense, not only a renewed interest in historical account, but a definite emphasis on narrative account and a conceptualization of narrative as central and crucial for the formation of

6. Charles I was also Charles V of the Austrio-Germans. He was the grandson of Isabel de Castilla and Fernando de Aragón. His mother Juana married the son of Emperor Maximilian of Austria, prince Philip, who was supposed to inherit the Habsburg Empire. However, Philip's early death and the mental insanity of princess Juana (questioned nowadays by some historians and by the Castilians at the time) gave the throne of Castilla, Aragón (Spain) and the vast Holy Roman Empire to Charles. Educated in Brussels by his aunt Margherite of Austria, Charles arrived in Spain followed by a cohort of Flemish counselors. Shortly thereafter, a revolution broke out led by the followers of his brother Fernando who was educated in Castilla and more in tune with the Castilian way of governing by *comunidades*, a kind of parliament formed by the estates which formed the *Cortes*. The *Revuelta de los Comuneros* (Comuneros Revolution) started in the *Cortes*, and was crushed by the imperial forces.

consciousness and identity, both of persons and communities. Unamuno (1905/1966) would come to say that Don Quijote has more historical factuality than Cervantes himself, as long as it is the narrative personality of Don Quijote, the one that influenced Spanish thinking and passed from fictional process to a real (material, social, psychic) formative historical process.

The analysis of the "histori-cal" and "story-cal" narrative account of Spanish identity by *la generación del 98* resulted in a line of political, sociological and historical thinking, which developed into a reflection on narratives or the role of novels in making individual and social life and biographies.

The analysis of the cultural and psychological account of Spanish identity led to a line of ethnographic and cultural-historical thinking about the architectures of mind *avant la page*. One distinctive trait of the cultural debate about Castilian identity is that it emphasized both narratives and cultural settings with the same force, establishing a deep and dense relation between history-story, on the one hand, and *país, paisaje y paisanaje* (country, landscape and people) on the other. Unamuno refers to both as the history and the infrahistory of people and peoples. The spirit of Castilla is thought to exist in its stones, streets, fields, paths, objects, activity settings and scenarios with the same force as in the narratives (myths and poetry, novel and popular culture). This is an essential point: The cultural structures of activity and consciousness are integrated in a historical complex in which the material, the psychological, the setting for being, and the model of being are merged. This view leads us to an ecological research of cultural-historical architectures that takes into account both the body and the spirit of culture.

### The "Body" and Extension of Castilian Identity

We try here to convey the main ideas and assumptions that guide our work on the identities of the Castilian people.

*La generación del 98*'s approach to the cultural infrahistory of Castilla and the Castilians is syncretic, having strong intuitive and cultural tools ranging from the poetry of Antonio Machado (whose poems are, in Vygotskian words, "real traps for catching feelings," in the case of the Castilian-situated soul) to ethnographic research developments and sociological or philosophical analysis.

When we use the term *body* to speak of the situated part of the psyche, we do not only use it metaphorically: A Castilian's psyche has extracortical extensions linked to the organism itself and the cultural shells or contexts made by and for ourselves. These are a culture's cortical territories.

Both Lorenz (1992) and Wallon (1942) warned us about the biological roots of human psyche. The territory of cultural mediations is still the territory of animal behavior. Psychological tools are placed and organized in physical, biological environments and used from a biological-postural system. In our approach, we have not changed the biological nature of the environment, but we have enriched it allowing for a combination of the same elements in new functional structures that support higher psychological functions (see del Río, 1990, for the concept of *zone of syncretic representation*, which provides a model for the integration of biological space and functions with mediating and higher processes; and del Río, 1994a, 1994b for the associated concept of *external brain*, which analyzes the cultural extracortical components of the situated psyche). Our identity, our cognitive and directive functions are distributed in these territories, which come to be new natural-plus-human environments. When we travel to another country or move to another cultural context, then we are obliged to leave the cultural tools that activate external to the functional system. If these tools are taken out of our zone of syncretic representation, then we feel "like a fish out of water," and have difficulties recognizing ourselves. For example, our favorite food or drink are real bio-psychological handles for activating the first block of the functional system (i.e., activation). Most of these basic cultural tools are socially used and shared, and might be considered as essentials of cultural identity, although they may appear less explicitly than the grand legitimating narratives.

The different psychological tools that allow us to connect this basic, territorialized culture to wider symbolic contexts also have an embedded nature. Orality is embedded in the structure of kitchens, public squares (*plazas*), and other places where people commonly meet. Literacy is embedded in libraries and classrooms, in suitcases and tables. Audiovisuality is embedded in cinemas and living rooms, and so on. There is a real, not only mental-abstract embeddedness whose mechanics are guaranteed by cultural connectors and sophisticated processes of triangulation — like the joint action made possible in the convergent looking at an object by mother and child, or the complex processes of shared television viewing.

## The Spirit and Time of Castilian Identity

Living in situated identity and functions is very easy: Our functions are literally at hand. Because our cultural body is so dense and coherent, it is difficult for most of us to look upon it, see oneself and then construct a decontextualized symbolic context of identities. Religions, like Catholicism; psychological cultural tools, like psychoanalysis; and philosophical models, like existentialism; allow us to build a model and narrative of our connected selves. We also find great help in small cultural tools, like the mirror, the diary, photograph albums, or social commemorative meetings (anniversaries, baptisms, weddings, reunions and so on).

To elaborate and deepen this conception of spirit and time, the symbols and history of identity, let us examine Miguel de Unamuno's conception about levels of novel.

## Three Levels of Novel in Miguel de Unamuno's Writings

For Unamuno, the planes of personal, national and human identity are linked through the idea of *novela* (Unamuno, 1927/1990a, footnote 5). He conceived of a novel as a model of life, and a life as a novel written by that life's protagonist. This theme was explored in one of his most outstanding works, where the boundary between personal construction in the fictional model and personal construction in the mental realities of readers or writers becomes blurred (Unamuno, 1914/1990b). This idea in Unamuno's novel is a recurrent problem in this century's literature (cf. Sabato, 1984).

Unamuno was concerned with transcending that first level of situated identity, which raises a fundamental problem in consciousness: it is more phenomenal and historical-symbolic than a priori noumenal, and this opens the way to real and important changes in history. We could say, in Luria's style, that narratives create neurons, change the brain, and that symbols change the real materiality of humans, aside from changing their environment.

Unamuno refers to three different types of novelizing, or "writing life," interconnected in turn: the novel of personal life, the novel of national life, and the novel of humanity. We will sketch each type by using quotations from Unamuno's (1927/1990a) *Cómo se Hace una Novela*.

*Personal novel as project*. The relationship between novels, personal identities and narratives is a continuing feature in Spanish literature. Unamuno was especially celebrated for the way in which his novels focused on the opposition between the character that is read by the reader and the reader who in reading the novel is also "writing" himself as the argument.

¿Hay novela más novelesca que una autobiografía? (p. 114)

[Is there a novel more novelistic than an autobiography?]

Y yo quiero contarte, lector, cómo se hace una novela, cómo haces y has de hacer tú mismo tu propia novela. (p. 192)

[And I want to tell you, reader, how a novel is made, how do you make and should make yourself your own novel.]

Sé que hipócrita significa actor. ¿Hipócrita? ¡No! Mi papel es mi verdad y debo vivir mi verdad, que es mi vida. (p. 159)

[I know that hypocrite means actor. Hypocrite? No! My role is my truth and I must live my truth, which is my life.]

Presumo que algún lector, al leer esta confesión cínica, ... se indigne diciendo que no hago sino representar un papel, que no comprendo el patriotismo, que no ha sido seria la comedia de mi vida. Pero a este lector indignado lo que le indigna es que le muestro que él es, a su vez, un personaje cómico, novelesco y, nada menos, un personaje que quiero poner en medio del sueño de su vida. Que haga del sueño, de su sueño, vida y se habrá salvado. Y como no hay nada más que comedia y novela, que piense que lo que le parece realidad extra-escénica es comedia de comedia, novela de novela, que el noúmenos inventado por Kant es lo de más fenomenal que puede darse y la sustancia lo que hay de más formal. El fondo de una cosa es su superficie. (pp. 175-176)

[I presume that a reader, while reading this cynical confession ... will be annoyed, seeing me as an actor that represents a role, that I do not understand patriotism, that the comedy of my life is not serious. But the reason why this reader is annoyed is that I am showing to him that he also is a comical and novelistic character, moreover that he is a character that I want to place in the middle of his life dream. What he makes of the dream, of his dream, life and he will be saved. Because there is nothing but comedy and novel, the reader should consider that what seems like reality offstage is comedy of the comedy, novel of the novel, that the noumenon invented by Kant is one of the most outstanding realities that can exist and the substance something from the most formal. The bottom of anything is its surface.]

El lector que busque novelas acabadas no merece ser mi lector; él está ya acabado antes de haberme leído. (p. 176) ... ¿Y cómo acabarás tú, lector? Si no eres hombre, hombre como yo, es decir, comediante y autor de tí mismo, entonces no debes leer, por miedo de olvidarte de tí mismo. (p. 177)

[The reader who wants finished novels does not deserve to be my reader; he is already finished, before reading me. ... And, how will you finish, reader? If you are not human, human like I am, that is to say, an actor and author of yourself then, you must not read, not being the case that you forget yourself.]

In the last quotation, Unamuno confronts two effects of the novel: distracting, escapist stories versus consciousness-forming stories. In a sense, Unamuno forces his readers to the second, to construct their own stories as a novel story, to integrate the events that happen to them as "free events," that is to say, with novelized, prewritten, voluntary, predefined happenings. The novel would be a model for a self-written story, a self-designed life.

This vision of life as dream appeared in the Spanish dramatist Calderón de la Barca (1635/1992). It finds a Vygotskian complement in Unamuno: Conscious dream, mediated activity and arguments must become life to escape from the realist dream of unconsciousness.

In this perspective, Unamuno writes novels to pose a problem to his readers. Unamuno uses the etymology of *problem*[7] to make an equivalence between problem and project. Solving the problem is not finding a single solution, but constructing, creating something. Unamuno's novels are nothing but projects of consciousness. His rejection of the sociological and pedagogical models of his time is based on a rejection of their a priori definition and limitation of human novel, of their inability to think of children, persons and peoples as projects of identity, projects of humanity (Unamuno, 1986a). He pointed to the nation — homeland

---

7. From Greek *proballein*: pose, meaning "put something forward" and from Latin *proiicere*, meaning "to project."

— as the transition between the personal novel and the humanity novel (Unamuno, 1927/1990a).

*Nation's novel.* For Unamuno, the personal novel leads unavoidably to the national novel: "You cannot make politics without novel or novel without politics" (Unamuno, 1927/1990a, p. 195). Unamuno linked his own life, as writer and as reader, with active engagement in politics. He reminded those who told him to give up political activities and devote himself to literature, science and life, that they did not know that "my studies, my novels, my poems, are politics" (p. 171). (In a complementary and equivalent way, Sabato, 1984, said to those who criticized him for making literature instead of politics, that profound politics is good literature.)

Vivir en la historia y vivir la historia, hacerme en la historia, en mi España, y hacer mi historia, mi España, y con ella mi universo y mi eternidad, tal ha sido y sigue siendo la trágica cuita de mi destierro. La historia es leyenda, ya lo con-sabemos. (p. 132)

[To live in history and to live history, to make myself in history, in my Spain, and to make my history, my Spain, and with it my universe and my eternity; this has been and still is the tragic affliction in my exile. History is legend, that we all co-know.]

Y yo estoy aquí, en el destierro, a la puerta de España y como su ujier, no para lucir y lucirme, sino para alumbrar y alumbrarme, para hacer nuestra novela, historia, la de nuestra España. (p. 210)

[I am here, exiled, at the gates of Spain and like its usher not to shine and shine myself, but to enlighten and illuminate myself, to make our novel, history, the one of our Spain.]

Hay una leyenda de la realidad que es la sustancia, la íntima realidad de la realidad misma. La esencia de un individuo y la de un pueblo es su historia, y la historia es lo que se llama la filosofía de la historia, es la reflexión que cada individuo o cada pueblo hacen de lo que les sucede, de lo que se sucede en ellos. (p. 130)

[There is a legend of reality that is the substance, the intimate reality of reality itself. The essence of an individual and the one of a people that is their history and history is what is called philosophy of history; it is the reflection that each individual or each people make of what happens to them, of what happens in them.]

   This legend of the people is a cultural reality, a real entity that builds up the new generations that use them. That is why Unamuno says that the Spain shown by Cervantes in *El Quijote* becomes more real today than the Spain of the 16th century described in historical accounts. The Spain of Cervantes is his daughter (the product of his writing) and not his mother (the starting point for his writing.)

   *Humanity's novel.* As a cultural existentialist, Unamuno tried to link his personal life-project to the Spanish cultural project, and to the project of humanity. His reflections on religion and science are meant to complement them by looking to explain the future, rather than the past.

y sobre la congoja del posible acabamiento de mi novela, sobre y bajo ella, sigue acongojándome la congoja del posible acabamiento de la novela de la Humanidad. (p. 179)

[and about the grief about the possible ending of my novel, upon and underneath it, continues to distress me the grief of the possible ending of the novel of Humanity.]

   Jean Cassou (1924/1990) interpreted Unamuno's writings and self-written life as a prototype of the Spanish cosmological view, of the Spanish novel concerning humanity. What really matters here is the idea of the culture of nations making novels about the world and trying to convince other readers, not whether it is realistic or scientific. These novels are not about what the world or humanity as it is now (descriptive models, positivist and rationalistic thinking), but about what we wish, or conceive that it may or should be. Collective identities can grow bottom-up and may become integrated with complex hierarchical structures[8] or they can be manufactured by groups or institutions that generate top-down discourses. There may also be an identity that is "recovered" or rediscovered by someone belonging to the community and redirects the unconscious popular identity to it as a conscious identity (e.g., the case of the *la generación del 98*, or the Catalonian reconstruction).

8.  Unamuno called them *patrias de los pueblos*, peoples' homelands, nations with a real communitarian historical cultural structure.

| Identity planes/levels | General characteristics | Specimen records | Data collection methods |
|---|---|---|---|
| Situated | Extracortical activity and consciousness scenarios | Religious imagery in everyday contexts (e.g., photographs in the house, clothing) | Ecological analysis and video-recording |
| Symbolic | Life's novels and narratives | Christian and historical narratives vs. mass-media narratives | Discussion groups Life stories; content analysis; ecological analysis |
| Socially-mediated | Groups of consciousness | Ritualized shared activities (e.g., ro-merías, cofradías, sewing and embroidering women's groups) | Mainly through life stories |
| Instrumentally-mediated | Tools em-bedded in a scenario of consciousness | Dialogical-oral vs. individual-literate discourse construc-tions: Oral traditions such as praying in church, folk singing and dancing versus writings, school productions | Ecological analysis; content analysis |
| Conscious | Popular beliefs, stereotypes brought to consciousness | | Questionnaire survey |

Figure 16.2. Units of analysis for different planes/levels of identity.

## Castilian Cultural Identity: Being, Acting, Feeling or Thinking Different?

Cultural-economical globalization coincides historically and cul-turally — not casually it seems — with a recovery of consciousness about cultural identities (see Turner, this volume). In Europe this process merges with that of the European Union's own development and design. Similarly, the recent Spanish democracy is organized explicitly in relation to its cultural-historical and story-cal regions: Basque, Catalan, Galician, Castilian, Andalusian, and so on. It has been said frequently that in the process of cultural construction of identities, some groups choose to do it according to a "creation of enemy-based identity" processes, in which a cultural identity's dramatics structurally demand the existence of a "bad guy" in order to uphold a definite and positive role for the chosen identity.

In contrast, steady, definite functionally-situated identities, which do not operate on an explicit and narrative level as "enemy" identities, can also be found in Spain. For instance, Castilians and Andalusians do not see a need for claiming a distinctive national public narrative (as do Basques, Catalans and Galicians), and would feel comfortable with a "Spanish" identity. Nevertheless, an analysis of their situated and practical identity's functional cultures should reveal a less conscious but not weaker identity system.

Starting from the assumption that cultural identity may only be approached through a systematic functional analysis of activity, identity and consciousness's levels — conscious and unconscious, historical and present, situated and symbolic — a research model has been employed in which a set of methodologies are considered for capturing the hypothesized levels or planes of identity constitution (see Figure 16.2).

Among the techniques mentioned in Figure 16.2, the questionnaire has been used widely and overused in psychology and sociology, causing an overestimation of conscious cognitive processes (narratives included) in identity research. The central functional identity processes and the situated activity-consciousness system's of cultural directivity have been omitted, and their social distribution and ecological situatedness ignored. Content analysis, the other technical resource widely recognized in mass-media research, is not used extensively, if used at all, in the domain of psychology, and certainly not for cultural-historical analysis of those mediators responsible for the functional-psychological construction of identity.

From a cultural-historical point of view, we have hypothesized that cultural projects about identity operate mainly through the cultural tools found in mass communication, while situated identities act through the more embedded and transparent mediations of everyday culture and activity, in "consciousness scenarios." The former may not be noticed unless we make a detached global analysis of the process of mass culture from a technical and systemic perspective. The latter, as historically-accumulated products of cultural psyche, may not be seen and usually remain implicit, or may appear as spontaneous constructions, unless revealed through an ecological-psychocultural analysis. Taking both methodological constraints as a starting point, we are working on the distinctive traits of the cultural-historical typologies for three generations of men and women in rural and urban settings in Castilla y León. The data sources include: (a) a discussion group with 60 participants in 12 sessions, (b) ecological specimen records and content analysis of cultural shells for three generations of five families, (c) situated life stories via audiovisual records of a rural man and an urban women, and (d) a questionnaire survey of 150 people (youths and their parents and grandparents).

A first glance at the raw data reveals, as expected, a similar fuzzy-situated nonconscious lived identity, but also quite different historical ways of living and feeling identity among the three generations of Castilians. These historical ways also reflect the "story" meaning of *historia*. As a first, provisional conclusion, we can say that the elder Castilians construct their identity mainly in rituals and actions embedded in their daily-life activity systems, while the younger Castilians rely mainly on mass-media models proposed for action. Not surprisingly, changes in identity construction reflect broader changes in the social sphere, and these changes are the focus of our current research. But that is another story that shall also be told...

### Appendix

*The Psychological Functional System*

Many of the European developmental psychologists who adopt a bio-functionalist approach (i.e., Claparède, Piaget, Wallon, Vygotsky, and Luria), postulate that in an environment–organism interaction not only is the organism incorporated to the environment, but the environment is also modified — and therefore incorporated to the organism. Psychic life's "organization" (cultural functional construction biologized in the re-construction of mental organs), is the main structuring process of the general function that these psychologists identify with life itself. Therefore, a dialectic structuring between organism and medium yields development's dynamics, at ecological, cultural, social and biological levels. Vygotsky (1989) extended this perspective: The cultural reconstruction made by humans of natural functions into higher functions is also organic and biological, but created through external means.

Tools are outside the person; organs are within the person. The essence of intelligence lies in tools. Instinct is a capacity to use and construct organized instruments; intelligence is unorganized. It has its merits and its shortcomings. But constructive psychological activity (will) is something fundamentally new — a synthesis of one or another kind of activity. Because organic structures and functions are constructed in the brain using external, unorganized means, instincts are built. See Ukhtomskii: the system of neurological functions is in an organ. In this sense, man *builds* new organs, but organic ones, with the aid of instrumental activity. (pp. 55-56)

Finding the cultural and psychological organizing principle, and how it evolves from generation to generation (see del Río & Álvarez, 1995a; Sternberg, 1996; Stokols, 1995) are therefore central goals for bio-functionalist psychologies, including the cultural-historical approach (Álvarez, 1996). We now consider the cultural-historical approach, paying special attention to the different levels of psychological construction that have to be taken into account to avoid the traps of reductionism and dualism that Vygotsky (1927/1982) criticized in the 1930s and which still pervades psychological science at the doors of the 21st century.

### Some Cultural-Historical Assumptions about Functional Systems

The Vygotskian theses about the cultural roots of psychological construction assert that there is no unique or universal functional system, individually structured, mental, internal and detached from culture, and genetically guaranteed. Functional psychological research therefore cannot be approached over an isolated sample of individuals of a certain culture nor over a single historical cohort, and no individual's functional system should be extrapolated to any other.

Because the higher psychological systems are cultural constructions, they share a certain number of universal laws:

*Sympsychical character.*[9] Psychological functions are socially constructed, shared and distributed. Differences are found in the organization of intrapsychological and interpsychological functions because of different cultural models in which individuals are embedded. The units of analysis at this level should be *symbiosis* (Wallon, 1942), *sympsyche* (Unamuno, 1986b), or *group of consciousness* (del Río & Álvarez, 1995a, 1995b).

*Cultural situatedness.* The instrumental system of mediations which underlies psychological construction is symbolic systems, structures of representation, myths and narratives, all of them are articulated in systems of shells by the cultural *mise en scène* (Álvarez, 1996; del Río & Álvarez, in press). The unit of analysis at this level should be *cultural shells*.

*Cultural-historical and ontogenetic cultural character.* The psychological systems' construction is tied to the specific historical and cultural conditions that change and evolve both on individual and social planes. The unit of analysis at this level should be the *cortical/cultural neoformation* (Luria, 1978/1983).

*Distributed.* Psychological development consists of a complex process of sharing, appropriating and interiorizing of the cultural-historicalsocial distributed functions never totally nor perfectly performed. The unit of analysis at this level should be the *law of double formation* (Vygotsky, 1934/1984).

These universals lead us to identify some of the tasks for a culturalhistorical psychology research, already advanced by Vygotsky, which imply:

1. The flexible and heterogeneous character of functional psychological systems within every human culture should be considered (del Río & Álvarez, 1995a; Tulviste, 1988).

2. The specific and functional psychological diagnosis at the individual plane implies functional diagnosis at the cultural level. Psychological assessment therefore has to be culture-bound, never "culture-free" (Laboratory for Comparative Human Cognition, 1983/1988).

3. Derived from the previous point, the most appealing and urgent task for cultural-historical psychology remains, as in Vygotsky's

9. Sympsychical, term derived from Greek συν–ψυχοζ (united in the same feelings). Unamuno used this term in a sense very close to the Wallonian symbiosis.

time, to make a functional inventory and diagnosis of the cultural practices that are responsible for the present and active psychological functional systems (Tulviste, this volume, expresses a similar view). If this is correct, then it is as important to know the human culturome[10] as it is to know the human genome to understand the functional role of each relevant cultural architecture for the construction of human psyche and avoid "malformations" or troubles in development.

## References

Altamira, R. (1997). *La psicología del pueblo español*. Madrid: Biblioteca Nueva. (Original work published 1901)

Álvarez, A. (1996). Los marcos culturales de actividad y el desarrollo de las funciones psicológicas. Unpublished doctoral dissertation. Universidad Autónoma de Madrid, Spain.

Calderón de la Barca, P. (1992). *La vida es sueño*. Madrid: Club Internacional del Libro. (Original work written 1635)

Cassou, J. (1990). Retrato de Unamuno (M. de Unamuno, Trans.). In M. de Unamuno, *San Manuel Bueno, mártir* and *Cómo se hace una novela* (pp. 91-102). Madrid: Alianza. (Reprinted from *Mercure de France*, 1924, *188*, 5-12)

del Río, P. (1990). La zona de desarrollo próximo y la zona sincrética de representación: El espacio instrumental de la acción social. *Infancia y Aprendizaje, 51-52*, 191-244.

del Río, P. (1994a). Extra-cortical connections: The sociocultural systems for conscious living. In J.V. Wertsch & J.D. Ramírez (Eds.), *Literacy and other forms of mediated action* (pp. 19-31). Madrid: Fundación Infancia y Aprendizaje.

del Río, P. (1994b). Re-present-acción en contexto: Una alternativa de convergencia para las perspectivas cognitiva e histórico-cultural. In A. Rosa & J. Valsiner (Eds.), *Historical and theoretical discourse* (pp. 129-146). Madrid: Fundación Infancia y Aprendizaje.

10. Culturome is the word and the task we suggest that should be adopted by cultural-historical disciplines in order to complement the task of geneticists. This task would also confront the cultural-historical thesis with the pervasive, implicit, innatist attempts to reduce human inheritance to the genetic or organic, and deny or ignore any possible contributions from history and culture. Through cultural and biological processes, human beings reconstruct natural functions into higher functions and in doing so, they reconstruct the eco-biological setting as a neurocultural organ.

del Río, P., & Álvarez, A. (1995a). Tossing, praying and reasoning: The changing architectures of mind and agency. In J.V. Wertsch, P. del Río, & A. Álvarez (Eds.), *Sociocultural studies of mind* (pp. 215-247). Cambridge: Cambridge University Press.

del Río, P., & Álvarez, A. (1995b). Directivity: The cultural and educational construction of morality and agency. Some questions arising from the legacy of Vygotsky. *Anthropology and Education Quarterly, 26,* 384-409.

del Río, P., & Álvarez, A. (in press). El entorno sincrético: El medio perceptivo y la puesta en escena socio-cultural. In *La mediación cultural: Una aproximación histórico-cultural a las tecnologías y a la naturaleza humana.* Madrid: Fundación Infancia y Aprendizaje.

Ganivet, A. (1996). *El idearium español.* Madrid: Biblioteca Nueva. (Original work published 1897)

Laboratory for Comparative Human Cognition (1988). Cultura e inteligencia (C. Girad, Trans.). In R.J. Sternberg (Ed.), *Inteligencia humana, III* (pp. 1001-1111). Barcelona: Paidós. (Translated from *Handbook of human intelligence,* pp. 642-719, by R.J. Sternberg, Ed., 1983, Cambridge: Cambridge University Press)

Lorenz, K. (1992). Die Naturwissenschaft vom Menschen: Eine Einfuhrung in die vergleichende Verhaltensforschung. Das "russische Manuskript" (1944-1948) (A. v. Cranach, Ed.). München: Piper.

Luria, A.R. (1983). La organización funcional del cerebro (L. Kuper, Trans.). In A.A. Smirnov, A.R. Luria, & V.D. Nebylitzin (Eds.), *Fundamentos de psicofisiología* (pp. 113-142). Madrid: Siglo XXI. (Original work published 1978)

Sabato, E. (1984). *Abaddón el exterminador.* Barcelona: Seix Barral.

Sternberg, R.J. (1996). Myths, countermyths and truths about intelligence. *Educational Researcher, 25*(2), 11-18.

Stokols, D. (1995). The paradox of environmental psychology. *American Psychologist, 50,* 821-837.

Tulviste, P. (1988). Kulturno-istoricheskoe razvitie verbal'nogo myshlenija. Psikhologicheskoe issledovanie. Tallinn: Valgus.

Unamuno, M. de. (1966). *Vida de Don Quijote y Sancho.* Madrid: Círculo de Lectores. (Original work published 1905)

Unamuno, M. de. (1986a). *Amor y pedagogía.* Madrid: Espasa Calpe. (Original work published 1902)

Unamuno, M. de. (1986b). *Diario íntimo.* Madrid: Alianza.

Unamuno, M. de. (1990a). *Cómo se hace una novela.* In M. de Unamuno,

*San Manuel Bueno, mártir* and *Cómo se hace una novela* (pp. 83-210). Madrid: Alianza. (Original work published 1927)

Unamuno, M. de. (1990b). *Niebla*. Madrid: Espasa Calpe. (Original work published 1914)

Unamuno, M. de. (1996). *En torno al casticismo*. Madrid: Biblioteca Nueva. (Original work published 1895)

Vygotsky, L.S. (1982). Istoricheskij smysl psikhologicheskogo krizisa [The historical meaning of the crisis in psychology]. In L.S. Vygotsky, *Sobranie sochinenie: Tom I. Voprosy teorii i istorii psikhologii* (pp. 291-346). Moscow: Pedagogika. (Original work written 1927)

Vygotsky, L.S. (1983). *Sobranie sochinenie: Tom 3. Problemy razvitie psikhii.* [Collected works: Vol. 3. Problems in psychological development]. Moscow: Pedagogika.

Vygotsky, L.S. (1984). Aprendizaje y desarrollo en la edad escolar. *Infancia y Aprendizaje, 27-28,* 105-116. (Original work written 1934)

Vygotsky, L.S. (1987). *Psikhologiia isskusstva* [Psychology of art]. Moscow: Pedagogika. (Original work written 1916. Spanish trans., in press, Madrid: Fundacion Infancia y Aprendizaje).

Vygotsky, L.S. (1989). Concrete human psychology. *Soviet Psychology, 27*(2), 53-77.

Wallon, H. (1942). *De l'acte à la pensée*. Paris: Flammarion.

Zaporozhets, A.V. (1977). *Vospratie i deistvie* [Perception and action]. Moscow: Prosveschenie.

Zazzo, R. (1954). Espace, mouvement et cinémascope. *Revue International de Filmologie, 5* (18-19), 209-219.

# 17  Recent Trends in the Development of Education in Russia and the Role of Activity Theory for Schooling

*Vitaly V. Rubtsov*

This chapter deals with special aspects of the innovative developmental education that has resulted from political and social reforms in Russia. The future development of this type of education is so important at present in the country that many administrators and specialists from different institutions and organizations are involved in its discussion. This chapter will (a) briefly review factors that influence current educational policy in Russia, (b) point to the existence of a growing tradition of educational innovation, (c) make a short review of different innovative educational approaches, and (d) give a longer discussion of the *cultural-historical* type of school, with a specific focus on the first two levels.

### Innovative Education: Sociocultural Analysis

The formation and existence of innovative educational institutions in Russia has resulted from a variety of factors and circumstances that have evolved in the political and economic reforms happening in the country. The most important, primary factors are:

— differences between social and state strategies for the development of education. These differences act as a constant source for development and change in the educational system;
— objective conditions in the changing socioeconomical and political situation in Russia that make it difficult for timely reactions by the official structures;
— special demands by certain societal groups (i.e., religious, professional, and parent groups, among others) for the creation of educational institutions that will suit their special interests and needs;
— increased demands by teachers for "new education." These teachers did not have a chance to realize their models and interests during the Soviet system of education. These people are oriented towards

the creation of new educational techniques or a different use of currently existing ones;

— the existence of many different kinds of enthusiasts who would like to create many different kinds of schools. These people are actively working on the creation of their own approaches for the organization of educational processes, and they would like to see these processes removed from the regulation and control of educational professionals and state educational entities;

— the lack (under the traditional educational system) of administrative, research, and practical centers that are capable of determining conditions and means for implementing the most promising educational models;

— the previous blockade of practical interaction between the Russian system of education and other national pedagogical systems. As a result, other systems of education are imported into Russia, sometimes uncritically, and not always with justifiable results.

All these factors show the necessity for creating new educational institutions in Russian society — kindergartens, schools, colleges. These institutions should define and solve the problems that appear as a result of social reforms, and react to societal demands and changes. Initially, all the different institutions that form the major complex of innovative education create the demand for educational services. New educational types and models will be created and implemented in response to this complex.

These conditions indicate that innovative education is becoming more common in the Russian system of education. This type of education develops as an alternative to the bureaucratically-rigid state system of education, which does not readily tolerate changes from existing traditions of practice. This state system is incapable of solving a number of problems that have developed because of radical changes of life in Russia. Innovative educational institutions have become an essential part of the system, stimulating its development and carrying out important state objectives such as including teenagers who have dropped out of existing state schools.

Innovative schools have widened the spectrum of the educational possibilities in Russia. For example, a religious school reflects a response to the restriction on implementing religious and confessional education. The same principles lie behind the creation of national or ethnic schools. The denial of national traditions and the cultural-histori-cal background of peoples who are living in different parts of the coun-try but who are at the same time educated in the same, universal system of state education leads to the creation of national, innovative (state and nonstate) schools. This type of school is directly oriented to the solution of an important national problem that has not been addressed for decades.

Innovative education becomes the basis for new experiments that guarantee the development of innovative teaching methods, which are necessary for solving regional problems of education. Innovative edu-cation must still guarantee conformity to the state standard of educa-tion, which in turn guarantees the rights of students to move freely from one area of education to another. It guarantees the quality of the education by attracting highly-skilled people from the intelligentsia, who would like to contribute their knowledge, and stimulates the development of the material basis, attracting additional investments in education from the private sector, which leads to an increase in the number of people working in state classrooms.

The number of gymnasia and lycées that are now being opened can be understood in relation to the loss of the classical and gymnasium education that existed in Russia before the 1917 Revolution. These insti-tutions openly declare that their goal is to restore the best traditions and examples of Russian classical education.

At the same time, it has become obvious that perspectives for the de-velopment of education in Russia have to deal with the problem of moving innovative education from the realm of alternative education into educational institutions that can support the "zone of proximal de-velopment" for the whole educational system in Russia.[1] These per-spectives have to deal with the support of the new innovative systems that are being developed and implemented in different sectors of Rus-sian education. In other words, these perspectives have to deal with the changes needed to build new educational models on the basis of inno-vative institutions and with the institution's own participation (primar-ily through their innovative activity).

---

1. It should be noted however that there is some state support for innovative educa-tion. For example, the Moscow Bureau of Education has a "Department of Inno-vative and Experimental Education."

## How to Create a System of Innovative Education: Strategies and Mechanisms

### Innovative Education as a System

State policy in the field of innovative education should be formed in accordance with the special needs for different types of education. A number of levels must be considered when forming a goal-oriented program of innovative education in the system of state education in Russia. At the governmental and administrative level, the question should not be about opening a particular innovative or private school, college, or kindergarten, but about how to give a form to social initiatives in the form of independent educational institutions, while preserving their innovative nature.

The image of this type of educational institution implies the existence of a well-designed conception or strategy for these institutions. This conception should include an approach to the content of education, an adequate approach for fulfilling goals, and methods and techniques for working with the contents. It is also important to supply the institution with specially-trained teachers, educational materials, and a system of scientific and methodological support.

### Conceptualization and Scientific Expertise

The development of a system of innovative developmental education requires specific scientific and administrative work in order to move from the declaration of formal goals by educational institutions to the creation of concrete educational environment. The final result of this process will be the creation of an institution that would correspond to a particular social initiative. Special research work on the educational goals and the formulation of the corresponding contents is needed at the microlevels for these schools, kindergartens, and colleges. As a result of these works, teachers should begin to understand what kind of educational institution they are building or want to build. The final result of this work should be an elaborated plan of development for a particular educational institution.

It is absolutely clear that the organization of special scientific support, primarily psychological and pedagogical, is necessary, along with the creation of a special network of centers that would deal with the development and expertise of these institutions. These centers would be formed according to the actual state of the institution, and its declared goals, so that the center's conceptual basis is designed to support these goals. The center would also help in the formulation and development of new educational programs and in the organization of psychological and pedagogical support necessary for the retraining of teachers.

This collaboration will give form to the social and personal initiatives that are associated with the creation of an educational institution, and a way to transform these initiatives into a particular type of school. As a result of coordinated collaboration of the centers, social initiatives and teachers, even at the level of a particular educational institution, it will be possible to change the quality of the educational activity, raise the standards for the government regulations about the new types of innovative schools, and preserve their independence.

### Developmental Pedagogy to Realize Innovative Educational Processes

Long ago, it seemed obvious that there was no evolution in a society determined by its different types of educational institutions. Each educational institution had its own world, with little or no coordination between them, such that preschools, schools, technical colleges, and colleges each functioned independently of each other.

Today there is a process of integration between the school and the kindergarten (the so-called "school-kindergarten" system), and integration between the school and university (the so-called "school-university" system). There are also colleges, gymnasia, lycées, technical schools, and so on. In 1993, in Moscow and St. Petersburg and other cities, some schools were united with research institutions — so-called "schools-laboratories." The special interest that appeared in this system of experimental education was the unique system where the child comes himself to knowledge and creativity driven by his own interest and motives.

The administrative organs of the educational system should facilitate a reasonable integration of different types of educational institutions, which is extremely important for the new educational institutions. This step in overcoming the alternative nature of innovative education is the creation of diversity in the system of developmental education, preserving at the same time the unity of the whole system. The diversity in education, based upon the restoration of the spiritual, cultural, national, historical, and professional roots and ways of living of the Russian people, guarantees the self-definition of the personality and creates conditions for its self-realization. The pedagogy of development that has been formed currently is child-centered and goal-directed in terms of the acquisition of norms of life in particular regions. This pedagogy can serve as a basis for creating a system of innovative teaching methods that broaden the possibilities for the development of an individual during learning and upbringing. In other words, pedagogy development reflects a school that supports diversity in education, especially in its innovative part. Today, when support is given to many different types of innovative institutions it is necessary to evaluate them.

The present-day educational space includes at least seven types of school; each type represents a particular model for instruction and upbringing for the next generation. These types are: (a) the traditional school, (b) the specialized school (providing intensive study of one or a complex of subjects); (c) the gymnasium-lyceum, (d) the instrumental innovative school (based on proprietary methods that have been discovered during practical activities by the talent of the teacher; the use of specific pedagogical technologies, new methods and tools of instruction, and so forth); (e) the school oriented toward a particular established pedagogical system (e.g., the Waldorf School, the Montessori School); (f) the developmental-teaching school (Davydov, 1986; Elkonin, 1989); and (g). the history-culture school (named after the school that provides an intensive humanities component of knowledge in the "dialogue of cultures" school, Bibler, 1969).

I will now examine those aspects for each type of school that directly or contrastively delineate the contours of the cultural-historical type of school, which will be discussed in the next section.[2]

The traditional school, oriented toward the transmission of ready-made knowledge, essentially reproduces the empirical type of thinking and ultimately deprives the student of the ability to assimilate the cultural-historical point of view. No effort is made to explore the conditions of the origin of the object, the modes of action or understanding,

---

2. There are other experimental schools in the Russian educational system, inspired by the cultural-historical tradition, that require attention: the didactic system of development education (Zankov, 1963; 1975/1977); "Development" by Zaporozhets-Venger, "activity theory of education" by Galperin (1974/1975) and Talysina. There still remains the task to evaluate these directions and schools, with the aim of integrating and preserving their best features.

and their cultural-historical context; this makes it impossible to examine the ideal plane of processes and phenomena. At the same time, thanks to the practices of the traditional school, the society has developed particular ideas concerning what the student ought to know and be able to do, and at what age. This must not be ignored when designing a school of a new type.

The specialized school is usually a secondary school. It provides intensive study in one or several subjects, and is oriented primarily to the schoolchild's mastery of particular methods of working with the subject-matter content to be studied. Most often, this is accomplished by increasing the number of exercises and school hours allocated in the syllabus for the detailed study of the material. In the majority of cases, the difference between this type of school and the traditional school is quantitative not qualitative.

Practical experience has shown that, given particular abilities and prior training, youngsters — basically students in the middle and upper grades — can assimilate considerably more complicated subject material than in the traditional school and can quickly specialize in a particular activity (mathematics, physics, foreign languages, and so forth).

The modern gymnasium or lyceum represents an attempt to recreate an academic level of education (in style, form, and method) that existed in the prerevolutionary period. This form of education justifiably enjoys a high prestige. In practice, the organization of this type of educational institution generally involves substantial changes in the syllabi, through the addition of new subjects. Changes of this sort, as a rule, are made by increasing the number of humanities subjects (e.g., philosophy, logic, culture, ancient and modern languages) and by enlisting top-rated specialists to participate in the process of instruction (teachers from leading higher educational institutions, research institutes, and science centers).

The experience of existing gymnasiums testifies to the fact that in many cases the incorporation of new material leads to an overload of the curricula. The instructors who have been brought in are not specialists in public-school education; they structure their work with the aim of transmitting large amounts of information and fail to consider the age characteristics of the pupils. It needs to be pointed out that thanks to the gymnasia, higher standards have been established for the level of general secondary education and the method of organizing the educational environment. Most importantly, the public has come to realize that every new school has to have an idea that is not merely declared but is expressed in the array of school subjects and their content.

There are also serious problems confronting an innovative school, which is oriented toward the creation of its own concepts or the adoption of ready-made pedagogical technologies. Exploratory and research work is a necessary first step for developing new educational systems. However, the absence of precise criteria by which to judge which concepts and teaching methods may or may not be utilized in the new school, and the lack of wholeness and systematicity in the testing of the substantive foundations of each specific school, makes it impossible to examine the distinctive character of this type of school.

Schools that are oriented toward a particular established pedagogical system (e.g., the Waldorf School or the Montessori School) shape the pupils to have a rather limited mode of vital activity. Proceeding exclusively from the actual level of the child's development and his associated needs and interests, the designers of these educational systems omit the sociocultural level and cultural-historical context of development. Consequently, they fail to deal with the question of the individual's assimilation of the variety of historical types of consciousness and activity, and thereby block his way to various forms of social communities. At the same time, the appearance of these schools in Russia's system of educational institutions has substantially broadened the pedagogical community's understanding of the forms and content of youngsters' schooling, enhanced the importance of ideas and endeavors proceeding from the youngster himself, and highlighted the question of the link between methods of instruction and the physical and spatial organization of the educational institution.

The developmental-teaching school (V.V. Davydov, D.B. Elkonin) constitutes a definite accomplishment by Russia's psychological science and practice. This approach enables the youngster to reconstruct ideal patterns of action and master concepts from the standpoint of the conditions of their origin (which is in keeping with the tasks of the cultural-historical school). This system is reflected most completely in the way in which younger schoolchildren are taught mathematics, Russian, and art. In these subjects, youngsters engage in special forms of interaction with their peers and adults and engage in the kinds of activities that have served historically to produce products of culture, such as mathematical and linguistic concepts and art works. As a consequence, the youngsters come to acquire the foundations of theoretical thinking and creative imagination. Hence, developmental instruction is oriented toward the mastery of an important type of consciousness. This is not however the only meaningful type for this system of education, namely, scientific and artistic consciousness as forms of theoretical consciousness. The system of developmental instruction offers a model for the school of the cultural-historical type, though to be sure one that is limited in terms of its goals and tasks, and geared solely to the instruction of younger schoolchildren. It does not adequately address how to accomplish the task of integrating the mastery of cultural-historical forms of consciousness and activity. It should be pointed out that the theory and practice of developmental instruction has demonstrated clearly the inseparable link between the goals and tasks of education, and the actual methods of instruction, as well as the manner of scientifically designing a new type of school under specific socioeconomic conditions.

The history-culture school of today represents a rather broad spectrum of schools, all the way from educational institutions providing intensive study of the subjects in the humanities, to the dialogue-of-cultures school. In most schools of this type, the cultural-historical contents of activity for acquiring knowledge in the humanities has been reduced to a process of sequential assimilation of knowledge about the history and culture of particular periods or civilizations. The task of mastering historical types of consciousness and activity is not, as a rule, addressed in the framework of schools of this type.

One exception to the general rule, and a school that is closest in concept to the cultural-historical school, is the dialogue-of-cultures school, in which the declared orientation is toward the necessity of a person's mastery of the entire cultural-historical space, while the individual's development is linked to a dialogue of corresponding types of thinking that have been objectivized in various forms of dialogue of cultures. However, the history-culture school fails to explore the conditions of mastery of corresponding historical forms as forms of special educational work having substantive content, and as forms of organizing the development of child-adult interactions that define the life of the youngster in school. These forms are reduced to the traditional forms of interaction between adult and child in the classroom (for a broader context of the concept "cultural-historical school," see Bruner, 1996; Carpay & van Oers, 1998).

## The Cultural-Historical School

The main conception of the cultural-historical type of school is that the principal directions of the child's development should involve: (a) mastery of the actual forms of consciousness and activity that represent historical types of consciousness and activity that arose at some time and still retain their relevance; (b) mastery of various historical forms of learning; and (c) mastery of and participation in various child-adult communities that, by virtue of the modes of their organization, model a particular historical type of school.

The cultural-historical type of school can be constructed as a system of schools of different levels, where each level provides conditions that necessarily model the forms inherent to a specific historical type of consciousness and activity. For each level of school, the students focus primarily on mastering one of the forms of consciousness and the corresponding type of activity. The sequential transition from one level of school to another is correlated with the periodization of the leading types of children's activities, and this determines the characteristics of the children's education.

It is reasonable to speak of at least four basic historical types of consciousness and activity: mythological, workshop, scientific, and productive. Analysis shows that each of these types of consciousness and activity arose within the framework of a particular type of historical community that provided the individual with the necessary means to structure his activity effectively, and under the conditions of a particular type of school that replicated both the appropriate type of activity and the social community itself.

The modern cultural-historical school, oriented toward the mastery of the four historical types of consciousness and activity, must model in compressed form the conditions in which these types of activity and consciousness were replicated in the corresponding historical type of school. The idea is to model and copy the actual form of consciousness and activity through the form in which instruction is organized, rather than directly transferring and reconstructing the historical types of schools in the present-day school.

In summary, the cultural-historical type of school, which is oriented toward the preparation of the individual to master the multidimensional sociocultural norms of the current society as cultural-historical norms, can be structured as a system of schools that enable the individ-

| | Myth-making school | Workshop school | Laboratory school | Project/design school |
|---|---|---|---|---|
| Subject content | Properties and relations of things as given in immediate sense perception and visual representations. Modes of expressing them in sign-symbolic form | General properties and relations of the environment as reflected in historically formed cultural and specialized types of activity. Socially signifi-cant signs. | Models, theories, methods of staging experiments. | Methods of interfacing the data of various sciences and experience of various types of activity in practice. |
| Modes of action to be assim-ilated | Action with respect to scenario in accordance with role. | Reconstruction of methods for deriving general properties and relations from immediately given properties of things. Exercises in skills. | Exploration, research, experimenta-tion. | Project-designing. Creation of experi-mental patterns. Practical calcula-tions. Formulation of programs of actions for coordi-nation of multi-person activity. |

Figure 17.1. Interconnection between content and modes of action for the different levels in the cultural-historical school.

ual, in compressed form, to master a particular type of consciousness and activity in a form that reflects its present-day existence.

### A Theoretical Proposal for a Cultural-Historical Type School

In our case, this system consists of schools of four levels (Rubt-sov & Margolis, 1996). These levels are the *myth-making school* (level 1, ages 5-6); the *workshop school* (level 2, ages 7-9); the *laboratory school* (level 3, ages 10-14); and the *project/design school* (level 4, ages 15-17). The sequence of levels of instruction, and each school's functional place in it, is determined primarily by the phylogenetic line of development of forms of consciousness and activity.

Figure 17.1 shows the interconnection between the content that is assimilated in the school at each level, and the generalized modes of action that come into being as a result of the educational process at the appropriate stage of instruction.

The sequence of schools is determined by the necessity to master the particular manner of action at one level, so that it can be used as a means of action at the following level. Thus, in order for the child in the laboratory school to be able to construct models of a particular phenomenon and engage in studying it, he must have already formed the corresponding culturally-shaped pattern of action at the preceding level (the workshop school in our system), and in order for the youngster to be able to assimilate that pattern of action, he must also have already mastered an action with a certain substantive content with respect to a particular story or scenario on the preceding age level (i.e., the myth-making school in our system).

In this conception, the results of the mastery consists of a system of properties and relations serving to determine the visually perceivable content of objects (level 1); a system of culturally-given patterns and modes of action with objects (level 2); a system of concepts, models, and theories and the means appropriate to this system (level 3); and a system of project/designs (level 4).

It is necessary to distinguish between the object the children are to study and the content they are to assimilate. Thus, in the myth-making school, the children are acting with the story of a task and, in accordance with the story, acting with an imaginary, mythological, play object; this is in keeping with their age characteristics. The real content of their work, meanwhile, consists of modes of action that are necessary for the following level of instruction (the mode of systematizing objects, joining and separating parts of the object, putting parts of the object into the whole and removing them, and so forth).

In the workshop school, the youngster studies the purposes of the action as reflected in the objects, and masters special skills and abilities that make these actions possible (e.g., an understanding of numbers and, at the same time, how to count). An understanding of the patterns of objects (ideas) and generalized modes of action corresponding to these patterns is characteristic of the historical type of artisan's consciousness.

Later on, in the laboratory school, the content of the subjects to be studied by the students is assimilated on the basis of the construction of the models, concepts, and theory of that content; this is characteristic of the scientific type of consciousness. It is here that students start to assimilate the foundations of scientific theories and encounter experimentation and scientific writings. In the project school, the students assimilate the subject content by constructing a design or a pattern of activity that relates to the project/design type of consciousness. Project designing and, later, devising a program, constitute a modern means of organizing the activities of a collective group of people and coordinating the actions they are to undertake (see Davydov, this volume). In the process, one important objective of the endeavor is the emerging community, and the modeling of its goals, tasks and means of functioning.

The forms by which youngsters record the results of their work at each stage of instruction are far from random. These forms preserve the cultural-historical context and, therefore, have their own specific character. In the myth-making school, for example, it may take the form of a kind of museum of things, a collection of objects that the children gather on the basis of certain general considerations such as the properties, characteristics, and relations that qualify as essential to particular sets. The workshop school may also have the children make a museum consisting of a collection of technologies for working with objects, as well as appropriate tools for these technologies (measuring instruments, apparatus for observation, methods for making costumes, techniques for writing, drawing, and so forth), as well as students' own creative and study assignments (notebooks and drawings). In the laboratory school, students write a system of "scientific" texts to record the results of their work in the different school subjects. And, finally, in the project/design school, students may design and implement a system of projects. At each level of their schooling, the students are mastering particular systems of knowledge, instead of isolated types of knowledge in particular subjects, and more complicated systems of skills specific to particular types of activity rather than merely simple skills.

The assimilation of a particular historical type of consciousness and activity in a cultural-historical school proceeds through modeling the actual forms of organization of learning situations as they were historically conditioned. For example, the form of interaction between teacher and students in the workshop school should be based on a mode of teaching and learning that replicates the principles of interaction between master and apprentice, and should thereby shape the particular form of child-adult interaction that is specific to the given type of school. When we organize the conditions for instructional interactions that are specific to the particular historical school, then we are, in accordance with special laws, recreating this school through the form of the child-adult community that is specific to it, and through a preplanned mode of interaction among the participants involved in it. In effect, the cultural-historical school serves to institute forms of community that model the type of historical consciousness (on each specific level of schooling) as a special environment in which the child-adult community is a zone of immediate development for the subsequent community and its associated type of historical consciousness and activity (cf. Vygotsky).

### Educational-Methodological Implementation of a Cultural-Historical Type of School

We are able to offer a sketch of the educational-methodological implementation of this conception for only two levels: the myth-making school and the workshop school. This conception is currently being implemented in an experimental educational center in Ulan Ude in the Buryat region. Victor Gurughapov is the scientific research advisor for the school.

*The myth-making school (level 1 of instruction).* Instruction in the myth-making school consists of two stages:

1. Five- and six-year-old children, proceeding on the basis of the given mode of mythological or imaginative description of an object, work with that object as a system of properties, relations, and means.

2. The children proceed to the mastery of an action that is in the opposite direction and transform the set of objects given to them into some kind of integral system based on a general mythological mode of description. In this stage, the children proceed from the immediate perception of the object to an understanding of the characteristics of that perceived object in some mythological context — that is, to the development of the object's substantive properties and to the structuring of these properties into a system on the basis of an appropriate explanatory principle that enables them to unite these different properties into a whole.

In the myth-making school, the children structure their activity in accordance with a particular scenario (on the basis of their familiar rituals). In the process, the instruction makes extensive use of mythological and story material. The teacher directs the development of the actual story that the children will act out and directs changes in the children's functional-role interactions. The adult makes extensive use of discussions and debates that are typical for children of this age, and the children take positions that are determined by their roles.

There are no school subjects in any traditional sense, nor traditional positions of teacher and pupil. The content to be assimilated is acted out jointly in accordance with the scenario and the assignment of roles. This mode of description retains the structural integrity of the object's system, in such a manner that the properties of that system are structured and retained by the children. (Children know how to construct categories of relations, how to relate objects to one another, and how to describe these relations by means of painting and music.) The way out of the play situation must be provided within the play itself. For example, one can have the children prepare a special "text" in which a collection of things demonstrate various "qualities." For example, a group of children composes a story about a town constructed entirely out of hard materials that have different characteristics. Fairy tale (symbolic) creatures live in that town, and the children must describe how they act (live) there. An important level of sign mediation occurs for children in this period (see also Elias, 1991).

The instructional sequence in the myth-making school is:

1. Reconstruction of substantive content based on the discernment and construal of relations among things, and their properties.

2. Recording of the content that is discerned, both in the form of the children's special compositions and texts of various kinds (metamyths), and in the form of topical collections.

3. Specific museums, collections of objects, and so forth that have been gathered by the children themselves in accordance with the properties and relations they have discerned.

4. The mastery of a ritual-type mode of action that has substantive content given by the corresponding mythological story that describes that content.

5. Preparation for the transition to the workshop school and its mode of consciousness, and formation of action in accordance with the culturally-given pattern.

The result of the first level of schooling does not consist so much in the kinds of knowledge about particular subject content; rather it consists in shaping a child's ability to consciously make the transition from the mythological mode of working with an object to the construction of a systematic description of the object itself, and the ability to independently construct some imaginable context, and in accordance with it, his own texts about the nature of things. This new formation is a vital pre-requisite for youngsters to proceed further to the study of scientific concepts in the workshop school, and of models and theories in the laboratory school.

*The workshop school (level 2 of instruction).* The task of the workshop school is to organize instruction for children ages 7 through 9 so that they can assimilate culturally-given patterns of action and skills that prepare them to work with the kind of subject content that is inaccessible to direct perception. These patterns serve as the object of the students' special work under the supervision of the teacher. At this level, new positions come into being: the position of the teacher (the adult who possesses the culturally-given pattern of action) and the position of the student (the youngster who is supposed to make that pattern his own).

The orientation toward shaping 7- to 9-year-olds' generalized modes of action and corresponding concepts is consistent with the goals of Elkonin and Davydov's system of developmental instruction, which substantially facilitates the task of designing an integral educational environment on this level of instruction.

Formation of younger schoolchildren's generalized patterns of action, and the corresponding concepts, is impossible outside of a collectively-distributed form of organization for the process of transmitting patterns from the teacher to the student (see Perret-Clermont, 1980; Rubtsov, 1987/1991, 1994). The collectively-distributed form makes it possible to objectify the idea of the actual mode of action through modes of coordination of individual object operations. In the process of this work, full utilization can be made of the prerequisites for the organization of instruction that were laid down specifically in the myth-making school. Thus, children's ability to correlate their actions with the rules of the story make it possible, under conditions of the collectively-assigned form of instruction, to effect the coordination of actions with modes of constructing the object itself. Collective forms of work that formerly involved the assignment of roles, as mediated by the mythological mode of describing a subject, are being transformed into the assignment of individual operations with the object. A systematic understanding of a subject, as reflected in children's ability to describe connections and relations among its properties (within the framework of a story or a myth), comes to be transformed into a systematic mode of reconstructing the mode of action and the object itself.

Another process that takes place in the workshop school is the mastery of a system of particular skills that require an automatic level of execution. Here the form of instruction involves exercise in accordance with the given pattern and does not need so much mediation by collective forms of schoolwork.

Within the framework of the cultural-historical school, there also arise several fundamentally new tasks for designing the educational environment for children ages 7 through 9:

— the creation of joint forms of action between adults and children, and between the children themselves. These actions, which shape the child-adult community, provide the foundations for the laboratory school;
— the use of culturally-oriented contexts of action under conditions of the school work, relating primarily to the use of up-to-date sign-symbolic and model tools;
— the formulation of the content of instructional tasks in connection with new conditions for the children's development on the preceding level of instruction in the myth-making school.

## Prospects for the Creation of the Cultural-Historical School

It would make no sense to design a cultural-historical school if locations had not already been designated in today's educational space within which this type of educational institution could take shape (e.g., the recently established "kindergarten-school" complexes). As a rule, these locations are private or sponsored all-day educational institutions. Parents and sponsors are demanding higher standards for children's level of knowledge and abilities, and for the organization of the whole educational environment in accordance with changing sociocultural conditions of present-day life. The necessity of constructing an educational process that starts a child's education from five years-old, the necessity of assuring the continuity of education at different levels of age development, and of ensuring a high degree of students' adaptation to existing educational institutions (with their basically fixed demands), compels persons who will design new complexes to design a new type of school that is distinct from those that already exist. A model for that kind of school is what was proposed in this chapter.

Making this model into a practical reality will require substantial organizational, financial, and personnel resources, solid scientific-methodological support, and commitment on the part of those who undertake this endeavor. This can occur by starting the effort simultaneously at several experimental sites while combining their resources. The methods of organizing such an endeavor constitute a topic that requires its own special discussion. For now, we can only point to the necessity of creating a structure that is new in relation to general education and secondary educational institutions: A design-analytical service whose basic task will be to preserve the general conceptual approach both in the organization of the practical, everyday work in specific schools, and in the implementation of methodological developments and applied scientific research.

At the present stage, we can point to at least four basic directions for work of a scientific-methodological and design-conceptual character. First, it is essential to undertake a serious revision of the content of school subjects according to the logic that is laid out in the cultural-historical approach (as described here) to the designing of educational environments, and that serve to facilitate the transition from the myth-making school to the workshop school. Second, it is necessary to determine the set of the school subjects themselves, which must differ substantially from those that now exist in secondary schools. Third, it is necessary to resolve the question of methods of school work and the characteristics of the organization of the child-adult communities that are to become specific to the school at each level. In this connection, the question arises of the adult's functional roles at various levels as instruction-teacher, upbringer, and class advisor (tutor). Fourth, it is necessary to seek out architectural designs for the buildings where the education as described can be carried out. On the assumption that the transitions from one school level to the next mark real milestones in the youngster's school life, then they will have to have their own corresponding buildings of a particular type, with their own type of equipment and furnishings. For every child, life in the school at each level must have its own independent importance and meaning.

## Preparation of Psychological and Pedagogical Personnel for Work in Innovative Institutions

The following aspect of the state policy towards education deals with the preparation of pedagogical and psychological staff for this system. Under the present conditions, when the majority of the Russian state universities are preparing graduates that are oriented toward the traditional system of education, the lack of staff who could work with and participate in the development of innovative models block the development of innovative education as a system. There is an obvious need for the creation of special higher-education institutions, corresponding to the needs of the system for the preparation and retraining of teachers.

The support of administrative organs can consist of the organization of pedagogical colleges based on already existing centers. For example, the Moscow Psycho-Pedagogical Institute was created as part of the Psychological Institute of the Russian Academy of Education. These institutions would distribute and develop new pedagogical methods. The goals of these centers should be the development of the new methods (based upon the demand of the particular type of school), training of teachers who are the codevelopers of these methods who will be able to work with these methods, and also the preparation of administrators who will be oriented towards the implementation of innovative models in education.

### Conclusion

The different steps described so far give a certain approach about the developments and creation of innovative education in the whole educational environment of Russia. This conception is offered for discussion as a way to realize the social phenomena described here.

### References

Bibler V. (1969). Tvortscheskoye myschelnye kak predmet logiki: Problemy i perspectivu [Creative thinking as a subject of logic: Problems and perspectives]. In S. Mikulinskogo & M. Yaroshevskogo (Eds.), *Nauchnoye tvorthestvo* (pp. 167-220). Moscow: Nauka.

Bruner, J.S. (1996). *The culture of education*. Cambridge, Mass.: Harvard University Press.

Carpay, J.A.M., & van Oers, B. (1998). Didactic models and the problem of intertextuality and polyphony. In Y. Engeström, R. Miettinen, & R.-L. Punamäki (Eds.), *Perspectives on activity theory* (pp. 298-313). Cambridge: Cambridge University Press.

Davydov, V.V. (1986). *Problemy razvivayushego obucheniya* [Problems of developmental learning]. Moscow: Pedagogika.

Elias, N. (1991). *The symbol theory* (R. Kilminster, Ed.). London: Sage.

Galperin, P.I. (1975). Changing teaching methods is one prerequisite for increasing effectiveness of the schooling process. *Soviet Education, 17*(3), 87-92. (Original work published 1974)

Elkonin, D.B. (1989). K teoriia nachal'nogo obuchenie [On the theory of elementary teaching]. In V.V. Davydov & V.P. Zinchenko (Eds.), *Izbrannye psikhologicheskie trudy* (pp. 199-212). Moscow: Pedagogika.

Perret-Clermont A.-N. (1980). *Social interaction and cognitive development in children*. London: Academic Press.

Rubtsov, V.V. (1991). *Learning in children: Organization and development of cooperation actions* (L.M.W. Martin, Ed.; M.J. Hall, Trans.). New York: Nova Science. (Original work published 1987)

Rubtsov, V.V. (1994). Social interaction and learning. In T. Husén & T.N. Postlethwaithe (Eds.), *International encyclopedia of education* (2nd ed., Vol. 9, pp. 5545-5548). Oxford: Pergamon Press.

Rubtsov, V.V., & Margolis, A. (1996). Activity-oriented models of information based on the instructional environments. In S.T. Kerr (Ed.), *Technology and the future of schooling* (pp. 172-199). Chicago: University of Chicago Press.

Zankov, L.V. (1963). The didactic foundations of teaching. *Soviet Education, 5*(4), 3-12.

Zankov, L.V. and others. (1977). *Teaching and development: A Soviet investigation* (B.B. Szekely, Ed.; A. Schultz, Trans.). White Plains, N.Y.: Sharpe. (Original work published in 1975)

# 18 When the Center Does Not Hold: The Importance of Knotworking

*Yrjö Engeström, Ritva Engeström, and Tarja Vähäaho*

## Introduction

Much recent ethnographic research on the organization of work practices has focused on temporally and spatially compact and stable "centers of coordination" (Suchman, 1997), typically different kinds of control rooms. We want to direct attention to another, in a sense almost opposite, type of work organization. We refer to work that requires active construction of constantly changing combinations of people and artifacts over lengthy trajectories of time and widely distributed in space.

Barley (1988) describes the work of hospital radiologists as follows:

Thus, the temporal organization of a radiologist's work was such that at any moment he could be drawn for a brief span of time into the work worlds of any of a large number of individuals. It was as if the radiologists existed at the nexus of a number of trains of action that ran on unpredictable schedules and made unanticipated stops. Since the temporal boundaries of the day were extremely fluid and the day's punctuation into segments was largely out of their control, radiologists usually accommodated to the temporal structure by treating the timing of events flexibly. All tasks would occur at their due moment. Since the nature of the work precluded the radiologists from dealing with one event at a time, they came to prefer multiple lines of simultaneous action. Most radiologists at both hospitals admitted that they found the hectic pace exhilarating and that other tempos bored them. (p. 142)

The radiologists described by Barley are clearly engaged in intensely collaborative work activity. But instead of being stable, the combinations of people collaborating to perform a task change constantly.

This constant change of the collaborative configuration is not unique to Barley's example. Airlines typically change the combination of the crew for every flight. In courts of law, the combination of the judge and the attorneys is different for each trial. These combinations of people, tasks and tools are unique and of relatively short duration. Yet, in their basic pattern, they are continuously repeated.

These forms of work organization do not fit standard definitions of a *team*. Teams are typically understood as relatively stable configurations. Barley's radiologists kept switching from one combination to another. The collaborative combinations themselves kept disappearing and re-emerging in new forms.

Neither do the examples fit standard notions of *network*. Networks are typically understood as relatively stable structures, which can be exploited more or less effectively by their individual or collective nodes. Barley's radiologists were not using a pre-existing network. They literally constructed the collaborative relations on the spot as the task demanded.

In a series of recent studies, we have encountered numerous examples of this type of work organization. We call it *knotworking*. The notion of knot refers to a rapidly pulsating, distributed and partially improvised orchestration of collaborative performance between otherwise loosely connected actors and activity systems. In this chapter, we will argue that knotworking is a historically significant new form of organizing and performing work activity, connected to the emergence of new co-configuration models of production. To examine the phenomenon more closely, we will first analyze a sequence of knotworking focused on a mental patient in primary health care. We will then move to an analysis of an attempt at institutionalizing knotworking among providers of children's medical care in the Helsinki area in Finland. We will conclude by discussing the challenges knotworking presents to activity-theoretical studies of work and organizational communication.

### Knotworking and Co-Configuration

Knotworking is characterized by a pulsating movement of tying, untying and retying together otherwise separate threads of activity. The tying and dissolution of a knot of collaborative work is not reducible to any specific individual or fixed organizational entity as the center of control. The center does not hold. The locus of initiative changes from moment to moment within a knotworking sequence. Thus, knotworking cannot be adequately analyzed from the point of view of an assumed center of coordination and control, or as an additive sum of the separate perspectives of individuals or institutions contributing to it. The unstable knot itself needs to be made the focus of analysis.

We may distinguish between more individually-based and more collectively-based forms of knotworking. Barley's radiologists apparently represent a form of knotworking based on the key role of an individual radiologist — at least this is the perspective offered by Barley, the analyst. On the other hand, in courts of law, expansive episodes of "teamwork between adversaries" (Engeström, Brown, Christopher, & Gregory, 1997) cannot be reduced to the guiding role of the judge. And in industrial settings dependent on quick horizontal problem solving, the fact that someone is a foreman or a supervisor may be temporarily all but irrelevant in the search and formulation of an innovative solution (Engeström, Engeström, & Kärkkäinen, 1995).

While examples of knotworking may be found in well established practices, such as legal work in courts of law, it seems that the rise and proliferation of this type of work is associated with ongoing historical changes in organizations. Victor and Boynton (1998) suggest that we can examine the recent evolution of work as a succession of five major types: craft, mass production, process enhancement, mass customization, and co-configuration. The last one of the five, co-configuration, is particularly interesting from the point of view of knotworking.

When a firm does co-configuration work, it creates a product that can learn and adapt, but it also builds an ongoing relationship between each customer-product pair and the company. Doing mass customization requires designing the product at least once for each customer. This design process requires the company to sense and respond to the individual customer's needs. But co-configuration work takes this relationship up one level — it brings the value of an intelligent and "adapting" product. The company then continues to work with this customer-product pair to make the product more responsive to each user. In this way, the customization work becomes continuous. ... Unlike previous work, co-configuration never results in a "finished" product. Instead, a living, growing network develops between customer, product, and company. (Victor & Boynton, 1998, p. 195)

A hallmark of co-configuration is "customer intelligence." To achieve it, a company will have to continuously configure its products and services to in interaction with the customer. Victor and Boynton (1998, p. 197) name medical devices and computer software systems as two leading industries where co-configuration is being implemented. The authors emphasize that co-configuration is more than just smart, adaptive products.

> The application of configuration intelligence to the product creates a system of customer, product or service, and company. The complex of interactions among all three, as a product or service adapts and responds to the changing needs of the customer, is the underlying, dynamic source of value. … With the organization of work under co-configuration, the customer becomes, in a sense, a real partner with the producer. (Victor & Boynton, 1998, p. 198-199)

Victor and Boynton give us a model of three interdependent components, or "actants" to use Latour's (1996) terminology: customer, product/service, and company. What is missing in this picture is interdependency between multiple producers forming a strategic alliance, supplier network, or other such pattern of partnership which collaboratively puts together a complex product or service (Alter & Hage, 1993; Moody, 1993). This extension adds to the complexity of interactions in co-configuration work. Against this background, knotworking may be seen as the emerging interactional core of co-configuration.

To summarize we may name six criteria of co-configuration: (a) adaptive product or service; (b) continuous relationship between customer, product/service, and company; (c) ongoing configuration or customization; (d) active customer involvement; (e) multiple collaborating producers; and (f) mutual learning from interactions between the parties involved.

While we appreciate Victor and Boynton's effort to conceptualize co-construction as a historically new form of organizing work, we do not subscribe to their use of corporate success stories as evidence. Besides being uncritical and sketchy, these stories focus exclusively on customer-intelligent products, such as sophisticated digital hearing aids, as examples of co-configuration. It is much more difficult to determine what kinds of services would be "customer-intelligent." Clearly standardized services delivered on the spot do not qualify. But what about long-term care relationships in a primary care health center or hospital? In the following sections, we will elaborate on this question by examining cases from medical-service organizations that provide continuous personalized care.

## The Case of a Mental Patient

In Finland, municipal health centers are responsible for the primary care services of the population. The services are organized on the principle of population responsibility, meaning that every citizen has a personal physician, a general practitioner at the health center, assigned to her or him. Each general practitioner is typically responsible for the population of a specified geographic area. In many health centers, general practitioners and other staff responsible for adjacent areas are organized into multiprofessional teams. The key virtue and achievement of this model is continuity of care. People do not have to drift from one physician to another, and many unnecessary visits are avoided. The first two authors have been heavily involved in the collaborative design and implementation of this model in municipalities in the 1980s and early 1990s (Engeström, 1990, 1993, 1994).

By the mid-1990s, several issues prompted us to begin to question the limits of this team-based model. First, many municipalities continued the reorganization by merging primary health care and social welfare services. This called attention to clients who use both health care and social welfare services. Sometimes it is possible to coordinate and improve these services by creating teams where all the health care and social welfare professionals responsible for a given geographic area are represented. However, such teams tend to become excessively large and complicated, and due to the differences in the nature of the work of the different professional groups, these teams sometimes become quite artificial ends in themselves, detached from the daily realities of frontline work (see Engeström, et al., 1995). In other words, stable teams do not seem to be a sufficient answer to the challenge of coordinating complex arrangements of multiple lines of substantially different services which do not rely on each other's assistance or advice on a daily basis.

The second reason for questioning the limits of the model emerged from discussions with general practitioners reporting on challenging new processes in their work. Occasionally, and apparently increasingly often, practitioners face situations where they have to contact a number of different professionals and nonprofessionals to quickly coordinate an ad-hoc collaborative effort in order to resolve a problem situation with a client. These efforts are clearly not manageable with the help or within the framework of the stable teams. Here is a condensed account of such a case, a 16-day sequence of events focused on a mental patient. The account is based on an interview with a general practitioner and on the written medical records concerning the case.

*Day 1*

1.  The general practitioner (GP) receives a phone call from the appointed custodian of a 32-year-old female mental health patient who resides at home and belongs to the population for which the GP is responsible. According to the custodian, the patient has called the custodian and yelled in a paranoid manner (e.g., "United Nations is watching me"). The patient has earlier been hospitalized for a psychosis. Possibly she has failed to take her medication.

2.  The GP and the custodian agree on a joint visit to the patient's home on the same day. As they ring the patient's doorbell, the patient shouts angrily behind the door but refuses to open it. She does not answer the phone either. The GP decides to consult the next day a psychiatrist of the regional hospital regarding the appropriate way to deal with the patient's problem. It seems clear that the patient is psychotic and needs care; what is unclear is whether there are sufficient grounds for forceful entry and involuntary hospitalization.

*Day 2*

3.  The GP together with a home-care nurse, the police, and an ambulance crew visit the patient's home. The patient refuses to open the door. The service technician of the apartment building is called to open the door but he fails because he does not have keys to the patient's safety lock. The patient shouts angrily from inside. She seems to be physically OK but mentally incoherent.

4.  The GP calls the hospital psychiatrist on call. When asked for instructions regarding forceful entry to the patient's apartment, the psychiatrist says: "Do so if you feel that the patient is so sick that it is necessary to take her into hospital care." The GP, in discussion with the others involved, decides to wait and see if there will be additional information and expressions of concern from the neighbors.

5.  The GP tries to call the patient's mother but fails to reach her. According to the medical records, the mother has herself been hospitalized for mental problems.

*Day 3*

6.  The GP discusses the situation with the custodian. The patient does not have other relatives. The situation has deteriorated after the patient's boy-

friend died about two years ago. The patient does not seem to keep in touch with her mother. The GP and the custodian agree that the custodian will keep an eye on possible signs of danger to the health of the patient or of others as the patient must periodically visit the custodian for official purposes (to get money for living).

## Day 5

7.  The GP telephones the patient. The patient answers, sounding physically fine. Her talk is incoherent but this time calm and not aggressive. The GP decides to wait and monitor the situation (e.g., messages from neighbors).

## Day 16

8.  The patient's neighbor calls the health center and reports that he has called the emergency call center concerning the patient.

9.  The patient's neighbor reports that the patient has yelled since 3:30 a.m., first to the mailman and continuing after that by banging on the walls aggressively. The neighbor says that he has understood that he should always call the personal doctor at the health center in a situation like this.

10. The emergency call center sends an ambulance to the patient's apartment.

11. The ambulance crew calls the GP from the patient's apartment and asks for legal permission to enter the apartment by force. The GP grants the permission.

12. The ambulance crew calls the police to come and assist them in taking the patient to the hospital.

13. The ambulance crew, assisted by the police, break the lock and take the patient into custody.

14. The patient is brought to the health center in handcuffs. She seems somewhat manic, talks incoherently and cries occasionally.

15. The GP writes a legal statement that is needed to take the patient into hospital care involuntarily. The patient is taken into the psychiatric ward of the regional hospital.

Activity theory takes a collective object-oriented activity system as its prime unit of analysis. Activity is realized in goal-oriented individual and group actions. What is a "knot" from an activity-theoretical point of view? Let us examine step 3 in the account given above.

In step 3, the general practitioner visits the patient's home together with a home-care nurse, the police, and an ambulance crew. Soon also the service technician of the building is included in the knot. The formation of this knot required a series of phone calls. On the spot, the knot performed at least the actions of ringing the doorbell, attempting to talk to the patient, calling the service technician, trying to open the door with the master key, and deciding to give up the attempt for the time being. This is clearly not an activity system in the sense of having a relatively stable object, motive, community, and division of labor. The half-life of the knot was far too short for such systemic infrastructure to evolve and stabilize. On the other hand, the knot is not just a singular action either. It performed a bundle of tightly interconnected actions. More importantly, it deliberately organized and dissolved itself to perform and terminate these actions. In other words, the knot functioned as a self-conscious agent.

Where did this self-consciousness reside? At the first glance, it may seem that the general practitioner was in control all through the events. However, this is not the case. Through steps 1 to 7, the GP's attempts to take control were frustrated by the patient's refusal to open her door. From step 8 to step 10, the GP was told about the events but he was not in control. Only in steps 11 and 14 the GP was directly making decisions that determined the course of the events.

Because the GP was not the constant center of control, the GP had to rely on other actors: the custodian, the neighbor, the ambulance crew, the police, the service technician, the psychiatrist — and not the least, the patient herself. None of these was the center of control either. The center just did not hold. Thus, knotworking differs from an action in that the subject is not fixed — the subject is the pulsating knot itself, or in other words, subjectivity is dynamically distributed within the knot.

Knotworking is not reducible to a single knot, or a single episode. It is a temporal trajectory of successive task-oriented combinations of people and artifacts. In the case described above, the important artifacts included the door, the keys, the handcuffs, the medical records, and the legal documents authorizing involuntary hospitalization.

Knotworking situations are fragile because they rely on fast accomplishment of intersubjective understanding, distributed control and coordinated action between actors who otherwise have relatively little to do with each other. Weick and Roberts (1993) talk about "heedful interrelating" as the central quality of such collective action. But their example — work on an aircraft carrier — is about collaborative work in which people stay physically together for relatively long periods of time

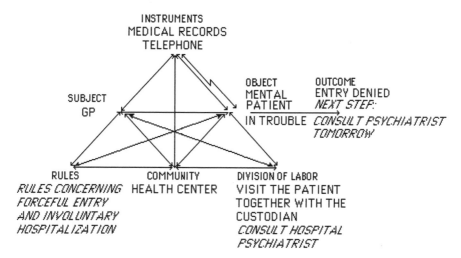

Figure 18.1. The activity system of the GP in the second step of the knotworking trajectory.

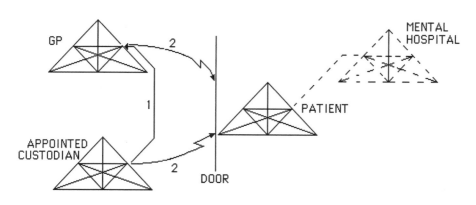

Figure 18.2. Steps 1 and 2 in the knotworking trajectory.

and go through large numbers of iterations of the same basic tasks. Such settings are indeed classical examples of the robustness of collective activity systems or communities of practice (Wenger, 1998). In knotworking, the combinations of people and the contents of tasks change constantly. This highlights the importance of communicative actions and tools for the success of knotworking.

### Dimensions of Knotworking

In the case of the mental patient, some actors seem to be individual (e.g., the GP), some are collective (e.g., the ambulance crew, the police). However, the seemingly individual actors represent their respective collectives (e.g., the GP represents his health center), and correspondingly, the collectives act through individuals. Thus, each thread in a knot may be understood as a collective activity system.

Knotworking is dependent on fast accomplishment of intersubjective understanding and distributed control. Intersubjectivity is not reducible to either the *inter*action between or the *subjectivity* of each participant. Both are needed. Thus, we need to be able to analyze the internal dynamics and tensions of the activity systems that partake in a knotworking trajectory. For this, we use the model of an activity system (Engeström, 1987).

Figure 18.1 depicts schematically the structure of the general practitioner's activity in the second step of the knotworking trajectory. The GP is facing a mental patient in trouble, a particular instance of the relatively stable general object of his work — patients with medical problems. The GP has two main tools available to deal with this particular object, the telephone and the medical records. These tools turn out to be insufficient as the patient refuses to open her door — thus the lightning-shaped arrow indicating a disturbance in Figure 18.1.

The failure to gain entrance to the patient's residence prompts the GP to anticipate and plan the next steps. These anticipations are marked in italics in Figure 18.1. They include a plan to consult the hospital psychiatrist by telephone and the consideration of rules of forceful entry and involuntary hospitalization.

Figure 18.1 alone represents knotworking from the point of view of a single participant's activity. This is clearly insufficient. Knotworking needs to be represented along several complementary dimensions (see Engeström, 1999). First, we need a *socio-spatial* dimension to depict the relations between the different activity systems involved in forming a knot at any given point of time. An example of this dimension is schematically represented in Figure 18.2. The figure contains three activity systems that are actively involved in the interaction in steps 1 and 2 of the networking trajectory: that of the GP, that of the appointed custodian, and that of the patient. Step 1 is the phone call from the custodian to the GP. Step 2 is the joint visit of the GP and the custodian to the pa-

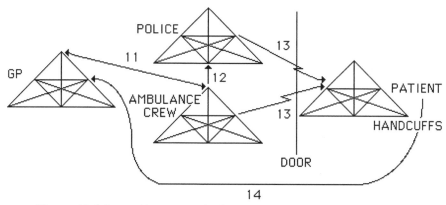

Figure 18.3 Steps 11 to 14 in the knotworking trajectory.

tient's apartment. The key artifact mediating and triggering a disturbance between the three activity systems is the patient's door. From the point of view of the patient, it serves as her instrument for refusing access to her apartment. In addition to the three presently active activities, the mental hospital where the patient once was kept is depicted with broken lines, indicating that it is involved indirectly, as a piece of historical record that influences the GP's (and possibly other participants') judgment of the situation.

We also need a *temporal* dimension to depict successive steps or episodes in a trajectory of knotworking. Figure 18.3 depicts the knot in steps 11 to 14 of the trajectory. A comparison between Figure 18.2 and Figure 18.3 offers a view into the evolution of the knot over time, from its initiation to its termination. Among other things, the comparison reveals how the combination of participating activity systems has shifted. The appointed custodian — a lay person — has been replaced by two professional systems of enforcement, the ambulance crew, and the police. By inserting representations of the steps in between, we would get a complete series of evolutionary moments in the trajectory.

The spatial and the temporal dimensions are fairly obvious. What is less obvious is the need for an *ethical* dimension. Knotworking regularly calls for a redistribution and reconceptualization of control, responsibility, and trust. In the mental patient's example, the physician had to give up his attempt to take control over the situation. This does not imply that knotworking is automatically a benign phenomenon of empowerment — in the example, the patient ended up being hospital-ized against her will. Our claim is simply that the emergence of knot-working shakes and makes questionable the given forms of hierarchy and segmentation of professional and organizational authority.

Is the case of the mental patient an example of co-configuration? It meets the first three criteria: the service was adaptive, the relationship was continuous, and the service was constantly configured and custom-ized. The fourth criterion — customer involvement — is problematic. In step 7, the physician did negotiate with the patient, but in most of the steps the patient was incoherent. The fifth criterion, multiple collaborat-ing producers, is strongly present through the sequence. After the fail-ures in steps 2 and 3, entrance to the patient's home succeeded in step 13. This may be regarded as a microlevel indication of learning from the interaction — the sixth and final criterion of co-configuration. To assess whether mutual learning occurred in a broader sense, more longitudinal evidence would be needed.

So the case of the mental patient is a mixed bag from the point of view of co-configuration. We suspect that there are no pure cases. Even when co-configuration is based on a new customer-intelligent techno-logical product, the relationships and interactions will carry historical baggage from earlier forms of organizing work.

## Can Knotworking Be Institutionalized? The Care Agreement

In the case of the mental patient, knotworking was initiated and carried out relatively informally, with few if any rules and tools explic-itly designed to structure the interaction in this particular type of cases. We might say that the relevant activity systems relied on the strength of weak ties among them (Granovetter, 1973). However, there are many domains where the informal relations do not work. In such cases, one may attempt to institutionalize knotworking by introducing appropriate rules and tools. We now turn to an analysis of such an attempt.

The Helsinki University Central Hospital (HUCH) is divided into a number of hospitals and clinics. All of them, including the HUCH Hos-pital for Children and Adolescents (hereafter called simply HUCH chil-dren's hospital), are struggling with the need to cut the disproportionally high costs of care typical to the Helsinki region. The current phase of their change efforts is focused on coordination and collaboration between the HUCH children's hospital outpatient clinic, the hospital wards, the other hospitals in the area, and, most importantly, the health centers of Helsinki and the other cities in the area.

This phase has been facilitated by our research group, using a method called *Boundary Crossing Laboratory*. Approximately 60 invited representatives of physicians, nurses, other staff, and management from the various institutions responsible for children's health care in the Helsinki area met in ten three-hour sessions, the last one of which was held in mid-February 1998. The participants viewed and discussed a series of patient cases videotaped by the researchers. The cases demonstrated, in various ways, troubles caused by lack of coordination and communication among the different care providers in the area. The troubles took the form of excessive numbers of visits, unclear loci of responsibility, and failure to inform other involved care providers (including the patient's family) of the practitioner's diagnoses, actions and plans.

The historical background behind these troubles was identified and discussed. In municipal health centers, the personal doctor principle and multiprofessional teams have effectively increased the continuity of care, replacing the isolated *visit* with the long-term *care relationship* as the object of the practitioners' work activity. The notion of care relationship has gradually become the key conceptual tool for planning and recording work in health centers.

A parallel development has taken place in hospitals. Hospitals grew larger and more complicated in the postwar decades. Fragmentation by specialties led to complaints and was seen to be partially responsible for the rapidly rising costs of hospital care. In the late 1980s, hospitals began to design and implement *critical paths* or *pathways* for designated diseases or diagnostic groups.

These paths are a crucial part of a team's (physician, nurses, and support professionals) efforts to manage and/or coordinate the patient's care. A critical path should be developed based upon diagnoses with similar patient care needs. The critical path should then be organized to help the health care team know what intervention on any given day of a patient's hospitalization is most likely to produce the best outcomes for a given patient population. (McDonald, 1994, p. 141)

With these reforms spreading and taking root, should not the problems with coordination and collaboration be under control? Evidence presented and discussed in Boundary Crossing Laboratory sessions led to the conclusion that this was not the case. Care relationships and critical paths were solutions created in response to particular historical sets of contradictions. These contradictions are rapidly being superseded by a new, more encompassing configuration of contradictions.

Care relationships and critical paths respond to contradictions internal to the respective institutions. Care relationships are seen as a way to conceptualize, document and plan long-term interactions with a patient inside primary health care. Their virtue is that the patient can be seen as having multiple interacting problems and diagnoses that evolve over time; their limitation is that responsibility for the patient is practically suspended when the patient enters a hospital. Correspondingly, critical paths are constructed to give a normative sequence of procedures for dealing with a given disease or diagnosis. They do not help in dealing with patients with unclear and multiple diagnoses, and they tend to impose their disease-centered worldview even on primary care practitioners. Fundamentally, both care relationships and critical paths are linear and temporal constructions of the object. They have great difficulties in representing and guiding horizontal and socio-spatial relations and interactions between care providers located in different institutions, including the patient and his/her family as the most important actors in care.

The need for such horizontal and socio-spatial coordination across institutional boundaries was spelled out powerfully in an article titled "A Health Lesson I Never Wanted" by Eric Caines, a former high-ranking official involved in the market-oriented reform of the British National Health Service. He encountered the contradictions when his own father-in-law became terminally ill:

What was absolutely clear to us, ... was that each episode of illness had been treated separately on the basis of what appeared to be the distinctive characteristics at the time. ... The glaringly obvious problem was that nobody was in overall charge of the case. (Caines, 1997, p. 24)

The experiences Caines had with the care of his father-in-law are common among child patients who suffer from multiple parallel medical problems or whose diagnosis is unclear. Asthmatic and allergic children with repeated respiratory problems are the clearest case in point. Such a child may in the course of one year have a dozen hospital visits, including some stays of a few days in a ward, and even more numerous visits to a primary-care health center. Some of these visits are for serious

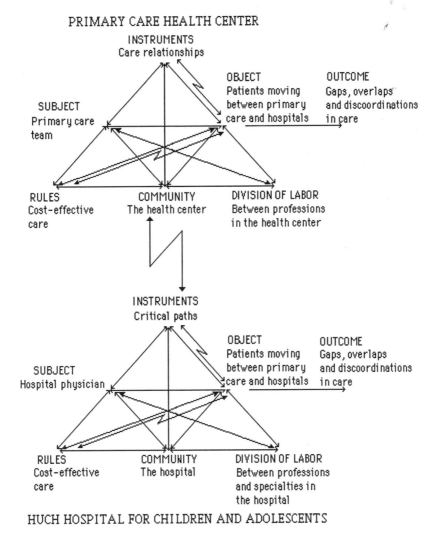

Figure 18.4. Contradictions in children's health care in the Helsinki area.

emergencies, some of them are for milder but urgent infections, and some are for tests, control, and follow-up.

One of the cases we presented in the Boundary Crossing Laboratory was Simon, age 3. In 1997, he had three visits to the district hospital of his municipality, 11 visits to the HUCH ear clinic, 14 visits to his personal physician at the local health center, and one visit to the outpatient clinic of the HUCH children's hospital. Another case we presented, Andrew, age 4, had in 1997 four visits to the HUCH hospital for skin and allergic diseases, nine visits to his local district hospital, and 14 visits to his primary care health center.

The newly emerging constellation of contradictions is schematically depicted in Figure 18.4.

A contradiction emerges between an increasingly salient aspect of the object — namely patients moving between primary care and hospital care — and the rule of cost-efficiency. This contradiction is about to reach a crisis. In Finland, the costs of health care, including hospital care, are basically covered by the municipal health centers who are supposed to monitor the referrals to hospital care. In Helsinki, these costs are clearly above national averages, largely due to the excessive use and high cost of services provided by the central university hospital HUCH, of which the HUCH children's hospital is a part. Thus, there is an aggravated tension between the primary care health center and the university hospital. Health centers in the Helsinki area are blaming the university hospital for high costs, while the university hospital criticizes health centers for excessive referrals and for not being able to take care of patients who do not necessarily need hospital care.

Finally, a contradiction emerges between the new object (patients moving between primary care and hospital care) and the recently established instruments, namely care relationships in primary care and critical paths in hospital work. Being linear-temporal and mainly focused on care inside the institution, these tools are inadequate for dealing with patients who have multiple simultaneous problems and parallel contacts to different institutions of care.

Through painstaking debates and design efforts, which included explicit discussions of the idea of knotworking, the participants of the Boundary Crossing Laboratory constructed an expansive solution to this set of contradictions. The solution, centered around the idea of *care agreement*, distinguishes between two layers of responsibility: each practitioner's traditional responsibility for his or her patient's specific care, and the shared responsibility for the formation, coordination and monitoring of the patient's overall network and trajectory of care. This expansion of responsibility concerns not only the socio-spatial and temporal dimensions of work; the third, ethical dimension of the object of work is unavoidably also involved.

To ensure that the expansion is achieved, four interconnected solutions were created. First, the patient's personal physician — a general practitioner in the local health center — is designated as the *coordinator* in charge of the patient's network and trajectory of care across institutional boundaries. Secondly, whenever a child becomes a patient of the

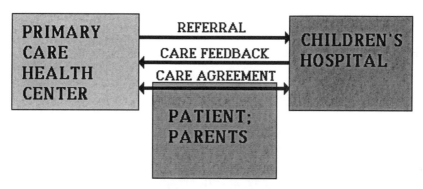

Figure 18.5. Conceptual model of the care agreement procedure.

HUCH children's hospital for more than a single visit, the hospital physician and nurse in charge of the child draft a care agreement which includes a plan for the patient's care and the division of labor between the different care providers contributing to the care of the child. The draft agreement is given to the child's family and sent to the child's personal health center physician (and when appropriate, to the physicians in charge of the child in other hospitals) for their scrutiny. Thirdly, if one or more of the parties find it necessary, they will have a *care negotiation* (by e-mail, by telephone, or face to face) to formulate a mutually acceptable care agreement. Fourthly, *care feedback*, in the form of a copy of the patient's medical record, is automatically and without delay given or sent to the other parties of the care agreement after the patient's unplanned visit or changes in diagnoses or care plans. Figure 18.5 depicts a simplified model of the care agreement. The model was designed by participants of the Boundary Crossing Laboratory and is used to inform practitioners of the new practice.

The projected care agreement practice aims at resolving the contradictions depicted in Figure 18.4 by creating a new instrumentality. This instrumentality, when shared by practitioners across institutional boundaries, is supposed to expand the object of their work by opening up the dimension of horizontal, socio-spatial interactions in the patient's evolving network of care, making the parties conceptually aware of and practically responsible for the coordination of multiple parallel medical needs and services in many patients' lives. This does not replace but complements and extends the linear and temporal dimension of care. The solution also aims at relieving the pressure coming from the rule of cost-efficiency and the tension between the HUCH children's hospital and health centers by eliminating uncoordinated excessive visits and tests and by getting the health center general practitioners involved in making joint care decisions that are acceptable to all parties.

### The Case of Jim

Jim was born prematurely together with his twin brother John. He is regularly checked and treated for his lungs (for a condition called bronchopulmonal dysplasia or BPD) at the HUCH children's hospital. In May 1998, at the age of 16 months (corrected age 12 months), Jim and John visited Doctor M at the HUCH children's hospital for lung control. M is the lung specialist responsible for Jim's and John's ongoing care at the hospital. Figure 18.6 is a reproduction of the actual care agreement proposal written by Dr. M for Jim after the visit. The care agreement text is included in a box in the patient's medical record chart, still a manual document waiting to become computerized.

The crucial idea in this care agreement proposal is that Jim should gradually start to visit also his personal physician at the primary health care center, mainly "in acute situations, for example resp[iratory] infections and suspected *otitis* etc." This implies a stepwise "normalization" of Jim's health care services and an increased role for the personal physician and health center. In an interview conducted two weeks after the care agreement proposal was prepared, Jim's mother commented on the issue as follows.

Mother:      Well, now it was our latest visit to M [the hospital physician], that's when she talked me into it a bit, and it was actually after that discussion that she took up this care agreement. And she said that she'll send some of the boys' paperwork to this personal physician, so she can sort of get acquainted, and that way, if, if we could get to know each other a bit...

Researcher:   Have you received this care agreement, so that you'd know what it means?

Mother:      Well, I haven't received it... I haven't thought about it, except that we must go and visit the personal physician, and actually it is to our advantage, too, if, if it would develop into a good relationship, and why not. One must of course trust that, that the physician also tells herself if she feels that now we are

Care agreement proposal for the personal physician discussed with the mother, suggesting that care responsibility in the long-term illness, developmental follow-up of the small prematurely born and the follow-up of the bronchopulmonal dysplasia is still for the time being in the hospital for children and adolescents, both in the neurological hospital and in the children's clinic, the next control to be after half a year. In acute situations, for example in resp. infections and suspected otitis etc., contact to primary care and when needed for instance in breathing difficulties to the hospital for children and adolescents.

Responsible physician in hospital care M.K. At the lung outpatient clinic and responsible nurse M.H., In addition developmental follow-up consultations and primary care personal

Physician:_____,
Personal Nurse:_____
and the personal physician as coordinator.

Signed *M. K.*

Distribution: copy to be sent to the personal physician at the S. Health Station.

Figure 18.6. The care agreement proposal for Jim.

moving into areas which do not belong to her, or about which she cannot say much.

Notice how the mother hesitates when describing the possibility of a care relationship with the personal physician: "if, if we could get to know each other a bit" and "if, if it would develop into a good relationship." The hesitation seems to be grounded in uncertainty concerning the general practitioner's competency when "moving into areas that do not belong to her." This issue of trust is clearly one of the first barriers to be overcome if this form of knotworking is to succeed.

In her interview, Dr. M gave the following account.

Dr. M:      This [care agreement proposal] was made during a visit on May 12. At that point, they had the development control for the corrected age of one year, and also the control for this lung disease of prematurely born babies, this BPD, here at the lung clinic. And in this connection we found that Jim had an ear

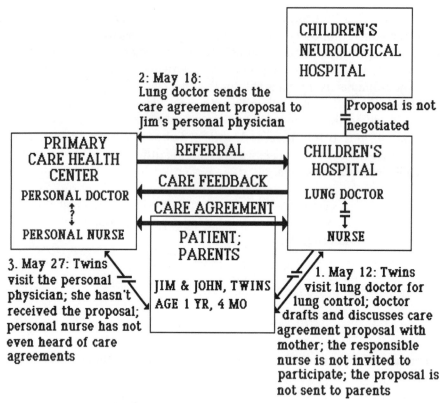

Figure 18.7. The first three steps in Jim's care after the launching of the care agreement procedure.

infection. And it seemed that, well, the follow-up control of that would be quite natural to conduct by the personal physician. And this idea emerged from the realization that now is sort of an appropriate moment to connect with them [the primary-care health center] and to establish contact with them.

Researcher:     Did you take this matter up, or did the family?

Dr. M:          I took it up, with the mother ... the mother was here with the boys. And when we found this ear infection, and realized that it requires a follow-up, I suggested that now it's easiest and most convenient for you to go to the place nearest to you. And that's when we agreed that we'll send copies of paperwork on the boys to the personal physician, so she will also get familiar with the boys' background, on paper, too. And then as agreed the mother reserved an appointment with the personal physician.

Interestingly enough, the physician saw Jim's ear infection as the springboard that enabled her to initiate the preparation of the care agreement. Even as a formalized care agreement procedure, knotworking was triggered by a contingent impulse.

We will now examine the first steps in Jim's trajectory of care after the care agreement proposal was drafted (see Figure 18.7). These actual steps may be compared with the ideal model depicted in Figure 18.5. The actual steps are constructed from extensive interviews with all parties involved, from medical records, and from fieldnotes and videotapes recorded as the researchers have observed patient visits to the hospital.

In Figure 18.7 (and later in Figure 18.8), the actual steps of care are depicted with numbered thin arrows. Ruptures in communication and collaboration are marked with a break in the middle of an arrow: ←||→. Correspondingly, possible ruptures are marked with a question mark: ←?→. Thin lines with no arrows and no numbers indicate connections that were not realized but were named as relevant in interviews.

There are four significant ruptures in the first three steps of care. In the first step, Dr. M prepared the care agreement proposal in discussion with the patient's mother — but failed to invite the participation of the hospital nurse responsible for Jim. She also failed to send a copy of the care agreement proposal to Jim's parents. Notice an interesting interplay of initial hesitation ("perhaps") and rapidly emerging certainty ("of course") in her reflection on this — a small action of reflective learning.

Dr. M:     Well, as a matter of fact, not to the family, no... Now a copy has only been sent to the personal physician. So that's right, perhaps a copy should of course go to the family, too, so they'd see it on paper, what's in it, yes.

Finally, Dr. M realized that she had also failed to send the care agreement proposal to the neurologist in the adjacent neurological hospital, responsible for the monitoring of Jim's development as a prematurely born child.

Researcher:     As you prepared this care agreement, did you negotiate with the neurologist who monitors the development?

Dr. M:     No, no. I did not even try. No, no... somehow not, time didn't seem to allow it, and it didn't... it seemed it was most important now to negotiate with the mother.

Researcher:     Do you think the neurologist might in his own location think of preparing a care agreement, too?

Dr. M:          Now I cannot say, because I actually don't know to what extent they have been implementing this care agreement idea in the Neurological Hospital. In our house it is timely and everyone is talking about it, but...

In the third step, as the boys visited their personal physician two weeks later, it turned out that the personal physician and the twins' personal nurse had not received the care agreement proposal. We showed the care agreement proposal to Jim's personal nurse at the health center and asked for her reactions.

Personal nurse: Well, this says here that the personal... they've written "primary care, personal physician colon, personal physician as coordinator." But it doesn't say here that I should... Probably if I only get this, I wouldn't send anything forward to anywhere. I mean, if they don't directly ask for this information.

Thus, while the aim of establishing contact between the patient and the personal physician was achieved, the continuity of knotworking between the primary care health center and the hospital was severely hampered.

We also showed the care agreement text to Jim's parents after their visit to the personal physician. They expressed some disappointed in the contents of the care agreement.

Father:         Isn't this ... this the medical record, what has happened. But how is this to be regarded as any kind of agreement, that I cannot understand.

Mother:         Well, if... it does mention there that it was discussed in the consultation. But we of course understand an agreement as a clear paper that would tell us... This doesn't make it clear what it contains.

Father:         Yes, this mentions the persons responsible in the children's hospital, so that's of course good, and we'll know whom to turn to when something happens.

Researcher:     Yes. Can you think of some improvements to this?

Mother:         You mean to the agreement?

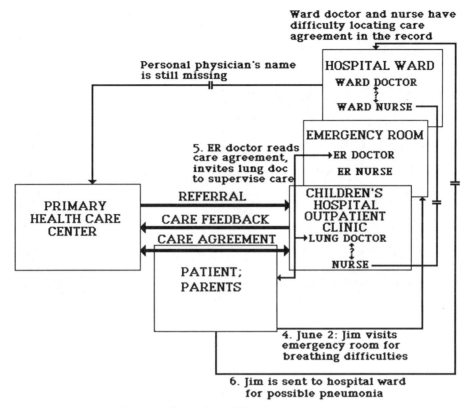

Figure 18.8. Steps 4 through 6 of Jim's care.

Researcher: Yes.

Mother: Well, it could be clearer. But then again, one asks whether it is something we should in the first place... Should we know more about it, or are we just one part of the system. But on the other hand, we are the practical part which is ... which has quite a big role.

The next three steps in Jim's care trajectory add to the complexity of the configuration (see Figure 18.8). In June, Jim visited the emergency room of the HUCH children's hospital for breathing difficulties (step 4). The attending physician noticed the care agreement text in Jim's medical record; prompted by the text he contacted Dr. M, the lung specialist responsible for Jim's ongoing hospital care, and invited her to come and supervise Jim's examination in the emergency room (step 5). Although limited to communication within the hospital, step 5 nicely demon-

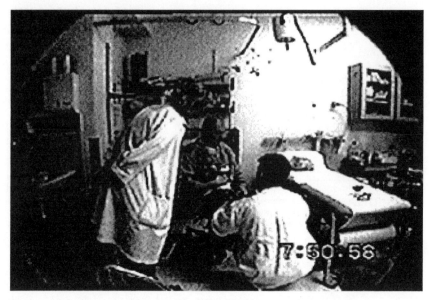

Figure 18.9. Knotworking around Jim in the emergency room.

strates the power of the care agreement in facilitating knotworking.
Attending emergency room physician: Yes, I've seen in practice how
this care agreement works. I noticed in the patient's papers that there
was a designated physician responsible for his care in the hospital, so I
called to consult with her. And it happened so well that she could come
to the spot herself. Now it's important that the personal physician gets
informed about the patient's phases here, now that she is also involved
in the care.

Figure 18.9 captures an event of knotworking in the emergency
room. Jim is sitting on his father's lap, being examined by Dr. M (on the
left) and the emergency room nurse (on the right); the attending emergency room physician has just left to see another urgent patient.

In step 6, Jim was sent to the hospital ward for suspected pneumo-
nia. The ward physician and the ward nurse responsible for Jim
reported that they did receive and make use of the care agreement text.
However, they pointed out three ruptures. First, the care agreement text
is hidden inside the thick medical record folder and easily escapes the
attention of the physician and the nurse. They both suggested that there
should be a sign on the cover of the folder indicating that the record
contains a care agreement.

| Researcher: | Can you say who is responsible for Jim's care? What would you say? |
|---|---|
| Ward nurse: | Physician, nurse. Well, I would of course see it in these papers, but I wonder where I can find the care agreement. How do I know that a care agreement has been done for this particular child? I think it should be visible somewhere. Either in the computer, so that when a patient comes, I will see it there right away, it's registered. Or somewhere in these medical records, somewhere here it should be marked that this patient has a care agreement. So that I know to look it up. |

Ward physician: One clear thing is of course how this particular group of patients is distinguished from other patients. And there the easiest is perhaps to put on the cover of the medical record file some sort of a stamp. It could have a text, "care agreement." Or it can be a black circle with a green triangle or some such sign that makes it visible at a glance, that here is a care agreement, and then you proceed accordingly.

Secondly, the physician pointed out that the name of the primary care personal physician was still missing in the care agreement, which made it difficult for him to inform the health center of the most recent steps in Jim's care. Thirdly, the ward nurse realized that there is no communication between her and the hospital outpatient clinic nurse responsible for Jim on a continuing basis. This realization led her to start to reconfigure the interaction. Notice that here the nurse takes over the questioning and turns it into self-interrogation — another small action of reflective learning.

| Ward nurse: | Well, yes. So is it our task? It says here [in Jim's care agreement text] that N is the responsible nurse, to inform N that Jim is now here, or how does it work? |
|---|---|
| Researcher: | Yes, aha. |
| Ward nurse: | And would it be the task of the ward nurse responsible for Jim to contact this responsible nurse in the outpatient clinic? |
| Researcher: | Yes. Can you think what would be the advantage of doing that? |
| Ward nurse: | It may be that if the responsible nurse in the outpatient clinic knows better this family and child. If he comes to us for the |

first time, then... So if she [responsible nurse in the outpatient clinic] wants to send us some information, something we, too, should know.

Researcher:     Yes.

Ward nurse:     So in that sense.

Researcher:     Yes.

Ward nurse:     And the responsible nurse of the outpatient clinic could... We could have a small discussion, for instance that now the responsibility is transferred to this person for the period of ward care, for instance.

### Lessons From Jim's Case

The care agreement procedure was designed to help solve the contradictions depicted in Figure 18.4. While offering a glimpse into the potentials of knotworking (especially in step 5), Jim's case also reveals that early implementation of the new instrumentality looks very different from the ideal picture of Figure 18.5.

Seven communicative ruptures were identified in the first six steps of Jim's care after the initiation of the care agreement procedure. Out of these seven, three were directly linked to the hospital physician's habit of working and carrying responsibility alone: she did not involve the nurse, she did not send the proposal to parents, and she did not negotiate it with the neurologist. Another, analogous rupture stemmed from the ward nurse's realization that she and the hospital nurse responsible for the patient on an ongoing basis never interacted. These ruptures are representative of a large number of similar ones in other cases we have recorded and analyzed.

These ruptures reveal a deep-seated historical layer of images and practices of professional autonomy and individualism in medical work, among physicians but also among nurses. The ruptures are manifestations of a contradiction emerging with the implementation of the care agreement. This contradiction takes shape as a tension between the new instrument requiring distributed and negotiated knotworking on the one hand and the deep-seated division of labor perpetuating solo performance and the equally persistent rule of solo responsibility on the other hand. This double contradiction is marked with number 1 in Figure 18.10.

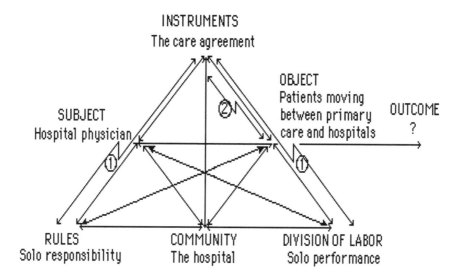

INSTRUMENTS
The care agreement

OBJECT
Patients moving
between primary
care and hospitals

OUTCOME
?

SUBJECT
Hospital physician

RULES
Solo responsibility

COMMUNITY
The hospital

DIVISION OF LABOR
Solo performance

Figure 18.10. Emerging contradictions in the care agreement practice.

Most of the other ruptures we have recorded reflect inadequacies of the care agreement itself as an instrument for knotworking. Typically, practitioners in the hospital as well as in the health centers have found it difficult to notice and locate the care agreement text embedded in the traditional medical record chart. This often explains why the personal physicians do not respond to the care agreement proposal in a timely manner; the proposal has simply gone unnoticed. Similarly, parents repeatedly complain that the care agreement text does not look like an agreement between equal parties and is not written in a language useful and informative for the parents. In other words, there is a tension between the new instrument (or rather its old-fashioned features) and the demanding new object of children with long-term illnesses moving between hospitals and primary care.

These ruptures are not merely technical shortcomings in the narrow sense of the word. They reflect a real asymmetry among the parties involved in the knotworking effort. The care agreement instrument is still primarily an initiative of the hospital (that is why we have put the hospital physician in the subject position in Figure 18.10). This contradiction, marked with number 2 in Figure 18.10, will be transcended as primary care practitioners and parents begin to suggest modifications to the artifact and its use procedure.

Is the care agreement an example of co-configuration? In principle, the care agreement is supposed to a collaborative tool for continuous configuration of long-term personalized care. All six criteria of co-configuration are supposed to be built into the design of this instrumentality. However, there is large gray area between design principles and practical application. Instead of lamenting this fact, we celebrate it and recommend continuing participatory analysis of ruptures and contradictions of activity as a source of mutual learning.

### Knotworking as a Research Challenge

Activity-theoretical studies of work and communication have thus far mainly dealt with development and learning within well-bounded singular activity systems. If knotworking is indeed a historically significant new way of organizing work, associated with the rise of co-configuration, activity theory must expand its methodological repertoire to cope with the challenge.

The first direction of methodological expansion concerns reworking the relationship between discourse and practice, between communicative and instrumental aspects of activity. In knotworking, these two are inseparably intertwined. This implies, on the one hand, that activity-theoretical studies of work and organizations must work with discourse data employing and further developing the sophisticated tools of the trade. On the other hand, this implies that activity-theoretical studies of work and organizations must conduct critical dialogue with varieties of discourse and conversation analysis that neglect or ignore the object to be produced as the central driving force and glue of practical-discursive human activity (for an attempt in this direction, see Engeström, in press).

Another direction of methodological expansion is the development of conceptual tools for analyses of sequences and trajectories of knotworking. In this paper, we have presented two preliminary case studies in which we operated with different representations of such sequences. For Strauss (1993) the concept of trajectory "refers to a course of action but also embraces the interaction of multiple actors and contingencies that may be unanticipated and not entirely manageable" (p. 53). While compatible with an activity-theoretical viewpoint, this characterization is still far too vague. On the one hand, we need to develop ways to analyze and conceptualize the specific actions and interactions of which trajectories and their internal turning points are made, including small but significant actions of reflective learning and reconfiguration. On the other hand, we need to identify and characterize different types of trajectories, their overall shapes and developmental potentials.

A third direction of methodological expansion is implied in our discussion of the three dimensions of knotworking: the socio-spatial, the temporal, and the ethical. The idea of *pulsation* integrates the socio-spatial and the temporal dimensions: knots are tied and untied in various rhythms which need to be represented along both dimensions simultaneously. Pulsation also compresses and releases the different participating activity streams in ways that tend to disrupt and shake given notions of responsibility and power, opening up the ethical dimension of work for analysis and intervention.

### References

Alter, C., & Hage, J. (1993). *Organizations working together*. Newbury Park, Calif.: Sage.

Barley, S.R. (1988). On technology, time and social order: Technically induced change in the temporal organization of radiological work. In F. Dubinskas (Ed.), *Making time* (pp. 123-169). Philadelphia: Temple University Press.

Caines, E. (1997, May 9). A health lesson I never wanted: Need for National Health Service reforms. *New Statesman, 126,* 24.

Engeström, Y. (1987). Learning by expanding: An activity-theoretical approach to developmental research. Helsinki: Orienta-Konsultit.

Engeström, Y. (1990). Learning, working and imagining: Twelve studies in activity theory. Helsinki: Orienta-Konsultit.

Engeström, Y. (1993). Developmental studies on work as a testbench of activity theory. In S. Chaiklin & J. Lave (Eds.), *Understanding practice: Perspectives on activity and context* (pp. 64-103). Cambridge: Cambridge University Press.

Engeström, Y. (1994). The working health center project: Materializing zones of proximal development in a network of organizational learning (pp. 233-272). In T. Kauppinen & M. Lahtonen (Eds.), *Action research in Finland*. Helsinki: Ministry of Labor.

Engeström, Y. (1999). Expansive visibilization of work: An activity-theoretical perspective. *Computer-Supported Cooperative Work, 8,* 63-93.

Engeström, Y. (in press). Communication, discourse and activity. *The Communication Review.*

Engeström, Y., Brown, K., Christopher, L.C., & Gregory, J. (1997). Coordination, cooperation, and communication in the courts: Expansive transitions in legal work. In M. Cole, Y. Engeström, & O. Vásquez (Eds.), *Mind, culture, and activity: Seminal papers from the Laboratory of Comparative Human Cognition* (pp. 369-385). Cambridge: Cambridge University Press.

Engeström, Y., Engeström, R., & Kärkkäinen, M. (1995). Polycontextuality and boundary crossing in expert cognition: Learning and problem solving in complex work activities. *Learning and Instruction, 5,* 319-336.

Granovetter, M.S. (1973). The strength of weak ties. *American Journal of Sociology, 78,* 1360-1380.

Latour, B. (1996). On interobjectivity. *Mind, Culture, and Activity, 3,* 228-245.

McDonald, J.C. (1994). Inpatient flow management: A collaborative approach. In R.S. Howe (Ed.), *Case management for healthcare professionals* (pp. 131-142). Chicago: Precept Press.

Moody, P.E. (1993). Breakthrough partnering: Creating a collective enterprise advantage. Essex Junction, Vt.: Omneo.

Strauss, A.L. (1993). *Continual permutations of action.* New York: Aldine de Gruyter.

Suchman, L. (1997). Centers of coordination: A case and some themes. In L.B. Resnick, R. Säljö, C. Pontecorvo, & B. Burge (Eds.), *Discourse, tools, and reasoning: Essays on situated cognition* (pp. 41-62). Berlin: Springer

Victor, B., & Boynton, A.C. (1998). Invented here: Maximizing your organization's internal growth and profitability. Boston: Harvard Business School Press.

Weick, K., & Roberts, K.H. (1993). Collective mind in organizations: Heedful interrelating on flight decks. *Administrative Science Quarterly, 38,* 357-381.

Wenger, E. (1998). *Communities of practice: Learning, meaning, and identity.* Cambridge: Cambridge University Press.

# Index